CW01401722

COMBATING POVERTY IN EUROPE

Combating Poverty in Europe

The German Welfare Regime in Practice

Edited by

PETER KRAUSE
DIW Berlin

GERHARD BÄCKER
University of Duisburg

WALTER HANESCH
University of Applied Sciences Darmstadt

ASHGATE

Published by
Ashgate Publishing Limited
Gower House
Croft Road
Aldershot
Hants GU11 3HR
England

Ashgate Publishing Company
Suite 420
101 Cherry Street
Burlington, VT 05401-4405
USA

Ashgate website: http://www.ashgate.com

British Library Cataloguing in Publication Data
Combating poverty in Europe : the German welfare regime in
  practice. - (Studies in cash and care)
  1.Public welfare - Germany 2.Poverty - Germany 3.Public
  welfare - Europe 4.Poverty - Europe
  I.Krause, Peter II.Bäcker, Gerhard III.Hanesch, Walter,
  1947-
  361.6'5'0943

Library of Congress Cataloging-in-Publication Data
Combating poverty in Europe : the German welfare regime in practice / edited by Peter
  Krause, Gerhard Bäcker and Walter Hanesch.
    p. cm. -- (Studies in cash & care)
  Includes bibliographical references and index.
  ISBN 0-7546-3222-9
    1. Poor--Services for--Germany. 2. Poor--Services for--European Union countries. I.
  Krause, Peter, 1965- II. Bäcker, Gerhard, 1947- III. Hanesch, Walter. IV. Cash & care.

HV4099.C66 2004
362.5'094--dc21

                                                                        2003045234
ISBN 0 7546 3222 9

Printed and bound by Athenaeum Press, Ltd.,
Gateshead, Tyne & Wear.

Contents

List of Contributors

Hans-Jürgen Andreß is Professor for Social Research Methods at the Faculty of Sociology in Bielefeld. His major research interests are the sociology of labour markets, social policy, social stratification and the application of multivariate statistical models.

Gerhard Bäcker is Professor for Applied Social Sciences at the Gerhard-Mercator University Duisburg-Essen. His main research interests are social policy, family policy and labour market.

Bea Cantillon is the Director of the Centre for Social Policy, University of Antwerp and Professor at the Faculty of Political and Social Sciences at the same University. Her major research interests are the welfare state, social inequality and poverty.

Michael F. Förster is an Administrator at the OECD Directorate for Employment, Labour and Social Affairs and a Research Fellow at the European Centre for Social Welfare Policy and Research. His publications and research focus on poverty and income inequalities in OECD countries and in transitional economies.

Jan Goebel is a Research Associate at DIW Berlin with the German Socio-Economic Panel Study (GSOEP) in Germany. His major interests are poverty, inequality and income dynamics.

Walter Hanesch is Professor of Social Policy and Social Administration in the Department of Social Work at the Fachhochschule Darmstadt, University of Applied Sciences, Germany. His main areas of research are the analysis of poverty and social exclusion as well as of social policies in Germany and in Europe.

Richard Hauser is Professor of Economics, specializing in Social Policy at the Johann Wolfgang Goethe University in Frankfurt am Main. His main research interests are social policy, comparison of social security systems, income and wealth distribution and poverty problems.

Bruce Headey is a Principal Fellow of the Melbourne Institute of Applied Economic and Social Research at Melbourne University. His two main interests are in research on happiness/subjective well-being, and on welfare states and welfare reform. He co-authored a book in 1992 on 'Understanding Happiness: A Theory of Subjective Well-Being' with psychologist Alex Wearing. His most recent book, co-authored with Robert E. Goodin, Ruud Muffels and Henk-Jan Dirven is 'The Real Worlds of Welfare Capitalism' published in 1999. He is editor of the Australian Social Monitor.

Bjørn Hvinden is Professor of Sociology at the Norwegian University of Science and Technology (NTNU), Trondheim, and Senior Scientific Advisor to the Research Council of Norway. His main research interests include activation, employment and disability policies, comparative welfare and social security, self-organization among marginal groups and the situation of Romanian people.

Peter Krause is a Senior Research Fellow with the German Socio-Economic Panel Study (GSOEP) at DIW Berlin, Germany. His major research interests are income, poverty, subjective indicators, inequality and welfare dynamics.

Michael Maschke is a Research Associate at the Institute for Social Science, Humboldt-University Berlin, Germany. His major research interests are disability policies, poverty and social exclusion.

Ruud Muffels is Professor of Socio-Economics at Tilburg University, Director of the Tilburg Institute for Social and Socio-Economic Research (TISSER) and Research Director at the Institute of Labour Studies (OSA). His primary interests concern welfare and labour market economics, socio-economic policy and comparative analyses of the welfare state.

Brian Nolan is a Research Professor at the Economic and Social Research Institute, Dublin. He has published widely on income inequality, poverty, public economics, social policy, and health inequalities.

Birgit Otto is a Junior Research Fellow at DIW Berlin (German Institute for Economic Research). Her major research interests are income and wealth distribution, European comparison of poverty problems and family policy.

Mark Pearson is the Head of the Social Policy Division at the OECD. He has researched the reform of tax/benefit systems in order to make work pay; welfare reform strategies and policies to promote the reconciliation of work and family life.

Armindo Silva is the Head of Unit at the Directorate-General for Employment and Social Affairs of the European Commission. He is presently responsible for social protection and inclusion policies, and has also worked in the departments for industrial policy and employment policy.

C. Katharina Spiess is a Senior Research Fellow of the DIW Berlin (German Institute for Economic Research) and Lecturer at the Berlin University of Technology (TUB). Her major research interests are family economics, public finance and regional inequality.

Karel Van den Bosch is a Senior Researcher at the Centre for Social Policy, University of Antwerp and Lecturer in the Faculty of Political and Social Sciences at the same University. His major research interests are poverty, income inequality and the welfare state.

Gert G. Wagner is Professor of Economics at the Berlin University of Technology (TUB) and Research Director at DIW Berlin (German Institute for Economic Research). From 2002 continuing on through 2003 he is serving on the Federal Commission for 'Sustainability of Financing the Welfare State'. His major research interests are labor and population economics and survey statistics.

Claudia Weinkopf is a Senior Researcher at IAT, Gelsenkirchen, Germany. She coordinates the research group "flexibility and security". Her major research interests are labour market policies, employment and the service sector.

Acknowledgements

This book presents strategies for combating poverty and exclusion within the German welfare regime, and summarizes the debate for an international audience. It also contains chapters on comparative international research into poverty in Europe, and the role of the European Union in combating poverty and exclusion in the EU Member States. The book thus offers both a national and an international perspective.

We would like to thank all the authors for their expert and committed contributions, and for their professional collaboration. Special thanks go to Armindo Silva, for his insider's view into the EU Commission's anti-poverty policies. We also extend particular thanks to the OECD for permission to reprint the chapter by Michael F. Förster and Mark Pearson: 'Income Distribution and Poverty in the OECD Area: Trends and Driving Forces', *OECD Economic Studies* (34), 2002/1, OECD Copyright, 2002/1.

This book arose out of a research project on 'Poverty and Inequality in Germany', which was commissioned and sponsored by the Hans Böckler Foundation, the German Trade Union Federation, and the *Paritätischer Wohlfahrtsverband* (a non-denominational German welfare association). It could not have been published without the financial support of the Hans Böckler Foundation, and we would therefore like to express particular thanks to the head of the department for research funding, Dr Erika Mezger.

Most of the German texts required professional editing or translation, for which we thank Susan Richter, Anke Middelmann-Beal and especially the Language Technology Centre Ltd. in London.

Finally, no book can be completed without the hard work, commitment and motivation of the staff involved. Ingrid Tucci, a graduate sociologist in Berlin, held the threads of the project together, editing the individual chapters, patiently resolving technical problems, dealing with correspondence, and compiling the index listings for the completed volume. We extend our special thanks to her.

Berlin, Darmstadt and Duisburg, January 2003

Peter Krause
Gerhard Bäcker
Walter Hanesch

Chapter 1

Combating poverty
in Europe and Germany

Gerhard Bäcker, Walter Hanesch and Peter Krause

Welfare regimes and combating poverty: a European comparison

When we consider the welfare regimes which exist in the Member States of the European Union, there appear, at first sight, to be more points in common than differences. All states have a democratic political system, an economic system conforming to the type of a socially responsible market economy, and a developed social security system. The national benefits systems in the EU states provide protection against general risks to livelihood, as well as specific needs. Although these systems have come under some pressure to converge in recent years, both to ensure freedom of movement and to bring working and living conditions across the European Union closer together, regulatory competence within the European Union has nevertheless remained at the level of the individual Member States. There are still substantial national differences in the organization, the financing, the degree of cover and the level of payments offered by the various social security and benefit systems (see Hauser, 1997).

In comparative international welfare research, repeated attempts have been made to develop a comprehensive typology for so-called welfare or social state regimes. The best known is the approach proposed by Gösta Esping-Andersen (1990), whose book 'Three Worlds of Welfare Capitalism' has had a lasting influence on international debate. Esping-Andersen uses complex explanatory models to distinguish three types of regime, the liberal, the corporatist-conservative and the social-democratic. The distinguishing features he uses are the relative significance of the three support institutions (state, market and family), the quality and scope of social rights (degree of 'decommodification', defined as freeing labour from the status of a commodity), and the degree to which the welfare state determines social distribution.[1] If we incorporate the proposal made by Stefan Leibfried (1990) to add a further type of regime, the 'rudimentary', we can distinguish four types of regime:[2]

- the 'social-democratic' welfare regime, typical of the Scandinavian countries;
- the 'corporatist-conservative' welfare regime, which characterizes most of the countries of continental Europe;

- the 'liberal' welfare regime, found in the Anglo-Saxon countries and;
- the 'rudimentary' welfare regime, applicable to the states of southern Europe.

These welfare state types reflect ideal normalizing assumptions, and also specific conditions for access to the individual safeguards provided by the various national social security systems. The use of state benefit systems to protect the individual against social risks is given a particularly high priority in the social-democratic and conservative welfare regimes, while the liberal type 'places more emphasis on the role of the free market and the family', and provides protection only in the event of short-term loss of income. The rudimentary type applies especially to countries where the process of economic and social modernization began relatively late (and which were also integrated relatively late into the European Community), and whose social security systems themselves are in the process of modernizing and 'catching up' (see, for example, Schmid, 1996).

From the standpoint of comparative research into poverty, the central flaw in existing typologies is that they gloss over poverty policy. Given the growing importance of policies for combating poverty in the European welfare states, Voges and Kazepov have urged that the organization and intensity of such policies should be considered as an additional dimension (see Voges and Kazepov, 1998, p. 7) – a call that has not yet been acted on, however (see also Eardley et al., 1996).

In respect of their social security systems, the welfare regimes mentioned are characterized by specific model types (see also European Commission, 1996):

1. The states with the Scandinavian social security model (Denmark, Sweden, Finland) are characterized by the fact that social security is defined as a civil right, and all citizens are entitled to the same tax-financed social security services. People in paid employment receive additional income-related payments from company systems. Only unemployment insurance is separate from the state benefits system, and is generally based on voluntary contributions. The overall level of social security benefits is comparatively high; financing is predominantly through (correspondingly high) taxes.
2. Germany, Austria, France and the Benelux countries represent the continental European social security model. Here, social insurance forms the core of the social security system, and so social benefits are coupled to employment status, either directly or indirectly (for family members). Systems financed through contributions predominate, dependent on previous earned income and in part on membership of particular professional groups. Gaps in the cover provided by this primary network are bridged by a separate safety net of welfare services.
3. Great Britain and Ireland represent the Anglo-Saxon social security model. This is characterized by the existence of a comprehensive social security system in which means-tested welfare payments play a major role alongside a low level of social insurance. Whereas the National Health Service in Great Britain is available free of charge to all citizens, this applies in Ireland only to those on low incomes.

4. Finally, the southern European states are in an exceptional position, associated with a social security model where universal social security systems have only been built up or expanded in the last decade or two in the wake of economic development and changes in socio-economic structure. In general, we find mixed insurance systems here, combining company and social insurance systems, with large gaps in cover and a comparatively low overall level of provision. In practice, the social security systems in these countries still work on the premise that additional cover is provided by primary networks (family and private charity), although this assumption is being increasingly undermined by economic and social changes.

Each of these models is thus characterized by a combination of different forms of social security and by different types of financing. Each has its own dominant pattern of goals and organizational principles, with all models falling back on the same fundamental forms (insurance, support and welfare). Because of this, the classification of individual countries is not always distinct and unambiguous (e.g. the Netherlands or Italy). We can, however, see that individual countries have generally continued to develop along the path they have embarked on, and although they may have modified their basic form, they have not departed from the fundamental model.

From the types of welfare regime set out above, and from the different models of social security, we can see that there is currently no uniform European welfare state or social security model. Rather, the European nations have developed quite different welfare regimes and social security models according to their respective levels of economic and social development and their individual social and cultural traditions. Leaving the southern European model to one side, we can distinguish three clearly defined social security models co-existing today in Western Europe, or in other words, within the European Union. While the Anglo-Saxon model is also widespread outside the European continent – particularly in the countries of the former British Empire such as the USA, Australia and New Zealand – the Scandinavian and continental European models can be interpreted as specifically European, and are mainly restricted to Europe itself.

Very different forms of welfare regulations and social security have therefore evolved in the individual member countries to implement the objectives of the welfare state. In each of the welfare regimes mentioned, or rather in the corresponding countries, we find specific mixtures of labour market intervention, family benefits and systems of income support, each contributing in their own particular way towards combating poverty.

1. The liberal model in the Anglo-Saxon countries is based on a largely deregulated labour market with a conspicuous spread in wage levels. Compared to universal social security systems with relatively modest cover, income support is evidence of a highly developed system of social assistance. The family-related infrastructure must be purchased privately on the open market.

2. The continental European countries within the conservative-corporatist model combine a highly regulated labour market with a developed system of social security dominated by social insurance. Social assistance here plays a rather marginal role. Family policy, at least as regards the public infrastructure for child support, is rather underdeveloped (with the exception of France).
3. The social-democratic model in the Scandinavian countries is characterized by a state-regulated labour market with extensive rights of access (integration through work). Moreover, the universal social security system provides a high level of income replacement payments, while social assistance traditionally plays a subordinate role. Family policy is characterized by a broad range of state payments for childcare.
4. Finally, the southern European countries are characterized by a largely unregulated labour market, combined with an only partially developed benefits system, where even the safety net of social assistance hardly exists at the national level, if at all (with the exception of Portugal). Family policy is not highly developed either, and its functions are supported by traditional family structures.

Analyzes carried out by the European Community Household Panel (ECHP) have shown that social transfer payments in all EU states help to reduce income poverty, albeit to very varying degrees. This applies least of all to the countries of southern Europe, while it is most marked in the countries with a social-democratic welfare regime, which also have the lowest poverty rates after transfer payments. In the countries with a liberal welfare regime, we also see a sharp reduction, but in these countries the poverty rate is very high both before and after state transfer payments. Against this, the countries belonging to the conservative welfare state type occupy the middle ground in terms of distribution effects (see, for example, Marlier and Cohen-Solal, 2000; Hanesch, Krause, Bäcker, Maschke and Otto, 2000; and also the chapter by Jan Goebel and Birgit Otto in this volume).

Overall, it is clear that the scope and organization of the transfer system have a significant influence on the extent of inequality and income poverty. It is clear that the Scandinavian countries with their social-democratic welfare regime, and the continental European countries with their conservative-corporatist model and its transfer systems, are the most successful in eliminating poverty and low income. At the same time, inequality before redistribution is not as marked as in the Anglo-Saxon and southern European countries. It is no coincidence, then, that those countries with comparatively successful poverty policies also have levels of social security provision above the EU average, while the countries with less successful poverty policies have below-average levels of provision. However – as already emphasized – these findings have to be seen in the overall context of interactions between the labour market, lifestyles, social benefits and social infrastructure.

Combating poverty by the European Union

Combating poverty in the Member States of the European Union is supported and assisted by poverty policy at the EU level. The founding of the European Communities and the evolution of the European Union were driven from the outset primarily by economic motives, and served to establish a common European internal market. In contrast, social policy played only a very subordinate role from the start. The European Community's competence in the field of social policy has remained limited to this day, and is mainly concentrated on promoting the mobility of labour and companies.

The limitation of the social policy competence of the EC/EU was and is motivated, not least, by the fact that social policy traditionally represents a key ground for securing mass loyalty, which national governments and parliaments are reluctant to give up. Moreover, national social security systems are marked by specific socio-cultural traditions, within which very different solutions have evolved to meet comparable objectives. Finally, there was and is a great fear that a shift of competence to the European level, and the establishment of uniform welfare benefit standards, would jeopardize national standards (for example in the Scandinavian countries) and lead to a general deterioration. Conversely, others (especially the southern European countries, and in the wake of EU enlargement, the Central and Eastern European countries in future also) fear that this alignment could force them to raise their standards and overburden them economically. In view of this, it is understandable that the primary competence for social policy regulation has remained with the Member States – in line with the subsidiarity principle.

At the same time, with a multi-level system, social policy in the Member States is faced with a growing pressure to adjust, in three ways (see, for example, Leibfried and Pierson, 1998). First, the last decade has seen wider opportunities for intervention granted to the EU in the social policy field as well, and this includes, not least, poverty policy. On the other hand, an increasing pressure towards convergence has grown out of regulatory systems based on voluntary contributions, especially in relation to the structuring of social insurance systems. Finally, increasing economic integration and the ever-closer alignment of economic, monetary and fiscal policy have imposed a growing pressure towards alignment on national social policy regimes as well.

If we consider poverty policy in the narrower sense at a European level, we see an area in which the European Commission, in particular, became involved at a very early stage. For example, since the mid 1970s (in conjunction with Ireland's accession), the EC has developed and implemented three poverty programmes. In the early 1990s, it also adopted a recommendation to Member States concerning the introduction of a national minimum income, and in the mid 1990s, it launched an admittedly rather unsuccessful attempt to anchor a catalogue of social basic rights in law and policy. Overall, these initiatives were driven by the intention of establishing uniform minimum standards in respect of social rights, minimum incomes and services across the European Union as a whole.

In connection with a planned fourth poverty programme, the early 1990s saw a blockade of poverty policy at the EU level, led by the governments of Germany and Britain. As a result of social policy arguments at that time, the problem of poverty has been supplanted in political debate at the European level by that of 'social inclusion'. At the same time, there have been greater efforts to broaden the legal basis for anti-poverty initiatives at a European level. The Maastricht Treaty, and particularly the Treaty of Amsterdam, completed this expansion of competence for European initiatives in the fight against poverty and social exclusion.

The latest phase in European Union poverty policy began with the Lisbon European Council in March 2000. At this meeting, the Heads of State and Government of the EU Member States resolved unanimously that, in the light of the strategic goal for the next decade, i.e. for the EU to become the most competitive and dynamic knowledge-based economy in the world, combating poverty and social exclusion should be a central objective in modernizing the European social model. With the 'open coordination' method and the action programme on combating poverty, two new initiatives were developed to address this new priority, supplemented and supported by the Structural Fund programmes (for more on the Community strategy to promote social inclusion, see the chapter by Armindo Silva in this volume).

The extension of social policy competence and the upgrading of poverty policy to the European level may be assessed in different ways. On the one hand, the EU's legal and political scope for action in combating poverty has been increased; on the other hand, this change is reflected in a paradigm shift in the social policy debate. The fact that the issue of poverty – or more accurately, the issue of social exclusion – has assumed a higher priority in the context of the Community strategy for modernizing social protection is noteworthy in three respects:

1. The upgrading of poverty policy is closely linked to an assumption of responsibility for social issues within economic policy. This has the primary objective of strengthening the structure of European economies as a defence against the pressures of increased global competition. On the other hand, an emphasis on the goal of cohesion also provides an opportunity to avoid the trade-off between efficiency and justice implicit in the mainstream economy, and to propagate a policy across the Member States that is not only economically efficient but also effective in social policy terms.
2. The prioritization of poverty policy (in terms of upgrading the role of the respective social 'safety nets') goes hand in hand with ever-decreasing emphasis on the principal social security networks and the questioning of more far-reaching social security standards (priority given to poverty policy over the earlier primacy of securing living standards). It remains to be seen whether the political upgrading of the fight against poverty and exclusion is not simply a fig leaf to conceal the wholesale dismantling of more far-reaching social standards.
3. Finally, we can observe a paradigm shift at the European level also, in terms of support for a move away from passive forms of benefit to active and integrative intervention models (services rather than transfers). There is some

evidence to suggest that European initiatives in poverty policy are also tending to move the European welfare regimes in the direction of workfare states. The problem here is not so much the emphasis on the goal of reintegration than the question of what conditions and perspectives will govern such moves towards integration (see Loedemel and Trickey, 2000).

Poverty in Germany – a long-neglected problem

When we attempt to analyze the common points and the differences between the European states, we find that academic and political interest in the subject of 'poverty' came quite late to all countries, and then only gradually. In the post-war period, which can be described as the expansion phase for social policy, social security provisions were systematically expanded on the basis of high economic growth rates and high employment – linked to the expectation that poverty (still present as a consequence of the war) could be reduced and ultimately overcome.

Germany offers a particularly good example of the way in which the subject of poverty has been driven out of political and academic debate. Until the 1980s, poverty research played only a subordinate and barely noticed role in the social sciences and economics (Hauser/Neumann 1992, pp. 237). Although some poverty and social reports and analyzes – generally local and regional in scope – on the disadvantaged living conditions of individual population groups did come to public notice, the dominant tone overall was that there could be no poverty in a generally prosperous state like Germany, which was also supported by a tight-knit social network. Germany was characterized more by the view that poverty could be successfully combated by the social security system. This official view also explains why Germany took a sceptical or even negative stance towards the poverty programmes set out by the European Union in the 1980s, and eventually ensured that they were terminated.

This attitude to the subject of poverty in Germany lasted right into the final phase of the conservative-liberal government under Chancellor Kohl. In the run-up to the 1998 German parliamentary elections, when the Report on Children and Young People commissioned by the German government reached the conclusion that children suffered particularly badly in situations of poverty, the government responded with the comment that while many families might have to make do on limited means, poverty was certainly not an issue. Poverty, it claimed, was a feature of developing countries, not of such a generally prosperous country as Germany (Stellungnahme der Bundesregierung / Opinion of the Federal Government, 1998, p. XII).

Times have changed: in early 2001, the red-green coalition government published the first report on poverty and wealth in Germany (Erster Armuts- und Reichtumsbericht / First Poverty and Wealth Report 2001). A second report is planned for 2004. The existence of poverty in the midst of prosperity is no longer disputed, but to some extent 'officially' confirmed at government level. This is the first step towards being able to analyze in detail the characteristics, causes and determining factors behind poverty, and above all to address the question of specific ways to combat it. This change has been introduced and accompanied by an increasingly far-reaching theoretical and empirical engagement with the problem of poverty. Overall, we can observe a great diversification in German poverty research today, within which new questions are being addressed, and a broad range of theoretical and empirical tools brought to bear.

Characteristic elements of the German welfare state

In the German version of the corporatist-conservative type of welfare state, the major risk areas (age, disability, illness, nursing care, accidents at work, unemployment) are mainly covered by category-based social insurance systems for which access, levels of payment, and funding are all linked to dependent paid employment. Another feature of this type of welfare regime is a conservative model of marriage and family life, which traditionally assumes that women do not work, or only work part-time, and makes social benefits for (married) women dependent on their husbands' insurance provision. The specific role of combating poverty is assumed by social assistance and by particular individual transfers (such as housing benefit and child allowance). Social assistance is a universal basic benefit covering all of Germany, to which the whole population (with very few exceptions) is entitled, but with recipiency subject to strict means-testing. Measured against overall welfare spending, the outlay on social assistance, at around 4 per cent of total welfare payments, remains comparatively low (Bäcker et al., 2000, p. 54).

However, to describe the specifically German version of the welfare state, it is not sufficient just to highlight the overwhelming importance of social insurance. The following features should also be noted, and are important for an understanding of poverty policy (Schulte, 2000, pp. 15):

- Germany's federal structure means that, beside the federal government itself, which is mainly responsible for social insurance and tax-funded transfers, the 16 federal states and the local authorities also function as independent 'welfare states'. The local authorities take responsibility for social and youth services, as well as providing social services and facilities outside the health system. Although social assistance is regulated by federal laws, and levels of payment are broadly consistent across the whole country, the local authorities still have to implement the regulations, and they are also responsible for financing.
- Only a small part of the responsibility for providing social services and facilities is assumed by the local authorities themselves; the structure of provision is typically dominated by non-profit-making welfare charities, and increasingly by private enterprise.
- The organization of the labour market and the setting of working conditions and wages are largely determined by agreements between the 'social partners' – employers' associations and trades unions. In the context of free collective bargaining, the state hands over regulatory competence in this area to the social partners, and, apart from providing the legal framework, remains in the

background. Hence, there are no nationally guaranteed minimum wages; this function is picked up by sector-specific and supra-regional wage agreements. The labour market is thus comparatively tightly regulated – in contrast to liberal welfare state regimes – and wage differences are limited. However, in the upheaval brought about by the transition to a service economy, the influence of wage agreements is dwindling, with an increase in the number of employees and businesses whose working conditions and pay are no longer regulated in this way.

- The federal government carries the main responsibility for unemployment cover (unemployment benefit and unemployment assistance), as well as for labour market policy. As benefits to the unemployed shift to municipally administered and financed social assistance (as described below), municipal authorities are also increasingly active in employment and labour market policy, especially for the long-term unemployed and hard-to-place persons.

- State social security to safeguard against life's ups and downs is supplemented by voluntary and statutory payments from employers and companies. Employers are involved not only in terms of their 50 per cent contribution to social insurance, but also in offering benefits such as supplementary retirement pension provision to their employees. The greatest beneficiaries of voluntary benefits of this kind are employees of large companies.

- A new trend is the development of supplementary cover provided by private enterprise, particularly retirement pension provision, which is designed to compensate for shortfalls in the area of statutory cover. The state promotes private provision by means of tax relief or by direct transfers.

- Access to health care, and the level of medical provision, are governed mainly by statutory health insurance. Although the number of people entitled to statutory health insurance is basically limited to those in dependent employment, the cover provided to wives and children free of charge, and the entitlement of pensioners to insurance, mean that over 80 per cent of the population is covered by statutory health insurance. All essential medical services are covered, and can be claimed without any restriction – although in some cases, specific extra payments are required. The provision and management of out-patient and in-patient services are handled overwhelmingly by private enterprise (i.e. doctors in private practice) and by non-profit-making service providers (in the case of hospitals).

- The level (and sometimes also the duration) of financial benefits from social insurance systems is based on the individual's earlier employment position, and the level of contributions paid. Benefits are coupled to the growth of the employee's net income, and are index-linked. As there are no basic or minimum payments in the individual branches of social insurance, the influence of the insurance and equivalence principle means that the level of unemployment benefits and pension payments may turn out to be very low. Where they fall below the socio-cultural minimum subsistence level, social assistance has to supplement the payments – albeit based on stringent means-testing.

- The scope of social insurance cover excludes the self-employed and also those employees who do not meet the legal requirements covering compulsory insurance contributions and payments.
- The marriage-oriented structure of social insurance (health and nursing care cover extended free of charge to non-working wives, and generous survivors' pensions), the fact that so-called 'mini-jobs' are exempt from contributions, the effect of specific tax-law regulations (combined assessment of married couples), and shortfalls in childcare provision for pre-school and schoolchildren, all lead to particularly poor conditions and low incentives for wives and mothers to go out to work. The German welfare state explicitly encourages women to take extended breaks in employment, and is built around the assumption of a return to low-paid part-time work after time off for child-raising.

Combating poverty within the German welfare regime

If we now summarize these structural features in relation to combating poverty, the German model exhibits specific advantages as well as risks and problems (Bäcker and Klammer, 2002, pp. 211):

The social insurance system provides a generally high level of benefits for standard risks. Administration by independent insurers with independent budgets, the dominance of the equivalence principle in setting payment levels, and funding through employers' and employees' contributions, all guarantee a comparatively high degree of autonomy and social acceptance for the individual branches of social insurance. However, funding based on paid employment makes the systems on the revenue side heavily dependent on trends in the labour market, so that rising unemployment very quickly creates a gulf between revenue and expenditure. In recent years, policy-makers have repeatedly tried to counter financial shortfalls by cutting benefits. In a heavily equivalence-based social insurance system with no minimum level of cover, any cuts in the level of income replacement payments and/or terms of entitlement increase the risk that individuals may not be entitled to payments, or that the level of payments may no longer be enough for subsistence. There is also the problem inherent in category-based systems that certain population groups are not included. However, the structural changes in the labour market that we have sketched out have precisely the effect of propagating those employment conditions – such as new kinds of self-employment, or mini-jobs – that are worthy of protection but fall outside the scope of social insurance cover.

In social insurance systems geared towards wage replacement, as in Germany, the level of benefits never covers more than a percentage of earlier net income. The increase of low-paid jobs that place the individual below or only just above the poverty line then leads inevitably to inadequate social insurance entitlements. As there are no national minimum wage regulations, and wage agreements increasingly fail to cover the segment dominated by insecure and low-paid jobs, a gap has become apparent in regulations addressing the labour market, working conditions and remuneration.

Later chapters in this volume make clear that the structure of the household is the crucial factor leading to poverty. Living together in a household can either decrease or increase financial burdens. The size of the household, particularly the presence and number of children, may increase the burden, as the income received has to be shared among several people. On the other hand, the burden may be decreased where many people contribute to household income, particularly through income from employment. The German marriage- and family-oriented model displays problems in this respect, as the still dominant gender role pattern (at least in the former West Germany) of a wife and mother going though phases of unemployment or part-time work makes household income heavily dependent on the husband's income, and so creates a latent risk of poverty. Income problems leading to poverty arise on the one hand with single parents (either unmarried or following a separation), where the breadwinner model with the marriage unit as the target of benefits no longer applies, while on the other hand, the husband's income in the middle and lower income bands is often no longer sufficient to cover the maintenance of children. Although the German welfare state supports families through child allowance and tax exemptions, which have actually significantly increased in recent years, there are also incentives for wives not to work, and the necessary preconditions for combining employment and child-raising still do not exist. Thirdly, if the husband loses his job, the impact of the loss of income is extremely serious if there is no second source of income from employment.

The gaps in cover inherent in the German welfare regime place an ever-increasing burden on social assistance at the local authority level, which provides a 'safety net' to ward off poverty. In Germany's federal state and fiscal structure, this shift of social policy responsibility also causes the financial burdens to shift from the central state to the local authorities. As local authorities are financially very weak, poverty policy as part of social welfare then comes up against very tight limits.

General economic and social factors affecting poverty in Germany

The current focus on the poverty problem in academic and public debate may be seen as a reflection of the changed economic, political and social conditions that have marked the situation in Germany since the 1980s, and which together have intensified income risks to the point where there is real danger of poverty. This upheaval in social structures, which may be observed in other European countries also, is occurring on several overlapping levels (see, for example, Kaufmann, 1997):

- *Mass unemployment:* Germany is in the grip of a persistent imbalance in the labour market, which has steadily worsened in the last few years in spite of all efforts made in labour market policy. Even in periods of economic recovery, it has not been possible to break down the core of mass unemployment, and one economic crisis after another has seen an increase in the number and proportion of long-term unemployed, who have almost no chance of re-employment and whose income level is crucially dependent on welfare state transfers. This general problem is overlaid with significant regional imbalances. In the old industrial regions, and in the former GDR in particular, the state of the labour market is extraordinarily bad.

- *Erosion of normal working conditions and increase in marginal employment*: As a consequence both of unemployment and of changes to economic structure towards a service economy, and against a background of changing lifestyles and careers, the German labour market is increasingly marked by working conditions that diverge to a greater or lesser extent from the norm of permanent full-time employment safeguarded by labour, social security and wage laws. Part-time work, mini-jobs, short-term work, new kinds of self-employment, contract work – these are the trends which ultimately lead to instability of employment and to increased income risks.

- *Gender role changes and increased employment among women*: The increase of new types of employment, particularly part-time work, is closely linked to the continuing increase in employment among women. This is true of the former West Germany, whereas the old East German states, where a high rate of female employment was part of the socialist norm, have if anything seen a decline in employment among women. It is typical of a large proportion of women's jobs that the income is not sufficient for individual subsistence; but where this income serves as 'extra earnings' for a couple, it does cushion the income risks for the household. However, with unstable relationships and/or new ways of life, the risks are still increasing.

- *Changing lifestyles*: Although marriage and family still represent the prevailing pattern of co-habitation in Germany, they no longer stand out on their own as they once did. Among new ways of living, single-person households, unmarried partnerships and above all one-parent families have grown in empirical significance. As shown by the consistently high rates of divorce and separation and the high numbers of births outside marriage, the traditional system of family protection, based on the male breadwinner model, has become fragile. This upheaval is also a factor in increasing income risk.

- *Migration*: Although Germany has never officially identified or perceived itself as an immigration country, migration has become a normal feature of society over recent decades. In contrast to neighbouring European countries, the principal groups of migrants include not only the classic economic migrants and their dependents from southern Europe, but also ethnic German refugees and emigrants from Central and Eastern Europe. Overall, migrants are impacted by particular problems of employment, and consequently of income.

- *German unification*: German unification represents a uniquely German problem. For the states of the former GDR, the abrupt transition from a planned economy to a market economy represents a radical economic and social break, which was and is associated with a clear increase in income and living standards, but has also led to persistent economic difficulties and high unemployment. An alignment of economic performance in the old GDR states with the level in the west is not yet in sight, nor is there much hope of rapid and sweeping improvements in the outlook for the labour market. From a social policy point of view, this upheaval can only be overcome by equally long-term and high transfer payments from west to east, which however also means that the German welfare state has very limited room for manoeuvre and that there is massive fiscal pressure to reduce welfare payments.

An employment-based restructuring of the German welfare state and the poverty problem

Empirical studies show that increasing unemployment, especially long-term unemployment, has contributed most to making income risk a reality. This is true not only of Germany, but of all the countries of Europe, cutting across all welfare state types. In Germany, this relationship is seen above all in the constant increase over the last 20 years in the number and proportion of people falling back on social assistance to support themselves in the absence of work. Although problems in the labour market are not the only reason for this trend – we must also consider the changes we have already mentioned in lifestyles and family structures (the increased number of single parents), and the consequences of migration – there are an increasing number of benefit recipients who could be considered employable. In this sense, social assistance in Germany is assuming more and more of a basic support function in relation to unemployment, and is supplementing statutory unemployment benefit as well as tax-funded, needs-based unemployment assistance.

Assuming that the level of employment under current macro-economic conditions does not increase, we may look for a solution to the problem of poverty attributable to labour market factors in higher and above all more targeted transfers to the persons or households affected. This approach fits the idea of a social and poverty policy aimed at stabilizing and improving actual living and income situations. When we analyze real social policy trends in Germany, as in most countries of Europe, it soon becomes clear that this approach has been outside the political mainstream for some time. In the last few years, policy has been characterized rather by a series of reductions in payment levels, in particular in the area of social security benefits for unemployment. This is not driven by fiscal motives alone. There has been an overall paradigm shift in connection with benefits for unemployment (Hanesch, 1999): persistently high unemployment, and above all the concentration of the risks of unemployment around unqualified, disabled and older people, may increasingly be interpreted (on the basis of neoclassical labour market theory) as a consequence of design faults in the social security system.

This line of argument, which dominates both academic (economic) and political debate in Germany, has its equivalent in most European countries, and also in the recommendations of the European Commission and of international organizations like the OECD The starting point is the realization that there are insufficient incentives to exchange unemployment and social assistance payments for a low-paid job, as the level of cover is too high in relation to achievable employment income, and employment income is taken too much into account in setting benefit levels As a consequence, Germany, in common with many other European countries, has seen a change in social security policy towards promoting employment Calls for an 'activating welfare state' and a new balance between 'encouraging and demanding' are behind support for measures stretching from reductions in benefits, higher voluntary contributions, compulsory employment and tighter penalties on the one hand, through to increased opportunities for integration, advice, training and placement on the other. It remains to be seen in the future whether the approaches implied by a mainly labour market related social policy are really suited to raising the level of employment and providing jobs for the unemployed. If this is not successful, or only succeeds for a limited time, there is a danger of growing disparities in income and increasing risks of poverty. Current social policy controversies in Germany focus precisely on this point.

Overview of the sections and chapters in this book

Combating Poverty in Europe: The European welfare regimes and the European Union

Regardless of specific national features, the existing social security systems in all European countries can be classified into different types of welfare regime, each applying different measures to combat poverty with varying degrees of efficiency. There are also growing efforts at European Union level to push through more strongly co-ordinated policies for combating poverty and social exclusion in the countries of the EU through national action plans.

In their chapter on *Welfare capitalism: The ten year impact of governments on poverty, inequality and financial risks in West Germany, The Netherlands and the USA*, Bruce Headey and Ruud Muffels use comparative panel data to review the short-, medium-, and above all long-term implementation of equity goals in three countries, each embodying one of the welfare regime types defined by Esping-Andersen. Here, the authors do not address the classical target population for social policy measures, but focus primarily on social security provisions for people of working age.

In their chapter *How successful are European countries in reducing poverty? A micro-simulation with the ECHP*, Birgit Otto and Jan Goebel also draw on Esping-Andersen's welfare typology. Based on data from the European Commission Household Panel (ECHP), they use a micro-simulation for selected countries to analyze the extent to which poverty has been reduced for different social groups by government action through taxation and social transfers. This takes account not only of the number of poor people in each case, but also of the intensity of poverty.

Armindo Silva's chapter on *National Action Plans to combat poverty in Europe* takes an in-depth look at the basis for a co-ordinated European anti-poverty policy. He explains in detail the 'Open Method of Coordination', set up to implement the action plans launched by all the EU Member States, and surveys future trends in the light of EU enlargement.

Finally, the use of indicators represents a major tool for the European Commission in pushing through national action plans for combating poverty and social exclusion. Brian Nolan's chapter on *Indicators for social inclusion in the European Union* reports on the concept underlying the European Commission's choice of indicators, and explains the individual items in detail. In this context, he also points to the need to compile suitable data to allow an adequate assessment of the ongoing process of poverty reduction.

Income inequality, poverty and redistribution

In the 1980s and 1990s, there was a trend towards increasing income inequality in many European countries, and as a consequence, an increased risk of relative poverty also. Analyzes based on annual income confirm this tendency in Germany too, although annual time series focus more on variability in income distribution; while the trend towards polarization, in light of more tightly defined income concepts in West Germany, is limited to specific periods. The associated social policy debate certainly revived the question of how well redistributive social policy measures actually work, and prompted the German government to publish its first 'Poverty and Wealth Report' in 2001 – to be produced regularly in future, in each legislative term. In the 1990s, the consequences of unification were the main focus of analyzes on income and poverty in Germany.

Peter Krause's chapter on *Income, poverty and dynamics in Germany* documents the differing income conditions in East and West Germany at the time of unification, based on data from the Socio-Economic Panel (GSOEP), and describes how income levels, distribution and dynamics, and the impact of social policy measures have changed since then.

Hans-Jürgen Andreß's chapter *Does low income mean poverty? Some necessary extensions of poverty indicators based on economic resources* refers to the distinction, introduced by Stein Ringen, between indirect measurement of poverty (based on resources) and direct measurement (focusing on the resulting living standards). He shows that the link between relative income poverty and deprivation in Germany – and in other countries – is rather tenuous, and calls for a corresponding widening of the concept of poverty.

Richard Hauser's chapter on *Distribution patterns and social policy options in Germany* uses data from income and consumption surveys (EVS) to look at long-term trends from 1973 onwards in the distribution of market and disposable income, and in the distribution of wealth. He points especially to the increase in poverty among children and young people, and proposes a number of social policy solutions.

Walter Hanesch's chapter on *Social assistance between social protection and activation in Germany* gives an overview of social assistance regulations, the most important social policy instrument for direct combating of poverty in Germany. He deals in detail with the current debate on the reorganization of the social security 'safety net', with a view towards greater integration of people of working age.

In the final chapter by Michael F. Förster and Mark Pearson, *Income distribution and poverty in the OECD area: Trends and driving forces*, the findings and trends previously shown for Germany are set in a European and international context. This chapter appeared previously in *OECD Economic Studies* (34), 2002/1. Further studies on the subject were published in Michael F. Förster, assisted by M. Pellizarri (2000), 'Trends and driving factors in income inequality and poverty in the OECD area', *OECD Labour Market and Social Policy Occasional Papers* (42), Paris. The analyzes compare the distribution of market and disposable income based on comparable income data, and break it down further in terms of socio-demographic groups and income components. In this way, Förster and Pearson give a solid overview of the background to trends in income inequality and income poverty in the 1970s, 1980s and 1990s in over 20 OECD countries.

Labour market related poverty – A challenge for social protection and integration strategies

In Germany, as in the other EU Member States, labour market related poverty is the focus of the employment and social policy debate. In his chapter on *Labour market related poverty in Germany*, for example, Walter Hanesch begins with an overview of empirical findings on poverty among the unemployed and in the households of unemployed people, addressing particularly the different types of household and income composition in this area. He then presents data on 'poverty in spite of employment', and also examines the significance of the household situation for the existence of the 'working poor'. Against this background, the chapter summarizes the current employment and social policy debate about the connection between the labour market and poverty, and presents approaches to overcoming labour market related poverty.

The analysis put forward by Michael Maschke in his chapter on *Immigrants between labour market and poverty* concentrates on the labour market position and income situation of immigrants in Germany. Based on an overview of the hierarchy of legal residence titles currently in force, he presents empirical findings on trends in participation in the labour market, welfare recipiency, income distribution and income poverty among migrants. In a final section, he examines the likely effects of the planned new Immigration Act on legal discrimination and the income situation of foreign migrants.

In her chapter on *Social protection and activation for the unemployed*, Claudia Weinkopf examines the points of departure and the strategic perspectives for an activation policy for the unemployed in Germany. She begins with a critical evaluation of the specific application of social benefits for the unemployed, the regulations for access to the labour market, and the penalties currently in force. She describes the experience of applying financial incentive measures, particularly in the low wage sector, and also addresses the question of what effects may be anticipated from current reform proposals to extend advisory and placement services. In her conclusions, she calls for the individual instruments to be incorporated into a comprehensive employment strategy aimed at raising the employment rate in Germany.

In his chapter on *Activation in the Western Europe of the 1990s: did it make a Difference?*, Bjørn Hvinden shows that the concept of activation can be interpreted in different ways. He also shows that the answer to the question as to how far activation has genuinely increased in the countries of Western Europe depends on which definition of activation is used. As Hvinden demonstrates, a positive correlation can be found between the scope of activation and trends in the labour market, although the impact of activation is also influenced by a whole bundle of other factors.

Families and children in poverty and concepts of family policy

Poverty among children and families with children is a growing social problem in almost all countries of the European Union. While the once close link between pension age and poverty risk has become much looser over the last few years, we now find a particularly high incidence of poverty among families with several children, and among single parents. This trend is noteworthy in that there is a general consensus in all countries that child poverty is particularly unacceptable. Since children are largely helpless victims of their situation, they are particularly dependent on secure living and income conditions.

This contradiction is picked up by Karel Van den Bosch and Bea Cantillon in their chapter on *Social policy strategies to combat income poverty of children and families in Europe*. Based on comparative data for Europe, he discusses which types of family composition are at particular risk of poverty, and analyzes the effects of various types of financial payment to families in helping to avoid poverty.

Gerhard Bäcker's chapter on *Child and family poverty in Germany* presents the findings for Germany. He demonstrates that the number and the age of children, and the different types of family situation, are crucial factors in determining the extent of poverty. However, another decisive factor is whether both parents contribute to family income from employment, or whether the traditional breadwinner model applies, with the husband alone responsible for earning an income. As the social security and tax regulations in Germany provide incentives for wives and mothers not to work, there is an urgent need for reform.

The employment rate for mothers is also heavily dependent on the provision of childcare facilities. C. Katharina Spiess and Gert G. Wagner highlight this problem in their chapter *Why are day care vouchers an effective and efficient instrument to combat child poverty in Germany?*, and emphasize that an expansion of daycare facilities is preferable to a further increase in financial transfers to families as a way of improving the chances of combining career and family. Spiess and Wagner call for targeted day-care vouchers to be issued, redeemable at accredited institutions.

Notes

1 The main insight gained from this approach is the recognition that social benefits are only one (doubtless important) factor in building a more comprehensive welfare state framework, whose effects only develop against the background of existing labour market, household and private network structures, and which is tightly bound up with other elements such as labour and tax policy. For the debate on the construction of this type of welfare regime in Germany, see, for example, Schmid, 1996; Lessenich and Ostner, 1998; Kohl, 2000.

2 In light of the imminent enlargement of the European Union, we must ask to what extent the countries of Central and Eastern Europe such as Poland, the Czech Republic or Hungary, which have left the planned economy behind and are in the process of changing their social benefits systems, form a fifth type, or whether they can be subsumed into the types already mentioned.

References

Allmendinger, J. and Ludwig-Mayerhofer, W. (eds) (2002), *Soziologie des Sozialstaats – Gesellschaftliche Grundlagen, historische Zusammenhänge und aktuelle Entwicklungstendenzen*, Juventa, München.

Bäcker, G. et al. (2000), *Sozialpolitik und soziale Lage in Deutschland*, Vol. I, Westdeutscher Verlag, Wiesbaden.

Bäcker, G. and Klammer, U. (2002), 'The Dismantling of Welfare in Germany', in Goldberg, and Rosenthal (eds) (2002).

Eardley, T. et al. (1996), *Social Assistance in OECD Countries: Synthesis Report*, DSS 1274 Social Policy Research Unit, University of York.

Erster Armuts- und Reichtumsbericht. (2001), 'Unterrichtung durch die Bundesregierung, Lebenslagen in Deutschland', Bundestags-Drucksache 14 and 5990, 8.5.2001.

Esping-Andersen, G. (1990), *The Three Worlds of Welfare Capitalism*, The Polity Press, Cambridge.

European Foundation (for the Improvement of Living and Working Conditions) (ed.) (1999), *Linking Welfare and Work*, Luxembourg.

Europäische Kommission (1996), *Soziale Sicherheit in Europa 1995*, Luxembourg.

European Commission and EUROSTAT (2000), *Die soziale Lage in der Europäischen Union*, Luxembourg.

European Commission and EUROSTAT (2000), *European social statistics. Income, poverty and social exclusion*, Luxembourg.

EUROSTAT (2000), *Social Protection Expenditure and Receipts. Data 1980-1997*, Luxembourg.

Goldberg, T., Rosenthal, M. (eds) (2002), *Diminishing Welfare: A Cross-National Study of Social Provision*, Auburn House, Westport, Connecticut.

Hanesch, W. (1999), 'The Debate on Reforms of Social Assistance in Western Europe', in European Foundation (ed.) (1999).

Hanesch, W., Krause, P., Bäcker, G., Maschke, M. and Otto, B. (2000), *Armut und Ungleichheit in Deutschland. Der neue Armutsbericht der Hans Böckler Stiftung, des DGB und des Paritätischen Wohlfahrtsverbands*, Rowohlt, Reinbek.

Hanesch, W. (2001), *Soziale Sicherung und Armut im europäischen Vergleich, in Deutscher Verein für öffentliche und private Fürsorge* (ed.) Europa sozial gestalten.

Dokumentation des 75. deutschen Fürsorgetages 2000 in Hamburg, Eigenverlag des Deutschen Vereins, Frankfurt am Main.

Hauser, R. (1997), 'Soziale Sicherung in westeuropäischen Staaten', in S. Hradil and S. Immerfall (eds), *Die westeuropäischen Gesellschaften im Vergleich*, Leske und Budrich, Opladen.

Hauser, R. and Neumann, U. (1992), 'Armut in der Bundesrepublik Deutschland. Die sozialwissenschaftliche Thematisierung nach dem Zweiten Weltkrieg', in Leibfried and Voges (eds) (1992).

Kaufmann, F.X. (1997), *Herausforderungen des Sozialstaats*, Suhrkamp, Frankfurt am Main.

Kohl, H. (2000), 'Der Sozialstaat: Die deutsche Version des Wohlfahrtsstaates – Überlegungen zu seiner typologischen Verortung', in S. Leibfried and U. Wagschal, (eds) (2000).

Leibfried, S. (1990), 'Sozialstaat in Europa? Integrationsperspektiven europäischer Armutsregimes', in *Nachrichtendienst des Deutschen Vereins* (10).

Leibfried, S. and Voges W. (eds) (1992), *Armut im modernen Wohlfahrtsstaat*, Westdeutscher Verlag, Opladen.

Leibfried, S. and Pierson, P. (1998b), 'Halbsouveräne Wohlfahrtsstaaten: Der Sozialstaat in der Europäischen Mehrebenen-Politik', in Leibfried and Pierson (ed.) (1998b).

Leibfried, S. and Pierson, P. (eds) (1998b), *Standort Europa. Europäische Sozialpolitik*, Suhrkamp, Frankfurt am Main.

Leibfried, S. and Wagschal, U. (eds) (2000), *Der deutsche Sozialstaat. Bilanzen – Reformen – Perspektiven*, Campus, Frankfurt am Main/New York.

Lessenich, S. and Ostner, I. (ed.) (1998), *Welten des Wohlfahrtskapitalismus. Der Sozialstaat in vergleichender Perspektive,* Campus, Frankfurt am Main/New York.

Lødemel, I. and Trickey, H. (ed.) (2000), *An Offer You Can't Refuse. Workfare in International Perspective*, The Policy Press, University of Bristol.

Marlier, E. and Cohen-Solal, M. (2000), *Sozialleistungen und ihre Umverteilungseffekte in der EU – Neueste Daten*, Luxembourg.

Mejer, L. (2000), 'Soziale Ausgrenzung in den EU-Mitgliedsstaaten', in *Statistik kurzgefaßt* (1), Thema 3, Luxembourg.

Mejer, L. and Linden, G. (2000), 'Persistent income poverty and social exclusion in the European Union', in *Statistics in focus* (3-13), Luxembourg.

Schmid, J. (2001), *Wohlfahrtstaaten im Vergleich*, 2. Auflage, Leske und Budrich, Opladen.

Schulte, B. (1998), *Europäische Sozialpolitik und die Zukunft des Sozialstaats in Europa*, Forschungsinstitut der Friedrich Ebert Stiftung, Bonn.

Schulte, B. (ed.) (1997), *Soziale Sicherheit in der EG*, Beck, München.

Schulte, B. (2000), 'Das deutsche System der sozialen Sicherheit – Ein Überblick', in Allmendinger and Ludwig-Mayerhofer (eds) (2000).

Stellungnahme der Bundesregierung (1998), *Zehnter Kinder- und Jugendhilfebericht – Bericht über die Lebenssituation von Kindern und die Leistungen der Kinderhilfen in Deutschland*, Bundestagsdrucksache 13 and 11368.

Voges, W. and Kazepov, Y. (eds) (1998), *Armut in Europa*, Chmielorz, Wiesbaden.

PART I

THE EUROPEAN WELFARE
REGIMES AND
THE EUROPEAN UNION

Chapter 2

Welfare capitalism: The ten year impact of governments on poverty, inequality and financial risk in West Germany, the Netherlands and the USA

Bruce Headey and Ruud Muffels

This paper assesses the ten year (1987-96) impact of taxes and transfers on poverty, income inequality and financial insecurity in the working age populations of the Netherlands, the USA and West Germany. These are the only countries for which ten consecutive years of socio-economic panel survey data are available, so they afford a unique opportunity to assess the medium to long term performance of governments in achieving key equity goals. It is indeed fortunate that Germany, the Netherlands and the USA are the three countries for which long running panels exist, because they can be taken as 'best cases' of Gosta Esping-Andersen's 'Three worlds of welfare capitalism' (1990). In Esping-Andersen's terms the USA is the prototypical liberal capitalist system and Germany is the clearest case of a conservative, corporatist welfare – capitalist state. The Netherlands from the mid-1980s onwards is classified by Esping-Andersen as a social democratic welfare-capitalist state, although it is clearly a borderline judgment, since the Netherlands has progressive social benefits but does not have the other defining characteristic of social democracy (according to Esping-Andersen's slightly Swedocentric view) of commitment to active labour market programs.

In any event, Germany, the Netherlands and the USA are the three cases available, and they may be regarded as the best countries from which to draw *policy lessons* because in the last ten years they have, in an economic sense, been the best performers of their type. Their economic growth rates per capita have all been about the same and have been higher than other large and medium-sized countries of their type. The USA has had a higher growth rate than the other liberal capitalist countries, namely Australia, Canada and Switzerland. The Netherlands has had higher growth than the other social democratic countries: Denmark, Norway and Sweden. Germany, despite the burden of reunification, has had higher growth than the other large corporatist countries of France and Italy, although it has not done as well as two very small countries, Austria and Belgium.

For the record ten year growth in real GDP per capita for 1987-96 (the ten years our data cover) was 20.6 per cent in the Netherlands, 16.4 per cent in West Germany and 14.4 per cent in the USA (OECD, 1998). In the Netherlands median disposable incomes (equivalent) increased 17.9 per cent in this period. In Germany the increase was 17.3 per cent and in the USA 17.8 per cent (source: the American, Dutch and German panels). Of course taxes and transfers are intended to promote equity goals as well as efficiency goals – and equity goals are the focus of this paper. But it is important to remember the efficiency record of these countries as we review their equity performance.

The equity goals we consider are those relating to income distribution. Welfare states, and by extension tax-transfer systems are intended to redistribute income both between persons (from the rich to the poor) and within person lifetimes, forcing people to save when they are earning for periods when they are not working. The equity goals pursued by income redistribution *between persons* are reduction of poverty and reduction of income inequality. The equity goal promoted by *within person* redistribution is reduction of financial risk, or, one might say, household income instability. This last welfare state goal receives less attention, certainly from sociologists, than they other two goals, but its historical and current importance in the development of the welfare state should not be forgotten.

Only households with prime age heads (25-59) – more or less the working age population – are included in the analysis. The reason for excluding the aged is that it is well known that they are the population group best catered for by welfare states (over two-thirds of expenditure is on them) and their programs have not yet been seriously challenged or cut by reformers. More seriously threatened in recent years have been programs for working age people where issues relating to work incentives are prominent. One central question for this paper is whether welfare state goals were being less well met in the later part of the decade than the earlier part.

In writing about equity goals, we do *not* imply that policy makers in the three countries are equally committed to all three goals, or as committed as each other. Historically, USA governments have prioritized economic efficiency and had some commitment to poverty reduction, not much to reducing income inequality, and considerable concern for stabilizing household incomes through social security (especially for the aged). In Germany, from Bismarck on, the highest equity priority was income stability, since this is believed to promote social stability. In the Netherlands, with its corporatist past and social democratic present, all three equity goals have been important.

Our aim, then, is to assess the impact of social insurance (social security in American parlance), social assistance (welfare) and taxes on poverty, income inequality and the financial risk of working age households. We will describe governments in the three countries as doing *more* or *less* to promote these goals, but we do not mean *better* or *worse*, since, plainly, we have no wish to substitute our values for the values of national policy makers.

A final introductory point: the impact of taxes and transfers (or the welfare state) matters much more in the medium and long term than the short term. Most previous studies, based on annual data, have only told us about short term impacts. But of course medium and long term poverty and inequality – and probably financial risk – are much more distressing and more damaging to people's life chances. The goals of the welfare state are mainly medium and long term goals, although of course short term poverty relief and income stabilization matter too.

The great advantage of the socio-economic panel data, in contrast to annual snapshot data, is that they enable us to assess the huge and cross-nationally divergent impacts of modern governments.

Methods

The American, German and Dutch panels

The American Panel Study of Income Dynamics (PSID) began in 1968 and has continued every year since. There are now over 33,000 respondents on file, one per household. Initially, the poor were over-sampled, partly because the study was sponsored by the Office of Economic Opportunity. This and other sample biases (some due, of course, to panel attrition) are adjusted by both cross-sectional and longitudinal weights, which are routinely provided by the data managers. The PSID, like the German and Dutch panels, is updated by including 'split-offs' in the sample'; that is people who leave their original household and form a new one (e.g. children who get married).

The German panel (GSOEP) began in 1984 in West Germany and, after reunification, was extended to cover all of Germany in 1990. Only West German data are used in this paper. The initial sample included over 16,000 respondents, with everyone aged 16 and over in sample households being interviewed. Special over-samples of five foreign (guest-worker) communities were included: Italians, Greeks, Yugoslavs, Spanish and Turks. Weights are used to adjust for this and other sample biases.

The Dutch Socio-Economic Panel also began in 1984 with around 11,000 respondents in 4,000 households, and has been enlarged on various occasions to get (and keep) it at a level of about 5,000 households. As in the German panel, all household member aged 16 and over are interviewed. Initially, interviews were carried out twice a year in April and October, but in 1990 it was decided to switch to annual interviews.

The German Institute for Economic Research and Syracuse University have produced matching files for the German and American panels in which key variables relating to income, labour force experience, taxes and transfers were coded identically to facilitate international comparisons. We have constructed a comparable Dutch file. The latest decade of data for all three countries is 1987-96; hence the time span of this paper.

Measures

We begin by detailing the components of income measured in the panels. This involves describing measures of pre-government (mainly market) income and post-government (i.e. disposable) income, and next indicating how governmental redistribution of income is calculated. We then describe how income is adjusted by household size and composition (equivalence scales) in order to try and provide valid comparisons between individuals' standard of living. It then remains to define poverty, income inequality and income stability – and say how they are measured.

Income, social insurance, social assistance and taxes

In measuring income, what we are trying to do is assess people's material standard of living, or, to be more exact, the potential level of consumption their income affords. The components of household pre-government (mostly market) income included in the American and German panels are household labour income, asset income (e.g. income from shares or renting out property), private transfers (e.g. payments from a separated father to an ex-wife looking after children) and owner-occupiers' imputed net rent. In the Dutch panel owner-occupiers' imputed net rent is not available, so we have removed this component from American and German pre-government incomes as well.

Post-government income, or what is more commonly called household disposable income, is defined here as pre-government income plus social insurance (social security) and social assistance (welfare) payments, minus direct taxes. Our measures of post-government income takes no account of indirect taxes or, on the transfer side, the value of non-cash benefits and services provided by government. However, the value of food stamps in the USA is included.

By social insurance programs we mean programs substantially funded by employee and employer contributions earmarked for specific eventualities: old age, widowhood, sickness, disability, unemployment. By social assistance we mean programs funded mainly from general revenue: general social assistance, non-means tested child allowances in Germany and the Netherlands and means tested Aid to Families with Dependent Children in the USA, public old age pensions, public widows and disability pensions, basic public unemployment assistance, food stamps in the USA, and student stipends in Germany and the Netherlands.

Governmental redistribution

For many purposes we want to estimate the impact of government – 'the welfare state' – on household incomes. What difference do taxes and transfers make to poverty, inequality income stability? The general formula is (Kakwani, 1986; Ringen, 1991):

(1) Governmental =   (pre-government income – post-government income) x 100
    redistribution (%)   pre-government income

This formula can be applied to a variety of concepts. For example, governmental reduction of income inequality is simply inequality measured in pre-government incomes minus post-government income inequality, divided by pre-government inequality and multiplied by 100.

Pre-government incomes are, in a sense, the incomes people would receive if government did not exist – if there were no taxes and transfers. Of course this is not intended as a serious counterfactual since, obviously, if there was no government, or only a nightwatchman state, economic behaviour and most other forms of behaviour would be very different (Ringen, 1987).

Adjusting for household composition to get equivalent incomes – equivalent standards of living

Clearly a family of two with an income of $100,000 a year is better off than a family of four, but not twice as well off, because the family of four reaps some economics of scale. Further, the family of four is probably better off if it consists of two adults and two children than if it consists of four adults, since children are generally cheaper to feed, clothe, etc. than adults. The question of how to adjust household incomes in order to get equivalent incomes (i.e. valid comparisons of standard of living) for households of different sizes and composition has sparked a great deal of debate. Different countries use different weights in calculating their welfare (social assistance) payments. The OECD, for purposes of international comparison, used to count the head of household as 1.0, other adults as 0.7 and children as 0.5. It then commissioned studies which showed that this equivalence scale overestimated the costs of maintaining both additional adults and children at a given consumption level (see particularly, Hagenaars, 1991). A new scale of 1.0 for the first adult, 0.5 for additional adults and 0.3 for children was proposed. An international group of experts noted that a partial consensus was emerging on scales with something like these weights and suggested that dividing income by the square root of household size would be a reasonable compromise (Buhmann et al., 1988). This 'International Experts' scale has been widely used in recent work; a quick calculation in fact shows it to be very close to the new OECD scale (Atkinson, Rainwater and Smeeding, 1995).

We shall use the International Experts' scale throughout the paper to adjust pre-government incomes, social insurance, social assistance, taxes and post-government incomes. It is important to record that detailed research has shown that, within a wide range, choice of equivalence scales does not significantly affect the rankings of countries in terms of their standard of living, poverty, or income inequality (Buhmann et al.; 1988; Coulter, Cowell and Jenkins, 1992).[1]

Poverty

In Western countries poverty is almost always defined in relative rather than absolute terms. Among academic commentators and social policy makers, poverty has come predominantly to refer to relative poverty, 'relative deprivation' or, more recently, 'social exclusion' (Runciman, 1966; Townsend, 1979; Jordan, 1996). Survey research has shown, similarly, that people see themselves and are seen by others as poor and excluded from a mainstream lifestyle if their incomes are below about 50 per cent of median income in the society in which they live (Hagenaars, 1986; Muffels, 1993; Rainwater, 1974; van Praag et al., 1982).

Our main measure of relative poverty is the conventional OECD one used during this period: a person is defined as poor if his/her post-government equivalent income is less than 50 per cent of median post-government equivalent income (OECD and the EU have now semi-officially adopted a poverty line of 60 per cent of median equivalent income, which is also approximately 50 per cent of the mean). It should be noted that this definition was *not* accepted by the any of the three governments whose performance is reviewed here. At the time the Netherlands and Germany had no official definition and the American food-based definition corresponded equivalent to about 40 per cent of median equivalent income.[2]

The percentage of the population below the poverty line, so calculated, is the 'poverty rate'. To give a more complete account of poverty one also needs data on the poverty gap; the average amount by which those who are poor fall below the poverty line. However, reports of very low incomes in surveys are notoriously unreliable. Frankly, we found poverty gap estimates generated from the three panels hard to credit. So we omit them.

Income equality

Our measure of income inequality is the Gini coefficient. Gini is the most widely used measure of inequality, running from 0 to 1, where 0 means that all incomes are equal and 1 means that one unit has all the income available. It should be noted that Gini is most sensitive to changes in the middle of the distribution, and not particularly sensitive to redistribution in favour of the poor.

Financial risk

Our measures of financial risk are based on the view that (1) in the short term prime age households would perceive themselves more insecure, or more at risk, the more their market income in a particular year declined compared with the previous year and (2) in the long term they would see themselves as being at risk the more their income fluctuated from year to year. So we calculated for each year the percentage of people whose real incomes declined ('losers') and the median losses involved. We also examined the coefficient of variation (the standard deviation divided by the mean) in each person's annual income during the decade. This was done for both pre- and post-government (equivalent) incomes; the difference being the impact (or insurance effect) of government in reducing risk.

Results

We now examine the short, medium and long term impact of the state on poverty, inequality and income stability, treating one year (1987 and 1996) measures as short term, five year measures (1987-91 and 1992-96) as medium term, and the ten year (1987-96) measure as long term.

In presenting results we will make the more or less (but not totally) correct assumption that tax-transfer systems work as follows:

• People first earn a market income (labour earnings, asset income etc.);
• Secondly, they collect social insurance benefits to which they are entitled;

- Thirdly, they receive any social assistance benefits they are entitled to, after government officials have assessed their market and social insurance income;
- Finally, they pay taxes on their total income.

This stylized account glosses over a number of exceptions and international differences. In the USA and the Netherlands family members file taxes separately and are primarily taxed on individual income. But entitlement to benefits is mainly determined by family size and household income. In Germany, by contrast, husband and wife file taxes jointly, and both taxes and transfers are mainly determined on a household basis.

Poverty

Table 2.1 shows the impact of social insurance, social assistance and taxes on poverty measured at the beginning and end of the 1987-96 period. The final row gives the percentage reduction in poverty effected by government. It can be seen that in the Netherlands and Germany lower percentages of people in these working age households would have been poor if they had to rely on market income alone. In the USA, as is fairly well known, the working poor are a considerably larger group. Furthermore, the Dutch and German governments, through their tax-transfer systems, reduce poverty substantially. The American government makes little impact; indeed it marginally increased poverty at the beginning of the decade.

In all three countries it appears that social assistance (transfers from general revenue) made the greatest contribution to poverty reduction. More detailed analysis (not shown here) indicates that in all countries a majority of people who were market income poor received at least some social assistance but zero social insurance. In fact, in all three countries social insurance only reduced poverty to a small extent, because it only helped people who had established a lengthy work record and so made substantial insurance contributions. It is sad and at first puzzling to see that direct taxes had the effect of moving some households, who would have been non-poor on the basis of transfers, back into poverty. Of course it should be remembered that the 'OECD poverty line' has not been adopted officially by any of these countries. It is also the case that nearly all the people taxed back into poverty were only just below the OECD poverty line.

It seems plain in all three countries that, despite a decade of good economic growth, there was more poverty at the end of the decade than the beginning. Market income poverty was nearly 50 per cent up in the USA and also well up in Germany. In the Netherlands, where growth was exceptional, market income poverty fell slightly.

Governments did little or nothing to counteract the trend. The American government continued to make no impact on poverty numbers. The German government did transfer more people out of poverty by the end of the decade than it had at the beginning, but disposable income (i.e. real) poverty was still higher. In the Netherlands there was a sharp fall in the percentage transferred out, so that disposable income poverty rose despite the favourable market trend.

We now assess the impact of governments on medium term (five year) and longer term (ten year) poverty.

Table 2.1   Impact of governments on poverty at the beginning and end of the decade: people in households with heads aged 25-59

Poor on basis of... (%)	USA		West Germany		Netherlands	
	1987	1996	1987	1996	1987	1996
Market income	14.3	21.3	8.6	13.3	11.9	9.7
Market and social insurance income	13.4	20.6	6.8	11.5	11.2	8.1
Market and social insurance and social assistance income	12.3	16.6	3.6	5.9	2.7	5.4
Disposable income (above – taxes)	14.9	21.0	6.9	9.6	4.1	6.5
Reduction in poverty by government* (%)	(+4)	1.4	19.8	27.8	65.5	33.0

*   *Reduction in poverty (%) = (market income poverty – disposable income poverty)/market income poverty x 100.*

The key finding in Table 2.2 is that the Dutch and German governments reduce poverty much more over five years than one, and somewhat more over ten years than five. Medium and long term poverty of course matter much more than short term, and it is important to record how effective the European welfare states are in this regard. The Dutch government comes close to abolishing five and ten year poverty, and the German government cut it to a very low level in the second half of the decade. American government, on the other hand, reduces the poverty of working age households no more in the medium and longer term than on an annual basis. People who are persistently or frequently poor lose benefits and/or fail to collect their entitlements. (Note that these data relate to a period before the 1996 welfare reform further reduced the period of entitlement.)

One reason for the European governments being able to reduce the poverty rate more effectively in the medium and longer term is that market incomes are quite volatile from year to year, so that not only are fewer people poor on a five or ten year basis than annually, but also those who are poor tend to be less far below the poverty line (i.e. the poverty gap is smaller). So fixed governments benefits can more readily pull them above the poverty line.

Table 2.2   Impact of governments on medium and long term poverty: people in households with heads aged 25-59

Poor on basis of... (in %)	USA			West Germany			Netherlands		
	1987-91	1992-96	1987-96	1987-91	1992-96	1987-96	1987-91	1992-96	1987-96
Market income	14.0	13.2	11.5	6.0	4.7	3.8	5.6	4.5	3.6
Market income and social insurance	13.2	12.4	10.7	5.1	3.5	3.3	5.4	3.8	3.4
market income and social insurance and social assistance	11.1	10.9	9.7	2.7	1.0	1.5	0.2	0.8	0.0[b]
disposable income (above – taxes)	13.6	13.2	11.7	4.1	1.6	2.6	0.9	1.7	0.8
reduction in poverty by government (%)[a]	2.9	0	(+1.7)	31.7	70.0	31.6	83.9	62.2	77.8

a   *See note *, Table 2.1.*
b   *Less than 0.1 per cent.*

Income inequality

We now assess the impact of these three governments on income inequality, remembering that our measure of inequality, the decile ratio, is simple the division of the 90th percentile's income by the 10th percentile's (Table 2.3).

Table 2.3   Impact of governments on inequality at the beginning and end of the decade: people in households with heads aged 25-59 – Decile ratios

Inequality on basis of... (in %)	USA		West Germany		Netherlands	
	1987 Gini	1996 Gini	1987 Gini	1996 Gini	1987 Gini	1996 Gini
Market income	.377	.402	.288	.315	.280	.306
Market and social insurance income3	.373	.397	.284	.301	.279	.302
Market and social insurance and social assistance income	.364	.391	.254	.268	.239	.276
Disposable income (above – taxes)	.345	.372	.234	.253	.223	.232
Reduction in inequality by government* (%)	8.5	7.5	18.7	19.7	20.3	24.2

*   *Reduction in inequality(%) = (market income Gini – disposable income Gini)/market income Gini x 100.*

The clear result here is that the Dutch 'social democratic' welfare-capitalist regime and the German 'corporatist' regime, despite having more equal market income distributions to start with, redistribute over twice as much as the 'liberal' USA. In contrast to our findings in relation to poverty, the inequality results indicate only small differences between the two European countries. The Netherlands has both a slightly more equal market income distribution than W. Germany and also redistributes somewhat more in the direction of low income families. Dutch social assistance benefits make the largest contribution to reduction of inequality, with direct taxes apparently playing an increasing role and social insurance virtually no role. In Germany also social assistance plays the largest role. In the USA the pattern is quite different. Market income inequality is much higher than in Germany and the Netherlands, or, one might say, returns to human capital are greater. Social insurance and social assistance make modest contributions to the reduction of inequality, with taxes doing a little more, but the total governmental reduction of inequality among prime aged households ('the undeserving poor') is still under 10 per cent.

In all three countries inequality of market incomes increased quite sharply during the decade. In the Netherlands and Germany transfers and taxes were having a somewhat more redistributive effect by 1996 than in 1987. This was due to (largely) unchanged entitlements rather than to any reforms intended to assist lower income groups. In the USA the redistributive impact of government did not rise in 1987-96, and since the Clinton welfare reforms redistribution has probably diminished further, although employment has risen (Ellwood and Dickens, 2002). Overall inequality rose quite sharply in the USA. In fact disposable income inequality actually rose more than market income inequality; the opposite pattern to the two European countries.

Table 2.4 shows the impact of governments on medium and long term inequality, and confirms the picture in the previous table.

In all three countries both market and disposable incomes are considerably more equal over five or ten years than in a single year. Market incomes tend to equalize over time both for labour market and family reasons. Labour market earnings usually rise until a person reaches the age of about fifty and then tend to fall as retirement approaches. Family membership changes due to marriage, divorce and children being born and later leaving home. So the number of family members who are in paid work changes and this has a big effect on family income.

The five and ten year perspective clarifies the importance of social assistance in effecting redistribution. In all three countries social insurance and taxes have about the same modestly redistributive impact, viewed over these longer periods. The difference lies in the different weights assigned to social assistance. In the USA social assistance is strictly means tested, and in most respects eligibility criteria have been tightened in recent years, especially at the beginning of the Reagan Presidency and since 1996. In Germany and the Netherlands people who lose their jobs or are disabled usually at first have some social insurance entitlements. However, these run out after a period (most commonly 6-12 months in Germany and 54 months in the Netherlands) and then people go on to social assistance if they are still unable to work (OECD, 1996). Social assistance is much more generous in the Netherlands than Germany. For example, a typical worker who used to be on average earnings and has a family of four still gets 79 per cent of previous earnings after five years out of work, whereas a German in the same situation gets 52 per cent (OECD, 1996). It should be mentioned that recent Dutch governments, following the OECD line, have come to regard this level of benefits as constituting a disincentive to work, and it is clearly the case that Dutch people tend to remain on benefits longer than Germans or Americans (Goodin et al, 1999).

The Ginis for 1992-96 compared to 1987-91 confirm that market income inequality has been rising in all three countries. This probably reflects increasing returns to skill in labour markets world-wide (Atkinson, Rainwater and Smeeding, 1995; OECD, 1998). The trend is not one that most governments would want to resist in the market itself for fear of creating inefficiencies ('distortions') in the allocation of labour. Having said that, it should be noted that the Dutch government has regularly (since the Wassenaar Accord in 1982) reached 'wage solidarity' agreements with employers and unions, which may have restrained increases in wage disparities (Hemerijck and van Kersbergen, 1997).

Table 2.4   Impact of governments on medium and long term inequality: people in households with heads aged 25-59

Inequality on the basis of... (in %)	USA			West Germany			Netherlands		
	1987-91	1992-96	1987-96	1987-91	1992-96	1987-96	1987-91	1992-96	1987-96
Market income	.360	.381	.359	.268	.289	.265	.254	.276	.253
Market income and social insurance	.358	.378	.356	.264	.282	.260	.252	.272	.250
Market income and social insurance and social assistance	.349	.371	.348	.244	.262	.241	.214	.239	.215
Disposable income (above − taxes)	.333	.353	.332	.223	.244	.224	.205	.212	.198
Reduction in poverty by government* (%)	7.5	7.3	7.5	16.8	15.6	15.5	19.3	23.2	21.7

* See note *, Table 2.3.

Governments can, however, more readily decide to redistribute more or less through their tax-transfer systems. The evidence in Table 2.4 suggests that only the Dutch government somewhat counteracted market trends, increasing its redistributive impact from 19.3 per cent in 1987-91 to 23.2 per cent in 1992-96.

Financial risk

Assessing the impact of government in reducing financial risk and thereby promoting household financial stability is more complicated than assessing its impact on poverty and inequality, so we adopt a somewhat different approach. In Table 2.5 we take a rather simplistic or at least a short term view by regarding a decline in income from one year to the next as evidence of risk. We examine the extent to which governments reduced risk by intervening to ensure that declines in real disposable income were less than declines in market income. The table deals with just the first and last years of the decade: the first row shows the percentage whose market income fell, the second row shows the median amount by which it fell, the third row shows the median amount by which the same people's disposable incomes fell, and the bottom row measures the impact of government in reducing risk.

Table 2.5   Government reduction of financial risk: insurance effects 1987 and 1996: People in households with heads aged 25-59

Income declines	USA		West Germany		Netherlands	
(in %)	**1987**	**1996**	**1987**	**1996**	**1987**	**1996**
Per cent whose market income declined	36.1	37.3	37.9	51.9	39.7	46.9
Median decline in market income[a]	13.1	13.6	11.4	9.7	12.3	7.3
Median decline in disposable income[b]	10.6	12.7	8.2	6.9	8.2	3.9
Government insurance effect[c]	19.1	6.6	28.1	28.9	33.3	46.6

a   As a percentage of the previous year's median market income (equivalent).
b   As a percentage of the previous year's median disposable income (equivalent).
c   Government insurance or risk reduction (per cent) = (Market income decline % – Disposable income decline %)/(Market income decline %) x 100.

Promoting household income stability is usually thought of as the highest equity priority of corporatist states, so we would expect to find the impact of governmental or welfare state 'insurance effects' to be greater in Germany than in the USA or the Netherlands. Table 2.5 shows that this expectation is not confirmed. The positions of Germany and the Netherlands are reversed. The median size of market income losses in the first and last years of the decade were about the same in all three countries but the Dutch tax-transfer system apparently did most to reduce these losses (but see Table 2.6), so that median disposable income losses were lowest in the Netherlands, followed by Germany, then the USA (It should be noted that results in this table are misleading in one respect; it was not in general true in this decade that fewer Americans than Germans and Dutch experienced losses of market income in one year compared with the previous one. That just happened to be true in 1987 and particularly 1996. The median percentage experiencing an annual income decline in this decade was between 40 per cent and 45 per cent in all three countries).

Table 2.6 gives a ten year picture of the impact of government on financial risk. We now take a slightly more sophisticated view of risk. A household's finances are viewed as being more at risk, the more their market incomes fluctuate from year to year. The welfare state is regarded as providing risk insurance by evening out these fluctuations and so compensating for the volatility of the market (Barr, 1998). The coefficient of variation (c.v.) is a straightforward measure of annual fluctuations in each person's income during the decade, but it does have one defect for our purposes. People whose incomes kept on rising throughout the decade record a high coefficient of variation, just like people whose incomes varied a lot, and those whose incomes declined a lot. But normally we would only consider people to be at risk, and perhaps in need of government assistance, if they were in the latter two categories. However more detailed analysis, using less convenient measures than the coefficient of variation, indicates that the results given in Table 2.6 require little modification (Headey, Goodin, Muffels and Dirven, 2000). The table gives results separately for all households and for those in the bottom half of the income distribution. The latter might be regarded as more in need of risk insurance (although this is perhaps more of a liberal or social democratic viewpoint than a corporatist one).

Table 2.6 indicates that market income instability was highest in the USA, and that American government, following its market creed, did least about it. Neither social insurance, nor social assistance, nor taxes in the USA did much to reduce financial risk for the population as a whole, although social insurance and social assistance made a modest impact on the fortunes of lower income people. This table provides a different and probably more correct comparison between the Germany and the Netherlands than was given by Table 2.5. It shows that market income instability was higher in Germany but that government did more there than in the Netherlands to even out fluctuations. Furthermore the German government, in line with corporatist values, assisted higher income households almost as much as lower income households, whereas the 'social democratic' Dutch regime helped the bottom half of the income distribution a great deal more.

It is of considerable interest that in all three countries, but especially Germany and the Netherlands, social assistance appears to do more to stabilize incomes than social insurance. This is a puzzle, since social insurance is usually thought of as being designed expressly to stabilize people's incomes at close to their normal market level in periods when market income is lost. In the event, it seems that during this decade not enough people under 60 who had stored-up substantial social insurance contributions (mainly for unemployment, disability or widowhood) suffered sufficiently serious declines in income to be eligible to collect their benefits. Market incomes certainly fluctuated a lot, but for many people the troughs were not so deep nor so long as to allow much insurance to be collected. Certainly, too, there must have been others whose incomes suffered severely but whose work history was such that they had not stored up much social insurance. Finally, remember that we are dealing here with the under 60s; social insurance kicks in mainly in retirement.

Table 2.6   Impact of governments on ten year income instability: People in households with heads aged 25-59

Instability on the basis of...	USA		West Germany		Netherlands	
	All: Median c.v.[b]	Bottom Half: Median c.v.[b]	All: Median c.v.[b]	Bottom Half: Median c.v.[b]	All: Median c.v.[b]	Bottom Half: Median c.v.[b]
market income	0.20	0.32	0.20	0.27	0.20	0.23
market income, social insurance	0.20	0.31	0.20	0.27	0.21	0.23
market income, social insurance, social assistance	0.20	0.29	0.20	0.22	0.20	0.20
disposable income (above – taxes)	0.20	0.29	0.21	0.21	0.20	0.18
reduction in income instability by government[a] (%)	13.6	9.4	20.0	22.2	9.1	21.7

a   *Reduction in financial risk by government (per cent) = (c.v. of market incomes – c.v. of disposable incomes)/(c.v. of market incomes) x 100.*
b   *People whose summed disposable incomes for the decade were below the national median.*

Discussion

Welfare states can work. The panel data show that in the medium and longer term – which matter more than the short term – the Dutch and German states very substantially reduce poverty and inequality, and also iron out financial risk (or income instability). This would have come as no surprise in regard to the retired population; the group best catered for by welfare states. What this paper has shown is that it is also true for the working age population; people whose programs have been under threat from recent welfare state reforms.

International differences in welfare state performance are huge. The Dutch 'social democratic' welfare-capitalist state reduces ten year poverty in the working age population to a small fraction (less than a tenth) of American levels and about one-third of German. Dutch disposable income inequality is also much lower than American and over 10 per cent lower than German. Household income stability is probably also highest in the Netherlands (for more detailed evidence see Goodin et al., 1999). Viewed over ten years, it is clear that social assistance programs contribute most to producing all three outcomes. It is crucial to understanding these international comparisons to realize that the Dutch 'social democratic' regime spends much more on social assistance (which is a higher proportion of the social policy budget) than governments in the other two countries. And of course Dutch outcomes can only be achieved because taxes and public expenditure are much higher as a percentage of GDP than in the USA (about 50 per cent higher) and quite considerably higher than in Germany. Consequently, disposable personal incomes are lower. The issue is what value for money people think they get for government expenditure.

A point of considerable practical importance is that, although the international differences remain vast, reduction of poverty and inequality were less effectively achieved in all three countries in the second half of the decade than the first. Plainly the change is a consequence of the policy push for cutting back welfare benefits to working age households in order to reduce work disincentives. The balance between equity and efficiency has shifted against equity.

Clearly, this paper has only scratched the surface in indicating *how* welfare state goals are achieved. We have disaggregated only to the extent of distinguishing between social insurance, social assistance and direct taxes. This is a first step but is probably too broad-brush to be useful for policy design and advocacy. The panel data allow us to disentangle the effects of specific social insurance and assistance programs and to ask, 'How effectively and efficiently do specific programs assist specific population groups faced with different life events and stages of the family life cycle?'

Notes

1   It does, however, affect estimates of the poverty rates of particular groups within countries. Clearly, poverty in large families is downgraded by giving lower weights to children, and would be upgraded if one reverted to higher weights.
2   The Federal Government defines a family as poor if it has to pay more than one-third of its income for an adequate diet.

References

Atkinson, A.B., Rainwater, L., and Smeeding, T.M. (1995), *Income Distribution in OECD Countries*, OECD, Paris.
Barr, N. (1998), *The Economics of the Welfare State*, Stanford University Press, Stanford.

Buhmann, B., Rainwater, L. Schmaus, G. and Smeeding, T.N. (1988), 'Equivalence scales, well-being, inequality and poverty: Sensitivity estimates across ten countries using the Luxembourg Income Study (LIS) database', *Review of Income and Wealth* (34), pp. 115-142.

Coulter, F.A.E., Cowell, F.A and Jenkins, S.P. (1992), 'Equivalence scale relativities and the extent of inequality and poverty', *Economic Journal* (102), pp. 1067-1082.

Dickens, R. and Ellwood, DT. (2001), 'Whither poverty in Great Britain and the united States? The determinants of changing poverty and whether work will work', *NBER Working Paper* (8253).

Esping-Andersen, G. (1990), *The Three Worlds of Welfare Capitalism*, Princeton University Press, Princeton.

Goodin, R.E., Headey, B., Muffels, R. and Dirven, H.J. (1999), *The Real Worlds of Welfare Capitalism*, Cambridge University Press, Cambridge.

Hagenaars, A.J.M. (1986), *The Perception of Poverty*, North Holland, Amsterdam.

Hagenaars, A.J.M. (1991), 'The definition and measurement of poverty', in L. Osberg (ed.) *Economic Inequality and Poverty: International Perspectives*, M.E. Sharpe, New York.

Headey, B., Goodin, R.E., Muffels, R. and Dirven, H-J. (2000), 'Is there a trade-off between economic efficiency and a generous welfare state? A comparison of best cases of the three worlds of welfare capitalism', *Social Indicators Research* (50), pp. 115-157.

Hemerijck, A. and van Kersbergen, K. (1997), 'A miraculous model? Explaining the new politics of the welfare state in the Netherlands', *Acta Politica* (23), pp. 258-280

Jordan, B. (1996), *A Theory of Poverty and Social Exclusion*, Polity, Oxford.

Kakwani, N. (1986), *Analysing Redistribution Policies*, Cambridge University Press, Cambridge.

Ministry of Social Affairs and Employment, The Netherlands (1996), *The Dutch Welfare State in International and Economic Perspective*, Ministry of Social Affairs and Employment, The Hague.

Muffels, R.J.A. (1993), 'Welfare Economic Effects of Social Security. Essays on Poverty. Social Security and Labour Markets: Evidence from Panel Data', *Series on Social Security Studies* (21), Tilburg University, Tilburg Netherlands.

OECD (1998), *Employment Outlook*, OECD, Paris.

OECD (1996), *Benefit Systems and Work Disincentives*, OECD, Paris.

Rainwater, L. (1974), *What Money Buys: Inequality and the Social Meanings of Income*, Basic Books, New York.

Ringen, S. (1987), *The possibility of politics*, Clarendon, Oxford.

Ringen, S. (1991), 'Households, standard of living and inequality', *Review of Income and Wealth* (37), pp. 1-13.

Runciman, W.G. (1966), *Relative Deprivation and Social Justice*, Penguin, Harmondsworth:.

Shorrocks, A.F. (1980), 'The class of additively decomposable inequality measures', *Econometrica* (48), pp. 613-625.

Townsend, P. (1979), *Poverty in the United Kingdom*, Penguin, Harmondsworth.

Van Praag, B.M.S., Hagenaars, A.J.M. and Van Weeren, J. (1982), 'Poverty in Europe', *Review of Income and Wealth* (28), pp. 345-359.

Chapter 3

How successful are European countries in reducing poverty? A micro-simulation with the ECHP

Birgit Otto and Jan Goebel*

Introduction

Using the fifth wave (1998) of the European Community Household Panel (ECHP), the purpose of this chapter is to analyze how successful the EU member states are in reducing poverty through the payment of cash social transfers. A similar analysis already has been performed by Heady et al. (2001). Their main focus was to show the impact of different kinds of social transfers such as means testing and flat rates on the reduction of overall inequality and poverty in European countries. Our analysis, however, focuses on the impact of social transfers as a whole (excluding pensions and survivor benefits) on the different dimensions of poverty. Moreover, since taxes and transfers are 'two sides of the same coin,' the reducing effect of cash social transfers cannot be measured by merely subtracting social transfers from disposable household income. In contrast to Heady et al. (2001) we therefore calculate a 'tax refund' and consider the aspect of tax payment reductions as a replacement for cash social transfers. In doing so, we follow the methodology used in Frick et al. (2000).

Since the headcount ratio, the 'classical' measurement of poverty, ignores important effects[1] of social policy, in this analysis a class of poverty measures defined by Foster, Greer and Thorbecke (1984) is applied (FGT), which measures the gap and the severity of poverty in addition to the incidence of poverty. Although this poverty measure stems from Sen's criticism of the headcount ratio (Sen, 1976), and especially satisfies his well-known poverty axioms,[2] the FGT measure is seldom used (for a discussion, see Myles, 1995; Myles and Picot, 2000).

Interestingly, cross-national comparisons of poverty and the welfare distribution have re-discovered this class of measures in recent years (DeFina and Thanawala, 2002; Heady et al., 2001; Frick et al., 2000). One reason might be that with the FGT a comprehensive poverty profile is obtained even though harmonized micro data such as the ECHP do not reflect the highly differentiated national systems of social insurance. Nevertheless, there is evidence from previous research that 'high expenditures on social protection are usually in line with lower national poverty rates' (Frick et al., 2000, p. 177; see also Heady et al., 2001; Kim, 1999).

From the recent comparative poverty research literature it is also well-known that single-parent families, couples with many children and households with an unemployed main breadwinner present typical poverty risk groups in most of the European countries (see e.g. Hanesch et al., 2000; Eardley et al., 1996). To analyze the poverty-reduction effect for these groups, a decomposition of poverty by population subgroups is examined for three household characteristics. While the 'household type' and the 'main activity of the head of household' describe the social-structural background of poor households, information about how many of the poor households are 'able to make ends meet' gives insight into the subjective assessment of the current household income situation. Moreover, aware that we can only give a rough overview here, we select only six countries which are representative of the different welfare regimes (Germany, Austria, Denmark, the United Kingdom, Ireland and Greece) for the decomposition analysis.

The remainder of the chapter is organized as follow: A short overview concerning expenditures on social protection in countries of the EU is outlined in section 2. The data, methods and assumptions used to measure poverty are explained in section 3. Section 4 describes the empirical results. The final section concludes and highlights the main findings (section 5).

Expenditure on social protection in the European Union

The highest expenditures on social protection in 1999 were in the social democratic welfare regimes, as in Denmark and Sweden, and in the corporatist-conservative welfare regimes (see Table 3.1). Both types expend nearly one third of their gross domestic product (GDP) on social protection. In contrast to this, the Mediterranean welfare states expend only a quarter of GDP on social protection. Also remarkable is the low share of expenditures in Ireland in all years selected (less than 20 percent of the GDP) as compared with the United Kingdom, the second representative of the liberal welfare regime. This ranking of countries and welfare types does not change when the social protection expenditures for the years 1990 and 1996 are added.[3]

Given the differences between European welfare regimes, both in structure and in the extent of social insurance, the term 'social transfers' covers various definitions and functions of different transfers and allowances. Table 3.1 shows that the 'old age and survivor pension' transfer constitutes the largest relative share of expenditure on social protection in each country. This transfer is excluded from our analysis. Except for Ireland, all European countries expend more than one third of transfers on old age and pension benefits. In Ireland, transfers for sickness and health care comprise the largest relative share of expenditures. Social benefits in the form of specific transfers for combating poverty, such as housing and protection from social exclusion, have the lowest share of total benefits in the majority of countries considered here. The share of this function group is an average of less than four per cent of the total social expenditure across all countries.

Table 3.1   Social protection in countries of the European Union

	Expenditure on social protection (SP)							
	SPª as % of GDP			Social benefits by function group as % of SP in 1999				
	1990	1996	1999	Old age, survivors	Sickness/ health care, disability	Family/ children	Un-employ-ment	Housing, social exclusionᵇ
GER	25.4	30.0	29.6	42.1	36.0	10.5	8.8	2.6
FR	27.9	31.0	30.3	44.2	34.0	9.8	7.4	4.6
AUS	26.7	29.6	28.6	47.4	35.4	10.3	.4	1.6
B	26.4	28.7	28.2	43.0	33.6	9.1	12.1	2.2
NL	32.5	30.1	28.1	41.5	40.7	4.3	6.2	7.4
LUX	22.0	24.0	21.9	41.4	39.5	15.5	2.5	1.1
DK	28.7	31.4	29.4	38.0	31.7	13.0	11.2	6.1
SWE	33.1	34.5	32.9	39.5	36.9	10.5	8.1	4.9
FIN	25.1	31.6	26.7	35.1	37.2	12.8	11.3	3.7
UK	23.0	28.3	26.9	46.1	34.8	8.8	3.2	7.0
IRL	18.4	17.8	14.7	25.2	45.3	13.0	11.1	5.4
I	24.7	24.8	25.3	64.0	30.0	3.7	2.2	0.2
GR	19.9	21.8	20.0	46.2	37.0	2.1	12.9	1.9
SP	22.9	22.9	25.5	50.7	31.0	7.6	5.7	5.0
P	15.2	21.3	22.9	43.7	45.6	5.2	3.7	1.8

a   SP = Expenditure on social protection (as per cent of GDP).
b   Not elsewhere classified.

Source: Amerini (1999, 2000a, 2000b) and Abramovici (2002).

Data and methods

The data used in the analysis are extracted from the User Database (UDB) of the European Community Household Panels (ECHP), which has been collected for most countries since 1994 by public institutions under the supervision of the Statistical Office of the European Communities (Eurostat).[4] Currently, five waves (1994-1998) are available and fifteen countries are included. The analysis population includes all surveyed persons who are living in private households and for whom valid income information was collected in the fifth wave (1998). Since this wave does not contain data for Luxembourg and Finland, the comparative analysis includes the following thirteen countries: Germany, France, Belgium, Austria, the Netherlands, Denmark, Sweden, the United Kingdom, Ireland, Italy, Greece, Spain and Portugal.

To measure poverty, the disposable income information of the previous year is used.[5] The disposable income includes income from work (employed and self-employed), private income (rents, income from capital and private transfers to the household), as well as pensions and other social benefits directly received. Indirect social transfers (such as reimbursement of medical expenses), income in kind and imputed rents for owner-occupied accommodation are excluded (Marlier and Cohen-Solal, 2000, p. 7). In order to compare households of different structures and sizes, the disposable household income is transformed via the widely-used 'modified OECD equivalence scale' into an equivalent income.[6]

Social transfers in the analysis are defined as the sum[7] of public allowances and benefits excluding pension and survivor benefits (see also DeFina and Thanawala, 2002; Hölsch, 2002; Heady et al., 2001; Frick et al., 2000; Kraus, 2000).

For the micro-simulation of a 'world excluding social transfers,' we first deduct the amount of equivalent social transfers from the equivalent income. Second, since social transfers are financed by previously paid taxes, all persons with tax payments (EQTax) receive an equivalent tax refund given by the amount of the refund factor (RE). The source for estimating the refund factor is the gross-net factor, which is available in the household files of ECHP. This method could be also described as a 're-redistribution of resources', because the sum of equivalent social transfers (EQTrans) is redistributed to those who paid taxes previously. The tax refund is defined for each country separately as:

$$(1) \qquad RE = \left(\frac{EQTax_i}{\sum\limits_{i=1}^{n} EQTax_i} \right) \times \sum\limits_{i=1}^{n} EQTrans$$

Although all components of the micro-simulation are household information (disposable household income, social transfers, tax payment information), the components were transformed into equivalent components before the micro-simulation was examined. Although the correct method would be to transform these components after the micro-simulation, the latter method could produce a modified average income (mean) since the components may refer to different groups. The higher the overlap between tax-payer households and transfer-recipient households, the lower the difference between the mean of the real world and the mean of the simulated world. To determine the extent to which this problem could modify the empirical results of the analysis, we examined both methods. The results show only marginal differences and do not yield different poverty profiles of the countries included.

Since the term 'social transfers' is linked to specific histories and includes several function groups of social insurance, it is difficult to estimate the consequences of the absence of cash social transfers. Therefore we follow the assumption suggested by Heady et al. (2001) and Frick et al. (2000) and assume no differences between both worlds in the behavior of individuals concerning such aspects as changes in labor market participation.

The poverty threshold in the analysis is 50 per cent of the country-specific mean. Since the mean is not changed by the micro-simulation as described above, the poverty threshold in both worlds will be the same. To measure poverty, the class of poverty measures by Foster et al. (1984) is used. The FGT family is defined as:

$$(1) \qquad P_\alpha(y,z) = \frac{1}{n} \sum_{i=1}^{q} \left(\frac{z-y}{z} \right)^\alpha$$

In the above equation n describes the number of observed persons, q represents the number of poor, y is the equivalent income of the poor individuals, z describes the poverty threshold and α is the weighting parameter for the individual poverty gap. If the parameter α is equal to zero, the widely used head-count ratio or poverty incidence (FGT0) is produced. If it takes on a value of one ($\alpha = 1$), the sum of the poverty gaps is taken into account and divided by the whole population. These results in an average poverty gap (FGT1). Implementing an α which is greater than one ($\alpha > 1$) implies that the poverty measurement is sensitive both towards the poverty incidence and poverty gap (Slesnick, 2001, p. 159).

In accordance with Sen's poverty axioms, Foster et al. (1984) is often called the FGT2 measure 'poverty severity, because it measures the 'depth of poverty'. Because the most frequently used value of the parameter α for measuring poverty severity is 2, this measure is also known as the FGT2 measure. The average poverty gap (FGT1) is dropped from our analysis, because *poverty incidence* and *poverty severity* together give a sufficient or comprehensive picture of poverty for each country.

To show the impact of a population subgroup on the overall poverty measure, the FGT can be decomposed as follows:

$$(3) \qquad P_\alpha(y,z) = \sum_{j=1}^{m} \frac{n_j}{n} P_\alpha(y^j; z)$$

For any income vector y broken down into subgroup income vectors $\{y^1, \ldots, y^m\}$, P is additively decomposable with population share weights (n_j/n). '[...] In fact, increased poverty in a subgroup will increase total poverty at a rate given by the population share n_j/n; the larger the population share, the greater the impact. The quantity $T_j = (n_j/n) P_\alpha(y^j; z)$ may be interpreted as the total contribution of a subgroup to overall poverty while $100 \, T_j/P_\alpha(y^j; z)$ is the percentage contribution of subgroup j' (Foster et al., 1984, p. 764).

Empirical results[8]

Not surprisingly, we observe the lowest poverty incidence (HQ) as well as the lowest poverty severity (PS) in Denmark (6 per cent) and Sweden (7 per cent) (see Table 3.2, left column 'Real World'). In contrast to these countries, the Mediterranean countries (Italy, Greece, Spain, and Portugal) have a poverty incidence and severity more than twice as high (between 18 and 23 per cent). In these countries nearly each fifth person belongs to the poor population. A similarly high poverty incidence is reported in the table for the liberal welfare regimes (the United Kingdom, Ireland), but the poverty severity is considerably lower.

The lowest difference between the real world and the simulated world, excluding cash social transfers, can be observed for the Mediterranean countries. Only the overall poverty severity is reduced, with poverty incidence remaining approximately the same. Summing up, the impact of social transfers is very low, because the payment of social transfers reduces the poverty severity in all four Mediterranean countries only marginally (by 20 per cent). The largest differences in terms of poverty severity between the two worlds occurred for Denmark, Sweden and, surprisingly, Ireland. They would have by far the highest poverty severity in a world excluding social transfers and they exhibit by far the lowest poverty severity in the real world.

On the basis of the headcount ratio (poverty incidence), the United Kingdom and Ireland present similar poverty profiles in both worlds (around 19 per cent in the real world and around 28 per cent in the simulated world). Both countries reduce the headcount ratio to a similar extent. But from the perspective of poverty severity, one must argue that the poverty-reducing effect in Ireland (0.133 real world, 1.171 simulated world) is higher than in the United Kingdom (0.268 versus 1.100). The same effect can observed for Denmark and Sweden, the representatives of the social-democratic welfare regimes. Both countries reduce the headcount ratio to a similar extent (around 6 per cent in the real world and around 18 per cent in the simulated world). But the impact of cash social transfers differs considerably if one uses the poverty severity instead. From this perspective, Denmark is more successful than Sweden, because the poverty severity can be reduced from 0.879 down to 0.052. In contrast, Sweden reduces the poverty severity from 0.851 to 0.116.

Within the group of corporatist-conservative welfare regimes, France is the country with the highest poverty incidence and severity in a world excluding social transfers. One-quarter of the French population is poor. France therefore has the highest poverty severity after Denmark, the United Kingdom and Ireland in the simulated world. Similar to Ireland, through the payment of social transfers France obtains a reduction in poverty severity rather than a reduction in poverty incidence. The best result within the group of the corporatist-conservative welfare regimes, surprisingly, was attained by Austria, because it has both the lowest poverty incidence (15 per cent) as well as severity (0.358) in the simulated world, and the lowest poverty incidence (9 per cent) and severity (0.116) in the real world. A similar pattern of poverty and poverty reduction also can be reported for the Netherlands. But at 0.678, the poverty severity in the simulated world is considerably higher in the Netherlands than in Austria.

The TIP curve by Jenkins and Lambert (1997) paints a revealing picture of poverty for all countries in both worlds. By depicting the cumulated poverty gaps of the poor as a curve, it is possible to illustrate poverty incidence, poverty intensity and the inequality of individual poverty gaps for each country separately (see Figures 3.1 and 3.2). Poverty incidence is represented by the non-horizontal line which crosses the x-axis. The magnitude of poverty intensity is documented by the highest point of the curve (y-axis). 'The inequality dimension of poverty is summarized by the degree of concavity of the non-horizontal section of the TIP curve' (Jenkins and Lambert, 1997, p. 319). The lower the poverty gap of the poorest person in a country and the lower the inequality within the group of the poor population, the flatter the curve of the cumulative poverty gaps. Because incomes of the non-poor are not important within the agregation step[9], the poverty gap is set to zero for these individuals and each curve finishes parallel to the x-axis.

Table 3.2   Poverty severity and poverty incidence including and excluding social transfers, 1998

Countries	Real world		Simulated world excluding social transfers	
	Incidence (in %)	Severity	Incidence (in %)	Severity
Germany	13.3	0.151	19.0	0.678
France	13.5	0.158	25.0	0.706
Austria	9.2	0.116	15.0	0.358
Belgium	18.1	0.245	25.4	1.170
Netherlands	9.8	0.151	15.9	0.678
Denmark	5.8	0.052	18.6	0.879
Sweden	7.3	0.116	18.4	0.851
United Kingdom	19.3	0.286	27.2	1.100
Ireland	19.0	0.133	29.0	1.171
Italy	17.7	0.312	19.3	0.466
Greece	22.4	0.346	23.3	0.455
Spain	19.8	0.412	23.9	0.801
Portugal	23.1	0.371	27.6	0.635

Notes: Net equivalent disposable income, modified OECD equivalence scale, poverty line: 50 per cent of mean. The results of poverty severity are multiplied by a factor of 100.

Source: UDB ECHP 2002: Wave 5 (1998), weighted.

With the exception of the four Mediterranean welfare states, all European countries observed achieve considerable poverty reduction through the payment of cash social transfers (see Figures 3.1 and 3.2).

The results confirm previous empirical analysis by Defina and Thanawala (2002), Hölsch (2002), Kraus (2000), Heady et al (2001), but also emphasize the necessity of considering the different dimensions of poverty. First, as the cases of Ireland and UK have shown, the same reduction of poverty incidence does not imply the same reduction of poverty intensity. Second, the Mediterranean welfare states present rather 'rudimentary' welfare regimes with the following characteristics: 'earnings replacements are small, an unlimited guaranteed minimum income does not exist or varies according to local and regional regulations. Overall coverage is fragmented and means tests are of medium significance' (Kraus, 2000, p. 17).

Income including social transfers (1998)

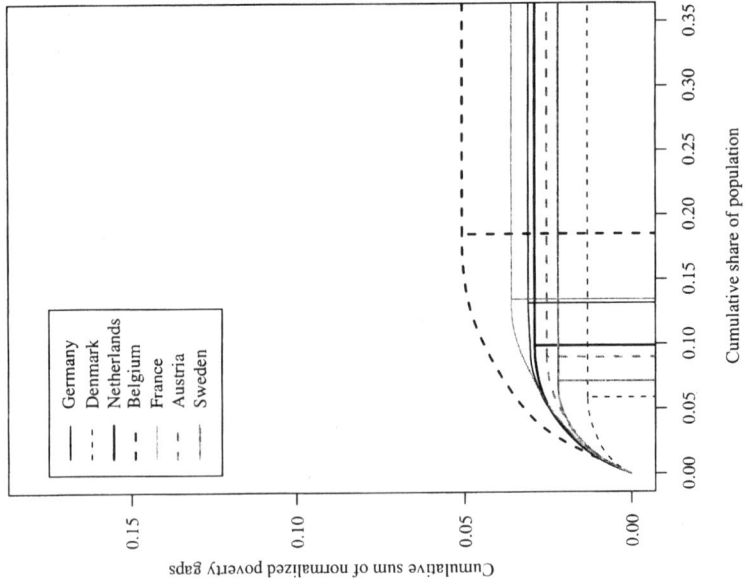

Germany
Denmark
Netherlands
Belgium
France
Austria
Sweden

Cumulative sum of normalized poverty gaps

Cumulative share of population

Income excluding social transfers (1998)

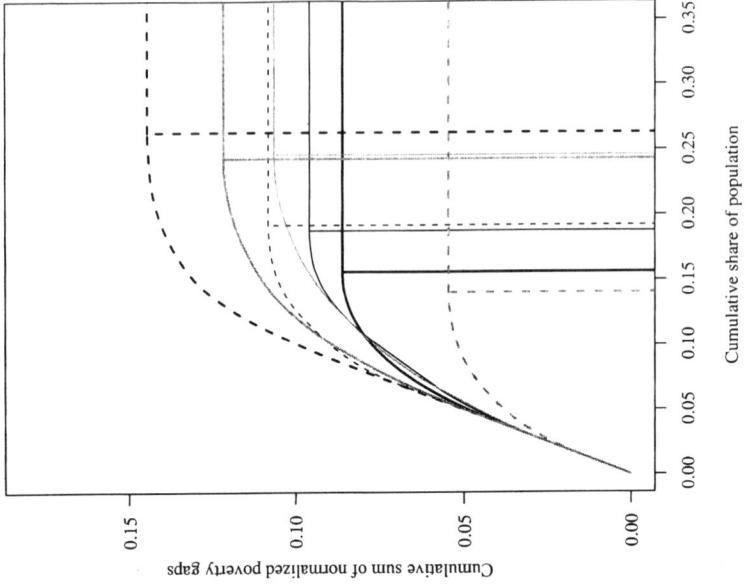

Cumulative sum of normalized poverty gaps

Cumulative share of population

Figure 3.1 TIP curves including and excluding social transfers

Figure 3.2 TIP curves including and excluding social transfers

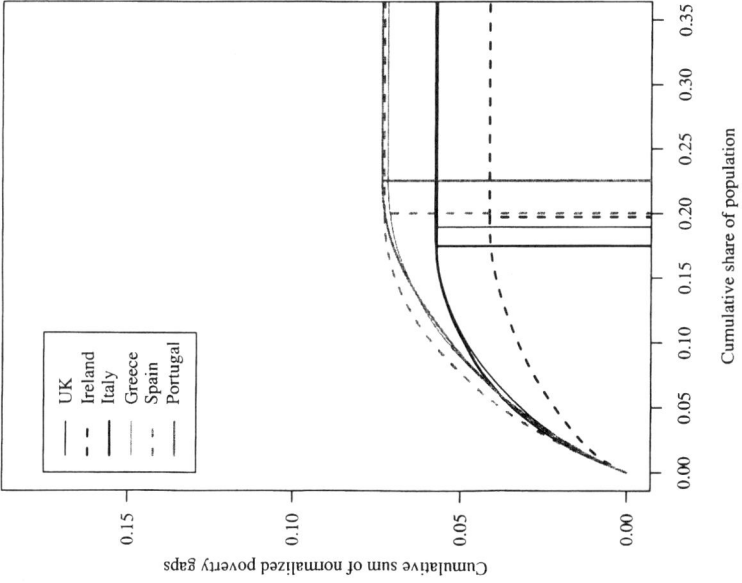

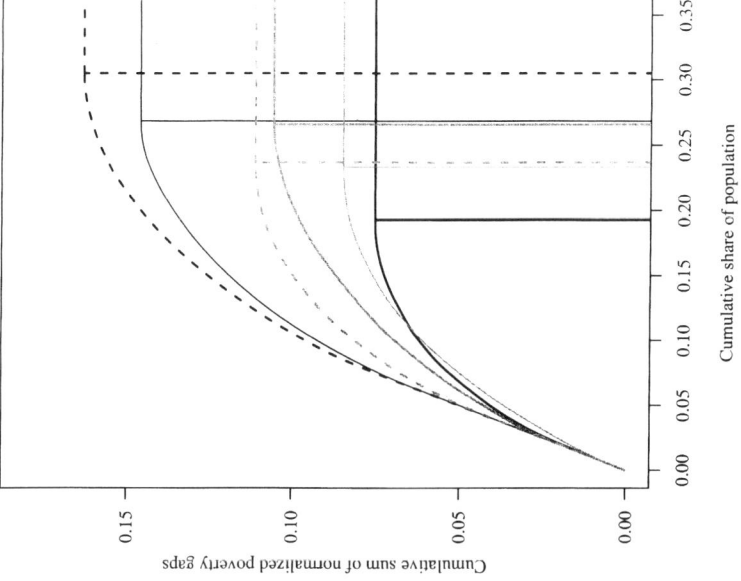

The poverty incidence and intensity in a world without cash social transfers would be lower than in the social-democratic and liberal welfare regimes. Third, Denmark and Sweden, both representatives of a comprehensive and universal welfare tradition with the goal 'to promote social integration and progress towards an equal and more secure society' (Kraus, 2000, p. 3) have among the highest poverty intensities in Europe in a simulated world without cash social transfers.

This result is remarkable, because these countries reach the lowest poverty incidence and intensity in the real world, and their total expenditures on social protection are not considerably higher than those of the conservative-corporatist welfare regimes. In other words, while these countries have the most successful poverty-combating policy, the comparative results of the simulated world also show also that their policies to combat poverty are linked with high welfare dependency among the population as a whole.

Decomposition of poor by household characteristics

The left column of the Tables 3.3, 3.4 and 3.5 shows the total population share of the analyzed characteristic. The other columns illustrate the 'poverty affection' based on poverty incidence or on poverty severity. 'The poverty affection index describes the relationship [contribution to total poverty / population share], with values above 1.0 indicating subgroups with an above-average poverty risk, and values below 1.0 indicating groups with a below-average risk' (Frick et al., 2000, p. 193). The larger the difference between both worlds, the larger the impact of social transfers on the income position of the respective subgroup.

Table 3.3   Decomposition of the poor by household type

Household characteristic of person	Poverty affection (contribution to total poverty/ population share)				
	Total population share (in %)	Real world		Simulated world excluding social transfers	
		Incidence (HQ)	Severity (PS)	Incidence (HQ)	Severity (PS)
Germany					
Single	16.8	1.42	2.38	1.19	1.63
Couple	27.1	0.47	0.87	0.55	0.54
Single-parent	2.73	3.39	3.97	3.05	5.29
Couple with children	30.0	1.43	0.48	1.39	1.17
Others	23.5	0.49	0.49	0.64	0.37
	100.0				
Austria					
Single	12.2	1.75	1.99	1.44	1.87
Couple	20.9	0.85	0.85	0.89	1.35
Single-parent	3.1	2.68	3.21	2.87	3.65
Couple with children	29.9	1.04	0.98	1.10	0.75
Others	33.7	0.63	0.54	0.65	0.43
	100.0				

Table 3.3 (cont)

Household characteristic of person	Poverty affection (contribution to total poverty/ population share)				
	Total population share (in %)	Real world		Simulated world excluding social transfers	
		Incidence (HQ)	Severity (PS)	Incidence (HQ)	Severity (PS)
Denmark					
Single	17.2	3.30	4.59	2.13	1.91
Couple	28.2	0.93	0.42	0.79	0.62
Single-parent	1.6	1.61	2.61	2.56	3.41
Couple with children	32.5	0.32	0.12	0.88	1.22
Others	20.4	0.18	0.04	0.41	0.21
	100.0				
United Kingdom					
Single	12.5	1.96	2.03	1.73	1.13
Couple	26.7	0.78	0.67	0.68	0.41
Single-parent	5.9	1.92	1.63	2.82	4.74
Couple with children	35.2	0.95	1.08	0.93	1.07
Others	19.6	0.50	0.45	0.54	0.45
	100.0				
Ireland					
Single	7.3	2.51	1.51	1.64	1.10
Couple	13.3	0.61	0.62	0.66	0.63
Single-parent	3.4	2.50	4.40	2.50	3.96
Couple with children	37.2	1.14	1.41	0.88	1.11
Others	38.7	0.57	0.33	0.98	0.74
	100.0				
Greece					
Single	8.2	1.35	2.20	1.39	2.37
Couple	20.8	1.19	1.46	1.24	1.45
Single-parent	1.4	0.58	0.86	0.59	0.61
Couple with children	35.3	0.60	0.53	0.56	0.42
Others	34.2	1.23	0.93	1.23	1.01
	100.0				

Notes: Net equivalent disposable income, modified OECD equivalence scale, poverty line: 50 per cent of mean.

Source: UDB ECHP 2002: Wave 5 (1998), weighted.

Poverty affection by household type Table 3.3 reports above-average poverty incidence affection in the real world, with the exception of Greece, for individuals from single households and single-parent households. In contrast to the situation in all other countries, Greek households with children have a below-average poverty affection. On the other hand, at a population share of 34 per cent in Greece, the category of 'other households' is quite large, such that the question emerges as to whether this group may also include some households with children.

Poverty affection by the main activity of the head of household The highest poverty severity affection occurs for individuals from households with an unemployed head of household and for individuals from households with an inactive head of household (see Table 3.4). Since the minority of employed persons work part-time, the household type 'employed head' is dominated by households with a full-time employed head of household. Although this group covers family types with different poverty risks, overall, the poverty severity affection is considerably below average in all countries. For all other household types we find national exceptions. For example, the poverty severity affection in Irish households with a retired head is below average (0.53), while this household type in the other countries in the analysis has above-average poverty affection. The highest poverty affection in the 'retired-head' households category can be observed in Denmark with a value of 2.21. On the other hand, individuals in this country from households with an 'unemployed head' have the lowest poverty severity affection (0.13).

The poverty severity affection in the group of individuals from 'inactive-head households' is, despite the generous welfare policy in Denmark, at a value of 6.72, higher than the poverty severity affection in Germany (6.44). In all other countries the poverty severity affection of individuals from 'inactive-head households' is considerably lower, with values ranging between 2.74 for Austria and 1.82 for Greece. Whether the post-harmonization processing of this information has yielded different definitions of 'retired-head household' and 'inactive-head household' remains an open question. It should be merely noted here that the relative population shares of these categories in Germany and Denmark are considerably lower than in the other countries (e.g. Austria 16 per cent versus Germany 4 per cent).

Table 3.4   Decomposition of poverty by employment status

Main activity status of the head of household	Poverty affection (contribution to total poverty/ population share)				
	Total population share (%)	Real world		Simulated world excluding social transfers	
		Incidence (HQ)	Severity (PS)	Incidence (HQ)	Severity (PS)
Germany					
Employed head	62.2	0.77	0.28	0.68	0.36
Unemployed head	6.0	2.93	3.38	3.36	5.73
Retired head	27.9	0.76	1.34	0.94	0.79
Inactive head	3.89	3.50	6.44	2.82	5.34
	100.0				
Austria					
Employed head	60.2	0.71	0.68	0.63	0.37
Unemployed head	2.7	2.97	1.79	4.12	7.44
Retired head	21.5	0.93	0.53	1.14	1.40
Inactive head	15.6	1.87	2.74	1.69	1.76
	100.0				

Table 3.4 (cont)

Main activity status of the head of household	Poverty affection (contribution to total poverty/ population share)				
	Total population share (%)	Real world		Simulated world excluding social transfers	
		Incidence (HQ)	Severity (PS)	Incidence (HQ)	Severity (PS)
Denmark					
Employed head	66.4	0.25	0.18	0.24	0.06
Unemployed head	6.75	0.52	0.13	3.62	6.25
Retired head	20.7	2.33	2.21	1.88	1.56
Inactive head	6.12	5.20	6.72	3.42	3.48
	100.0				
United Kingdom					
Employed head	62.9	0.46	0.37	0.37	0.17
Unemployed head	3.0	2.04	2.36	2.80	5.09
Retired head	17.4	1.80	1.46	1.52	0.54
Inactive head	16.8	2.01	2.63	2.50	3.85
	100.0				
Ireland					
Employed head	60.1	0.38	0.33	0.39	0.15
Unemployed head	11.0	3.11	2.54	2.87	4.11
Retired head	11.7	0.78	0.53	0.84	0.37
Inactive head	17.3	1.95	2.67	2.03	2.42
	100.0				
Greece					
Employed head	71.4	0.78	0.65	0.76	0.61
Unemployed head	1.49	2.73	3.53	2.72	3.30
Retired head	22.3	1.52	1.79	1.58	1.90
Inactive head	4.79	1.28	1.82	1.30	1.94
	100.0				

Notes: Net equivalent disposable income, modified OECD equivalence scale, poverty line: 50 per cent of mean.

Source: UDB ECHP 2002: Wave 5 (1998), weighted.

Furthermore, the decomposition of the poor population by the main activity of the head of household shows that social transfers in the largest sub-population – households with an employed head – have a rather low impact on the income situation in all countries. The poverty affection in both worlds is nearly the same for this group in all countries and is also quite low. For the group 'retired household head' we receive various patterns of effects. In most countries the individuals from this household type 'lose' in the real world. In Austria they 'win' through payments of cash transfers. Moreover, in Germany and Ireland the poverty incidence affection in this group decreases from the simulated world to the real world, while the poverty severity affection increases. Since the poverty gap within the poverty severity measure has a greater weight than the headcount ratio, again, this effect illustrates the limits of the headcount ratio.

Poverty affection by ability of the household to make ends meet   The last table (Table 3.5) reports the poverty affection of individuals from households with different assessments of their ability to make ends meet.[10] While the other two household characteristics present rather 'objective' and roughly categorized information about the household, this information directly reflects the current household information as interpreted by the reference person. It should be noted here that the poverty measurement refers to the disposable income of the previous year.

Table 3.5   Decomposition of poverty by subjective assessment status

Household is able to make ends meet	Poverty affection (contribution to total poverty/ population share)				
	Total population share (in %)	Real world		Simulated world excluding social transfers	
		Incidence (HQ)	Severity (PS)	Incidence (HQ)	Severity (PS)
Austria					
With difficulty	17.6	2.02	2.26	1.89	2.17
Both... and	62.1	0.94	0.86	0.97	0.86
Without difficulty	20.3	0.29	0.35	0.32	0.40
	100.0				
Denmark					
With difficulty	10.4	2.21	2.81	2.82	4.17
Both... and	58.7	0.86	0.74	0.91	0.78
Without difficulty	30.8	0.85	0.88	0.55	0.36
	100.0				
United Kingdom					
With difficulty	7.51	1.58	1.50	2.04	2.66
Both... and	60.7	1.12	1.07	1.10	1.07
Without difficulty	31.8	0.64	0.76	0.57	0.47
	100.0				
Ireland					
With difficulty	21.8	2.09	2.13	2.03	2.66
Both... and	67.5	0.75	0.71	0.78	0.57
Without difficulty	10.7	0.36	0.53	0.28	0.35
	100.0				
Greece					
With difficulty	44.2	1.51	1.58	1.52	1.61
Both... and	47.8	0.67	0.60	0.67	0.58
Without difficulty	8.0	0.16	0.18	0.12	0.14
	100.0				

Notes: Net equivalent disposable income, modified OECD equivalence scale, poverty line: 50 per cent of mean.

Source: UDB ECHP 2002: Wave 5 (1998), weighted.

However, the results show a clear relationship between the household income situation of the previous year and the current assessment of the household income situation. For the most countries the poverty affection of households with difficulty making ends meet is twice as high as in other households with lower difficulty making ends meet. Remarkable is that the country with the highest poverty incidence and severity among the group – Greece – has one of the lowest levels of poverty affection in the category 'with difficulty' (1.58). In contrast, the lowest poverty incidence and severity within Europe occurs in Denmark, where the poverty affection in households with difficulty has a value of 2.81.

Furthermore, the lowest differences between the group of households 'with difficulty' and the group of household 'with both: with and without difficulty', can be observed in the United Kingdom and Greece – both countries with a high overall poverty incidence and severity in the European comparison. Moreover, the poverty incidence and poverty severity affection indices are nearly the same in all countries. The additional consideration of the poverty gap within the poverty measurement therefore does not result in new findings for this household characteristic. If one compares the real world with a world excluding social transfers, the poverty profile changes considerably for only one country: Denmark. In Denmark the poverty severity affection of the group 'with difficulty' making ends meet rises in the simulated world, from a value of 2.81 up to 4.17 in the simulated world.

Conclusions

Using the fifth wave (1998) of the European Community Household Panel we analyze in this paper the impact of cash social transfers on poverty. For thirteen countries of the European Union we simulate a world excluding social transfers and reduced tax payments due to the absence of social transfers. The comparison of the real world with the simulated world is examined on the basis of the FGT Index (Foster et al., 1984), which satisfies Sen's widely-known poverty axioms (Sen, 1976).

For all countries, both the overall poverty incidence and poverty severity are generally higher in a world excluding social transfers than in the real world. The Mediterranean countries and the social-democratic countries represent extreme positions within the European Union. Not surprisingly, while the poverty-reducing effect of cash social transfers in the Mediterranean countries is very low, the impact in the social-democratic welfare regimes is quite high. Interestingly, although the Mediterranean welfare states present rather 'rudimentary' welfare regimes, the poverty incidence and severity in a world without cash social transfers would be lower than in the social-democratic and liberal welfare regimes. Denmark and Sweden, both representatives of a comprehensive and universal welfare tradition with the goal 'to promote social integration and progress towards an equal and more secure society' (Kraus, 2000, p. 3) have among the European countries some of the highest poverty intensities in a simulated world without cash social transfers. This result is remarkable, because these countries achieve the lowest poverty incidence and severity in the real world and the total expenditure on social protection are not considerably higher than in the conservative-corporatist welfare regimes. In other words, on the one hand these countries have the most successful poverty-combating policies, but on the other hand the comparative results of the simulated world show that these policies are linked with high welfare dependency among the population overall.

Furthermore, as the cases of Ireland and the UK have shown, the same reduction in poverty incidence does not imply the same reduction in poverty severity. Both countries confirm the impact of the 'poor law tradition' in these countries, though in a different manner. In contrast to the United Kingdom, Ireland is considerably more successful in reducing poverty through cash social transfers than the United Kingdom. After the social-democratic welfare regimes, Ireland attains the lowest poverty severity in the real world. The differences between both countries can be seen only when the FGT measure with α equal 2 is added. Given that in Ireland the share of expenditures on social protection in 1999 (15 per cent) is considerably lower than in the United Kingdom (27 per cent), this result emphasizes the necessity of a more differentiated perspective on both poverty and poverty-combating policies in cross-national analysis.

From the perspective of various groups at risk for poverty, such as families with children or households with an unemployed head, the results in all countries do not endorse inevitably a positive impact of cash social transfers on poverty affection – inasmuch as tax payments as funding basis of transfers are considered. The example of the single households, for which we found above-average poverty affection in all countries, illustrates that they are worse off in the real world than they would be in a world excluding social transfers. In contrast, single-parent households profit from the cash social transfers in the real world. They have by far the highest poverty affection but also by far the highest poverty reduction in most of the six countries. Exceptions are Greece and Ireland, in which a poverty reduction in this group cannot be observed.

Summing up, the application of the poverty severity measure first emphasizes the necessity of a more differentiated perspective on poverty profiles in European countries, second the limits of the headcount ratio within the scope of such analyses, and third the necessity of country-specific poverty thresholds (as De Vos and Zaidi, 1998, have stressed) and poverty-combating policies.

Notes

*   The empirical results of the analysis were presented at the ENEPRI conference on Policy competition and the Welfare State of the Netherlands Bureau for Economic Policy Analysis in The Hague (Netherlands), 29-30 November 2002. The authors would like to thank the participants of this conference as well as Walter Hanesch (FH Darmstadt) and Peter Krause (DIW Berlin) for their valuable comments. In addition, support by the European Centre for Analysis in the Social Sciences (ECASS, University of Essex, UK) is gratefully acknowledged.
1   '[…] government policies might affect not only the number of poor people, but also, and independently, the depth of their poverty and the distribution of resources among the poor (their relative deprivation).' DeFina and Thanawala (2002, p. 3). For a discussion of

the advantages and disadvantages of the headcount ratio as well as an excellent overview of applied alternative poverty measures, see also Myles (1995), Hagenaars et al. (1995).

2   Sen (1976, 1979) has formulated inter alia two axioms which a poverty measure should satisfy: Given other things, a reduction in the income of a poor household must increase the poverty measure (monotonicity axiom). A pure transfer of income from a poor household to any richer household also must increase the poverty measure, all other things being equal (transfer axiom).

3   Since expenditure on social protection is affected by both rises (declines) in paid transfers (e.g. in periods of mass unemployment) and modification in benefits, this table merely illustrates a rough stability of expenditures across included European countries.

4   Data collection is based on a sample of around 170,000 persons in 60,500 households (Mejer and Linden, 2000). The analyzes for Germany and the UK are based on the converted versions of the ECHP (Clemenceau and Wirtz, 2001). For a detailed description of the ECHP methodology, see Eurostat (1996); on survey attrition and non-response in ECHP data see Perracchi (2002) and on a comparative analysis of income data with the Luxembourg Income Study (LIS) see Beblo and Knaus (2001).

5   It should be noted here that the subjective assessment of household – whether it is 'able to make ends meet' – refers to the current income situation and not the household income situation of the previous year.

6   This modified OECD equivalence scale is used to assign the appropriate weight to each household member in the sample. This scale gives the first adult a weight of 1.0, additional adults (at least 15 years of age) a weight of 0.5, and children (under 15 years) a weight of 0.3. Concerning the measurement of poverty, De Vos and Zaidi (1997, p. 332) established a comparison of the 'old' and the 'modified OECD equivalence scale' with a subjective equivalence scale: 'The ranking of the member states in terms of poverty incidence remains largely unaffected by the choice of the equivalence scale.'

7   Specifically, we deduct from the ECHP variable HI130 'total social/ social insurance receipts (net, total year prior to the survey)' the content of variable HI132 'old age/ survivor benefits'. The difference illustrates therefore the sum of HI131 'unemployment related benefits', HI133 'family-related allowances', HI134 'sickness/ invalidity benefits', HI135 'education-related allowances', HI136 'any other (personal) benefits', HI137 'social assistance' and HI138 'housing allowance'.

8   A comparison with empirical results of previous waves have shown that for Belgium in the year 1998, the poverty incidence and, even more so, the poverty intensity are considerably higher than the rest of the values and do not appear realistic. For this reason the results for Belgium are presented but not described.

9   For a distinction between identification and aggregation within the measurement of poverty and the underlying focus axiom see Sen (1976).

10 The ECHP variable HF002 covers six categories covers six categories: (1) great difficulty, (2) difficulty, (3) some difficulty, (4) fairly easily, (5) easily and (6) very easily. However, it may be expected that there exist not only 'objective', but also cultural reasons for the distribution of the answers. For that reason, the six categories are summarized into three: (1) with difficulty, (2) both: with and without difficulty and (3) without difficulty. Since this information is not available for the converted version of Germany, the table covers only five countries. Unfortunately it was not available for Sweden either, the second representatives of the social-democratic welfare regimes (besides Denmark).

References

Amerini, G. (2000a), 'Der Sozialschutz in Europa', *Statistik kurzgefaßt* (3-15), Bevölkerung und soziale Bedingungen, Eurostat.

Amerini, G. (2000b), 'Der Sozialschutz in Europa', *Statistik kurzgefaßt* (3-2), Bevölkerung und soziale Bedingungen, Eurostat.

Amerini, G. (1999), 'Der Sozialschutz in der Europäischen Union, Island und Norwegen', *Statistik kurzgefaßt* (3-5), Bevölkerung und soziale Bedingungen, Eurostat.

Abramovici, G. (2002), 'Der Sozialschutz in Europa', *Statistik kurzgefaßt* (3-1), Bevölkerung und soziale Bedingungen, Eurostat.

Beblo, M. and Knaus, T. (2001), 'Measuring Income Inequality in Euroland', *Income and Wealth*, Series 47, No. 3, pp. 301-320.

Clemenceau, A. and Wirtz, C. (2001), 'Europäisches Haushaltspanel. Newsletter 01/01', *Statistik kurzgefasst* 3(14), Eurostat.

DeFina, R.H. and Thanawala, K. (2002), 'International Evidence on the Impact of Transfers and Taxes on Alternative Poverty Indexes', *LIS-Working Paper* (325), Maxwell School of Citizenship and Public Affairs, Syracuse University.

Eardley, T., Bradshaw, J., Ditch, J., Gough, I. and Whiteford, P. (1996), *Social Assistance in OECD Countries*, Vol. 1: Synthesis Report, Research report 46, Department of Social Security and the OECD, London, Paris.

Eurostat (1996), *The European Community Household Panel (ECHP)*, Vol. 1, Survey Methodology and Implementation – Theme 3, Series E, Technical Report, Eurostat, OPOCE, Luxembourg.

Eurostat (2001), 'Imputation of income in the ECHP', *DOC:PAN* 164/2001-12, European Commission.

Eurostat Task Force (1998), *Recommendation on social exclusion and poverty statistics*, Statistical Office of the European Communities, Document CPS/98/31/2, Luxembourg.

Foster, J., Greer, J. and Thorbecke, E. (1984), 'A Class of decomposable poverty measures', *Econometrica* 52(3), pp. 761-766.

Frick, J., Krause, P. and Büchel, F. (2000), 'Public Transfers, Income Distribution, and Poverty in Germany and in the United States: R. Hauser and I. Becker (eds), *The Personal Distribution of Income in an International Perspective*, Springer Verlag, Berlin, pp. 176-204.

Gough, I. (2001), 'Social assistance regimes: a cluster analysis', *Journal of European Social Policy* 11(2), pp. 165-170.

Goebel, J., Habich, R. and Krause, P. (2002), 'Einkommensverteilung und Armut (Teil II, Kap. 17)', in Statistisches Bundesamt (ed.), *Datenreport 2002 – Zahlen und Fakten über die Bundesrepublik Deutschland* (Schriftenreihe 376), Bundeszentrale für politische Bildung, Bonn, pp. 580-596.

Hagenaars, A.M., de Vos, K. and Zaidi, A. (1995), *Poverty statistics in the late 1980s: Research based on micro-data*, Eurostat, Reihe 3C, Amt für Veröffentlichungen der Europäischen Gemeinschaft, Luxemburg

Hanesch, W., Krause, P., Bäcker, G., Maschke, M. and Otto, B. (2000), *Armut und Ungleichheit in Deutschland (Poverty and inequality in Germany)*, issued by the Hans-Böckler-Foundation, Rowohlt Verlag.

Hauser, R. (1997), 'Soziale Sicherung in westeuropäischen Staaten', in S. Hradil and S. Immerfall (eds.), *Die westeuropäischen Gesellschaften im Vergleich*, Leske & Budrich, Opladen, pp. 521-545.

Hauser, R. (1999), 'Mindestregelungen für die Alterssicherung und Armut unter den Älteren in den EU-Ländern', in P. Flora and H.-H. Noll (eds), *Sozialberichterstattung und Sozialstaatsbeobachtung: Individuelle Wohlfahrt und wohlfahrtsstaatliche Institutionen im Spiegel empirischer Analysen*, Campus Verlag, Frankfurt am Main, New York, pp. 141-169.

Heady, C., Mitrakos, T. and Tsaklogou, P. (2001), 'The Distributional Impact of Social Transfers in the European Union: Evidence from ECHP', *Fiscal Studies* 22(4), pp. 547-565.

Hölsch, K. (2002), 'The Effect of Social Transfers in Europe: An Empirical Analysis Using Generalized Lorenz Curves', *LIS-Working Paper* (317), Maxwell School of Citizenship and Public Affairs, Syracuse University, Syracuse.

Jenkins, S.P. and Lampert, P.J. (1997), 'Three 'I's of Poverty Curves, with an Analysis of UK poverty Trends', *Oxford Economic Papers* 49, pp. 317-327.

Kim, H. (2000), 'Armutslinderung in Wohlfahrtsstaaten. Wirksamkeit von Steuern und Einkommenstransfers', *Internationale Revue für Soziale Sicherheit* 53(4), pp. 131-161.

Kraus, M. (2000), 'Social Security Strategies and Redistributive Effects in European Social Transfer Systems', *ZEW Discussion Paper* (40), Mannheim.

Marlier, E. and Cohen-Solal, M. (2000), 'Social benefits and their redistributive effects in the EU', *Statistics in focus* (9), Population and Social Conditions, Eurostat.

Myles, G.S. (1995), *Public Economics*, Cambridge University Press, Cambridge.

Myles, J. and Picot, G. (2000), 'Poverty Indices and Policy Analysis', *Review of Income and Wealth* 46(2), pp. 161-179.

Perracchi, F. (2002), 'The European Community Household Panel: A Review', *Empirical Economics* (27), pp. 63- 90.

Sen, A. (1976), 'Poverty: An Ordinal Approach to Measurement', *Econometrica* (44), pp. 219-231.

Sen, A. (1979), 'Issues in the Measurement of Poverty', *Scandinavian Journal of Economics* 81, pp. 285-307.

Slesnick, D.T. (2001), *Consumption and Social Welfare*, Cambridge University Press, Cambridge.

Tsaklogou, P. and Panopoulou, G. (1998), 'Who are the poor in Greece? Analysing poverty under alternative concepts of resources and equivalence scales', *Journal of European Social Policy*, pp. 213-236.

Voges, W. and Kazepov, Y. (eds), (1998), 'Armut in Europa', 2, in *Sozialpolitik in Europa*, Verlag Chmielorz GmbH Wiesbaden.

De Vos, K. and Zaidi, A. (1998) 'Poverty Measurement in the European Union: Country-specific or Union-specific poverty lines?', *Journal of Income Distribution*, 8(1), p. 77-92.

De Vos, K. and Zaidi, A. (1997) 'Sensitivity of Equivalence Scales for Poverty Statistics in the Member States of the European Community,' *Review of Income and Wealth* 43(3).

Chapter 4

National Action Plans
to combat poverty in Europe

Armindo Silva

Why a EU process for combating poverty and social exclusion?

Combating poverty and social exclusion ceased to be an exclusively national concern in 2001 when the European Council of Nice endorsed the proposal of a strengthened cooperation process based on National Action Plans, common objectives and indicators. The inclusion of poverty and social exclusion in the EU policy agenda is not entirely new however, as it had already been covered by the 1989 Social Charter and the 1992 Social Protocol. Furthermore, combating poverty and social exclusion had been the central aim of the three Poverty action programmes that the Commission implemented until the mid-nineties, when the Court of Justice ruled against the Commission for lack of substantive legal basis.

The legal uncertainties surrounding the Community competence in this field were lifted by the Amsterdam Treaty of 1997, which recognized a role for the Union in supplementing and completing the action taken by the Member States, to whom belong the key political responsibilities in promoting social inclusion. This legal clarification paved the way for the decision of the Council in December 1999 to strengthen policy cooperation with the aim of modernizing social protection in four domains:

- Making work pay and ensuring a secure income;
- Improving access and quality of healthcare;
- Ensuring the sustainability and the adequacy of pension systems;
- Combating poverty and social exclusion.

It was further decided that, instead of being launched simultaneously in the four domains, EU policy cooperation should progress stepwise, starting with what seemed to be the most urgent task and where progress could be more easily achieved: combating poverty and social exclusion. Such a decision reflected the very mature European dimension of poverty and social exclusion, both in terms of challenges and of political mobilization.

While in most EU Member States the old forms of poverty have been contained to a large extent by the development of social protection systems, especially through old-age pensions, unemployment benefits and minimum income guarantees, the emergence of new and more visible forms of poverty and social exclusion are posing acute problems of social justice and security. Such new forms were no longer associated with old-age, deprived rural areas or prolonged unemployment, but rather to family break-ups, drug addiction, ill-health, alcoholism, homeliness or vagrancy, extreme precarity in employment, immigration and discrimination based on ethnic grounds. They can also be associated the growing gulf between those holding the necessary skills for participating in the knowledge-based society and those missing them or unable to adapt (digital divide).

Such challenges are today common to all EU Member States, despite the diversity of social models and the very different dimensions of the problem. Also common is the perception that social protection ceased to be a solution to the problem and became part of the problem, as prolonged welfare dependency creates in many cases disincentives for breaking the vicious circle of the poverty trap and attempting to get a foothold in the labour market.

In figures, the challenge is illustrated by the fact that 18 per cent of the EU population, representing approximately 60 million people were at risk of poverty in 1998, living as they do below 60 per cent of the national equivalent income.[1] Half of that number lived in persistent poverty (i.e. had an income below that threshold in the current year and in 2 out of the 3 previous years). The risk of poverty tended to be significantly higher for particular groups such as the unemployed, single parents (most of whom are women), older people living alone (also women mainly) and families with numerous children. However the reality of material deprivation and lack of social participation for the groups affected by the new forms of poverty and social exclusion can hardly be traced by available statistics and remain to a large extent unchartered.

To the growing perception of common challenges corresponds the 'Europeanization' of the political debate and of the social movements that are active in combating poverty and social exclusion, including charities as well as interest groups. Especially among the latter, but also among many social scientists, there is a widespread belief that the drive towards the common currency and the consequent fiscal discipline inherent to the Stability and Growth Pact will tend to pull down social expenditure (including social services) in a sort of 'race to the bottom' and therefore exacerbate emerging inequities in society.

Such claims have not been substantiated by the available figures or in the literature (Scharpf and Schmidt, 2000). During the nineties, public social expenditure has not ceased to increase in real terms, both as a proportion of GDP and in per capita terms, although it has increased less than GDP in the second half of the decade (European Commission, 2002a). But other concerns have been voiced, for instance about the legal implications of Internal Market legislation on the national welfare systems. The growing awareness that economic objectives weigh far too much in EU policy making will continue to act as a powerful driver for the inclusion of social policy among the core areas of EU competence.

Adding a EU dimension to combating poverty and social exclusion represents a challenge for the EU institutions and in first place the Commission itself. Once sharing policy responsibilities with national governments, it is necessary to ensure that the Community is given the corresponding legislative and financial instruments to supplement effectively the national action. Otherwise, there is the risk that Brussels might be used again as a scapegoat for internal political difficulties or divergences between central and regional governments.

While recognizing a role for the Community in supplementing national action, neither the Amsterdam Treaty nor the Nice Treaty provided the instruments necessary for playing effectively that role and bringing about greater convergence in social protection systems. There was in particular the risk that Article 137 was be interpreted in a minimalist way, and that policy cooperation became limited to a simple exchange of information, which would be insufficient to tackle the emerging challenges.

The Open Method of Coordination

Since March 2000 the EU has at its disposal a new instrument to promote more effective economic and social policies across the Union necessary to underpin the transition of Europe into a knowledge-based society. The 'open method of coordination' was endorsed by the Lisbon European Council as a concrete way of developing modern governance using the principle of subsidiarity (Rodrigues, 2002). Its aim is to speed up real convergence in a variety of policy domains (education and training, R&D, social protection and social inclusion, economic reform, employment, and later environment) while respecting national diversity and keeping the distribution of competences as embodied in the Treaties.

The open method of coordination (OMC) should be based on common objectives agreed by all Member States, to be translated in national policies through action plans, including targets where appropriate, and monitored annually through peer review mechanisms on the basis of common indicators and benchmarks.

The OMC was attributed the role of supporting more effective policies by the Member States so that the Union could achieve its new strategic goal for the first decade of the 21st century – 'to become the most competitive and dynamic knowledge-based economy in the world capable of sustainable economic growth with more and better jobs and greater social cohesion'. In particular, the OMC should make a significant contribution to eradicating poverty by the end of the decade.

The Lisbon decision was influenced by the positive experience with the implementation of the European employment strategy since 1997 (the so-called Luxembourg process) that had run along very similar lines to what was now proposed as the open method of coordination. In the social area, the new method promises significant progress in fulfilling the following aims:

- To facilitate policy reforms in Member States, by widening the scope of policy solutions available. Mutual learning through the identification and exchange of good practice should be actively promoted by the OMC and made a regular component of policy-making in the social area.

- To give a concrete meaning to the concept of a European social model, thus avoiding that it becomes an empty ideological box. The common objectives agreed, first in the field of social inclusion, and more recently in the field of pensions, build up a consensus with which all Member States can identify themselves.
- To create a sense of urgency to tackle successfully the common challenges to the European social model, by exploring the positive effects of emulation based on comparison with accepted international benchmarks.
- To upgrade the social dimension in the EU policy coordination process, thus introducing a greater balance between policies promoting market efficiency and policies promoting social protection and inclusion.

More than two years after its introduction, the OMC remains a controversial issue, and its ability to meet the previously defined goals is disputed, or at least qualified, by many.

A frequently heard criticism highlights the lack of democratic legitimacy of the method and the risk of uniformity. Any social process based on European benchmarks would tend to ignore national or regional circumstances, as well as public preferences expressed through democratic means at national or regional level. While in some cases this criticism reflects a self-centred attitude that denies the utility of learning with the others' successes or mistakes, in most cases it is based on the assumption that there is little value in comparing social performance internationally. It is of course necessary to involve the representative political bodies in the process of selecting indicators and benchmarks, and in first place the European Parliament, if the new method is to be endorsed in the new Treaty. Also an explicit role should be granted to the organizations representing the civil society. But this should not lead to neglecting or dissolving the enormous potential of international comparison and emulation for driving reforms forward, particularly where these are being hampered by vested interests.

On the opposing side, there is the concern that the open method of coordination is ineffective, as it relies on the willingness of national governments and entails no sanctions. European social law, or at least the setting of European minimum standards, is necessary in order to avoid that the supremacy of market enhancing mechanisms in the EU constrains the development of national welfare systems (Scharpf, 2002). True, results may be slow to come by and a greater degree of convergence towards higher levels of social protection (as set in Article 2 of the Treaty) is by no means ensured through the implementation of the sole method. But, in a domain that is (legitimately) perceived by all EU Member States and their citizens as a matter of national sovereignty, it is difficult to envisage how progress can be achieved more effectively under the present Treaty rules.

So far, the Commission and the Member States have been fully committed to the implementation of the OMC in the social area. The method is proving its value in identifying a set of common values and to preserve them in times of difficult choices for the future. However, there are a number of aspects that should deserve particular attention for the future.

First, the OMC should not be considered as a panacea for all problems in the social area. The EU has at its disposal Treaty-based instruments, such as legislative action, social dialogue, the Structural Funds and Community action programmes. Different problems and dimensions call for different tools. There is a need to ensure that the right tools are used in each occasion and that they are adequately combined. For instance, in order to bring about greater consistency across Europe on the issue of portability of rights acquired under complementary pensions, the Commission has just launched the first phase of consultation of the social partners, in line with Article 137 of the Treaty. At the same time, this issue is covered also by the common objectives adopted in the field of pensions. A combination between the OMC and legislative action may prove useful in other fields as well (Scharpf, 2002). The Commission has included in its Social Policy Agenda for the period 2000-2005 an examination of the minimum standards for tackling exclusion from the labour market (Article 137), for which the lessons learned from the social inclusion and the employment processes could be pertinent.

Second, the OMC should not be seen as an example of inter-governmental cooperation, exempt from the Community method that applies in all matters subject to Treaty provisions. The Council and the Commission have their specific roles that should be played in respect for each other's competences. The Commission holds a right of initiative that should be used also in the framework of the OMC, as it is a crucial condition for the continued guidance and credibility of the process. The introduction of the OMC in the future Union Treaty could help in clarifying the roles of the different institutions and to legitimize the new process.

Finally, there are variations in the way the OMC has been applied to the different fields[2]. When compared with its immediate predecessor in the employment field, the social inclusion process justifiably provides for larger policy choice by the Member States. This is reflected in the rather broad nature of the common objectives, the lack of quantified common targets and the inexistence of recommendations. The more recent pension process reinforces some of these aspects. While such flexibility is a welcoming feature of the OMC and is necessary to respond to the different conditions of each process, it should not lead to a multiplication of processes with different rules and often overlapping objectives, and even less to a weakening of the method itself. There is therefore room for some streamlining and synchronization of the different processes in the social area.

Implementing the open method of coordination to combat poverty and exclusion

In December 2000 the Nice European Council decided to launch the new method in the field of combating poverty and social exclusion and defined a common set of four objectives:

- To facilitate participation in employment and access to resources, rights, goods, and services for all;
- To prevent the risks of exclusion;

- To help the most vulnerable;
- To mobilize all relevant bodies.

It also agreed on common working methods, thus launching a process that led all Member States to prepare their National Action Plans for social inclusion (NAPs/inclusion) during the first semester of 2001. The Commission supported this process actively by holding bilateral seminars in all capitals to discuss the plans with representatives of governments and other stakeholders. The Social Protection Committee, created by the Council in 2000, and including high-level representatives from all Member States and the Commission, acts as the main body for supervizing the implementation of the new process under the joint political responsibility of the Council and the Commission.

Following the submission of the NAPs/inclusion by all Member States in June 2001, the Commission examined the plans and made public its conclusions in a public report, which subsequently served as a basis for a discussion with the Member States in the Social Protection Committee. It was then possible to agree on a Joint Report on Social Inclusion that was submitted to the European Council of Laeken in December 2001. The European Parliament, the Committee of the Regions and the Economic and Social Committee also contributed by examining the NAPs/inclusion and adopting reports with recommendations.

In parallel, an expert group set up under the auspices of the Social Protection Committee in 2001 elaborated a list of common indicators on social inclusion, which was subsequently endorsed by the Council and submitted also at Laeken. The list comprises 18 indicators that measure the extent and depth of relative poverty, as well as long-term unemployment, health and education variables across all Member States.[3] Although many of such indicators could not be used systematically in the first report, it is hoped that the list will serve as a basis for the EU and each individual Member State to assess objectively progress of the multi-annual process on the basis of outcomes. Seven of such indicators integrate the list of 'structural indicators' that the Commission uses as a basis for its annual synthesis report on the economic and social situation of the Union, in preparation of the Spring Summits.

Another important achievement in 2001 was the adoption by the Council and the Parliament of the first Community action programme to encourage coordination in the fight against social exclusion. The programme, which will be implemented in 2002-2006, has a € 75 million budget, and is intended to support policy analysis and statistical improvements, the exchange of good practice and the promotion of networking across Europe among NGOs active in fighting poverty and social exclusion.

One of the most visible results of the implementation of the action programme in 2002 was the holding of the first Round Table on Social Exclusion, which took place in Aarhus on 17th October, the World Poverty Day, under the joint organization of the Danish Presidency and the European Commission. A large number of national and EU organizations representing civil society took part, alongside the representatives of national administrations. It provided an opportunity for stocktaking and debate about the future orientations of the EU anti-poverty strategy. Support for the continuation of the process and a more active role of EU institutions was expressed by many, as well as a wish to see the fight against poverty mainstreamed throughout other policies both in Member States and at the level of the Union.

It is fair to say that the new social inclusion process has been implemented in a steady fast way and that, two years after its launch, the progress achieved looks impressive, at least as regards developments at the EU institutional level. However, there are still no elements to evaluate the effectiveness of the new process at the level where it matters most. Since the social inclusion process has set itself long-term goals and is still at a relatively early stage, it is too soon to judge its actual impact on the eradication of poverty or the extent to which it has added value and urgency to the efforts of Member States to combat poverty and social exclusion. More importantly, the new process has not yet developed itself into a true strategy, acknowledged as decisive at national or regional level in order to provide a framework for action.

In the face of the evidence shown by the NAPs/inclusion of 2001, it is possible to identify strong and weak aspects. This debate is very timely as all Member States are now starting to prepare, often with the direct participation of non-institutional stakeholders, the second round of NAPs/inclusion to be submitted by July 2003.

The National Action Plans of 2001

The Aarhus Round Table was the largest of a series of public debates in which the Commission services have participated about the first NAPs/inclusion of 2001. Such debates have been organized throughout the Union on the initiative of national, regional or local authorities, social research centres, charities, NGOs and trade unions. While confirming the broadly positive assessment of the 2001 Joint Inclusion Report, such debates added in many cases a reserved judgement, with the hope that the second wave of plans will correct the weaknesses that were now detected.

The strong aspects

The endorsement by the European Council of common objectives and methods of work was not by itself a guarantee that the Member States would accept them when drafting their NAPs/inclusion. The open method of coordination is based on voluntary acceptance and entails no legal or financial sanctions. The first real test for the common objectives was to demonstrate that they were sufficiently comprehensive to frame all the major policies and measures taken in the 15 Member States to combat poverty. The effort spent in preparing the NAPs/inclusion is also to be seen as a demonstration of the will to share efforts with the other EU countries and of the recognition that the EU process adds value to national policy. With the first NAPs/inclusion, the open method of coordination in the social inclusion field gained widespread acceptance by all major stakeholders. This was the first strong aspect of the process so far.

Secondly, the NAPs/inclusion provided a wealth of information on institutions, policies and actions developed by the 15 Member States to combat poverty and social exclusion. They contain numerous examples of initiatives that have met with relative success and that deserve being shared and disseminated as examples of good practice. The plans can be therefore a reference tool for further use. Under the Community action plan 2002-2006 it is now envisaged to start in 2003 a series of peer reviews centred on such policy examples and hosted by the authorities that first designed and implemented them.

Thirdly, the NAPs/inclusion confirmed that, beyond the apparent diversity of situations and policy approaches, there was a core of common challenges that face the Union and the Member States. The Joint Report on Social Inclusion (European Commission, 2002b), the first document adopted by the Council featuring a full analysis of issues and policies concerning poverty and exclusion across the Union, identified eight core challenges:

- Developing an inclusive labour market and promoting employment as a right and duty for all;
- Guaranteeing an adequate income and resources to live in human dignity;
- Tackling educational disadvantage;
- Preserving family solidarity and protecting the rights of children;
- Ensuring good accommodation for all;
- Guaranteeing equal access to quality services (health, transport, social care, cultural, recreational and legal);
- Regenerating areas of multiple disadvantage;
- Improving delivery of services.

Fourthly, the preparation of the NAPs/inclusion represented an opportunity to develop a more strategic and integrated approach to combating poverty. National anti-poverty strategies, were already in place in a few Member States (Ireland, France) or in the process of being developed (Portugal, Belgium). The EU strategy encouraged such efforts, as well as those of countries seeking to introduce greater consistency in their anti-poverty policies, in cases where competences had been largely de-centralized (Spain, Italy) or where a segmented target group approach still prevails (Greece).

The support given by the EU process to more strategically minded and integrated anti-poverty policies aims to respond to the twofold need of conceiving policies that tackle the roots of poverty (joblessness, discrimination, the digital divide) rather than its most visible consequences, and of aiming at the multiple dimensions of social exclusion, rather than focusing too narrowly on just a few headline-hitting phenomena. However, the drive towards greater integration and strategic content should not be misunderstood. The goal is not to produce 15 homogeneous plans but rather to encourage Member States to introduce or reinforce such aspects in their policy-making process. This involves *inter alia* greater attention being paid to information, mobilization and consultation of stakeholders and better intra-governmental coordination.

Finally, the NAPs/inclusion contributed to placing the fight against poverty and social exclusion among the key objectives of social and economic policy in the EU. The Lisbon conclusions had already placed the eradication of poverty among the key strategic goals to be met throughout the transition into a knowledge-based society. This commitment will have to be monitored annually in the Spring Summits. For such a 'reserved seat' to be more than a ceremonial process, two conditions are however necessary: I) that the indicators for assessing progress over the long run are strengthened (which includes a more timely data delivery process); and II) that poverty is mainstreamed into the other economic and social policies at EU level. This is vital if the Lisbon strategy is to pursue the goal of improving the coordination of economic and social policies at the level of the Union.

The weak aspects

For Member States, it is clear that the priority of anti-poverty policies varies with the political orientations of each government and the extent and seriousness of poverty and social exclusion. Whereas in some countries poverty is still endemic and affects large sections of the population, in others it is concentrated on well-defined groups. The pervasiveness of social protection systems, as well as the quality and universality of access to basic services (health, housing, education) has contributed in most Member States to reduce traditional poverty to a bare minimum (in rural areas, among old-age people, the disabled, etc.). However, the new forms of poverty and social exclusion above mentioned are a threat to all Member States, and should have pressed them to use the new EU initiative to gather more resources and efforts at all levels of responsibility.

However, and while in some Member States the preparation of the NAPs/inclusion served this ambition, it is probably fair to say that in most they still play a very minor role in domestic policy making. Many national administrations tend to consider the NAPs/inclusion as a policy document with relevance for Brussels but not for the domestic policy debate. Some viewed the preparation of the NAPs/inclusion just as an exercise of displaying best practice to their EU partners. They did not seem aware of the opportunity provided by the new EU process for putting more ambition or integrating better with other policy branches. Others have a difficulty with the concept of social or economic planning or indeed of partnership involving government and civil society, and for that reason, did not sufficiently involve stakeholders or associated other government departments in the preparation of their NAPs/inclusion.

Secondly, there seems to be a generalized lack of public debate and awareness of the new process. While this can be attributed to a large extent to the previously described attitude of neglecting the domestic policy role of the NAPs/inclusion, there was a genuine problem of lack of time in the preparation of the plans. The Nice European Council adopted the common objectives and mandated the Member States to prepare and submit the NAPs/inclusion within a delay of six months. This was too short for national administrations to mobilize, inform and consult with representatives of civil society, especially in those countries with a federal or regionalized political structure.

Thirdly, many Member States limited the ambition of their NAPs/inclusion to achieving a well structured presentation of policies and institutions, highlighting some examples of good practice. In these cases, the NAPs/inclusion gave a fair reflection of the status quo but did not sufficiently present new initiatives or set new ambitions. As a result, target setting was more an exception than a rule. While certainly the Lisbon goal asks for more efforts from those countries that show higher risks of poverty (Portugal, Greece, Ireland, UK) it should nevertheless induce improvements in developed welfare systems to respond to the new challenges. And, as the conclusions of the Barcelona European Council recognized, the setting of targets, based on careful analysis of trebds and causes, is an important element in the national plans, as it helps to increase transparency, accountability and prioritization in national policy-making.

Finally, there were some neglected issues, some of which were specified in the Nice objectives, such as access to culture and justice, sport and leisure, access to rights and ensuring that moving from welfare to work results in increased income (thereby avoiding poverty traps). Others were not specified in the Nice objectives but could be said to be implicit in them. These include the gender dimension of poverty, illiteracy, access to financial services, social capital and problems faced by particularly vulnerable people such as ex-prisoners and families, drug addicts, immigrants and refugees, or people living in institutions.

The perspectives of the EU anti-poverty process for 2003

The immediate perspectives of the new process will depend crucially on how Member States will improve the role, the ambition and the mobilization capacity of their second NAPs/inclusion. The EU institutions, and in the first place the Commission, can also play an important supporting role. But the responsibility in driving the process forward will fall mainly on the side of Member States. Finally, it is clear that the enlargement of the EU will play a crucial role in the future development of the process, and more generally of the open method of coordination.

The conditions look more favourable now than two years ago, as lessons can be learned from experience, and there will be more time now than in 2001 to prepare the second round of NAPs/inclusion for delivery in July 2003. Reflecting a wide consensus about the robustness of the common objectives adopted in Nice, the Council has decided to introduce few substantive changes:

- The invitation to Member States to include national targets in their NAPs/inclusion (in fulfilment of the conclusions of the Barcelona European Council);
- The emphasis placed on gender differentiation in the analysis of social exclusion and in assessing policy impact;

- The highlighting of the special difficulties facing immigrants as regards their social inclusion.

If the social inclusion process is to match its ambitions and start delivering, Member States will have to make the preparation of their second NAPs/inclusion a key moment in the development of effective policy responses to combat poverty and social exclusion. This requires:

- That appropriate efforts and time are spent in informing, mobilizing and consulting domestic stakeholders, including the local and regional authorities. Considerable investment may be required to achieve this, especially in those countries where policy competences are dispersed by many different authorities at regional and local level. Spain has set the example of using the open method of coordination internally by encouraging the *Comunidades Autonomas* to develop Regional Action Plans;
- That the progress achieved since the first NAPs/inclusion is evaluated on the basis of national indicators as well as the common indicators adopted in Laeken. Using these indicators as tools in the national policy-making process will constitute the real test as whether these are appropriate to capture the key dimensions of poverty and social exclusion also at the national level.
- That new initiatives and more ambitious goals, commensurate with the challenges facing each Member State, are envisaged in the plans. In this connection, it is particularly important that the national targets included in the 2003 plans are sufficiently comprehensive, and that they are quantified. Drawing targets from the existing set of commonly agreed indicators would help in enhancing mutual learning and transparency in the EU context.
- That the NAPs/inclusion serve to mainstream poverty and social exclusion into the national policy making process. This involves better coordination between government departments, and the creation of proofing mechanisms, so as to ensure that policies in such crucial areas as employment, healthcare, education, justice or housing have a positive effect on eradicating poverty and social exclusion. It may also involve closer links between anti-poverty strategies and budgetary and fiscal policies to ensure that sufficient resources are available to meet the targets.

The Commission supports in several ways the action of Member States. It plays an important role as a catalyst by co-ordinating and providing guidance to the whole process through its involvement in the work of the Social Protection Committee. It presents proposals on objectives and indicators, organizes the exchange of good practice, provides support to monitoring and peer reviews, and mobilizes European organizations active in combating social exclusion through networking. And it holds a key responsibility in the management of the Community action programme to encourage coordination between Member States in combating social exclusion, which will be fully operational in 2003.

Looking beyond – the impact of enlargement

With enlargement, the Union will have to face new and comparatively greater challenges in combating poverty and social exclusion. Large sections of the populations in the applicant countries live on low income, and lack access to some basic services and facilities. In most applicant countries unemployment is high, and social protection systems are unable to provide secure income to elderly, sick or disabled people. In some, the social situation of some ethnic minorities, of children and of mentally ill persons raises serious concerns. On the other hand, income inequality is generally lower than in the present Member States, and many will consider the eradication of poverty as a secondary goal subordinate to accelerating economic growth and job creation. Hence, a relatively low priority has been attributed to anti-poverty policies in many applicant countries. In addition, the concept of social exclusion is still rather recent in most applicant countries, especially those that have gone through socialist centralized planning, where poverty and exclusion were individually stigmatized.

For these reasons, it is important to start involving applicant countries in the EU social inclusion process as early as possible so as to prepare the conditions for their full participation after accession. The Commission started in 2002 to co-operate bilaterally with the 12 applicant countries that have formally started negotiations, by holding seminars in each country and by inviting them to participate in the Community action programme on a voluntary basis. A method of work has been agreed, based on the preparation of Joint Inclusion Memoranda, with the aims of identifying the key social problems, setting out the major policies in place or envisaged to combat poverty and social exclusion, and selecting a few key issues for further review. These policy documents will be ready by the end of 2003 and will pave the ground for the first national action plans to be submitted by the new Member States after accession.

While the acceptance of the social inclusion process by the new Member States will have an effect on the way anti-poverty strategies and policies are designed and implemented in these countries, it is also to be expected that enlargement will spur changes in the process itself. It will be necessary to assess whether the balance and focus of the present four common objectives are appropriate for countries with very diverse social and economic conditions. It will also be necessary to revisit the list of commonly agreed indicators, to check if they are appropriate to measure the new realities. In this connection, it is a particular challenge that applicant countries tend to use indicators based on the concept of absolute poverty while the EU common indicators rely entirely on relative poverty. The new Member States will also have to adopt the statistical methodologies necessary to participate in the EU-SILC and in the ESSPROS.[4] This is crucial if the whole Union is to be covered by comparative data in the second half of the current decade.

However, the impact of enlargement will not be limited to the instruments of coordination, and will be reflected also on the structure and aims of the open method of coordination. The increasing number of countries involved will add to the complexity of the process, and this will invite proposals for simplification and synchronization. It does not seem reasonable or indeed necessary to ask all

25 Member States to present and discuss their national plans every two years after 2005. A streamlined process should however leave intact the possibility to continue to assess progress towards the common objectives and targets.

Such a review of the social inclusion process is also called for by the need to improve the consistency of the different processes launched after 2001 in the social area (social inclusion, pensions) as well as the actions taken in the other two areas that had been earmarked by the Council for strengthened policy co-operation (healthcare and 'make work pay'). Common challenges are transversal to all four areas, such as demographic ageing, the difficulty to keep with the pace of technological change, immigration or the changing role of the family, which justify a more integrated treatment. Also the underlying objective in the Lisbon strategy of a greater balance between economic, employment and social protection policies at EU level will not be reached until the policy recommendations derived from the different processes in the social area are jointly formulated so as to reach a larger impact and visibility.

Notes

1 Data from the European Household Panel, Eurostat, 1998 (the data refer to 1997 incomes).
2 More recently, the European Council decided to extend the method into the field of pensions (Laeken, December 2001), and asked the Commission and the Council to start co-operating in the field of healthcare and long-term care for the elderly along the principles of the OMC (Barcelona, March 2002).
3 The Belgian Presidency contributed to the work of the group by sponsoring a study by international scholars (Atkinson et al., 2002) and an international conference on social inclusion indicators.
4 SILC – Survey on Income and Living Conditions. ESSPROS – European System of Social Protection Statistics.

References

European Commission (2002a), *Social Protection Report 2001*.
European Commission (2002b), *Joint Report on Social Inclusion*.
Rodrigues, M.J. (2002), 'For a European strategy at the turn of the century', in M.J. Rodrigues (coord.), R. Boyer, M. Castells, G. Esping-Andersen, R. Lindley, B. Lundvall, L. Soete, M. Telò and M. Tomlinson, *The New Knowledge Economy in Europe – A strategy for international competitiveness and social cohesion*, Edward Elgar, Cheltenham.
Scharpf, F. and Schmidt, V. (eds) (2000), Welfare and Work in the Open Economy, vol. I: From vulnerability to competitiveness, *Oxford University Press*, Oxford.
Scharpf, F. (2002), *The European Social Model: Coping with the challenges of diversity*, Max-Planck-Institut für Gesellschaftsforschung, Working Paper, July 2002.

Chapter 5

Indicators for social inclusion in the European Union

Brian Nolan

Introduction

In December 2001, the European Council held at Laeken in Belgium adopted a set of commonly agreed and defined indicators of social inclusion, which will in the future play a central role in monitoring the performance of the Member States in promoting social inclusion. These indicators are intended to allow the Member States and the Commission to monitor progress towards the goal set by the European Council of Lisbon of making a decisive impact on the eradication of poverty by 2010. This represents a major step forward in the development of European social policy, and has the potential to transform the context in which poverty and social exclusion are addressed. This chapter discusses how this happened, the basis on which the indicators were selected, and the implications for the future development of policy-making in Europe.

The decision to adopt social inclusion indicators

For many years from the original establishment of the EEC, its main objective was to create an area where free movement of goods, services, capital and people would enhance economic growth. The predominant focus was economic rather than social. However, in more recent years that focus has shifted, with the Union having an increasing interest in and competence on social policy, partly in the light of the perceived need to offset some of the potential negative effects of creating the Single Market. Important landmarks in the development of that competence were the 1989 Social Charter, the Social Protocol of the Maastricht Treaty in 1992, and Articles 136 and 137 of the Amsterdam Treaty requiring the Community to support member states' action to combat social exclusion. The concerns of European policy now encompass raising living standards and improving living and working conditions, strengthening social cohesion and combating exclusion, promoting equal opportunities, and sustainability. Thus the social policy agenda has expanded and deepened in scope, and the Amsterdam Treaty in particular assigned the fight against social exclusion a central role in the social policy agenda.

This is however occurring in a context where the links between economic and social spheres are increasingly seen as of central importance. The linkage between different policy domains is highlighted in the identification at the European Council held in Lisbon in March 2000 of a fresh set of challenges which must be met so that Europe can become 'the most competitive and dynamic knowledge-based economy in the world capable of sustainable economic growth with more and better jobs and greater social cohesion'. Promoting competitiveness, employment and social cohesion are now clearly identified as the central aims of European policy. This reflects *inter alia* the economic context, and in particular the persistence of high unemployment in Europe, the acknowledged need to co-ordinate macro-economic policies in the framework of EMU and the Growth and Stability Pact, and the perceived importance of adaptability and removing structural impediments to flexibility which place Europe at a competitive disadvantage. A guiding principle of the Social Policy Agenda adopted in 2000 is thus strengthening the role of social policy as a productive factor.

The Lisbon Council explicitly stated that the extent of poverty and social exclusion in the Union is unacceptable, and that building a more inclusive European Union is an essential element in achieving the Union's ten year strategic goal of sustained economic growth, more and better jobs and greater social cohesion. The common objectives on poverty and social exclusion subsequently agreed by the Nice European Council in December 2000 were:

- To facilitate participation in employment and access to the resources, rights, goods and services for all, via social protection systems and policies focused on housing, basic services, healthcare, education, justice and other services such as culture, sport and leisure.
- To prevent the risks of exclusion, including in relation to new information and communication technologies, the needs of people with disabilities, life crises which can lead to social exclusion, and family solidarity.
- To help the most vulnerable focusing on women and men at risk of persistent poverty, social exclusion among children, and areas marked by exclusion.
- To mobilize all relevant bodies by for example promoting the participation and self-expression of people suffering exclusion, mainstreaming the fight against exclusion into overall policy, and encouraging the active engagement of all citizens in the fight against social exclusion.

At the Nice Summit, a number of fundamentally important decisions about process were also made. In seeking to make a decisive impact on the eradication of poverty and social exclusion by 2010, it was agreed to adopt what is called the 'open method of coordination'. The key elements in the open method of coordination are the agreement of *common objectives* on poverty and social exclusion; the preparation of *National Action Plans (NAPs)* on poverty and social inclusion (NAPsincl); the preparation of a regular *Joint Report on Social Inclusion* by the Commission and the Council; and the adoption of *common indicators* to monitor progress towards the common objectives and comparing best practice across Member States.

Until recently, policy co-ordination at EU-level has mostly been applied to economic policy, with multilateral surveillance of national economic policies provided for in the 1992 Maastricht Treaty, and to employment, via the so-called Luxemburg process formalized by the 1997 Amsterdam Treaty and fine-tuned by the Luxembourg European Council the same year. Under that process the European Council agrees employment guidelines for the member states on an annual basis, and progress towards achieving the objectives laid down in the guidelines is monitored by the Council through an annual review of National Action Plans for employment describing how the guidelines are being put into national practice. The Commission and the Council jointly examine the NAPs and present a Joint Employment report to the Council. (See for example EU Employment and Social Policy, 1999-2001; European Communities, 2001.)

This process in the employment field has served to demonstrate the role which co-ordination, with agreed objectives and monitoring procedures, can play and this broad approach is in effect now being extended to poverty and social exclusion. Thus the Stockholm European Council in March 2001 not only reaffirmed that 'the fight against social exclusion is of utmost importance for the Union', but also gave a clear mandate to the Council to improve monitoring of action in this field by agreeing on a set of social exclusion indicators by the end of 2001, that is by the end of the Belgian Presidency of the Council of the EU in the second half of 2001. We turn in the next section to the way in which these indicators were indeed produced and agreed.

Agreeing on indicators of social inclusion

The Lisbon Council, having set the Union the 'strategic goal for the next decade of becoming the most competitive and dynamic knowledge-based economy in the world capable of sustainable economic growth with more and better jobs', acknowledged the need to regularly discuss and assess progress made in achieving this goal on the basis of commonly agreed structural indicators. The Commission now draws up an annual synthesis report on progress on the basis of structural indicators relating to employment, innovation, economic reform, social cohesion and the environment, and the coverage and content of these indicators continue to develop. (See for example Communication from the Commission on 'Structural indicators', 2001.) These high-level structural indicators are however complemented by more detailed sets in different fields, in particular playing a central role in the Employment Strategy as we have seen. The task of developing a corresponding set of indicators in the field of poverty and social exclusion was assigned to the EU's Social Protection Committee, which comprises high-level officials from the relevant ministries in each Member State, and a technical sub-group it set up for the purpose. (As a contribution to this complex exercise being carried out during its Presidency of the EU, the Belgian Government sponsored a scientific study on the subject and organized an international conference to discuss it; that study was subsequently published as Atkinson, Cantillon, Marlier and Nolan, 2002.) This Indicators Sub-Group worked on the topic for much of 2001, and the fruits of their labours were seen in the report subsequently endorsed by the Laeken European Council, meeting the commitment to adopt a set of commonly agreed social inclusion indicators by the end of that year. Before turning to the specific indicators selected, it is worth emphasizing some general features of the approach adopted (which shared a great deal of common ground with the Atkinson et al. study). First, the Social Protection Committee stressed that the portfolio of EU indicators should command general support as a balanced representation of Europe's social concerns and, because of this, the proposed set of indicators should be considered as a whole rather than a set of individual indicators.

Secondly, the Social Protection Committee recommended a focus on common indicators that address social outcomes rather than the means by which they are achieved (for instance, the level of education attained, not total spending on schools). This does not of course obviate the need for policy and context indicators to help in understanding the observed outcomes and assessing the role of policy in each country, but the fundamental distinction between goals and policy effort – all too easily conflated – is made and progress is to be judged on the basis of outcomes. (Apart from analytic clarity, this serves to bring out that Member States, while agreeing on the indicators by which performance is to be judged, are left free to choose the methods by which these objectives are realized.)

Thirdly, the Social Protection Committee also adopted a set of methodological principles to guide the selection of indicators. These first refer to the individual indicators:

- an indicator should capture the essence of the problem and have a clear and accepted normative interpretation;
- an indicator should be robust and statistically validated;
- an indicator should be responsive to policy interventions but not subject to manipulation;
- an indicator should be measurable in a sufficiently comparable way across Member States, and comparable as far as practicable with the standards applied internationally by the UN and the OECD;
- an indicator should be timely and susceptible to revision;
- the measurement of an indicator should not impose too large a burden on Member States, on enterprizes, nor on the Union's citizens.

Three more then refer to the portfolio of indicators as a whole:

- the portfolio of indicators should be balanced across different dimensions;
- the indicators should be mutually consistent and the weight of single indicators in the portfolio should be proportionate;

- the portfolio of indicators should be as transparent and accessible as possible to the citizens of the European Union.

Finally, recognizing that a large number of indicators are needed to properly assess the multidimensional nature of social exclusion, the Social Protection Committee recommended that they be presented in three tiers:

- *Primary indicators* consisting of a restricted number of lead indicators which cover the broad fields that have been considered the most important elements in leading to social exclusion;
- *Secondary indicators* supporting these lead indicators and describing other dimensions of the problem. Both these levels would be commonly agreed and defined indicators, used by Member States in their National Action Plans on Social Inclusion and by the Commission and Member States in the Joint Report on Social Inclusion.
- Member States themselves can then include a *third level of indicators* in their National Action Plans on Social Inclusion, to highlight specificities in particular areas, and to help interpret the primary and secondary indicators; these are not to be harmonized at EU level.

The Committee also took as starting-point the social cohesion indicators that, as already noted, are included among the EU's broader structural indicators. The seven included in the synthesis report presented by the European Commission to the Stockholm European Council were as follows:

- Distribution of income (income quintile ratios);
- Low Income rate before and after social transfers;
- Persistence of poverty;
- Jobless households;
- Regional cohesion (variation in unemployment rates across regions);
- Early school leavers not in further education or training;
- Long term unemployment.

The selected indicators of social inclusion

With these objectives, principles and point of departure, the Social Protection Committee and its Indicators Sub-Group grappled with an intimidating variety of conceptual, methodological and data-related issues, and ended up recommending the set of Primary Indicators shown in Table 5.1, and the set of Secondary Indicators shown in Table 5.2. The specific indicators selected are worth discussing in some detail, before focusing on the areas where gaps clearly exist and then turning to how the indicators are to be used.

Table 5.1   Primary indicators

	Indicator	Definition
1	Low income rate after transfers	Percentage of individuals living in households where the total equivalent household income is below 60 per cent national equivalent median income with breakdowns by age and gender, most frequent activity status, household type, tenure status
2	Distribution of income	S80/S20: Ratio between the national equivalent income of the top 20 per cent of the income distribution to the bottom 20 per cent
3	Persistence of low income	Persons living in households where the total equivalent household income was below 60 per cent median national equivalent income in year n and (at least) two years of years n-1, n-2, n-3 (incl. gender breakdown)
4	Relative median low income gap	Difference between the median income of persons below the low income threshold and the low income threshold, expressed as a percentage of the low income threshold (incl. gender breakdown)
5	Regional cohesion	Coefficient of variation of employment rates at NUTS 2 level
6	Long term unemployment rate	Total long-term unemployed population (≥12 months; ILO definition) as proportion of total active population (incl. Gender breakdown)
7	Persons living in jobless households	Persons aged 0-65 (0-60) living in households where none is working out of the persons living in eligible households
8	Early school leavers not in education or training	Share of total population of 18-24-year olds having achieved ISCED level 2 or less and not attending education or training (incl. gender breakdown)
9	Life expectancy at birth	Number of years a person may be expected to live, starting at age 0, for Males and Females
10	Self defined health status by income level.	Ratio of the proportions in the bottom and top quintile groups (by equivalent income) of the population aged 16 and over who classify themselves as in a bad or very bad state of health (incl. gender breakdown)

Low income

The Primary Indicators begin with the most obvious and widely-used indicator of poverty, namely the percentage falling below income thresholds. The Indicators Sub-Group emphasized that this was to be seen as a measure of people who are 'at risk of being poor', not a measure of poverty. This reflects a growing realization that low income, on its own, may not always be a reliable indicator of poverty and social exclusion. Those observed as on the same income level at a point in time may have quite different living standards, because both the other resources and the needs of households vary. (This has been the focus of my own recent work with ESRI colleagues, see for example Layte et al., 2001). The availability of other resources, notably savings and other assets as well as assistance from friends and families, will be influenced in particular by how long the current low income has persisted. Differences in needs can arise due to a variety of factors other than the differences in household size and composition which are taken into account in measuring low income by the use of equivalence scales – with ill-health and disability perhaps the most obvious example. This means that while low-income households are best considered as being at high risk of poverty, we also need complementary information, such as the length of time spent at these levels of income and other indicators of resources and living standards.

Table 5.2   Secondary Indicators

	Indicator	Definition
11	Dispersion around the low income threshold	Persons living in households where the total equivalent household income was below 40, 50 and 70 per cent median national equivalent income
12	Low income rate anchored at a moment in time	Base year 1995 1. Relative low income rate in 1997 (=indicator 1) 2. Relative low income rate in 1995 multiplied by the inflation factor of 1994/96
13	Low income rate before transfers	Relative low income rate where income is calculated as follows: 1. Income excluding all social transfers 2. Income including retirement pensions and survivors pensions 3. Income after all social transfers (= indicator 1) (incl. gender breakdown)
14	Gini coefficient	The relationship of cumulative shares of the population arranged according to the level of income, to the cumulative share of the total amount received by them
15	Persistence of low income (below 50 per cent of median income)	Persons living in households where the total equivalent household income was below 50 per cent median national equivalent income in year n and (at least) two years of years n-1, n-2, n-3 (incl. gender breakdown)
16	Long term unemployment share	Total long-term unemployed population ($\geq$12 months; ILO definition) as proportion of total unemployed population (incl. gender breakdown)
17	Very long term unemployment rate	Total very long-term unemployed population ($\geq$24 months; ILO definition) as proportion of total active population (incl. gender breakdown)
18	Persons with low educational attainment	Educational attainment rate of ISCED level 2 or less for adult education by age groups (25-34, 35-44, 45-54, 55-64) (incl. gender breakdown)

In addition to the way low income measures are to be interpreted, many significant choices have to be made in producing them, and the Sub-Group devoted considerable time to the fundamental one, namely the choice of low income threshold. The decision to place the main emphasis on relative rather than absolute or fixed thresholds does not appear to have been particularly contentious, although a low income threshold anchored at one point in time and updated only in real terms over time was adopted as a secondary indicator. The choice of which relative income threshold to prioritize is however more problematic, since practice varies across the Member States. Eurostat, for statistical reasons and reflecting the advice of the Task Force on Poverty and Social Exclusion, has adopted 60 per cent of median income as the basic low income threshold. This was clearly influential in the recommendation that 60 per cent of median income be the threshold employed in the Primary low income indicator. However, the Sub-Group however also concluded it was necessary to report as secondary indicators on the number of people living in households with incomes below 40 per cent, 50 per cent, and 70 per cent of median income, to capture the shape of the income distribution around the 60 per cent threshold. They were clearly concerned however that people falling below 60 per cent and even more so 70 per cent of median income should not be taken on that basis as poor.

The Primary low income indicator, of numbers falling below the 60 per cent of median threshold, is to include breakdowns by age and gender, most frequent activity status, household type, and tenure. Tenure is particularly important because the data from which these low income indicators are derived currently comes from the European Community Household Panel Survey (ECHP), which does not include imputed rents for home owner-occupiers in the income measure. The breakdown by tenure status allows people who have a low income but do not have to pay a rent, and thus are in a relatively better position, to be distinguished. The breakdown by activity status allows the position of such groups as the unemployed and retired to be distinguished, and also those who are working but living in a low-income households.

The research literature on poverty measurement has emphasized for many years that simply measuring the numbers falling below an income threshold can give misleading signals, failing to distinguish between the situation where they are all just below versus very far below that threshold. Finding the best way of measuring this depth aspect of low income is more difficult, particularly in the light of the known unreliability of very low incomes in household surveys. The measure recommended by the Committee was the difference between the median income of persons below the low income threshold and that threshold. (More conventional measures of the depth of low income incorporate the gap between each of the incomes below the threshold and the threshold itself, but will be more sensitivity to mis-measurement.)

Income distribution

The issue of the reliability of measured low incomes is also relevant to the choice of indicator of the distribution of income. One of the structural indicators already in use by the Commission, as we saw earlier, is an income distribution measure, namely the ratio of the share of total income going to the top versus the bottom quintile. While this is also potentially seriously affected by mis-measured low incomes, the Committee recommended its use as a Primary Indicators. (A less sensitive alternative would have been the percentile ratio, that is the ratio of the income cutting off the top quintile to the corresponding income threshold for the bottom quintile.) The Committee also recommended that the Gini co-efficient, widely used as a summary income inequality measure though less transparent than the quintile shares ratio, as a secondary indicator.

Persistence of low income

Persistent low income is a defining characteristic of poverty and the current EU structural indicator to measure this uses data from the ECHP. The structural indicator in use measured the number of people who have lived for 3 or more years in households below 60 per cent of median income. This was modified in the Committee's recommendations to the number of people currently below 60 per cent of median income, who had also been below that income line for (at least) two of the previous three years. This is intended to capture people living below the poverty line persistently but not necessarily continuously.

Jobless households

The structural indicators in use by the Commission as the Social Protection Committee's sub-group began its work included an indicator of the number of jobless households. This is particularly important because of the emphasis in the EU policy agenda on increasing employment and on jobs as the best way to tackle social exclusion. It is recognized however that employment alone will not tackle poverty if it is unevenly distributed among households, and some countries have been particularly concerned about a growing divide between 'work-rich' versus 'work-poor' households. The Committee's Sub-Group agreed that an indicator measuring the number of people in jobless households was more appropriate than the number of jobless households, but had more difficulty deciding what should count as 'jobless'. The existing structural indicator defines a jobless household as a household where no one works and where at least one person is unemployed, but the Sub-Group preferred a measure of the number of people who live in households where there is no paid employment income, regardless of whether the people who do not work are unemployed or inactive. This still left the issue of how students and the retired should be treated, which was particularly difficult since for example normal age of retirement varies a good deal across countries. It was decided not to count those aged 15-24 and in full-time education as potentially qualifying a household as jobless, and that two different upper age limits (60 and 65 in the other) would be used in distinguishing the elderly for the same purpose.

Long-term unemployment

The long-term (a year or more) unemployment rate is also included as an indicator of social cohesion in the broad structural indicators reported by the Commission to the Council, and this was simply adopted by the Social Protection Committee. (A variety of other employment-related indicators are of course employed in monitoring the Employment Strategy, but long-term unemployment is seen as a key cause of poverty and social exclusion). The long-term unemployment share (within total unemployment) and an indicator of very long-term unemployment (at least 2 years) were also recommended as secondary indicators.

Regional disparity

Another indicator 'inherited' by the Social Protection Committee, that is already in use among the structural indicators, was the variation of the unemployment rate across regions within Member States. The Committee's Sub-Group was in favour of a specific indicator of regional cohesion, but recognized that comparing the degree of regional disparities across Member States faces very real problems given the differing numbers and sizes of regions. They expressed a preference for the coefficient of variation of *employment*, rather than *unemployment,* at NUTS 2 level, and this is one of the Primary Indicatorss recommended. It also agreed that one structural indicator did not do justice to all the issues concerning territorial disparities, and that this was among the areas needing further development.

Education and training

While considering the selection of indicators in the areas of low income and unemployment in considerable detail, the Social Protection Committee and its Sub-Group were in a position to deal only in a more preliminary fashion with areas such as education and health. On low educational attainment, the structural indicators used by the Commission in 2001 included the share of the total population of 18-24-year olds having achieved ISCED level 2 or less and not attending education or training. (ISCED, the International Standard Classification of Education, is a framework for comparing educational programmes across countries, which of course differ greatly in terms of institutional structures; ISCED 2 is lower secondary level.) This indicator is also used in monitoring the employment process. The Social Protection Committee recommended that this indicator should be used as a Primary Indicators for social exclusion. They also recommended as complementary secondary indicators (also used in the Employment process) the proportion of the population of working age with a low educational attainment (ISCED level 2 or less) distinguishing gender and age classes.

Health

On health, the Social Protection Committee faced the very real difficulty that while there is a good deal of comparative data on health, very little of it has a specific focus on poverty and social exclusion. At this stage two health-related indicators are included among the Primary set, namely life expectancy at birth (for males and females) and a measure of inequality in self-assessed health. This inequality measure is the ratio of the proportions in the bottom and top income quintile groups of the population aged 15 and over who classify themselves as in a bad or very bad state of health.

Priority areas for further development of indicators

Arriving at agreement among EU Member States on a set of common indicators on social inclusion in a relatively short space of time, across a very wide range of areas all involving very real conceptual, methodological and practical difficulties, represents a major achievement. We turn to its potential importance for the future development of social policy in the Union shortly. First, though, it is important to discuss the areas which the agreed indicators do not cover or where they are in need of significant development.

Major gaps in the areas and topics covered at this stage – recognized by the Social Protection Committee and its Indicators Sub-Group reflect a combination of data unavailability and absence of clear conceptual underpinning in particular areas. The Committee stressed that the portfolio of indicators needs to command general support as a balanced representation of Europe's social concerns, and the agreed set does cover the key areas of income, employment, education and health. However an important area not currently covered by the agreed indicators is housing. The Committee could only recommend that individual Member States in their National Action Plans should present quantitative information on decent housing, housing costs, and homelessness and other precarious housing conditions, and that better comparable data and reporting on these topics be a priority.

Homelessness is of course the most pressing concern in the housing area, and clearly one of the most serious forms of exclusion. It is however particularly problematic from a measurement point of view, since people who are homeless or living in very precarious and temporary accommodation tend not to be included in household surveys, the primary source of data for indicator construction in most countries (except in the Nordic countries, which make greater use of administrative records). As well as the homeless, those living in institutions such as old age homes, prisons, orphanages are also often excluded from the coverage of household surveys, and their situation would have to be captured in a comprehensive portfolio of indicators. Other areas where the Committee felt indicators need to be developed as a matter of priority included social participation, access to public and private essential services, indicators at local level, indebtedness, benefit dependency, and family benefits. They were also anxious to examine further how the gender dimension of poverty and social exclusion can be perceived and measured in a more satisfactory manner.

Although some education and health indicators are included among the current set, development of further indicators in those areas is also a clear priority. As far as education is concerned, functional literacy and numeracy are clearly necessary to operate in modern societies, and illiteracy and innumeracy can be direct causes (as well as correlates) of poverty and exclusion. Substantial progress has been made in recent years in developing comparative data on literacy, notably through the International Adult Literacy Survey (IALS), but there remain some serious concerns about comparability of the results and not all EU countries are included. The OECD has recently launched a new Programme for International Student Assessment (PISA), a survey of students' skills and knowledge at age 15 being administered in 32 countries, including all the EU Member States, which should be very useful. Another important issue with respect to education is access, and the influence of socio-economic background on that access. Comparing the educational attainment level of parents and their children, for example, sheds some light on this issue and the related one of the intergenerational transmission of educational disadvantage and thus poverty and social exclusion. Once again truly comparable data is essential but not currently available.

As far as health is concerned, inequalities in health and access to health services are now widely seen as key aspects of broader socio-economic inequalities and social exclusion. Here again data limitations are very real. The lack of comparative measures of socio-economic mortality differentials is a particularly serious gap in the knowledge base for indicators of social inclusion, although Eurostat is currently seeking progress towards harmonized measurement using administrative sources. The two health indicators now adopted as Primary Indicatorss undoubtedly have serious limitations – it is not clear what an aggregate measure of life expectancy at birth indicates about poverty and social exclusion, and interpreting self-assessed health status can also be problematic – but they provide a starting-point.

The Social Protection Committee expressed particular interest in the development of measures of quality-adjusted life expectancy (taking prevalence of disability into account), premature mortality by socio-economic status, and access to healthcare. Ideally one would want variation in life expectancy, and in quality-adjusted life years, across socio-economic groups to be captured since the focus in this context is firmly on poverty and exclusion. The variation in healthy life-years by socio-economic status is important in its own right, but it is also instrumentally significant. From a social inclusion perspective, the impact that illness and disability have on ability to participate fully in the life of society is also critical. Those with a chronic illness or disability may well face severe obstacles in obtaining access to schooling, employment, independent housing and other aspects of participation. This is difficult to capture in comparable way across countries, given the problems in measuring disability in a harmonized way, but is of central importance to a significant group. Similarly in seeking to capture inequalities in access to health care, failure to access care due to financial constraints is particularly salient from a social inclusion perspective, although once again difficult to measure.

Another area in need of development is the use of non-monetary indicators, now in use in various Member States. The key rationale underlying the growing emphasis on non-monetary indicators is that income, while a key component, does not tell us everything we need to know about the resources or living standards of households. Some households on low income may actually be doing very much worse than others on the same income, for a variety of reasons relating to both how their resources and their needs have evolved over time. (This is evident from a variety of national studies as well as from analysis of data for all the EU Member States participating in the ECHP). The Social Protection Committee's Sub-Group saw considerable value in the development of these measures at EU level, on the basis that they can augment income-based measures in identifying those at risk of poverty, they provide a better understanding of the living conditions of the poor, and they give information about those domains where income based indicators are least helpful. It agreed to focus efforts on the possibility of defining a concise portfolio of indicators measuring the extent to which basic needs are satisfied across Member States.

The current treatment of regional variation also requires development. In the structural indicators 'inherited' by the Social Protection Committee, the European Commission sought to give weight to the regional dimension by specifying a specific indicator of regional disparities, namely the variation in regional unemployment rates. The Committee did as we have seen adapt this to the variation in employment rates. However, the logic of having a specific regional disparity indicator may be questioned. An alternative (proposed by Atkinson et al., 2002) would be to give regional breakdowns for all indicators of social inclusion where it is meaningful and data allow.

The final point to be noted about the further development of social inclusion indicators at EU level is about the nature of the indicators involved and the process by which they are arrived at. As the European Anti-Poverty Network (2001) put it, 'the best indicators are those which gauge changes in the everyday lives of people living in poverty and social exclusion'. The importance of increasing the involvement of excluded people in the development of indicators, and the need to explore the most effective means of giving a voice to the excluded, was emphasized by the Social Protection Committee – though the best ways of bringing this about, at Member State and EU levels, are still being developed.

Statistical capacity-building

In discussing the social inclusion indicators which have now been adopted and the areas where further development is clearly required, the crucial role played by availability of suitable data has been obvious. One of the major challenges faced in developing and producing a comprehensive portfolio of indicators of social inclusion is the absence of a single reliable data source available across all Member States and covering the wide range of areas involved. This is in sharp contrast to for example economic indicators, where National Accounts allow cross-country comparisons to be made, and the Employment Strategy where the Labour Force Survey serves as a common and reliable data base. Building of statistical capacity is an essential investment if the EU is indeed to become a knowledge-based economy – a point also made in the December 2001 Summit in Laeken, where Heads of State and Governments stressed, in this context, 'the need to reinforce the statistical machinery'.

In it important in this context that the current set of Primary and Secondary indicators rely quite heavily on the European Community Household Panel (ECHP) as data source – notably for the core low income indicators. The ECHP is a panel survey organized by Eurostat, based on a standardized questionnaire that involves interviewing a representative sample of households in each country, covering a wide range of topics, including income, health, education, housing and employment. The first wave was conducted in 1994 in the then 12 EU Member States, and Austria and Finland subsequently joined although Sweden is not participating. While there remain important gaps in the available information and the reliability of the income data for a few countries has been questioned, the fact that the survey is harmonized has been crucial in getting beyond the very serious difficulties that can arise through non-comparability of figures from national sources. It has been particularly important in allowing income dynamics and persistence of low income to be tracked.

The ECHP has however now been discontinued, the last wave of surveying having been carried out in 2001. It is to be replaced by a rather different approach to producing data across all the Member States, known as the EU Statistics on Income and Living Conditions (EU-SILC), which will become the EU reference source for income and social exclusion statistics. This will allow Member States to draw on national sources where they already exist and also to separate the cross-sectional element from the longitudinal, panel element if they so wish, and to use both surveys and administrative registers. The objective is to 'anchor' EU-SILC in the different national statistical systems.

While this is a valid aim, the data approach now being adopted has its risks. It is not difficult to see serious problems relating to harmonization and non-comparability arising – since even the way a household is conventionally defined may vary from one country to the next. In addition, one of the key aspects of social exclusion into which data must provide a window is its multidimensionality, the extent to which a particular individual or household is affected by a variety of types of exclusion. It is then essential that data be collected in a way which allows linkage of the information for an individual across different dimensions. Data access arrangements are also important, since use of micro-data by researchers – apart from shedding light on key causal processes at work in creating and sustaining exclusion – can highlight data limitations and feed back into improvement of the data and its comparability. In addition, many countries clearly need to develop their national statistical systems, in particular to try to cover groups that are particularly vulnerable to social exclusion but inadequately captured or missed entirely by current data sources.

The role and potential of EU social inclusion indicators

Finally, we turn to the role which indicators of social inclusion can play and their potential importance in the development of EU social policy, and indeed the strategic direction of the Union more broadly. As we have seen, the specific indicators adopted at the Laeken Council at end-2001 arise out of the political agreement reached at earlier European Councils in Nice and Stockholm. These indicators are intended to allow the Member States and the Commission to monitor progress towards the goal set by the European Council of Lisbon of making a decisive impact on the eradication of poverty by 2010, to improve the understanding of poverty and social exclusion in the European context, and to identify and exchange good practice.

As part of the open method of co-ordination, Member States have already submitted their first National Action Plans on Social Inclusion, in mid-2001. These have been examined in the first Joint Report on Social Inclusion (2002). This has served to illustrate quite emphatically the need for common indicators, with enormous variation across the National Action Plans in the use made of indicators and in the specific indicators employed. In the absence of commonly defined and agreed indicators, Member States used national definitions of core indicators such as poverty and inadequate access to housing, health care and education. In measuring the core risk of poverty, for example, countries focused on different relative income thresholds, or used indicators of 'absolute' poverty which again differed across countries, or focused on benefit dependency.

With commonly agreed indicators now having been adopted, the open method of co-ordination can become fully operational. These common indicators will have to be used by Member States in preparing their next round of National Action Plans, by mid-2003. This will mark a fundamental sea-change in the way policy with respect to social inclusion is framed. It will provide policy-makers for the first time with a basis on which the starting positions and progress over time in the different Member States in terms of key areas of social concern can be reliably compared. While evaluating the contribution of specific policy initiatives will always be extremely difficult, the scope for policy learning will be considerably enhanced. Most productively, though, as in the Employment Strategy Member States will pursue the policies they regard as most likely to succeed in their particular circumstances, but the spotlight will be firmly placed on concrete outcomes.

A review of the common objectives on social inclusion that were agreed at the Nice European Summit is also under way. This review may focus on issues such as the mainstreaming of the gender issue in the inclusion process, highlighted in the Joint Report. What is as yet unclear is precisely when and how the step will be taken from agreeing common indicators against which progress is to be measured to setting national poverty and social inclusion *targets*, which can be linked to the commonly agreed indicators. The objective of greater social cohesion can only be made concrete by setting such targets for the reduction of poverty and social exclusion, similar to those that have evolved the macro-economic and employment fields as part of the Maastricht process and the Employment Strategy.

This is going to be particularly challenging in the context of enlargement of the Union. (At present, issues of social inclusion do not appear to have been at the forefront of concerns in the consideration of enlargement.) While the adoption of an initial common set of social inclusion indicators represents a major achievement, social inclusion may only be given the same weight as employment and the macroeconomy in EU and national decision-making when such targets are in place.

References

Atkinson, T., Cantillon, B., Marlier, E. and Nolan, B. (2002), *Social Indicators: The EU and Social Inclusion*, Oxford University Press, Oxford.

European Anti-Poverty Network (EAPN) (2001), *The European strategy for combating poverty and social exclusion: EAPN proposals for evaluation, monitoring and indicators*, EAPN, Brussels.

European Commission (2001), *Structural Indicators, Communication from the Commission*, COM (2001) 619 final.

European Commission (2001), *EU Employment and Social Policy, 1999-2001*, Office for Official Publications of the European Communities, Luxembourg.

European Commission (2002), *Joint Report on Social Inclusion*, Office for Official Publications of the European Communities, Luxembourg.

Layte, R., Maître, B., Nolan, B. and Whelan, C.T. (2001), 'Persistent and Consistent Poverty: An Analysis of the First Two Waves of the ECHP', *Review of Income and Wealth* 47(4), pp. 357-372.

PART II

INCOME, INEQUALITY, POVERTY AND REDISTRIBUTION

Chapter 6

Income, poverty and dynamics in Germany

Peter Krause

Introduction

Unification has had a crucial impact on income trends in Germany over the last decade. In contrast to other reformed states in Eastern Europe, the transition to a market economy in the old East Germany was driven primarily by the social policy priority of aligning living conditions with those in the West, and only incidentally by pure economic logic. The living conditions of the population in the East of the united Germany were to be brought into line with the higher level of prosperity in the western part of the country as quickly as possible. An East/West divide in the shape of a prolonged disparity in affluence within the country was to be avoided at all costs. There was general agreement on this point between all influential political groups at the start of the 1990s.

This chapter documents the progress of income trends since the mid 1980s for West Germany, and since 1990 – the year of unification – for the East also. It begins with a description of the database used, the Socio-Economic Panel (GSOEP), and income measurement, then goes on to describe the growth and distribution of income for Germany as a whole, and for the former West and East German Länder (states) separately. This allows a clear picture of the process of alignment between living conditions in both parts of the country to emerge (Section 2). Attention is drawn particularly to the low-income bands and relative income poverty, which is also reflected in deep socio-demographic divisions (Section 3). These analyzes are supplemented by a description of trends in income dynamics (Section 4), and a brief discussion of the impact of redistributive welfare state measures (Section 5).

Database and measures

Income trends in Germany since 1984 can be depicted as an annual time series, using data from the Socio-Economic Panel (GSOEP).[1] The GSOEP is the only data source providing detailed annual information on income trends in private households representative of the entire German population since the mid-1980s (Wagner, Schupp, Rendtel, 1994; Burkhauser, Kreyenfeld, Wagner, 1997). This scientific longitudinal study began in the former West Germany with a random sample of just 6,000 households representing approximately 16,000 people; by

2000, the progressive addition of further random samples had brought this up to over 12,000 households with more than 30,000 people. As early as June 1990 – immediately before the introduction of economic, monetary and social union, and four months before actual unification, which took place on 3 October 1990 – the SOEP was extended to cover the former GDR. This provides a unique opportunity for a micro-analytical review of the income trends and adjustment processes triggered from the very outset by unification, based on socio-economic characteristics.

The annual GSOEP surveys collect income details in two ways: on the one hand, they capture *monthly* household net income, i.e. regular income after deduction of taxes and contributions, and including social transfers received; at the same time, they sum up individual (gross) income for all current household members over the previous year, and a tax and benefit deduction model is then used to derive the *net annual income for the previous year*. Annual income thus explicitly takes account of one-off special payments (salary payments for the 13th and 14th months, Christmas bonuses, holiday pay etc), as well as tax rebates.[2] These components are not considered in monthly incomes, which provide more of a picture of the current income stream for any given month. These two views of income differ not only in respect of the time periods covered, but also conceptually (Canberra Group, 2001; Böheim and Jenkins, 2000; Hauser and Wagner, 2002). This chapter mainly uses monthly household net income taken directly from the survey, as this gives a figure consistent with the socio-demographic composition of the household. The same is not necessarily true for the previous year's income calculated on the basis of people currently living in the household, as there may have been additions to the household, or changes to the source of income in the course of the year (e.g. due to unemployment). Annual incomes are used to determine the redistributive effects of welfare state measures by comparing market and disposable incomes.

It should be noted that direct surveying of all incomes in the household typically results in under-counting and missing values (the proportion of missing values is around 9 per cent). The problem of under-counting has been reduced by adjustments based on the sum of ongoing individual monthly incomes in the household.[3] Missing values are imputed by means of a comprehensive regression calculation using the IVEware program[4] (Raghunathan, Solenberger, van Hoewyk, 2002).[5] In generating the previous year's income, missing values are imputed using a different process (Little and Su, 1989), which also takes into account information from longitudinal analyzes.

To allow comparison of incomes taking account of the needs of households of differing size and structure, the incomes are converted into so-called equivalent incomes (Faik, 1995). The equivalence scale used here is the one recommended by Citro and Michael (1995, p. 161):

$$(1) \qquad eq = (\text{N-Adults} + 0.7*\text{N-Children})**0.7$$

This equivalence scale combines the advantages of the OECD scales, which assign lower weights to children than to adults, and the international expert scale6, which uses decreasing individual weights for increasing numbers of people living in the household. The calculated weights per household fall between those of the old and revised OECD scales (Annex Table 6.8).

All household incomes are divided by household-specific equivalence weightings. The resulting equivalent incomes may be characterized as modified per capita incomes, adjusted for household-specific needs. This measure allows us to compare levels of affluence derived from income across households of differing size and composition. This equivalent income is applied to all individuals within the household, including children. It is assumed that the available resources within the household are redistributed in such a way that every member of the household shares the same level of economic welfare (the pool assumption).

The unit of analysis is the individual rather than the household, as only individuals can be tracked over time where they change households. The findings therefore apply to the whole population living in private households. Non-private households (old people's homes etc) are not included in the analysis; nor are homeless people, prisoners, etc.

As there were still significant price differentials between East and West Germany immediately after unification, the former GDR states also enjoyed greater purchasing power, which has to be taken into account in a common measurement of income. For this reason, the bulk of the analyzes use real incomes, separately adjusted for price trends in East and West respectively. With reference to the base year of 2000, it is assumed retrospectively that differences in purchasing power have been eliminated, by virtue of the fact that prices in the East have risen faster than in the West; the use of real incomes thus provides an implicit check on purchasing power discrepancies also. From 2000 onwards, it is assumed that any remaining price differences between East and West are no different from those that may be found between urban and rural regions of Germany.

Income poverty as defined by the EU is measured relative to the mean income for the population. In line with recommendations from Eurostat, we can thus define the income-poor as all persons living in households whose equivalent income does not exceed 60 per cent of the median value for the population.[7]

Income – trends and distribution

Income levels – differences between East and West Germany

When we consider income trends for Germany as a whole since unification, we find a strong rise in incomes initially, tailing off distinctly in the course of the 1990s. The average equivalent disposable incomes of private households have risen from a nominal 944 euros a month in 1991 to 1,276 euros in 2000 (Table 6.1). The corresponding annual incomes – income figures here always referring to the preceding year – have increased in the period from 1992 to 2000 from an average of 14,226 euros to 15,499 euros.

Table 6.1   Household net incomes for the population in private households in Germany (in Euros)

Germany – All		1985	1988	1991	1994	1997	2000*
Monthly income							
Mean	Nominal			944	1,092	1,186	1,276
	Real			1,155	1,187	1,228	1,276
Median	Real			1,022	1,057	1,096	1,129
Top 90 line	Real			1,853	1,903	1,955	2,045
Bot 10 line	Real			583	610	635	657
4-year% increase – Mean nominal					15.68	8.61	7.59
4-year % increase – Mean real					2.77	3.45	3.91
4-year % increase – Median real					3.42	3.69	3.01
4-year % increase – Top 90 line real					2.70	2.73	4.60
4-year % increase – Bot 10 line real					4.63	4.10	3.47
Equivalent income previous year				1992	1994	1997	2000*
Mean	Real			14,226	14,675	14,778	15,499
(3)4-year % increase – Mean real				(3.16)	0.70	4.88	
West Germany		1985	1988	1991	1994	1997	2000
Monthly income							
Mean	Nominal	809	884	1,036	1,146	1,233	1,326
	Real	1,077	1,161	1,244	1,244	1,276	1,326
Median	Real	964	1,034	1,125	1,111	1,141	1,185
Top 90 line	Real	1,697	1,814	1,934	1,996	2,018	2,095
Bot 10 line	Real	539	578	642	621	650	672
4-year% increase – Mean nominal			9.27	17.19	10.62	7.59	7.54
4-year % increase – Mean real			7.80	7.15	0.00	2.57	3.92
4-year % increase – Median real			7.26	8.80	-1.24	2.70	3.86
4-year % increase – Top 90 line real			6.89	6.62	3.21	1.10	3.82
4-year % increase – Bot 10 line real			7.24	11.07	-3.27	4.67	3.39
Annual income previous year		1985	1988	1992	1994	1997	2000*
Mean	Real	13,408	14,411	15,209	15,275	15,206	16,061
(5,3)4-year % increase – Mean real			7.48	(5.54)	(0.43)	-0.45	5.62
East Germany		1985	1988	1991	1994	1997	2000*
Monthly income							
Mean	Nominal			528	862	985	1,055
	Real			754	947	1,019	1,055
Median	Real			718	898	977	982
Top 90 line	Real			1,092	1,396	1,459	1,574
Bot 10 line	Real			462	534	584	598
4-year % increase – Mean nominal					63.26	14.27	7.11
4-year % increase – Mean real					25.60	7.60	3.53
4-year % increase – Median real					25.07	8.80	0.51
4-year % increase – Top 90 line real					27.84	4.51	7.88
4-year % increase – Bot 10 line real					15.58	9.36	2.40
Annual income previous year				1992	1994	1997	2000*
Mean	Real			10,199	12,146	12,929	13,021
(3)4-year % increase – Mean real				(19.1)	6.45	0.71	
Price indices		1985	1988	1991	1994	1997	2000
West Germany		75,1	76,1	83,3	92,1	96,6	100,0
East Germany				70,1	91,1	96,7	100,0

*   *Excl. Subsample F. – Top 90 line, Bot 10 line = income thresholds separating the poorest/richest 10 percent of the population from those on lower/higher incomes.*

Source: GSOEP.

However, these average findings for the whole of Germany do not take account of differing price trends, or of the significant differences in purchasing power between East and West, particularly immediately after unification. On the basis of real incomes, where incomes in East and West are separately adjusted in line with their respective price trends, we see only moderate overall income growth in the course of the 1990s, with four-year growth rates between 2.5 per cent and 4 per cent.

A differentiated view of real income trends makes it clear that the increases in real income that were observable in the early 1990s were mainly in the East – and starting from a much lower level of affluence. In the West, four-year real income growth from the mid 1980s to the early 1990s was still 7-8 per cent, but from then on, there has been little evidence of income growth. From the income threshold values at the upper and lower ends of the income distribution scale, also shown in Table 6.1, it is clear that the 1980s and the second half of the 1990s saw increases mainly in lower incomes, while higher incomes increased more at the beginning and end of the 1990s.

In the East, the incomes of private households grew by more than 25 per cent in real terms in the four years immediately following unification. As the 1990s progressed, income growth here also gradually slowed to below 4 per cent, and since the late 1990s, the ongoing reduction of income differentials compared to the former West Germany has largely ceased.

Income details based on previous year figures display a similar trend (cf. the chapter by Hauser in this volume; Becker et al., 2002). In the West, the 1990s saw an even lower income growth rate than in the monthly figures, with an increase towards the end of the decade; on this measure, income growth in the East at the end of the 1990s is distinctly lower than in the West.

Income inequality before and after unification

A general indicator used to describe income inequality gives the income shares belonging to a given part of the population ordered by income level (Table 6.2). This shows that the poorest 10 per cent of the population in 2000 had just 4 per cent of total monthly income at their disposal, while the richest 10 per cent of the population had around 22 per cent of the total. If we take annual income figures as a basis, the inequality stands out rather more strongly; here, the income share of the bottom income group is a little lower, and that of the top income group is a little higher. Based on real income, this inequality declined during the 1990s, but increased again towards the end of the decade. All summary measures of inequality (the decile ratio, the Gini coefficient, MLD, Theil(1); cf. Cowell, 2000) agree on this. This surprisingly stable pattern in Germany as a whole, given the differences in income distribution and growth in West and East, is the result of opposing trends in the two parts of the country.

In the West, income inequality began by falling slightly in the second half of the 1980s, then rose sharply, particularly in the early 1990s; there was then a period of stagnation in the later 1990s, followed by a fresh increase in inequality at the end of the decade. Based on previous year's income, the increase in inequality in the West, as measured by the Gini coefficient, is more conspicuous than with monthly disposable income, which is more tightly constrained by ongoing income flow.[8]

In the East, incomes have always been far less unequally distributed than in the West, and there was little change in this up to 2000. Although there was an increase in inequality from the start of the 1990s, this slowed more and more, and it is only at the end of the 1990s that we see a fresh increase in inequality in the East. In contrast to the West, inequality figures based on annual incomes are only

Table 6.2   Income inequality in Germany

Germany – All				1991	1994	1997	2000
Monthly equivalent income (real)							
Quantile share	Poorest 10%			3.93	3.91	4.05	3.84
	Richest 10%			21.67	21.74	21.53	21.52
Decile Ratio 90:10				3.177	3.119	3.078	3.240
Gini				.265	.262	.255	.262
Theil (1)				.121	.123	.116	.120
MLD				.118	.117	.110	.119
Annual income previous year (real)				**1992**	**1994**	**1997**	**2000**
Quantile share	Poorest 10%			2.94	3.02	2.93	2.22
	Richest 10%			21.42	22.08	21.83	24.74
Gini				.277	.279	.274	.313
West Germany		**1985**	**1988**	**1991**	**1994**	**1997**	**2000**
Monthly equivalent income (real)							
Quantile share	Poorest 10%	3.86	3.79	4.04	3.85	3.98	3.80
	Richest 10%	21.93	21.84	21.15	21.82	21.65	21.48
Decile Ratio 90:10		3.147	3.137	3.012	3.213	3.103	3.236
Gini		.265	.264	.254	.265	.259	.263
Theil (1)		.126	.132	.113	.126	.119	.121
MLD		.120	.123	.110	.121	.113	.119
Annual income previous year (real)		**1985**	**1988**	**1992**	**1994**	**1997**	**2000**
Quantile share	Poorest 10%	3.33	3.39	2.86	2.79	2.75	2.04
	Richest 10%	22.40	21.10	21.07	22.13	22.00	25.33
Gini		.274	.259	.271	.284	.281	.323
East Germany				**1991**	**1994**	**1997**	**2000**
Monthly equivalent income (real)							
Quantile share	Poorest 10%			4.89	4.46	4.50	4.15
	Richest 10%			17.43	18.27	18.50	19.79
Decile Ratio 90:10				2.365	2.612	2.499	2.746
Gini				.191	.209	.208	.228
Theil (1)				.061	.075	.079	.091
MLD				.062	.076	.077	.097
Annual income previous year (real)				**1992**	**1994**	**1997**	**2000**
Quantile share	Poorest 10%			3.98	4.12	3.86	3.21
	Richest 10%			18.31	19.34	18.88	19.95
Gini				.216	.224	.221	.240

Notes: Quantile Shares = percentage of incomes of the richest/poorest 10 percent in the population. Decile Ratio = Relation of income thresholds separating the richest and poorest 10 percent in the population; Theil, Mean Logarithmic Deviation, and Gini are measures of inequality, (high values = high income inequality)

Source: GSOEP.

slightly higher than monthly values. The drop in inequality seen in both West and East in the second half of the 1990s is mainly attributable to two factors: the increase in child allowance, and tax exemption for income below the subsistence level.[9] Both measures have benefited lower incomes disproportionately.

Levels and distribution of income in East and West Germany

The convergence of income conditions between East and West can be graphically presented in terms of trends in different income thresholds (box plots) (see Figure 6.1).[10] This approach allows differences in income levels as well as in income distribution to be documented together. The chart makes clear how real incomes in the lower income bands in the East have gradually come into line with those in the West, particularly in the first half of the 1990s, while real incomes in the West have stagnated for long periods. However, this process of convergence has slowed down since the mid-90s. The chart also makes it clear that the spread of incomes is far less marked in the East, and that this is particularly true of differences in the upper income bands. Income thresholds in the bottom income band in the East are only slightly lower than in the West, whereas only 10 per cent of the population in the East achieve the kind of income levels that exceed the middle income bands in the West. The essential difference in distribution compared to the West is therefore less a question of lower income levels than of a smaller spread in the higher incomes.

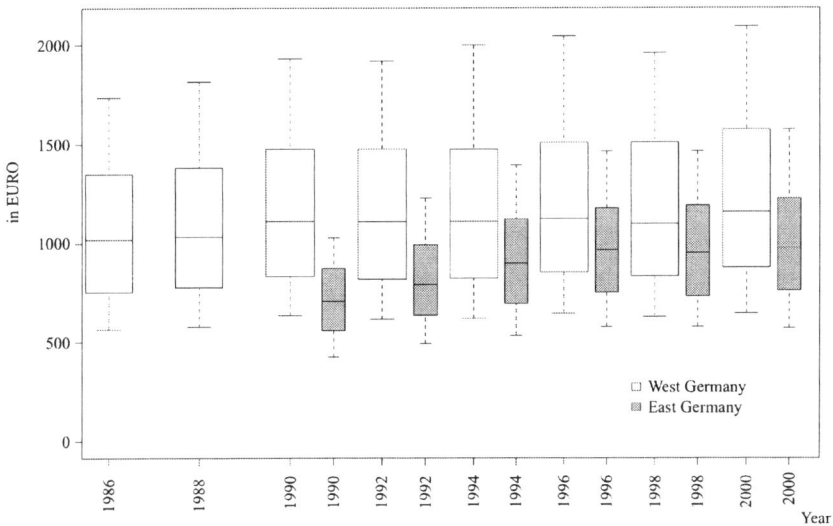

Figure 6.1   Income levels and distribution in East and West Germany, 1986-2000 (in Euros at prices of 2000)

Age profiles in income distribution

This side-by-side presentation of the level and distribution of income can also be applied to the breakdown by age groups (Figure 6.2).[11]

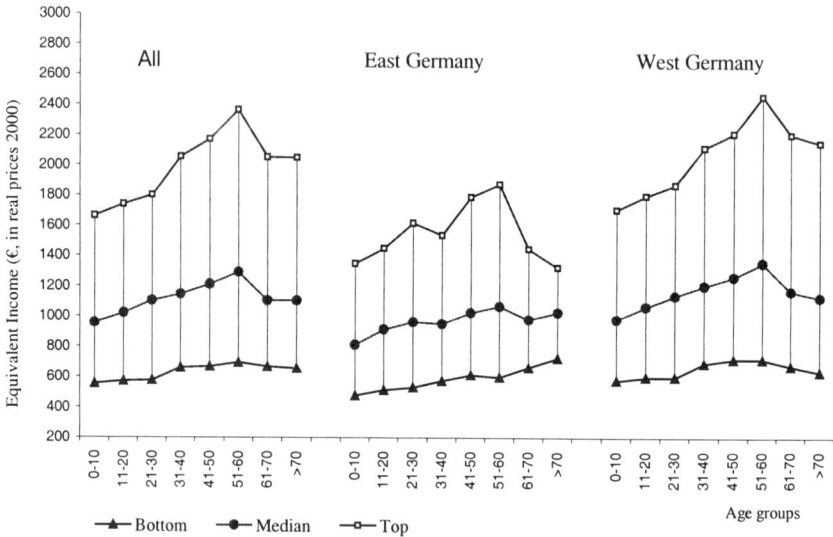

**Figure 6.2   Equivalent income in West and East Germany in 2000
                by age groups**

From the all-German overview (left-hand part of the chart), it is clear that the bottom threshold, delimiting the incomes of the poorest 10 per cent in each group, varies least with age. Even in the working years, the lower income thresholds are only slightly above those for other age groups. When we look at the middle (median) income threshold, we can already see a more distinct differentiation with age; the median income level rises with increasing age, and falls with the end of employment. This differentiation of income thresholds according to age is most clearly marked in the top income band. Children and young people are far less likely than other age groups to be living in (parental) households with higher incomes. The top income levels rise markedly with increasing age, and drop again with the onset of retirement. The gap between the upper and lower income thresholds, which represents the level of inequality (the decile ratio), is lowest for the youngest age groups, rises during the years of work, and drops again after the end of working life.

The middle and right-hand parts of the chart highlight the differences in income differentiation by age in the East. Although the lower income thresholds roughly match the comparative values for the whole of Germany, they differ much more in the way they change with age.

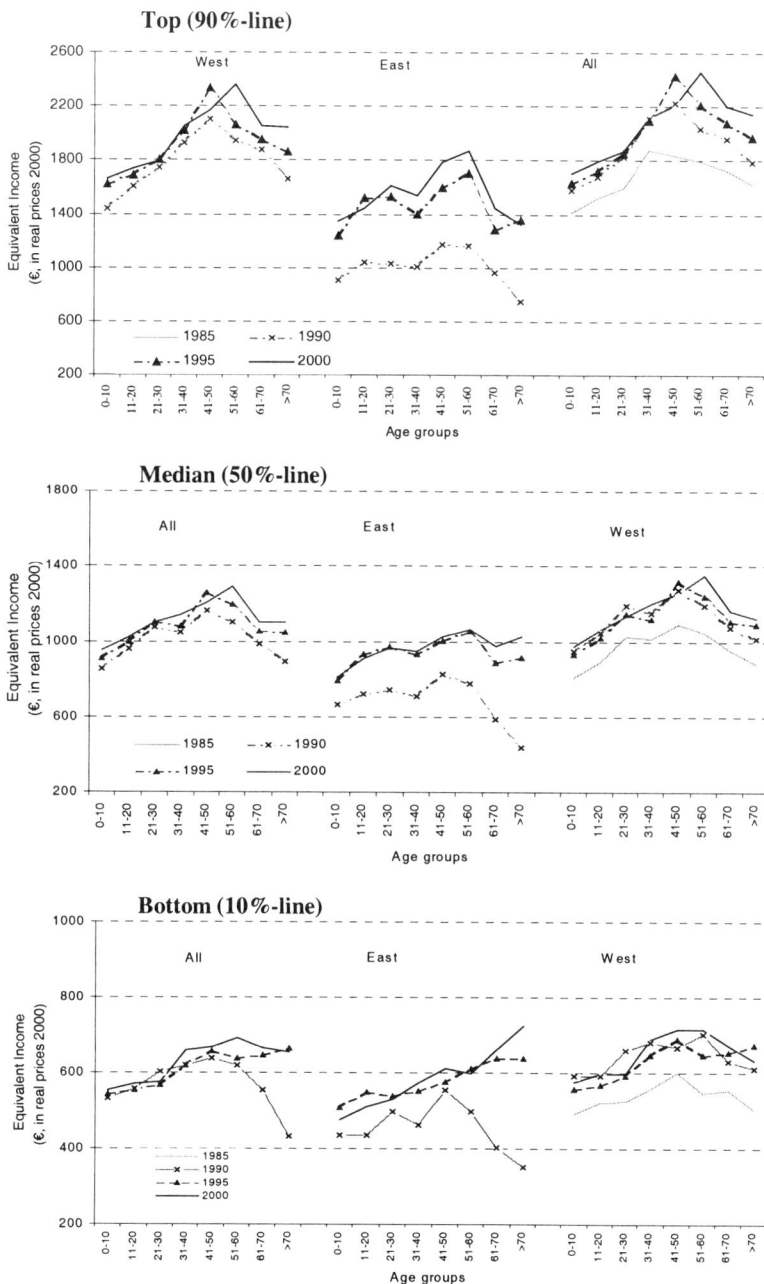

Figure 6.3   Shift of real income levels in top, median and bottom income thresholds

In the East, children and young people in particular are more likely to be living at lower income levels, whereas the lower income thresholds for elderly people actually exceed the corresponding values for the West. In 2000, therefore, children and young people in the East faced a disproportionate risk of low income and income poverty, while the elderly display below-average risk levels.

In contrast, the age differentiation in the thresholds in the middle and upper income bands is less marked than in the West. What is especially striking here is the much smaller spread in incomes among the elderly; for this age group, high incomes are distinctly under-represented in the East. It is apparent that the former systematic differences in income distribution between West and East are still having an effect.

Figure 6.3 documents how income thresholds have changed in real terms over time. The change to the lower and middle income thresholds (the lower and middle blocks on the chart) is somewhat magnified.[12] Essentially, these findings can be summarized in four points:

- In the East, incomes for all age groups underwent a sharp increase in the lower, middle and upper income bands in the early 1990s. In the later 1990s, there was a slight increase only in the thresholds for higher incomes during the working years.
- By far the biggest changes affected elderly people in the East of Germany. The transformation of the social security system here led to a particularly marked improvement in the bottom and middle income groups; but higher incomes are under-represented. The spread of incomes is also especially low in the East for this age group.
- In the West, incomes for all age groups in the lower, middle and upper bands all rose in the late 1980s; in the 1990s, on the other hand, incomes increased only for the middle and upper age groups, and mainly in the upper income band. For children and young people, the last decade has seen hardly any change in (parental) household incomes.
- Since the mid-1980s, a shift in income peaks in the highest income band has been discernible in the West: whereas the highest income thresholds in the mid-1980s could still be found among younger people of working age, in 2000 it is older people of working age who enjoy the highest income levels.

The trend for the whole of Germany in the 1990s is thus the outcome of changes in both parts of the country, as described above: an increase in lower income boundaries for the elderly, slight gains in real income for the middle and upper age groups in the middle income band, and a slight increase in the upper income thresholds for the youngest and oldest age groups, combined with a shift in peak income levels towards older people of working age.

Income poverty and low income

The concept of poverty used here is based on the idea of relative poverty as defined by the EU. This defines as poor anyone living in a household whose equivalent income does not exceed 60 per cent of the corresponding median income for the population as a whole. Rates of relative poverty (the 50 per cent threshold), and so-called 'precarious affluence' (the 75 per cent threshold), based on mean values, are also given.[13]

Median-based poverty rates are expanded using the FGT measure (Foster, Greer,Thorbecke, 1984; cf. the article by Otto and Goebel in this volume): beside the poverty rate (FGT(0)), which shows the size of the poor population and hence the extent of poverty, this takes account of the poverty gap[14] (FGT(1)) to indicate the intensity of poverty, and also inequality within the poor population (FGT(2)). The measure thus focuses on those people within the poor population who are most seriously impacted by poverty.

Poverty threshold values are derived exclusively on the basis of income distribution for the whole of Germany, using real income at 2000 prices; this applies to poverty definition in the East and West of Germany (Table 6.3). Older studies, where the two parts of the country are treated as independent units, lead to different results, especially immediately after unification (see Annex, Table 6.8; cf. Hanesch et al., 2000; Krause and Habich, 2000). In order to describe the growth of the poor populations in West and East independently of each other, additional FGT measures are used, based on established population quantiles for each region.

Incidence and intensity of low income and poverty

It emerges that 12 per cent of the population were suffering from income poverty in 2000, and this rate for Germany as a whole changed very little throughout the 1990s. The FGT measures show a decline in intensity of poverty in the late 1990s, but this was only short-term; the same is true for the mean-based poverty rate, whereas the proportion of the population in the lower income band overall (below the 75 per cent threshold) tended to decrease in this period.

The presentation of relative poverty over time, with poverty lines derived from distribution figures for Germany as a whole, is affected by the different income situations in West and East, especially in the early 1990s. Thus, poverty rates for the West in the early 1990s, based on an all-German reference value, show an increase in poverty; on this measure, the rate in the West in 2000 stands at 11 per cent, one percentage point lower than in Germany as a whole. If we look at the overall trend in the lower income range for the West, based on quantile groupings, we see a fall in the intensity of poverty in the early and late 1990s, each time followed by a fresh increase, but on this measure, the fluctuations are not very large. In the East, the poverty rate in 2000 stands at 16 per cent, four percentage points above the average for the whole of Germany. With the establishment of an all-German poverty threshold, we see a dramatic decrease in the early 1990s in the incidence of poverty, as a result of strong income growth.[15]

Combating poverty in Europe

Table 6.3   Incidence and intensity of poverty and low income in Germany

Monthly equivalent household income						
Germany – All			**1991**	**1994**	**1997**	**2000**
(All = 100%)						
75%- Mean (Low income)			35.3	35.0	33.4	33.0
50%- Mean (Poverty rate)			9.3	9.4	8.7	9.6
60%-Median						
FGT (0) – Poverty rate			11,9	11,6	11,7	11,9
FGT (1)			2,6	2,7	2,5	2,8
FGT (2)			1,0	1,0	0,9	1,1
(All = 100%)						
FGT(1) – Bot 10%			2.2	2.4	2.2	2.3
FGT(2) – Bot 10%			0.8	0.9	0.8	0.9
FGT(1) – Bot 20%			4.4	4.4	4.6	4.7
FGT(2) – Bot 20%			1.6	1.7	1.7	1.8
FGT(1) – Bot 40%			10.3	10.1	9.5	10.3
FGT(2) – Bot 40%			3.9	3.9	3.5	4.1
West Germany	**1985**	**1988**	**1991**	**1994**	**1997**	**2000**
(1991-2000: All = 100%)						
75% - Mean (Low income)	(34.8)	(34.9)	27.3	31.8	31.1	30.2
50% - Mean (Poverty rate)	(9.9)	(10.2)	6.2	8.3	8.0	8.7
60% - Median						
FGT (0) – Poverty rate	(13,5)	(12,0)	8,1	10,3	10,9	10,8
FGT (1)	(2,9)	(3,0)	1,8	2,5	2,3	2,5
FGT (2)	(1,1)	(1,2)	0,7	1,0	0,8	1,0
(West = 100%)						
FGT(1) – Bot 10%	2.3	2.4	2.2	2.3	2.2	2.3
FGT(2) – Bot 10%	0.9	1.0	0.8	0.9	0.8	0.9
FGT(1) – Bot 20%	4.6	4.7	4.4	4.4	4.6	4.9
FGT(2) – Bot 20%	1.7	1.8	1.6	1.7	1.7	1.9
FGT(1) – Bot 40%	10.6	10.6	9.8	10.5	9.8	10.2
FGT(2) – Bot 40%	4.1	4.2	3.7	4.1	3.7	4.0
East Germany			**1991**	**1994**	**1997**	**2000**
(All = 100%)						
75%- Mean (Low income)			71.7	48.7	43.6	45.3
50%- Mean (Poverty rate)			22.9	13.8	11.6	13.3
60%-Median						
FGT (0) – Poverty rate			29,1	16,9	15,3	16,3
FGT (1)			6,3	3,9	3,2	3,8
FGT (2)			2,1	1,4	1,1	1,6
(East = 100%)						
FGT(1) – Bot 10%			2.1	2.1	2.1	2.4
FGT(2) – Bot 10%			0.7	0.7	0.7	1.1
FGT(1) – Bot 20%			4.0	4.6	4.4	4.8
FGT(2) – Bot 20%			1.3	1.6	1.6	2.0
FGT(1) – Bot 40%			8.8	9.8	9.5	9.8
FGT(2) – Bot 40%			3.0	3.6	3.4	3.8

Note: All measures are based on real incomes. For poverty rates in East and West Germany independent of each other, see Annex, Table 6.9.

Source: GSOEP.

At the end of the 1990s, on the other hand, we can observe an increase in the poverty rate in the East. All region-specific quantile-based FGT measures also yield a concurrent increase in intensity of poverty for the East at the end of the 1990s, reaching and in some cases exceeding the relevant comparative values for the West.

Socio-demographic characteristics of the poor

This section addresses the question of what individual characteristics and what family and household types are associated with inadequate household income, and which socio-demographic groups experience a more or less than average incidence of poverty as a result. In addition to the median-based 60 per cent thresholds, we also show poverty rates based on non-adjusted income measurement, which are equivalence-weighted using the old OECD scale, with the poverty line set at 50 per cent of the mean (Tables 6.4 and 6.5). This alternative calculation provides consistency with other analyzes (cf. the chapters by Hanesch, Bäcker and Maschke in this volume; Hanesch et al., 2000), and also helps to check the reliability of the findings, especially where alternative equivalence scales are used. Poverty rates apply to the entire German population in 2000; the right-hand half of the table also documents the situation in the East of the country (Table 6.4).

We see very few gender-specific differences in the incidence of poverty; the poverty rate among women is slightly higher in the East only. There is a slight increase in the incidence of poverty with age, although the poverty rate for children and young people is much higher than for elderly people. On a median-based calculation, there is a further increase in poverty in later life. It is apparent that using a different equivalence scale for mean-based poverty rates understates the phenomenon of old-age poverty. However, both approaches agree in showing well below average poverty rates for elderly people in the East of Germany, which makes the very high incidence of poverty among children and young people all the more striking.

The lowest poverty rates are found in two-person households; the incidence of poverty then rises with increasing numbers of people in the household – disproportionately so from 5 people upwards. The poverty rate for one-person households is a little above the average, although using an equivalence scale with higher personal weightings gives distinctly below-average poverty rates for these households. This finding is also true for the East of Germany.

Differentiated by type of household, we find the lowest poverty rates in couples without children, in families with one child, and in households with grown-up children still living at home; in contrast, the highest poverty rates are seen in single-parent households, and in families with three or more children. Again, this applies to the East also. If we go on to look at different types of household over the course of life, it is noticeable that younger people living alone suffer somewhat more from poverty than those in middle age and older.

Table 6.4   Poverty and low income in Germany (2000, total population)

| | Population living in poverty or on low income (in %) | | | | | |
| | In Germany | | | East Germany | | |
	Pop. share	60% Median	50% Mean	Pop. share	60% Median	50% Mean
Total		11.9	9.1		16.3	11.7
Gender	100.0			100.0		
Male	47.8	11.1	9.1	47.9	15.0	10.8
Female	52.2	12.6	9.2	52.1	17.5	12.6
Age	100.0			100.0		
Up to 10 years	11.0	17.52	15.6	7.8	29.0	24.3
11-20 years	11.3	15.7	16.4	13.3	23.0	21.8
21-30 years	11.3	14.2	10.7	11.3	18.6	12.7
31-40 years	17.3	10.1	8.3	15.9	16.4	13.2
41-50 years	13.8	9.6	7.3	15.2	15.8	9.8
51-60 years	12.9	9.3	5.6	12.9	14.7	8.9
61-70 years	11.9	9.9	5.7	13.4	10.3	4.2
71 years and over	10.5	10.4	4.8	10.3	6.2	3.2
Household size	100.0			100.0		
1-Pers.- household	17.6	12.9	6.2	16.5	18.5	9.1
2-Pers.- household	30.1	9.3	5.4	32.2	13.4	7.5
3-Pers.- household	20.0	10.2	8.1	23.8	12.4	9.7
4-Pers.- household	21.3	11.3	9.4	21.0	17.5	14.3
5+.Pers.- household	11.0	21.2	25.6	6.6	35.2	39.0
HH-/Life-cycle	100.0			100.0		
HH up to 45 years						
Single household	6.7	14.8	9.8	6.0	23.7	15.4
Partner household	6.4	4.8	2.9	4.6	12.3	6.7
HH 46-65 years						
Single household	4.8	12.0	4.7	4.5	23.5	8,3
Partner household	11.9	7.5	3.5	14.5	12.6	5,2
Household w. underage child	*39.1*	12.1	*11.9*	*36.1*	16.7	*15.2*
With 1 child	15.9	7.0	6.6	18.8	8.8	8,4
With 2 children	16.0	12.2	9.8	13.8	20.7	17,4
With 3 or more children	7.3	23.0	27.9	3.7	42.4	45,1
Single parent household	4.2	37.0	30.6	5.9	49.1	42,6
Household with adult children	11.7	11.1	8.9	12.6	10.6	7,5
HH 66 years and over						
Partner household	8.6	8.0	4.5	9.1	5.3	2.3
Single household	6.7	12.3	4.8	6.8	10.6	5.2
Community size	100.0			100.0		
Under 2,000 inhabitants	9.0	14.6	11.8	23.2	15.9	13.1
2,000 to 20,000	32.2	12.3	9.7	31.3	16.0	11.8
20,000 to 100,000	26.6	11.0	7.8	17.5	20.3	12.4
100,000 to 500,000	18.4	11.0	8.3	19.5	14.7	10.0
over 500,000 inhabitants	13.8	11.9	10.1	8.5	14.4	10.9

Notes: See Table 6.5.

In the East, single-person households have high poverty rates in early and middle life, but lower rates in later life. Despite some clear divergences in the rates, this finding still applies when alternative poverty measures are used.

Classifying communities by size, higher poverty rates are found in smaller communities and in big cities, while rates are lower in smaller and medium-sized towns; in contrast, the incidence of poverty in the East is highest in small towns.

Table 6.5   Poverty and low income in Germany (2000, respondents)

| | Population living in poverty or on low income (in %) | | | | | |
| | In Germany | | | East Germany | | |
	Pop. share	60% Median	50% Mean	Pop. share	60% Median	50% Mean
Respondents	Population above 17 years					
Total		10.7	7.7		14.3	9.5
Nationality	100.0			100.0		
German	92.4	9.8	6.6	99.3	14.0	9.2
Non-German	7.6	22.7	21.6	(0.7)	(58.0)	(45.2)
Family situation	100.0			100.0		
Married / living together	56.9	9.1	6.8	55.0	11.2	7.1
Married / living apart	1.7	19.1	15.4	1.8	33.9	25.9
Single	25.1	12.6	9.6	25.3	18.2	13.1
Divorced	6.9	17.0	10.4	8.8	26.4	17.2
Widowed	9.4	9.7	4.8	9.1	6.9	3.5
Educational qualifications	100.0			100.0		
Hauptschule, no qual'n *	13.1	17.6	13.5	8.0	21.3	16.8
RS. FHS. Gymn, no qual'n *	4.5	10.4	8.4	3.1	14.1	10.6
Hauptschule (with qual'n) *	28.1	9.3	5.9	24.2	15.4	8.9
Realschule (with qual'n) *	24.0	8.5	5.5	37.9	15.0	9.6
FHS. Gymn. (with qual'n) *	9.0	11.0	6.7	5.2	13.1	10.7
Other	5.3	19.5	18.7	2.7	27.6	25.7
FH, University	14.1	4.34	2.4	16.8	6.4	3.3
In full-time education	1.9	12.5	14.8	2.1	15.8	13.7
Employment status	100.0			100.0		
Employed full-time	40.6	4.8	3.4	40.1	7.0	4.5
Employed part-time	14.1	10.4	8.5	10.6	18.2	14.2
Unemployed	5.6	38.0	27.3	12.3	40.4	27.5
In training	4.4	16.8	16.6	4.4	20.1	16.0
Not working	35.3	12.6	8.0	32.6	11.5	6.3

*   *Hauptschule = extended elementary school (classes 5-9); Realschule (RS) = secondary school; FHS, Gymnasium = secondary school (grammar school, classes 12-13); Fachhochschule (FH) = university of applied sciences*

Notes: Poverty rates for East Germany are based on the all-German threshold. 60 per cent-Median rates rely on adjusted monthly incomes (screener), equivalence-weighted by the Citro-Michael-Scale, whereas the 50 per cent-Mean rates refer to unadjusted incomes (screener), equivalence weighted by the Old OECD-Scale.

Source: GSOEP.

If we consider only the population from age 16 upwards (respondents), the poverty rate comes out slightly lower (Table 6.5).

Here, we find very high poverty rates among non-Germans; in the East, of course, these make up a very small proportion of the population. As might be expected, separated and divorced people show disproportionately high poverty rates – again, more so in the East. Widowed people, on the other hand, have a below average incidence of poverty; again this applies particularly to the East. With regard to levels of education, we see largely the expected gradations: people without any school or vocational qualification have a distinctly higher incidence of poverty, while university and college graduates have by far the lowest poverty rates. In Germany as a whole, middle and secondary school-leavers with vocational qualifications have lower poverty rates, although this is not necessarily true in the East.

As expected, people in full-time employment have a comparatively low incidence of poverty, whereas the risk level for the unemployed is well above average; again, this applies to the East also. Part-time workers are at medium risk, although they do show a disproportionate incidence of poverty in the East. For non-working people, poverty rates in Germany are somewhat above the average (but below average in the East because of the low rate of old-age poverty).

However, in assessing the extent of poverty, the proportion of poor people within each group is not the only factor; the size of the groups themselves is also significant. The groups with the highest incidence of poverty include non-Germans, and the unemployed – but non-Germans are hardly represented in the East, so that this problem is largely restricted to the West. Unemployed people are subject to roughly the same risk of poverty in West and East, but make up a much higher proportion of the population in the East.

Income dynamics and immobility

Thus far, our description of income trends in Germany has focused on cross-sectional findings over time, or on a socio-demographic breakdown. This section addresses the extent of the change itself, and the subject of income dynamics.

A general view of the scale of income dynamics is provided by the Fields-Ok index (Fields and Ok, 1996), which shows the sum of income differences between two points in time as a percentage of the sum of incomes at the starting point[16]. This index has the advantage over other measures, such as the Bartholomew index or the Glass-Prais index, that income dynamics are not defined in terms of pre-determined groupings, but rather by including all incomes. The Fields-Ok index is measured here in sliding three-year periods, on the basis of real income at 2000 prices. This allows us to read off the changing dynamics over time.

Income trends for the whole of Germany in the early 1990s were still strongly marked by the changes that resulted from the rapid convergence of the two parts of the country. Income dynamics have accordingly weakened somewhat since that time, and have now settled at a level of income change between 20 and 25 per cent.

In the West, the percentage change in incomes in the late 1980s was still significantly higher, at around 25-30 per cent, before falling back to the all-German level in the course of the 1990s. As might be expected, the income dynamics in the East during the process of transformation were initially high, standing at over 30 per cent at the beginning of the 1990s; this level of dynamics then gradually diminished into the late 1990s, and has now settled at around 20 per cent. On this measure, incomes in the East underwent less change in the late 1990s than in the West (Figure 6.4).

Percentage mobility

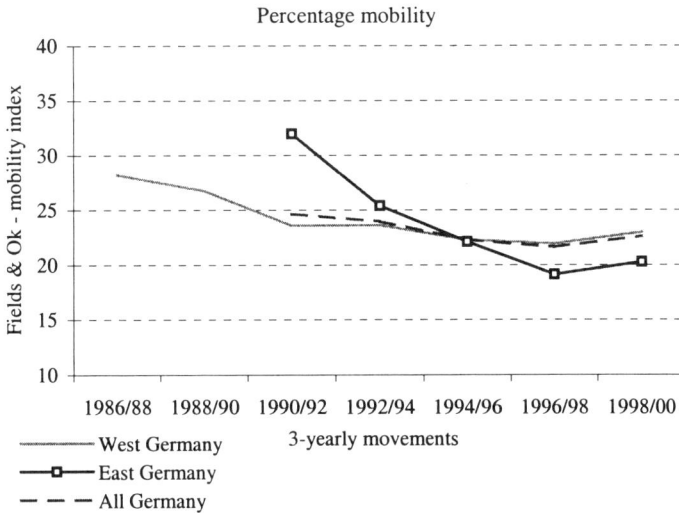

Figure 6.4   Income dynamics (3-year intervals of real income)

A more differentiated examination of the stability and mobility of different income bands may be carried out using quintile matrices, based on the respective regional distributions (Table 6.6). These depict the levels of stability and change in the lower, middle and upper income bands (at the first, third and fifth quintiles), measured over a period of four years.

Here we see that stability in the lowest income quintile increased slightly in the course of the 1990s. The proportion of the population falling into the bottom quintile over the four years rose from 52 per cent in 1990 to 56 per cent at the end of the decade; by the same token, the chance of climbing out of the bottom income quintile into the middle or upper income bands fell slightly in the equivalent period, from 21 per cent to 19 per cent.

In the middle income band, the numbers in the middle or adjacent quintiles showed a tendency to increase through the 1990s. In the period observed, the numbers dropping into the lower quintile hovered around 10 per cent, while the numbers rising from the middle into the highest income band declined slightly.

Combating poverty in Europe

Table 6.6   **Income dynamics: Quintile matrices**

		1985-1988	1988-1991	1991-1994	1994-1997	1997-2000
Germany – All:						
(Sum(Q): All=100)						
Low	$Q_1 \rightarrow Q_1$			51.8	54.3	55.6
	$Q_1 \rightarrow Q_2$			26.9	25.3	25.9
	$Q_1 \rightarrow Q_{3-5}$			21.3	20.4	18.5
Middle	$Q_3 \rightarrow Q_1$			9.4	10.5	9.8
	$Q_3 \rightarrow Q_{2-4}$			81.6	82.8	83.4
	$Q_3 \rightarrow Q_5$			9.1	6.7	6.8
High	$Q_5 \rightarrow Q_{1-3}$			13.8	15.6	15.1
	$Q_5 \rightarrow Q_4$			18.8	17.3	16.8
	$Q_5 \rightarrow Q_5$			67.4	67.1	68.1
West Germany						
(Sum(Q): West G.=100)						
Low	$Q_1 \rightarrow Q_1$	57.2	57.8	56.9	53.3	57.1
	$Q_1 \rightarrow Q_2$	24.0	22.1	22.9	25.8	27.5
	$Q_1 \rightarrow Q_{3-5}$	18.8	20.1	20.2	20.9	15.4
Middle	$Q_3 \rightarrow Q_1$	9.0	11.1	8.9	11.5	11.9
	$Q_3 \rightarrow Q_{2-4}$	83.0	81.7	84.0	83.2	80.9
	$Q_3 \rightarrow Q_5$	8.0	7.2	7.1	5.3	7.2
High	$Q_5 \rightarrow Q_{1-3}$	19.0	12.7	13.9	13.8	16.2
	$Q_5 \rightarrow Q_4$	19.2	22.4	19.9	18.1	19.4
	$Q_5 \rightarrow Q_5$	61.8	64.9	66.2	68.1	64.4
East Germany						
(Sum(Q): East G.=100)						
Low	$Q_1 \rightarrow Q_1$			41.1	46.2	51.3
	$Q_1 \rightarrow Q_2$			27.6	33.2	22.6
	$Q_1 \rightarrow Q_{3-5}$			31.3	20.6	26.1
Middle	$Q_3 \rightarrow Q_1$			14.2	10.7	13.7
	$Q_3 \rightarrow Q_{2-4}$			76.5	76.4	75.8
	$Q_3 \rightarrow Q_5$			9.3	12.9	10.5
High	$Q_5 \rightarrow Q_{1-3}$			21.7	18.6	19.0
	$Q_5 \rightarrow Q_4$			26.3	23.6	18.8
	$Q_5 \rightarrow Q_5$			52.0	57.8	62.2

Note: Quintile = 20 percent of the entire population with low (Q1), middle (Q3) or high incomes (Q5). The frames indicate the percentage of people remaining in (Q1, Q5) or near (Q3) the same quintile (diagonals of the matrices).

Source: GSOEP.

The numbers in the upper income range remained almost constant through the 1990s, but the stability rates are here much higher than in the lower income band. This implies that income changes into the middle and upper income ranges are less frequent, and at the end of the 1990s, they tended to go down.

In the West, no systematic change in the scale of income dynamics can be read from the quintile matrices; instead, the dynamic trend since the mid 1980s has taken more of an oscillating course. In the East, stability has increased since the beginning of the 1990s, particularly at the upper and lower ends of the income distribution scale, but stability rates overall are lower than in the West.[17]

Market income, disposable income and the redistributive impact of government

Market income includes the income earned from the market by household members, largely without direct involvement from the state (i.e. pre-government): it includes income from employment, income from capital, and private transfers. It follows that market incomes taking in the whole population are by their nature significantly more unevenly distributed than the resulting disposable incomes after state intervention in the form of tax and contributions, and after factoring in transfers (post-government).[18] The relationship between inequalities in income obtained from the market and disposable income for private households then gives an indication of the impact of redistributive welfare state measures over time. This comparison can, however, only be made on the basis of annual income figures.

Table 6.7   Market income, disposable income and the redistributive impact of government (annual incomes)

		Real income (2000)		Inequality (Gini)		Amount of state-related reduction
		Market income (Euro/year)	Disposable income (Euro/year)	Market income Gini (1)	Disposable income Gini (2)	((1-2) / 1)%
Germany - All						
All	1992	19,730	14,226	.416	.277	33.41
	1994	17,131	14,675	.429	.279	34.97
	1997*	17,510	14,778	.445	.274	38.43
	2000*	17,724	15,499	.466	.313	32.83
West Germany						
West	1985	15,992	13,408	.429	.274	36.13
	1988	16,979	14,411	.410	.259	36.83
	1992	18,240	15,209	.405	.271	33.09
	1994	18,247	15,275	.421	.284	32.54
	1997*	18,507	15,206	.437	.281	35.70
	2000*	18,799	16,061	.455	.323	29.01
East Germany						
East	1992	10,704	10,199	.382	.216	43.46
	1994	12,515	12,145	.432	.224	48.15
	1997	13,265	12,929	.462	.221	52.16
	2000	13,019	13,021	.497	.240	51.71

*   *Sample D (migrants) included as of 1996.*

Source: GSOEP.

Inequality in the distribution of disposable income, measured by annual Gini coefficients, increased in Germany at the end of the 1990s. For market income, on the other hand, we see an increase in inequality in distribution for the whole of Germany throughout the 1990s. The degree to which inequality was reduced by government measures then showed a sudden short-term increase in the second half of the 1990s (Table 6.7). As mentioned above, a possible cause for this is the raising of child allowance, as well as tax exemption for any income below the subsistence level; both measures have brought disproportionate benefits to lower incomes. However, this effect was quickly re-absorbed by the further increase in inequality of market incomes.

In the West, inequality in both market incomes and disposable incomes fell initially from the mid-1980s, but since the early 1990s, market incomes have shown a constant distinct increase in inequality. The level of inequality in 2000 is distinctly higher than in the 1980s and 1990s. Inequality of disposable incomes also increased in the early 1990s; it was held down in the later 1990s, only to start rising again at the end of the decade. In the West, the degree to which inequality has been reduced by government measures has therefore declined compared to the 1980s, except for a temporary increase in the late 1990s.

In the East, incomes were initially much less unequally distributed than in the West, but the level of inequality in market incomes still rose very steeply towards the end of the 1990s, and is now actually higher than in the West. At the same time, inequality in disposable incomes has only risen slightly in the same period, and they are still much more evenly distributed than in the West. The degree to which inequality has been reduced by government measures is thus much greater than in the West, and has gone on increasing in the course of the 1990s. In this way, welfare state measures have made a significant contribution towards bringing affluence levels in the East into line with those in the West.

Annex

Table 6.8   Equivalence scales

Equivalent scales	Old OECD scale[a]	Revised OECD scale[b]	International Expert Scale[c]	Citro & Michael[d]
1 Adult	1	1	1	1
+ 1 Child	1.5	1.3	1.4	1.4
+ 2 Children	2	1.6	1.7	1.8
+ 3 Children	2.5	1.9	2.0	2.2
2 Adults	1.7	1.5	1.4	1.6
+ 1 Child	2.2	1.8	1.7	2.0
+ 2 Children	2.7	2.1	2.0	2.4
+ 3 Children	3.2	2.4	2.2	2.7

a $Eqw = 1 + (Adults - 1)*0.7 + Children*0.$
b $Eqw = 1 + (Adults - 1)*0.5 + Children*0.3$
c $Eqw = (Household\text{-}Size)**0.5$
d $Eqw = (Adults + 0.7*Children)**0.7$

Table 6.9   Net household income of private households in Germany

Germany – All	1985	1988	1991	1994	1997	2000
Monthly income						
Mean Nominal			815	954	1,020	1,109
Real			963	1,031	1,055	1,109
(All = 100%)						
75%- Mean (Low income)			36.7	35.0	34.3	34.3
50%- Mean (Poverty rate)			10.0	9.1	8.1	9.1
West Germany	**1985**	**1988**	**1991**	**1994**	**1997**	**2000**
Monthly income						
Mean Nominal	684	768	893	1,001	1,057	1,149
Real	855	952	1,043	1,080	1,092	1,149
(West = 100%)						
75%- Mean (Low income)	35.8	33.9	34.9	35.2	35.4	35.5
50%- Mean (Poverty rate)	11.2	10.1	8.8	9.4	8.9	9.7
East Germany	**1985**	**1988**	**1991**	**1994**	**1997**	**2000**
Monthly income						
Mean Nominal			478	759	870	936
Real			621	827	899	936
(East = 100%)						
75%- Mean (Low income)			22.1	25.0	24.9	27.4
50%- Mean (Poverty rate)			4.1	7.5	6.2	5.8
Price indices	**1985**	**1988**	**1991**	**1994**	**1997**	**2000**
West Germany	75.1	76.1	83.3	92.1	96.6	100.0
East Germany			70.1	91.1	96.7	100.0

Notes: Unadjusted income screener, old OECD scale (mean in Euros).

Source: GSOEP.

Notes

1 For the period before 1990, data, however, are only available for the former West Germany.
2 Income benefits from owner-occupied residential property (imputed rent) are not factored in.
3 This takes into account income from employment and pensions (including widows' pensions), and from private transfers. In principle, these components are captured separately for each person in the household aged 17 and above.
4 The imputation of missing values with IVEware is implemented in SAS.
5 To ensure comparability with previously published findings, the Annex (Table 6.9) and the socio-demographic breakdown (Tables 6.4 and 6.5) also present findings based on the original Income Screener, using the old OECD scale.
6 Eq = Square root of household size (cf. Table 6.8).
7 The socio-demographic breakdown in Tables 6.4 and 6.5 also uses the 50 per cent mean threshold, albeit based on the unadjusted income screener, and applying the old OECD scale, which roughly matches the need bands used for social assistance (see Annex, Table 6.8 and 6.9, and Faik, 1997).
8 This indicates either that inequality has increased in the period under review (i.e. since the mid-1980s) in terms of one-off payments such as 13th month bonuses, tax rebates and income from capital, or that the volume of these more unequally distributed

components has grown faster than ongoing monthly income from employment, pensions and social transfers. For results from other datasets see Becker et al. (2002).

9   Before, the whole income was always taxable, but since the second half of the 1990s only incomes above the subsistence level have been taxable.

10 The breadth of the box plots records the size of the respective population groups, and the mid-line of each block indicates the relevant median – i.e. an income threshold value with half the population above and half below it. Similarly, the upper and lower limits of the middle blocks give the income thresholds which together cover 50 per cent of the population on medium incomes, and the outer lines show the decile thresholds bounding the richest and poorest 10 per cent of the population – i.e. the income range covering the affluence level of 80 per cent of the population, excluding the richest and the poorest groups.

11 This overview takes into account the median as well as the decile (90:50:10) threshold values. The outer threshold values show the upper and lower limits of income received by 80 per cent of the population in each age group.

12 In this overview, different scales are used for the lower, middle and upper income thresholds.

13 Median-based measurement is less sensitive to extreme values at the upper and lower ends of the distribution scale, and thus yields more reliable results than poverty rates derived from mean values.

14 This is the gap between actual income and the poverty threshold.

15 On a purely regional view, the small degree of inequality would produce a slow rise in relative poverty here, starting from a very low level (see Annex, Table 6.9)

16 Another variant of the Fields-Ok index relates the total amount of income differences to mean income differences per capita; this variant is not considered here.

17 However, this finding may also be attributed to the lower level of inequality in the East, as this produces a smaller absolute income difference between the quintile boundaries in the grouping, so the same income difference is more likely to cause a change of quintile in the East than in the West.

18 Market income does not include any public transfer payments (pensions, unemployment benefit, unemployment assistance, social assistance); for pensioners and other households with nobody in work, where the household receives no income from capital or private transfers, the minimum income figure is therefore 0; in this, it differs from disposable income.

References

Atkinson, A.B. (1997), 'Bringing Income Distribution In from the Cold', *The Economic Journal* 107, pp. 297-321.

Atkinson, A.B. (1998), *Poverty in Europe*, Blackwell, Oxford.

Becker, I. and Hauser R. (eds) (1997), *Einkommensverteilung und Armut*, Campus, Frankfurt am Main.

Becker, I., Frick, J., Grabka, M., Hauser, R., Krause, P. and Wagner, G.G., (2002), 'A Comparison of the Main household Income Surveys for Germany: EVS and SOEP', in R. Hauser and I. Becker (eds), *Reporting on Income Distribution and Poverty. Perspectives from a German and a European Point of View*, Springer, Berlin et al., pp. 55-90.

Biewen, M. (2000), 'Income Inequality in Germany During the 1980s and 1990s', *Review of Income and Wealth*, 46(1), pp. 1-19.

Böheim, R. and Jenkins, S.P. (2000), 'Do Current Income and Annual Income Provide Different Pictures of Britain's Income Distribution?', *DIW-Discussion Papers* (214), Berlin.

Büchel, F.; Diewald, M., Krause, P., Mertens, A. and Solga, H. (eds) (2000), *Zwischen Drinnen und Draußen - Arbeitsmarktchancen und Soziale Ausgrenzung in Deutschland*, Leske & Budrich, Berlin.

Büchel, Felix, Joachim R. Frick, Peter Krause and Gert G. Wagner (2001), 'The impact of poverty on children's school attendance – evidence from West Germany', in Koen Vleminckx and Timothy M. Smeeding (ed.), *Child well-being, child poverty and child policy in modern nations. What do we know?*, The Policy Press, Bristol.

Bundesministerium für Arbeit und Sozialordnung (2001), *Einkommensverteilung und Einkommensmobilität*, Wagner, G.G. und Krause, P., Bonn, Berlin.

Burkhauser, R., Kreyenfeld, M. and Wagner, G.G. (1997), 'The German Socio-Economic Panel Study: A Representative Sample of Reunified Germany and its Parts', *DIW-Vierteljahrshefte zur Wirtschaftsforschung* 66(1), pp. 7-16.

Canberra Group (2001), Expert Group on Household Income Statistics, *Final Report and Recommendations*, Ottawa.

Cowell, F.A. (2000), 'Measurement of Inequality', in Atkinson, A.B. and Bourguignon, F. (eds), *Handbook of Income Distribution* 1, Elsevier, Amsterdam, pp. 87-166.

Fabig, H. (1999), *Einkommensdynamik im internationalen Vergleich. Eine empirische Mobilitätsanalyse mit Panel-Daten*, Campus, Frankfurt am Main/New York.

Faik, J. (1995), *Äquivalenzskalen*, Duncker & Humblot, Berlin.

Faik, J. (1997), Institutionelle Äquivalenzskalen als Basis von Verteilungsanalysen – Eine Modifizierung der Sozialhilfeskala', in I. Becker and R. Hauser (eds), *Einkommensverteilung und Armut*, Campus, Frankfurt am Main.

Fields, G.S. and Ok, E.A. (1996), 'The meaning and measurement of income mobility', *Journal of Economic Theory* 71, pp. 349-377.

Frick, J., Büchel, F. and Krause, P., (2000), 'Public Transfers, Income Distribution, and Poverty in Germany and in the United States', in R. Hauser and I. Becker (eds), *The Personal Distribution of Income in an International Perspective*, Springer, Heidelberg, pp. 176-204.

Goebel, J., Habich, R. and Krause, P. (2002), 'Einkommensverteilung und Armut', in Statistisches Bundesamt (ed.), *Datenreport 2002*, Bundeszentrale für politische Bildung, Bonn, pp. 580-596.

Gottschalk, P. and Smeeding, T.M. (2000), 'Empirical Evidence on Income Inequality in Industrial Countries', in A.B. Atkinson and F. Bourguignon (eds), *Handbook of Income Distribution* 1, Elsevier, Amsterdam, pp. 261-307.

Hanesch, W., Krause, P., Bäcker, G., Maschke, M. and Otto, B. (2000), *Armut und Ungleichheit in Deutschland*, Der neue Armutsbericht der Hans-Böckler-Stiftung, des DGB und des Paritätischen Wohlfahrtsverbandes, Rowohlt, Reinbek bei Hamburg.

Hauser, R. and Becker, I. (eds) (2000) *The Personal Distribution of Income in an International Perspective*, Springer, Heidelberg.

Hauser, R. and Wagner, G.G. (2002), 'Economics of the Personal Distribution of Income', in K.F. Zimmermann (ed.), *Frontiers in Economics*, Springer, Berlin et al., pp. 311-370.

Jenkins, S. (2000), 'Modelling household income dynamics', *Journal of Population Economics*, 13(4), pp. 529-567.

Krause, P. and Habich, R. (2000), 'Einkommen und Lebensqualität im vereinigten Deutschland', in Zehn Jahre deutsche Währungs-, Wirtschafts- und Sozialunion', *Vierteljahrshefte zur Wirtschaftsforschung* 69(2), pp. 317-340.

Krause, P., Frick, J., Goebel, J., Grabka, M., Otto, B. and Wagner, Gert G. (2000), *Einkommensverteilung und Einkommensmobilität*, Gutachten im Auftrag des Bundesministeriums für Arbeit und Sozialordnung, Berlin.

Krause, P. (2001), 'Einkommen in Deutschland – Entwicklung, Dynamik, permanente Verteilung und Redistribution', in I. Becker, N. Ott and G. Rolf (eds), *Soziale Sicherung in einer dynamischen Gesellschaft*, Festschrift für Richard Hauser, pp. 418-439, Campus, Frankfurt am Main/New York.

Leisering, L. and Leibfried, S. (1999), *Time and Poverty in Western Welfare States, United Germany in Perspective*, University Press, Cambridge.

Little, R.J.A. and Su, H.L. (1989), 'Item Non-Response in Panel Surveys', in D. Kasprzyk, G. Duncan, G. Kalton and M.P. Singh (eds), *Panel Surveys*, John Wiley, New York, pp. 400-425.

Raghunathan, T.E., Solenberger, Peter, W. and van Hoewyk, John (2002), IVEware: Imputation and Variance Estimation Software. User Guide. University of Michigan.

Schwarze, J. (1995), *Simulating German Income and Social Security Tax Payments Using the GSOEP*, Cross-National Studies in Aging. Syracuse University Program Project Paper (19), Syracuse University, New York.

Wagner, G.G., Schupp, J. and Rendtel, U. (1994), 'Das sozio-oekonomische Panel – Methoden der Datenproduktion und -aufbereitung im Längsschnitt', in R. Hauser (ed.), *Mikroanalytische Grundlagen der Gesellschaftspolitik – Erhebungsverfahren, Analysemethoden und Mikrosimulation*, Akademischer Verlag, Berlin, pp. 70-111.

Chapter 7

Does low income mean poverty?
Some necessary extensions of poverty
indicators based on economic resources

Hans-Jürgen Andreß

Traditional poverty measurement: Inadequate income resources

Empirical analyses in western industrialized societies apply a variety of indicators to define persons affected by poverty. It is possible to differentiate between poverty indicators that either record the economic resources individuals have available to them, or indicators that study the outcome of how such resources are used, i.e., in terms of satisfying certain requirements and achieving a certain standard of living. This is illustrated in Figure 7.1 below: Individuals utilize individual, household, and external resources and with these create outputs generating well-being. The standard of living achieved is a result of their individual behaviour; the way in which people use the economic resources available to them for these purposes partly depends on their preferences. This implies that the same provision of economic resources does not necessarily lead to the same standard of living.

Following Ringen's (1988) differentiation, I, too, am referring to direct and indirect poverty indicators. Direct poverty indicators look at individuals' actual standards of living; indirect indicators, meanwhile, look at the resources available to these individuals. Disposable household income is a frequently applied resource indicator. Appropriate data on income, socially differentiated to a sufficient degree, is easily accessible from official statistics or scientific sources, even if it does not always provide the desired accuracy and reliability. Other resources, such as a person's professional, vocational, or educational qualifications, can possibly be ascertained with greater reliability; however, because of the lack in the type of uniform measure that is provided for incomes, it is more difficult to compare qualifications between different social groups. Furthermore, there is a certain legitimacy in applying income as a poverty indicator since, in free market societies, many goods and services needed for everyday living are purchased with money; the achieved standard of living is, therefore, determined in great part by disposable income. And finally, a lacking provision of financial resources can be compensated for through social security benefits in the form of money, so that all citizens have the same basic opportunities – this, at least, is the traditional social policy approach. By definition of the economic resource approach, individuals are poor if they dispose of an income lower than that required to cover a basic standard of living. I am therefore referring to income-based poverty measures.

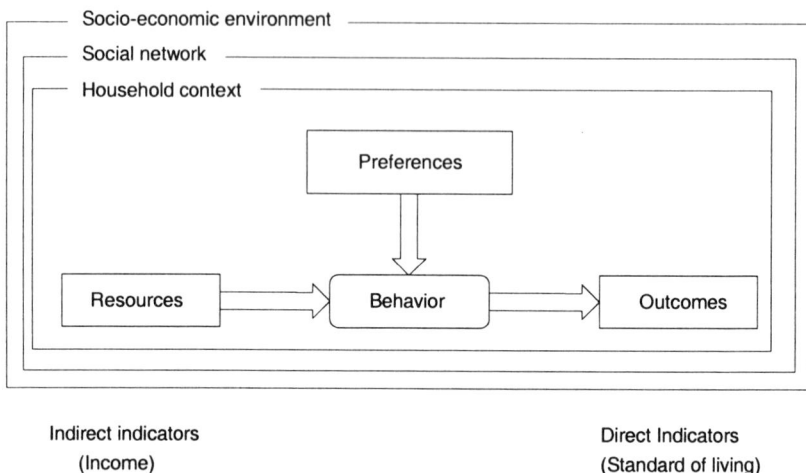

Figure 7.1   Direct and indirect indicators of poverty

The use of income data to measure poverty is common practice; however, it has also been frequently criticized. Some of the main objections are:

- The use of disposable income ignores other financial resources and monetary advantages, such as monetary assets, property ownership, or employer allowances.
- It also excludes certain financial burdens, such as rent and debt payments.
- Income determined for a specific point in time is subject to considerable temporal fluctuations. Therefore, if recorded at the 'wrong' time, it can either substantially over- or underestimate the actual income position.
- Information on income cannot always be ascertained reliably for specific groups, such as self-employed people.
- When using household income to measure poverty, far-reaching assumptions are necessary on whether, and in which form, the members of a household combine their individual incomes into a joint income pool, and how they then participate in this pool.
- Furthermore, a comparison between households of differing size and composition with the help of equivalent household incomes depends substantially on the chosen equivalence scale.
- Finally, a fundamental objection to the relative income limits used (e.g., 50 per cent of median income) is that they do not so much measure poverty but rather inequality. For, independently of the level of prosperity of a society, according

to this criterion, a certain percentage of people will (almost) always be poor where income-based inequality prevails.

One could add that income, however it is measured, obviously provides only one of a number of possible economic resource indicators. In this context, the attempts to estimate individuals' human capital and to perform poverty measurements on the basis of such concepts (Garfinkel et al., 1977) are a case in point.

The standard-of-living approach: Alternative or complement?

Given the critical objections concerning the economic resource approach, the question arises as to the possibilities provided by direct poverty indicators. In contrast to the economic resource approach, these study the outcomes of the behaviour of individuals based on how they utilize the resources available to them. They focus on the standard of living actually available to people in a given society at a specific point in time. Peter Townsend's 1979 study on 'Poverty in the United Kingdom' pioneered this 'direct' approach. In this study, Townsend's starting point was the population's observable standard of living (the community's style of living); he then studied which groups were able to participate in this style of living – and the extent to which they were able to do so. He defines the exclusion of more or less large groups of people from a generally accepted standard of living as deprivation; it therefore seems appropriate to speak of deprivation-based poverty measures in contrast to income-based poverty measures. According to this definition, those individuals who do not enjoy a generally accepted (minimum) standard of living are considered poor.

The concrete procedure of this approach can be summarized as follows: As a rule, the starting point of the standard-of-living approach is a list of items or activities, which, in the opinion of the respective researcher or a representative population sample, covers the essential features for a required standard of living (Table 7.1 outlines examples from a German survey; for details of this survey, cf. Lipsmeier, 2001). Then, either by observation or, more usually, by questionnaire, participating individuals are surveyed on whether they have these items at their disposal or whether they carry out these activities. Missing items, or activities not performed, thus provide an indicator for an insufficient standard of living. If there is an accumulation of lacking items, one speaks of a certain degree of deprivation, or poverty.

This approach is attractive for a number of reasons: It breaks up the one-sided fixation of poverty research on income, and makes the actual living situation of those affected by poverty the core of the analysis. Accordingly, the poverty concept used is multi-dimensional and more directly linked to the living conditions of the individuals studied. However, it must be noted that the standard-of-living approach is not free of conceptual and empirical problems, either (Andreß, 1999, p. 77; Andreß and Lipsmeier, 2001; Walker, 1987). Therefore, it must be emphasized that a 'correct' poverty indicator evidently does not exist.

Table 7.1   Standard-of-living features

General standard of living, basic requirements
 Ability to pay utility bills (gas, water, electricity, heating) without difficulty
 Living accommodation without damp walls
 Sufficient heating during the cold months
 Ability to eat healthily and sufficiently
 Ability to pay the rent for living accommodation/interest on property without difficulty
 Bath/shower in one's living accommodation
 Washing machine
 On average, one warm meal per day
 Ability to benefit from medical treatments not fully covered by health insurance
 Living in accommodation of sound building quality
 A completed professional qualification

Extended basic requirements
 Financial reserves, e.g., savings, life insurance
 Contact with other residents in the neighbourhood
 A telephone
 Ability to buy a present for family members/friends at least once per year
 A colour television
 A warm meal, with meat, poultry, or fish, at least every two days
 Living in a respectable neighbourhood
 Ability to generally pay greater attention to product quality than price
 Ability to afford a hobby
 At least one annual one-week holiday away from home
 A car

Additional/extra requirements
 Going out one evening every two weeks
 Garden or patio in living accommodation
 Ability to buy new clothing—even if current garments are not yet worn out
 Ability to replace used, but still functional, furniture
 A videocassette recorder

Workplace features (standard of living of employees and jobseekers)
 A job that includes sufficient retirement provision
 A place of work with no health and safety risks
 A job corresponding to one's qualifications, both in terms of activity and pay
 A secure place of employment

Standard of living of families with children
 Toys and other leisure items, e.g., bicycle, computer, sports equipment
 A separate bedroom for each child above the age of 10
 Extra-curricular learning activities for children, e.g., music, sports, language lessons
 Ability to celebrate birthday parties with many friends

Availability of local infrastructure near domicile
 Bus, tram, metro/underground stop
 Grocery
 Doctor's office
 Nursery/playgroup
 Pharmacy
 Bank or other financial institution
 Post office

Source: Sozialwissenschaften-Bus III/1996, Lipsmeier (2001, p. 13).

As long as the respective problems of the economic resource and standard-of-living approaches are not satisfactorily settled, I would argue for the simultaneous application of both direct and indirect poverty indicators to identify, on the one hand, the different effects of poverty, and, on the other, to be able to reciprocally control the respective results.

> 'Different methods produce different pictures of poverty. Despite differences in results, each of these pictures may be equally correct and realistic. They only map a different slice of reality. Therefore, a simultaneous use of various measures may be advisable. One measure gives one result, another reveals something else. By concentrating on one single "correct" measure, a great deal of valuable information may be lost. A full analysis requires a multidimensional method of measurement. In that way we can reveal the many faces of poverty and social exclusion that, in turn, can be combated by different remedies' (Kangas and Ritakallio, 1998, p. 199).

Low income and insufficient standard of living: Similarities and differences

In this section, based on the research results from different studies on poverty, both in Germany and abroad, I would like to illustrate the additional findings that can be obtained by combining both the economic resource and standard-of-living approaches. A research of the literature on the subject (Andreß and Lipsmeier, 2001) revealed 17 different studies that have applied the standard-of-living approach in one form or another, and have thereby obviously also recorded the classic information on incomes (cf. Table 7.2).

Low income: Only one of several causes for an insufficient standard of living

An important outcome from several of the studies is the relatively weak link between income and the extent of deprivation. A number of studies examined the correlation between the deprivation index and equivalent household income. Böhnke and Delhey (1999a, p. 24) reported a correlation of -0.35 for the German data; Nolan and Whelan found a similar value (-0.33) for the Irish data. Muffels (1993, p. 43) examined a number of deprivation indices for the Netherlands: The correlation with net household income was found to be between -0.18 and -0.33.

If the link between deprivation and income is tested under the simultaneous (statistical) control of other resource indicators, income can often be shown to be only one of several important influencing factors on the extent of deprivation. Desai and Shah, for instance, have found that income does not have a significant influence on all of the examined standard-of-living features (known, in their notation, as 'consumption events'):

> 'Income is one of the variables besides wealth, education, health, ethnic origin, etc., which defines the position of a household in the deprivation space. For some events, income has no influence; for others wealth does not. It would be a mistake therefore to look at just a single variable' (Desai and Shah, 1988, p. 519).

Table 7.2   Empirical studies on the standard-of-living approach

Study	Country/ies	Data Sources
A) Studies outside the Federal Republic of Germany		
Townsend (1979)	GB	Own survey 1966-1968, n=2,052 households with approx. 4,000 individually surveyed persons receiving income, or housewives.
Desai and Shah (1988)	GB	Secondary analysis of Townsend's data findings (1979)
Mack and Lansley (1985)	GB	Breadline Britain 1983, n=1,174 Persons
Gordon and Pantazis (1997)	GB	Breadline Britain 1990, n=1,831 persons
Nolan and Whelan (1996)	IRL	Own survey 1987, n=3,294 eligible voters in private households.
Muffels (1993)	NL	Dutch Socio-Economic Panel 1988, n=approx. 5,000 households, with approx. 15,000 individuals (over the age of 15) surveyed.
Leu et al. (1997)	CH	Own primary survey 1992, n=6,775 persons, permanent residents in Switzerland, over the age of 20.
Kangas and Ritakallio (1998)	FIN	Own survey, 1995, n =1,859 individuals, Finnish population between 18 and 70 years of age.
Halleröd (1995)	SE	Own survey, 1992 (Swedish Standard of Living Survey), n=793 persons, Swedish population between 20 und 74 years of age.
Mayer and Jencks (1989)	USA	Two surveys, 1983 und 1985, n (total of both surveys) =1,617, non-Hispanic or non-Asian households in Chicago.
B) Germany		
Andreß (1999)	D	Own survey, 1994, n=685 persons, in three towns/communes each in East and West Germany; individuals in private households between 26 und 66 years of age, plus an additional sample of social assistance recipients in nine communes (n=417 persons)
Andreß and Lipsmeier (1999)	D	Own primary survey (Buseinschaltung im Sozialwissenschaften-Bus III/1996), n=3,170 German persons in private households, 18 years and above.
Böhnke and Dehley (1999a)	D	Welfare survey (Wohlfahrtssurvey 1998, n=3,042, persons in private households, 18 years and above.

Table 7.2 (cont)

Study	Country/ies	Data Sources
C) International compararative studies		
Halleröd (1996, 1998)	SE, GB	SE: Swedish Standard of Living Survey 1992; GB: Breadline Britain 1990
Böhnke and Dehley (1999b)	D, GB	D: Welfare Survey ('Wohlfahrtssurvey') 1998; GB: Breadline Britain 1990
Dirven and Fourage (1998)	BE, NL	BE: Belgian Socio-Economic Panel 1985 und 1988, n (longitudinal section) = 10,755; NL: Dutch Socio-Economic Panel 1985 und 1988, n (longitudinal section) = 8,711 persons in private households.
Mayer (1995)	USA, CND, SE, D (West)	USA: Census (1980), Health Interview Survey (1980), Consumer Expenditure Survey (1984-85); CND: Survey of Family Expenditures (1982); SE: Level of Living Survey (1981); D: German Socio-Economic Panel (1984)

Source: Andreß and Lipsmeier (2001, p. 89).

Mayer and Jencks (1989) obtained similar results with U.S. data: Net household income alone explained only 14 per cent of the entire variation in the distribution of the material standard-of-living restrictions examined. If, in contrast, one includes further indicators of need, available resources, and domestic burdens (such as property ownership, health, age, size of household), the coefficient of determination rises to 37 per cent. For Swedish data, Halleröd (1994) demonstrated that the risk of deprivation-based poverty greatly depends on factors other than income. Especially the unemployed, single parents, and older people are often significantly more deprivation poor, even with controlled incomes. The higher poverty risk for these groups known from studies on income-based poverty is therefore not exclusively due to their lower income positions.

Income-based and deprivation-based poverty: The two are not identical

The observation that income and deprivation are only loosely linked is further supported by the fact that the same individuals are not identified as poor under both the income-based and deprivation-based indicators (Halleröd, 1995; Kangas and Ritakallio, 1998; Nolan and Whelan, 1996). This lack of 'overlap' between the two poverty populations can be illustrated on the basis of two examples. According to Halleröd's results (1995, p. 122), 33.6 per cent of the Swedes surveyed were considered poor according to at least one of the two measures, but only 8.8 per cent were considered poor under both poverty measures. Of those surveyed, only 12.4 per cent could respectively be categorised as being poor based on one of the measures. Halleröd puts this clear difference down to serious measuring faults in both indicators, illustrating this with a differentiated analysis of the two inconsistent groups, i.e., those who 'only' dispose of low incomes, and those who 'only' demonstrate an insufficient standard of living. It shows that a high degree of income-poor persons are not affected by deprivation and also, conversely, that about one-third of the deprivation-poor have an income above median level. He considers it unsatisfactory to apply a poverty definition that classifies as 'poor' people who have high incomes or those who experience no restriction on their standard of living. He considers it possible, however, to at least partially solve these problems through a combination of indirect and direct poverty measures.

Kangas and Ritakallio (1998) reach a similar result, but draw a different conclusion. In addition to relative income-based poverty (50 per cent of median income) and deprivation (i.e., where, for financial reasons, three or more items are lacking), they also examine the subjective perception of the shortage of resources, the subjective perception of excessive debt, and the receipt of social assistance. They also conclude that the overlap between the different poverty measures is low and that, depending on the indicator, different groups are affected by different degrees of poverty. However, instead of arguing, like Halleröd, for an application of the intersection of the indicators, they underline that it is the degree of lacking agreement and, in particular, the specific poverty risks demonstrated by the individual indicators, that are of particular interest for research into poverty. It is precisely the diverging results between the indicators that provide important pointers for social policy action, e.g., if it emerged that even individuals on incomes above the income limit were exposed to substantial poverty risks based on certain other indicators. Such a result would, for example, raise the question as to whether income transfers are sufficient social policy intervention strategies to combat poverty. Income-based poverty can – at least theoretically – be combated with income transfers. The low overlap of the income indicator with other poverty measures does show, however, that other aspects of poverty can be lessened only to a certain extent for some of those surveyed through income transfers.

Permanently low resources increase deprivation

The few longitudinal results point to the fact that the link between the degree of deprivation and disposable resources becomes much closer if one takes into consideration indicators on the duration of the lack of resources. Mayer and Jencks (1989) considered income information from two years for a section of the population in their U.S. survey. One of their survey findings is that the extent of the change in income over this period provides an important factor in explaining deprivation. If one compares persons on low incomes in one year, one will find that the degree of deprivation for those individuals, who had to manage on a similarly low income in the previous year, is substantially higher than for persons who still disposed of a sufficient income in the previous year.

In Nolan and Whelan's Irish study (1996, pp. 137), indicators of a continuous lack of economic resources (long-term unemployment) or a continuous surplus of economic resources (savings, property ownership) are significant features to differentiate between those individuals simultaneously affected by income and deprivation poverty and the rest of the poor population, which 'only' experienced low income. Overall, there is a clearly stronger link between such longer-term factors and the extent of deprivation than with the income position. Townsend (1997, p. 34) also showed that persons affected by poverty for longer periods of time in the past demonstrate substantially higher deprivation values at the time of the survey than those who reported no or only occasional episodes of poverty in their past.

International comparison

The standard-of-living approach also supplies important additional findings in international comparative studies, which could not be uncovered by focusing exclusively on income distribution. Thus, for example, Mayer (1995) showed that the standard of living among the poor in the United States was not much lower than in Canada, Sweden and Germany – despite the U.S.'s much more pronounced inequality in incomes compared to Canada and many European countries. A further result relates to the comparison between countries whose welfare systems are developed to varying degrees. Thus, for example, in a comparison of influencing factors on deprivation-based poverty between Sweden and Great Britain, Halleröd (1996; 1998) showed that long-term unemployment, even under the (statistical) control of incomes, had a much more negative effect on the standard of living in Great Britain than in Sweden. Halleröd puts this down to the fact that the Swedish social security system is more generous.

Results for the Federal Republic of Germany

Lastly, some findings should be reported for the Federal Republic of Germany, which are based on a combination of the economic resource and standard-of-living approaches. Interest is focused in particular on the overlap and differences between income-based and deprivation-based poverty. In the delimitation of segments of the population affected by poverty, I consider both criteria, i.e., lacking financial resources as well as an insufficient standard of living, as constitutive for poverty. Through the combination of income-based and deprivation-based poverty, three affected groups can be determined and delineated from the rest of the population. Table 7.3 below shows, in addition to the distribution of people to these four groups, the respective average value of the deprivation index, the average number of missing items and the average equivalent household income.

As is to be expected in a wealthy country like Germany, a large part of the population lives in relatively secure conditions. About 85 per cent of the population is affected neither by income-based nor by deprivation-based poverty. Based simply on the results of the welfare survey (Wohlfahrtssurvey), this share, at 78 per cent, is slightly lower in East Germany. However, this also means that, according to region and data base, between 15 per cent and 22 per cent of the German population live in a deficit situation of one form or another.

Table 7.3   Poverty situation in West and East Germany, 1996 and 1998

| | West Germany | | | | East Germany | | | |
| | No poverty | | Deprivation-based poverty | | No poverty | | Deprivation-based Poverty | |
	1996	1998	1996	1998	1996	1998	1996	1998
Share (%)	85	85	8	6	86	78	5	6
Index	0.2	0.4	3.4	3.0	0.3	0.5	2.8	2.9
Items	0.8	1	9.1	10	1.0	2	7.9	10
Income	2,623	2,750	1,964	1,890	2,100	2,310	1,718	1,700
	Income-based poverty		'Truly' poor		Income-based poverty		'Truly' poor	
	1996	1998	1996	1998	1996	1998	1996	1998
Share (%)	4	5	3	4	6	9	3	6
Index	0.5	1.2	4.4	3.7	0.5	1.1	2.9	3.4
Items	2.1	4	11.1	12	1.8	4	8.5	11
Income	943	1,000	893	910	989	950	884	880

Source: 1996 figures: Sozialwissenschaften-Bus III/1996, weighted calculations; 1998 figures: Welfare Survey (Wohlfahrtssurvey) 1998, according to Böhnke and Delhey (1999a, p. 26).

Here, three problem groups can be identified:

- The situation is particularly precarious for those affected both by income-based poverty and by an insufficient standard of living (defined in the Table 7.3 as the 'truly' poor, according to HallERöd, 1995). For both data sets and parts of the country, major restrictions in the way of life can be shown for this group, both in terms of the level of deprivation and in terms of average income. According to the results of the welfare survey (Wohlfahrtssurvey), a slightly larger number of people in East Germany (6 per cent) are affected by these severe limitations than in West Germany (where the share is 4 per cent). Our own survey discerned no differences between the two parts of the country; the respective share stands at 3 per cent.

The two remaining groups are marked by restrictions in one of the two poverty indicators respectively:

- I denote people as being exclusively deprivation poor if they demonstrate an insufficient standard of living but dispose of an income that is above the income poverty level. The medium income in this group is therefore also noticeably higher than in the two other groups, but is significantly below the overall average. Between 5 per cent (1996, East Germany) and 8 per cent (1996, West Germany) of the population lives in such conditions.

- I describe people as being exclusively income poor if their income is below the poverty line, but their standard of living is not noticeably restricted. The people in this group lack correspondingly lower standard-of-living features than the two other problem groups. Due to the differences in incomes between the two parts of Germany, this group is substantially larger in East Germany than in West Germany: Between 4 per cent (1996, West Germany) and 9 per cent (1996, East Germany) of those surveyed find themselves in such a situation.

I have already mentioned elsewhere some explanations for the comparatively low overlap of the different poverty measures. Income-based poverty is not always accompanied by deprivation-based poverty especially because the actual household income measures only a proportion of disposable economic resources. Family support measures, such as free childcare, can continue to secure an appropriate standard of living, even if income is very modest.

'A low income can also be a temporary side effect of a status passage. This is why the reduced financial resources have not (yet) had an effect on household provision and the situation of supplies' (Böhnke and Delhey, 1999a, p. 27).

Furthermore, a number of explanations are also feasible to support the observation that some of those persons described as exclusively deprivation poor do not also simultaneously demonstrate income-based poverty. Thus, there might be people in this group who, due to extraordinary financial burdens, such as debts, support payments or care costs, have such very limited disposable means, despite a nominally sufficient income, that their consumption is massively restricted.

'Likewise, the knowledge – or fear – of an income shrinking in the future (e.g., due to temporary employment or the threat of unemployment) could prevent people from transforming their relevant sufficient income into consumption' (Böhnke and Delhey, 1999a, p. 28).

Besides these arguments, it should be pointed out that both poverty indicators are not free of measurement error. An element of the low overlap can therefore probably be due to this. The fact that the 'truly' poor are a restricted group of people in a particularly precarious life situation, is vividly illustrated if one considers how these people evaluate their standard of living subjectively. A question relevant to this, in which a scale of school grades from one to six was provided for the assessment, was posed in connection with the 1996 survey on the availability of standard-of-living features. In the 1998 survey, meanwhile, the question asked whether, in an emergency situation, individuals would be able to procure a sum of 3,000 German marks at short notice, either from their own bank account, in the form of a bank loan, or from friends or relatives.

As anticipated, the 'truly' poor see themselves in a situation in which they are much more rarely able to procure a largish sum of money at short notice than those who find themselves exclusively in income-based or deprivation-based poverty (cf. Table 7.4). Likewise, they noticeably more often subjectively evaluate their standard of living as only 'sufficient or lower'. Those who are income poor, on the other hand, are more frequently able to procure money at short notice and thus also do not consider their standard of living as restricted as those who are deprivation poor. This proves the plausibility of considerations on the context only insufficiently recorded by income data, which decisively co-determines the actual level of the attained standard of living. If, finally, one were to ask about the socio-demographic structure of the groups 'truly' poor (Andreß and Lipsmeier, 2001, p. 62), then particularly the unemployed, single parents, and those with no professional qualifications are frequently affected by income-based poverty accompanied by a simultaneously severe restriction in the standard of living. This doubly precarious living situation can also be found, but not as frequently, in families with more than two children.

Table 7.4   Subjective assessment of the standard of living and short-term availability of a larger sum of money (percentage share)

Subjective assessment of the standard of living (1996)	No poverty		Deprivation-based poverty		Income-based poverty		'Truly' poor		Total	
	West	East	West	East	West	East	West	East	West	East
Very good or good	67	67	17	33	39	40	5	18	63	61
Satisfactory	30	28	51	36	49	39	48	36	30	31
Sufficient or lower	3	5	31	31	12	21	47	46	7	8
Ability to procure 3,000 German marks at short notice (1998)	82	77	23	24	50	35	14	10	74	65

Source: 1996 figures: Sozialwissenschaften-Bus III/1996, weighted calculations. 1998 figures: Welfare Survey (Wohlfahrtssurvey) 1998, according to Böhnke and Delhey (1999a, p. 26).

References

Andreß, H.-J. (1999), *Leben in Armut. Analysen der Verhaltensweisen armer Haushalte mit Umfragedaten,* Opladen / Westdeutscher Verlag, Wiesbaden.

Andreß, H.-J. and Lipsmeier, G. (1999), 'Lebensstandard nicht allein vom Einkommen abhängig. Ergebnisse einer aktuellen Umfrage', *Informationsdienst Soziale Indikatoren* 21, pp. 5-9.

Andreß, H.-J. and Lipsmeier, G. (2001), Armut und Lebensstandard, in Bundesministerium für Arbeit und Sozialordnung (ed.), *Lebenslagen in Deutschland. Der erste Armuts- und Reichtumsbericht der Bundesregierung,* Bonn.

Böhnke, P. and Delhey, J. (1999a), 'Lebensstandard und Armut im vereinten Deutschland', in *Discussion Paper FS* (III), Wissenschaftszentrum Berlin für Sozialforschung, Berlin, pp. 99-408.

Böhnke, P. and Delhey, J. (1999b), 'Poverty in a multidimensional perspective. Great Britain and Germany in comparison', in *Discussion Paper FS* (III), Wissenschaftszentrum Berlin für Sozialforschung, Berlin, pp. 399-413.

Desai, M. and Shah, A. (1988), 'An econometric approach to the measurement of poverty', *Oxford Economic Papers* 40, pp. 505-522.

Dirven, H.-J. and Fourage, D. (1998), 'Impoverishment and social exclusion: A dynamic perspective on income and relative Deprivation in Belgium and the Netherlands', in H.-J. Andreß (ed.), *Empirical poverty research in a comparative perspective,* Ashgate, Aldershot, pp. 257-281.

Garfinkel, I., Haveman, R.H. and Betson, D. (1977), *Earnings capacity, poverty, and inequality,* Academic Press, New York.

Gordon, D. and Pantazis, C. (eds) (1997), *Breadline Britain in the 1990s,* Ashgate, Aldershot et al..

Halleröd, B. (1994), 'A new approach to direct measurement of consensual poverty', *Discussion Paper* (50), *SPRC,* University of NSW, Sydney.

Halleröd, B. (1995), 'The truly poor: direct and indirect consensual measurement of poverty in Sweden', *Journal of European Social Policy* (5), pp. 111-129.

Halleröd, B. (1996), Deprivation and poverty: a comparative analysis of Sweden and Great Britain, *Acta Sociologica* (39), pp. 141-168.

Halleröd, B. (1998), 'Poor Swedes, poor Britons: a comparative analysis of relative deprivation', in H.-J. Andreß (ed.), *Empirical poverty research in a comparative perspective,* Ashgate, Aldershot, pp. 283-311.

Kangas, O. and Ritakallio, V.-M. (1998), 'Different methods – different results? Approaches to multidimensional poverty', in H.-J. Andreß (ed.), *Empirical poverty research in a comparative perspective,* Ashgate, Aldershot, pp. 167-203.

Leu, R.E., Burri, S. and Priester, T. (1997), *Lebensqualität und Armut in der Schweiz,* Haupt, Bern et al..

Lipsmeier E. (2001), 'Potentiale und Probleme des Deprivationsansatzes in der Armutsforschung', *Archiv für Wissenschaft und Praxis der Sozialen Arbeit* (32), pp. 3-30.

Mack, J. and Lansley, S., (1985), *Poor Britain,* George Allen and Unwin, London.

Mayer, S.E. and Jencks, C. (1989), 'Poverty and the distribution of material hardship', *The Journal of Human Resources* (24), pp. 88-113.

Mayer, S.E. (1995), 'A comparison of poverty and living conditions in the United States, Canada, Sweden, and Germany', in K. McFate, R. Lawson, W.J. Wilson (eds) *Poverty, inequality and the future of social policy: Western states in the new world order,* Sage, New York, pp. 109-151.

Muffels, R.J.A. (1993), *Welfare economic effects of social security. Essays on poverty, social security and labour market: evidence from panel data,* Tilburg University Press, Tilburg.

Nolan, B. and Whelan, C. T. (1996), *Resources, deprivation and poverty,* Clarendon Press, Oxford.

Ringen, S. (1988), 'Direct and indirect measures of poverty', *Journal of Social Policy* (17), pp. 351-365.

Townsend, P. (1979), *Poverty in the United Kingdom. A survey of household resources and standards of living*, University of California Press, Berkeley / Los Angeles.

Townsend, P. (1997), 'The poverty line: methodology and international comparisons', in D. Gordon, C. Pantazis (eds), *Breadline Britain in the 1990s*, Ashgate, Aldershot et al., pp. 49-69.

Walker, R. (1987), 'Consensual approaches to the definition of poverty: towards an alternative methodology', *Journal of Social Policy* (16), pp. 213-226.

Chapter 8

Distribution patterns and social policy options in Germany

Richard Hauser

Introduction

At the lower end of the personal *market income*[1] distribution scale, we see the whole range of social policy problems magnified. Here are the unemployed and the chronically sick; the long-term disabled and the elderly; many single parents and couples with several children; those just starting work and those in casual work, normal citizens and marginalized people – not forgetting all their dependants with no income of their own. This is the dominant sphere of activity for social security policy. However, it is questionable whether social security policy is doing enough, and whether it is doing it efficiently, i.e. with the minimum of disincentives for both benefit claimants and taxpayers; not providing services to those who do not need them; and with adequate safeguards against abuse.

The upper end of the market income distribution scale is also of special significance for social policy, but from a quite different viewpoint. Here the question is: do the well-off contribute enough towards financing social policy measures, or are they escaping their socio-political responsibilities through tax evasion or refuge in tax havens, with the consequence that the burden on more responsible citizens becomes even greater?

The tax and transfer system reduces the spread of net incomes quite significantly; but does it reduce it for everybody in the lower market income range, and does it reduce the gaps sufficiently? Plato, no less, had something to say on this question. To quote Frank Cowell, who cites this passage in his 1977 book 'Measuring Inequality' (p. 26):

'if a state is to avoid ... civil disintegration ... extreme poverty and wealth must not be allowed to rise in any section of the citizen-body, because both lead to disasters. This is why the legislator must announce now the acceptable limits of wealth and poverty'.

Plato suggested that the maximum discrepancy between the income and wealth of the rich and the poor should not exceed 4:1. What party today would dare to adopt such a principle in its political program?

The following pages begin with a rough sketch of trends in personal income distribution, in terms of market income and of net income[2] as modified by the tax and transfer system. I base this on the results of income and consumption surveys from the Federal Statistical Office, which do have some limitations: very wealthy households, and people in institutions, are not included, and the assessment is restricted to German households, as the income and consumption surveys have only covered foreigners since 1993.[3] I then discuss the second element of economic welfare: the net wealth of households and its distribution. I conclude by discussing some suggestions for social policy reform.

Of course this field is far too wide for all social policy problems to be addressed and all options debated. I do not concern myself with the five branches of social insurance[4] that are financed by contributions from employees and employers, and by supplements from the state. Social insurance provisions already provide many groups with a net income that is based on earlier income from employment, and cover the costs of sickness, rehabilitation and care. I restrict myself to transfers financed through taxation, which require no explicit advance payment in the form of contributions based on employment income, and which are more strongly targeted at the lower income range. The most prominent are the family benefits, unemployment and social assistance. The means-tested pension supplement assistance for the disabled and the elderly that comes into force from 01.01.2003 is also part of this group.

Distribution trends and current situation

The starting point for our consideration is the distribution of gross income from employment across employees. The first question here is: has the distribution of this most important category of market income become more unequal?

To answer this question, we need a distribution measure. A comprehensive measure, which expresses the degree of inequality in income distribution in a single number, is the Gini coefficient. This coefficient has the value 0 per cent when income is distributed completely equally, and rises to 100 per cent when the whole income is drawn by one person while all others go without – in other words, a situation of maximum inequality. Figure 8.1 shows the values of the Gini coefficient for the distribution of gross income from employment across recipients (line in the middle).

It can be seen that in West Germany, the Gini coefficient for the distribution of gross income from employment across recipients showed a gradual rise from 29.7 per cent to 32.0 per cent over the whole period from 1973 to 1998. This is a small but significant increase. In East Germany the Gini coefficient is lower than in West Germany, but it rose much faster in the five-year period from 1993 to 1998, without however reaching the West German level.

The answer to our question is this: notwithstanding the many factors influencing the distribution of income from employment, inequality has increased only slightly. This is surprising when one considers the changes which have taken place in terms of sector structure, shifts in regional economic priorities, the increasing number of women in employment, the increase in part-time and casual work, the general shortening of annual working hours, and changes to wage structures.

It has to be said that the Gini coefficient does not react strongly to changes at the upper and lower ends of the range. Distribution indicators that are especially sensitive at the lower end, like Theil's measure or the Atkinson Index, show that this is where inequality has become greater.[5]

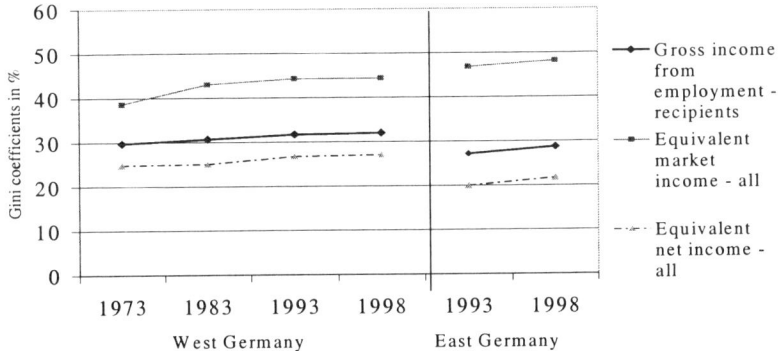

Figure 8.1   Change in the Gini coefficient as a measure of personal income inequality in Germany 1973-1998

The unemployed do not appear in this picture, as they receive no salaries or wages. Personal income distribution for other types of income cannot be seen either. To see the changes caused by these factors, we have to sum all market incomes at the household level and artificially distribute it across all members of the household. Only then do we see how far the unemployed and their dependants are affected by the loss of employment income, and how far other types of market income may cushion this loss.

However, when we distribute household market income across all members of the household, we are not looking at a simple per capita distribution, but taking into account savings from shared housekeeping, and the more modest needs of children. The OECD has developed a scale for this purpose, which assigns a weighting of 1.0 to the head of the household, 0.7 to other people over 14 years old, and 0.5 to younger children. This scale also roughly matches institutional data in Germany. Personal income recalculated using this scale is described as equivalent market income.

At this stage we can ask a second question: has the overall distribution of equivalent market income changed, taking account of the unemployed, the disabled, children and old people? Referring again to Figure 8.1, we see from the top lines that this view gives a much higher Gini coefficient, which has also risen more steeply. The increase in West Germany from 1973 to 1998 was 11.5 per cent. In this area, the distribution in East Germany is even more unbalanced than in the West, and it increased somewhat in the five-year period from 1993 to 1998. These differences can be attributed to higher unemployment and lower incomes from assets in the new federal states. Thus, from this perspective one can speak of a clear increase in inequality.

But this is an artificial distribution, because it does not yet take into account the effects of social security and the taxation system.[6] Benefits are paid out as a substitute for wages where income is lost because of social risks, or where the expense of child maintenance or the costs of sickness and care are too high, or where there is not even the minimum needed to live. Income tax also has a compensating effect, acting through tax-free allowances and through its progressive structure. In considering the extent of differences in standard of living, we must look at the distribution of equivalent net income.

The third question then arises: whether inequality in the personal distribution of equivalent net income has increased strongly in the last 25 years. The Gini coefficients for the personal distribution of equivalent net income, also given in Figure 8.1 (bottom lines), show two things. First, the inequality of equivalent net income distribution across persons is distinctly lower than the distribution of gross income from employment across employees and also much lower than the distribution of equivalent market income across persons. Second, the Gini coefficient for equivalent net income distribution rose only slightly in this quarter-century, by 8.7 per cent in total. This is a much smaller increase than those observed in Great Britain or the USA. So there is an increase in inequality, but so far it has been kept within bounds by the compensating effects of the social security and tax systems.

Gini coefficients are not very transparent. The distribution situation can be seen more clearly if we arrange people in ascending order by equivalent net income, divide them into groups of 10 per cent each, and look at the percentage of the total equivalent net income accounted for by each group. Just such a decile representation – for West and East Germany separately – is shown in Figure 8.2.

From this it can be seen that in West Germany the income shares of the lower five deciles decreased from 1973 to 1998, and the shares of the upper four deciles increased. In East Germany a similar process went on from 1993 to 1998, though at a lower level of inequality. The shares of the lower six deciles decreased and shares of the upper three deciles increased.

One could interpret the quotation from Plato as applying particularly to the ratio between the top and bottom deciles. In West Germany, this ratio stood at 1:4.67 in 1973 – not so far away from Plato's thinking. However, a quarter of a century later it had shown a distinct rise, standing at 1:5.55 in 1998 In East Germany the ratio between these extremes deteriorated from 1:3.55 to 1:4.0 in the five-year period from 1993 to 1998. Again, even within the top and bottom deciles there are large differences of income, which have grown larger.[7] When one considers that the income and consumption surveys used for this assessment did not include the wealthiest group, one can conclude that the danger of 'civil disintegration' has grown.

West Germany

East Germany

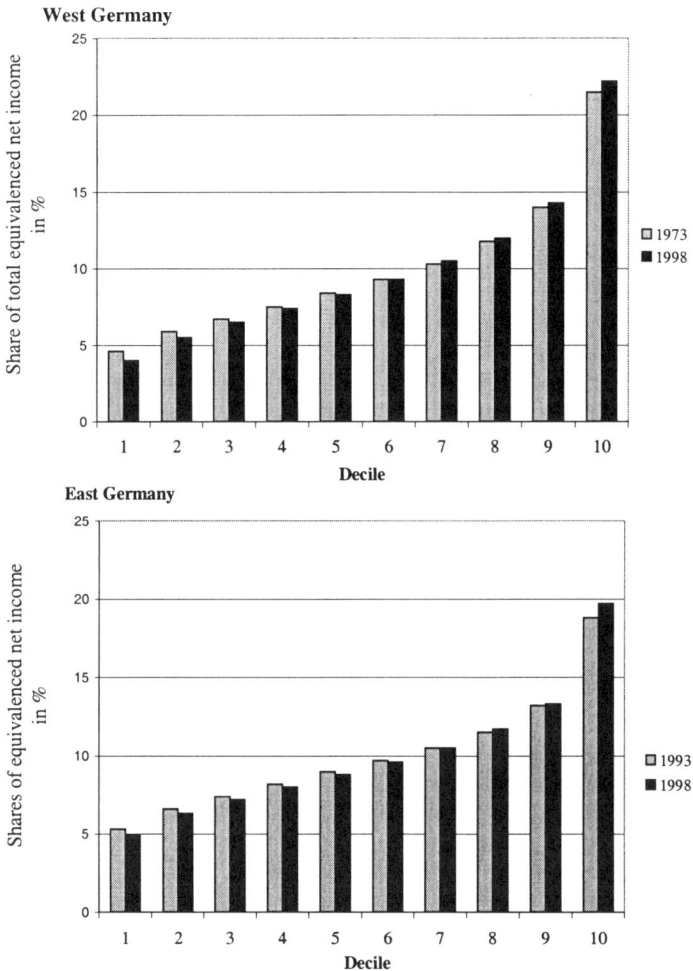

**Figure 8.2   Trends in equivalent net income distribution, by decile:
West Germany 1973-1998, East Germany 1993-1998**

Source: Hauser and Becker (2001a), Tab 6.2.6, p. 104.

A look at the wealth distribution

Apart from its importance in generating investment income, wealth has other
functions that make it an important second element in the welfare of households. It
has to be admitted that the state of knowledge about wealth distribution is not very
good; in particular, very little is known about the distribution of wealth within the
business sector, much of which also belongs to households. Only public share

ownership can be determined, while the value of titles in companies of limited liability, partnerships and one-man businesses remains obscure. Leaving aside this element of wealth, together with household consumer assets, and excluding also the richest households (net monthly income above DM 35,000), which are especially hard to pin down, one can make a number of observations about the distribution of total net wealth in West and East Germany for the years 1993 to 1998.

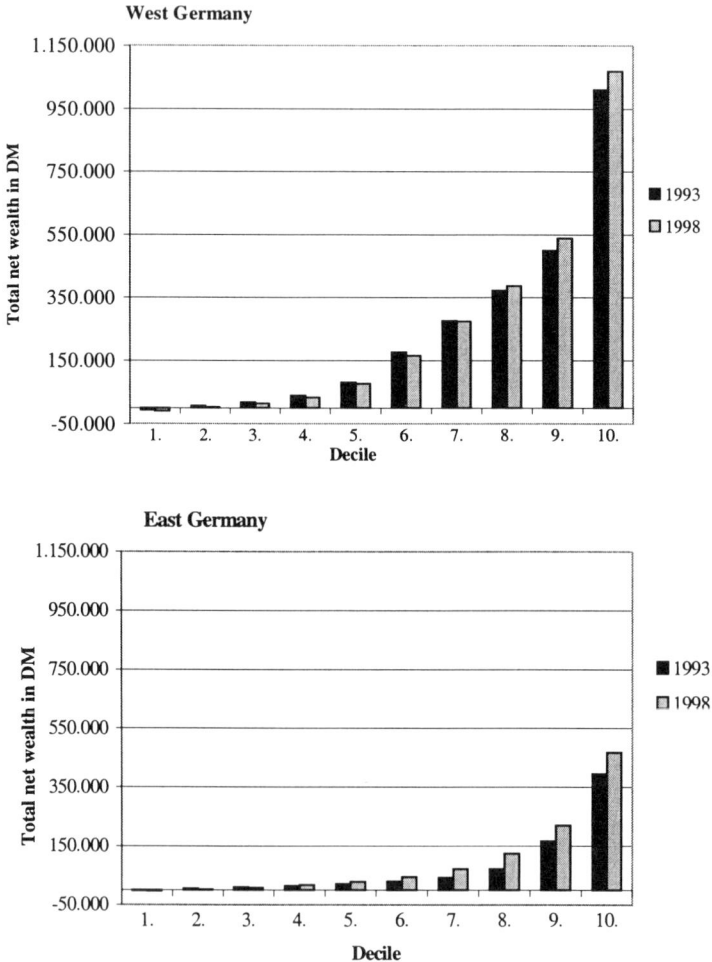

Figure 8.3   Distribution of total private household net wealth in West and East Germany 1993-1998

If one orders households by net wealth, derived by subtracting their respective debts from gross wealth, and then divides them into groups of 10 per cent each, one arrives at another decile representation, shown in Figure 8.3. This time however, each decile represents the average value of net wealth per household, not (as in the previous example) the share of total net wealth.

This decile distribution shows that, on average, the bottom 10 per cent of all West German households are in debt while the top 10 per cent of all households have average assets of more than DM 1 million. Similarly, in East Germany, the bottom 10 per cent are in debt, but the net wealth of the top 10 per cent is less than half as much as in the West. The average indebtedness of the bottom 10 per cent most likely represents consumer credit taken out to finance the consumer assets not included here, such as consumer durables, cars etc.

From Figure 8.3 it can be seen that inequality in wealth distribution is much greater than inequality in income distribution; the Gini coefficient for household net wealth is more than twice as high as that for personal equivalent net income.[8] Moreover, the inequality of wealth distribution is even greater in East than in West Germany.

In the period from 1993 to 1998 inequality of wealth distribution in West Germany increased further: While the bottom seven deciles suffered a decline in their average wealth in these last five years, the averages of the top three deciles continued to grow. In the former GDR a distinct increase could be seen in the top seven deciles from 1993 to 1998, while the bottom three deciles fell back.

The great discrepancy between households in respect of their net wealth becomes even clearer if we group the bottom 30 per cent, the middle 40 per cent and the top 30 per cent and determine the shares of total wealth for these groupings.

Table 8.1   Shares of bottom, middle and top wealth groups in total net wealth in West and East Germany, 1993-1998 (per cent)

Wealth group	West Germany		East Germany	
	1993	1998	1993	1998
Bottom 30%	0.7	0.3	1.5	0.6
Middle 40%	23.2	21.5	14.1	16.4
Top 30%	76.1	78.2	84.4	82.8
Total	100	100	100	100

Source: Income and consumption survey database of the Faculty of Economics (distribution and social policy studies), Goethe University, Frankfurt am Main; author's own calculations.

Table 8.1 shows that the top 30 per cent of households account for around 80 per cent of net wealth of all households. In West Germany, this share is somewhat lower than in the East; in East Germany there was a slight decrease over the last five years. While in West Germany the share of the top group increased slightly, in the West, the middle 40 per cent of households own a good fifth of the total wealth, in the East only a sixth. In both parts of the country, the bottom 30 per cent of households do not own any significant share of total wealth. The term 'two-thirds society' coined by Glotz is thus quite accurate, at least with regard to net wealth.

Given this lack of wealth among the bottom 30 per cent, it also appears very unlikely that there will be any significant voluntary wealth creation to supplement state-funded pensions provision. We may assume that the middle 40 per cent will grasp this opportunity and drain off potential state funding resources by virtue of additional saving. The top group can provide for security in old age out of existing wealth, switching into subsidized forms of investment. This can produce very profitable results.

Are the top and bottom income groups expanding at the expense of the middle class?

We have seen that inequality in equivalent net income distribution has increased slightly, but we do not yet know where in the income pyramid these changes have occurred. Does the theory of a thinning middle class propounded in the USA apply to Germany also? To tackle this problem, we must ask two questions:

First, has the proportion of people who have to get by on less than half of the mean equivalent net income increased or decreased? Second, has the proportion of people who have more than twice the mean equivalent net income at their disposal increased or decreased? Figure 8.4 supplies answers to both these questions.

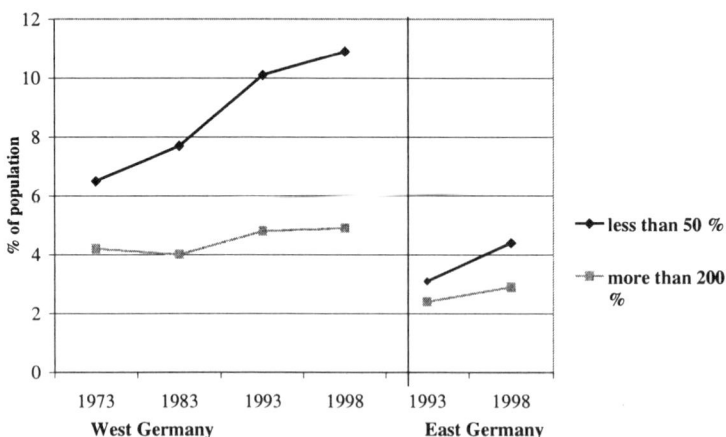

Figure 8.4   Proportion of people in the low-income and affluence bands in West and East Germany, 1973-1998

Source: Hauser and Becker (2001a), Tab. 6.1.8, p 92 and Tab. 8.2.1, p 177.

In West Germany we can detect a clear rise between 1973 and 1998 in the proportion of people who have to get by on less than half the mean equivalent net income. By 1998, 10.9 per cent of the German population had already fallen below this threshold. In D-Mark terms this means that in 1998, a single person living below this threshold had less than DM 1,462 per month at his disposal. For larger households, the threshold was correspondingly higher. In many social policy studies, people living below this threshold are regarded as relatively income-poor.

East Germany too showed an increase in this group of people between 1993 and 1998, but the percentage was still distinctly lower than in West Germany. However, one has to bear in mind that even in 1998 mean equivalent net income in East Germany was only about 75 per cent of the value for West Germany. Anyone under the 50 per cent threshold had less than DM 1,106 per month at his disposal.[9] If we took an average for the whole of Germany as a reference point, the proportion of people in this bottom group would be much higher in the former GDR than in the West. I will return to this point later.

At the upper end of the income distribution scale we do not see such a large increase in the respective percentages. In 1973, 4.2 per cent of the population in West Germany had more than double the average at their disposal, while the figure for 1998 was 4.9 per cent. At a lower level, East Germany showed a similar increase, from 2.4 per cent to 2.9 per cent.

These findings do give weight to the conclusion that the middle class is in fact thinning out in Germany, but that this is caused more by people falling into the bottom income band than rising into the top band.

Groups disproportionately affected by poverty

The social policy-maker focuses on the lower and middle income bands. Particular notice must be taken of people in the 'income-poor' band, the threshold of which I have set – despite some reservations – at 50 per cent of mean equivalent net income. More than 10 years after reunification there no longer seems to be any distinction between West and East Germany on this subject of poverty; for subjective expectations with regard to desirable minimum incomes converged some years ago[10]; welfare benefit levels differ only slightly; and child allowance and child-raising allowance are at the same level. Only wages and wage-related benefits still differ significantly.

If we calculate mean equivalent net income for Germany as a whole, the 50 per cent threshold for a single person stood at DM 1,394 in 1998. If we included foreign as well as German households in the calculation, a slightly lower threshold would result.[11]

The group of people who have to get by on an equivalent net income below this threshold is very heterogeneous. An above-average number of families of unemployed people, families with several children, and single parents can be found among the 'income-poor'. A uniform poverty threshold also produces a higher poverty rate in East Germany than in the West – 15 per cent against 9 per cent.

At this point I would like to pick out just one aspect, as it highlights a problem that I believe requires especially urgent social policy intervention (which would not, however, face any insurmountable barriers). This concerns the poverty rates for children and young people.

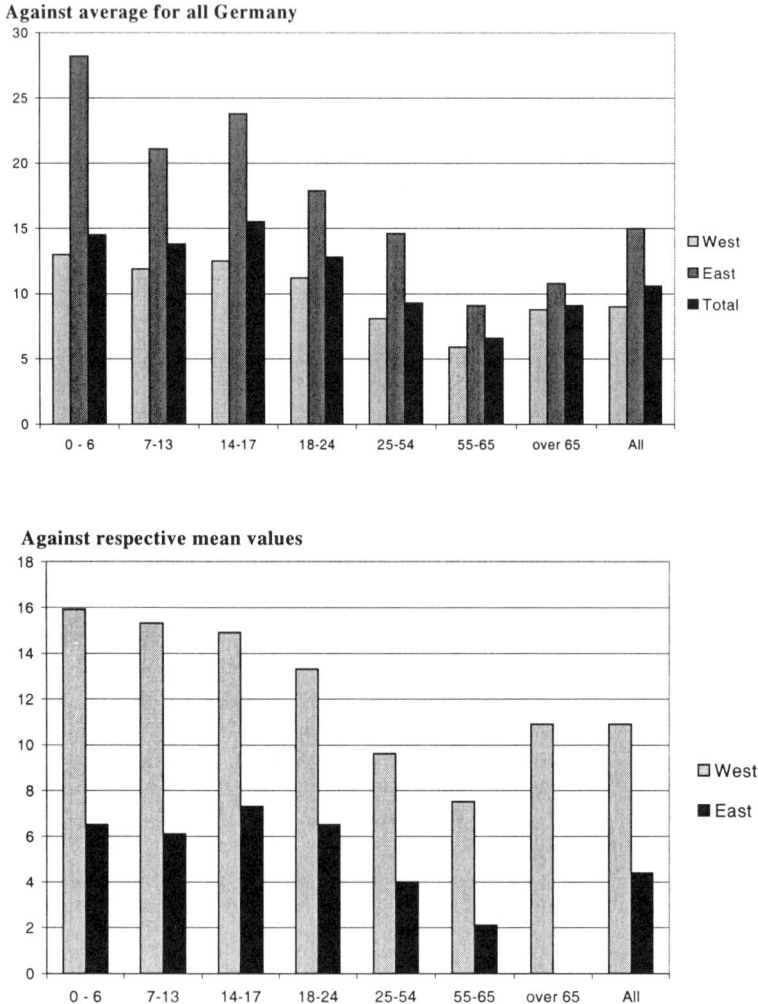

Against average for all Germany

Against respective mean values

**Figure 8.5   Poverty rates by age at the 50 per cent threshold
                (old OECD scale)**

Source: Hauser and Becker (2001a), Tab 7.2.4, p 147.

Figure 8.5 shows the poverty rates for West and East Germany by age-group, calculated separately on the basis of their respective mean values, and together on the basis of a mean value for the whole of Germany. From a comparison of the two representations, one can see how the choice of mean value affects the result.

Irrespective of this, it is clear that children and young people show poverty rates far above the average.

If we calculate poverty rates for children between 0 and 17 on the basis of an average for the whole of Germany, they lie between 21 per cent and 28 per cent (depending on age group) for East Germany, and at 12 per cent to 13 per cent for West Germany. A similar tendency for children to be particularly impacted by poverty can also be derived from social assistance statistics.[12]

Findings from the Socio-Economic Panel, presented by Wagner and Krause, show that poverty rates for children decrease only slightly if one uses average income over four years instead of annual income.[13] In the great majority of cases therefore, we are talking not just about short-term poverty, but about deprivation persisting over the medium term. Regardless of any possible statistical inaccuracy, this finding should alarm us.

Some thoughts on social policy options

The problem of high poverty rates among children has several causes. The most important of these are:

- First, the state of the labour market – i.e. high unemployment – which means that single parents and couples with children cannot obtain sufficient income from work.
- Second, social changes that have led to an increase in the proportion of single parents with low earning potential and poor social security coverage.
- Third, insufficient willingness or ability of those liable for maintenance to pay for children, and in some cases also for previous spouses following divorce or separation.
- Fourth, inadequate family compensation, which does not guarantee children a socio-cultural minimum subsistence level. The contribution towards child maintenance needed from parents in the lowest income band leads to the whole family falling into the poverty zone.

From a social policy perspective, we must then ask what options exist to combat the problem of child poverty.

There is no doubt that a successful employment policy will significantly alleviate the problem. Certainly, we can say at the outset that the problem would not be completely solved even in what would today be almost utopian conditions of full employment *at current wage levels*; first, it is not possible to take account of the number of children in setting wage levels; second, the earning potential of unskilled and semi-skilled workers is insufficient to cover maintenance for several children, even at current wage levels; and thirdly, there are obstacles to both parents (or single parents) taking work, as childcare facilities are not sufficiently well-established.

Any expectation that the problem of child poverty might be completely solved by employment policy measures is even less justified if we proposes to increase employment by reducing the minimum wage, with or without wage subsidies, as this would only reduce the wage income of the bottom band (compared to full employment at current wage levels). The same is true of any explicit promotion of part-time employment or other forms of flexible working arrangement.

Notwithstanding their limited effectiveness, measures to increase employment are an essential part of any policy for combating poverty. Their effectiveness in eliminating child poverty should, however, be increased by extending childcare facilities, for infants under three years old as well as children between three and six, and children of primary school age, to the point where no parent is prevented by the need for childcare from taking a part-time or full-time job when one is available. As the German Government's Poverty and Wealth Report has again shown, *West Germany* in particular, with childcare places for 2.8 per cent of infants below the age of three, lags far behind countries like Denmark (with 48 per cent), and Sweden (33 per cent). The same is true of all-day care in the primary school. In the former GDR the situation with crèche places is a lot healthier, with a 36.3 per cent provision rate. Added to under-provision is the remarkable fact that many childcare institutions – oriented towards school holidays – close altogether at certain times. Just imagine if grocery stores were to behave in the same way – and all at the same time.

It is apparent that it will take some time to establish childcare facilities, even if they got the go-ahead immediately, and besides, it is questionable whether we will return to a higher rate of employment in the medium term. Therefore measures are needed which could have some immediate effect in reducing or even eliminating child poverty. If skillfully constructed, they need not be at all incompatible with employment policy and measures to extend childcare facilities, as is sometimes maintained.

Two measures in the field of family compensation can help towards this. The first involves expanding the services of the maintenance allowance office. This office makes supplementary advance maintenance payments to children of single parents, when the person liable for maintenance does not make the payments; these payments are then recovered from the parent liable. Benefits are also paid retrospectively, where this is possible. This little-known social service has increased substantially in scope in the last few years, as only about a quarter of those liable for maintenance pay up regularly and in full. In 1997, 1.7 billion DM were paid out, taking some of the burden away from social security.

However, the maintenance allowance is only available for a maximum of 6 years to children between 0 and 12 years old. Thereafter, the person who cares for the child is thrown back on normal legal procedures to press his or her claims, always assuming the person liable for maintenance can actually pay, and can be reached – and is even still alive. To solve this problem, which has now become a huge risk area, the payment period should be extended to cover the whole time from birth to the end of compulsory schooling age for those children entitled to maintenance; for further education, student grants would then kick in and guarantee no gaps in financial cover for children of single parents.

The second measure involves introducing a means-tested child support supplement, which would bring normal child benefit up to the socio-cultural minimum subsistence level for a child of approx. DM 600.[14] This supplement should be subordinate to maintenance payments and all social benefits (including the maintenance allowance); only social assistance would be subordinate to the child benefit supplement. Means-testing should be graduated. For every DM above the parents' minimum subsistence level, the child benefit supplement would go down by 50 pfennigs – i.e. a benefit reduction rate of 50 per cent. This would prevent any parents who could meet at least their own socio-cultural minimum subsistence level out of their income from becoming dependent on social assistance. According to our estimates for 1998, this sort of provision, requiring net expenditure of approx. DM 6.3 billion, would remove about a third of children and their parents currently drawing social assistance benefits from the welfare system. Many of them would then cross the 50 per cent threshold defined above, and would no longer be classed as 'income-poor'. Altogether about 3.7 million children and their parents would benefit from this supplement, and it would also help parents on low incomes above the social assistance threshold, and their children.[15]

Closing remark

The problem of child poverty is present in all developed OECD countries; in Germany, however, the problem is greater than in the majority of EU countries.[16] This should spur us to more vigorous action, because widespread and enduring poverty in the childhood years can do lifelong damage both to the victims and to society as a whole.

Annex

Table 8.2   Gini coefficients as a measure of inequality of personal income distribution in Germany (in per cent)

	West Germany				East Germany	
Distribution	**1973**	**1983**	**1993**	**1998**	**1993**	**1998**
1 Gross income from employment, for recipients	29.72	30.65	31.69	31.97	27.11	28.71
2 Equivalent market income, all	38.60	43.01	44.25	44.35	46.78	48.13
3 Equivalent net income, all	24.81	25.02	26.70	26.96	19.94	21.70

Source: Income and consumption survey database of the Faculty of Economics (distribution and social policy studies), Goethe University, Frankfurt am Main; author's own calculations.

Table 8.3 **Distribution of total private household net wealth in West and East Germany 1993-1998 (average values, rounded to 1,000 DM)**

Households by total net wealth in ascending order	West Germany		East Germany	
	1993	1998	1993	1998
1st Decile	-7,000	-10,000	-2,000	-4,000
2nd Decile	7,000	3,000	5,000	2,000
3rd Decile	18,000	14,000	9,000	8,000
4th Decile	40,000	34,000	14,000	17,000
5th Decile	81,000	77,000	20,000	28,000
6th Decile	176,000	166,000	29,000	45,000
7th Decile	267,000	274,000	43,000	71,000
8th Decile	373,000	387,000	72,000	123,000
9th Decile	500,000	538,000	167,000	220,000
10th Decile	1.011,000	1.069,000	395,000	468,000
Total	248,000	255,000	75,000	98,000

Source: Income and consumption survey database of the Faculty of Economics (distribution and social policy studies), Goethe University, Frankfurt am Main; author's own calculations.

Table 8.4 **Poverty rates by age at the 50 per cent threshold (old OECD scale) 1998, in per cent**

Age group	Respective mean values		Mean value for all Germany		
	West	East	West	East	Total
All	10.9	4.4	9.0	15.0	10.6
0-6 years	15.9	(6.5)	13.0	28.2	14.5
7 - approx. 13 years	15.3	6.1	11.9	21.1	13.8
approx. 14 - approx. 17 years	14.9	(7.3)	12.5	23.8	15.5
approx. 18-24 years	13.3	6.5	11.2	17.9	12.8
25-54 years	9.6	4.0	8.1	14.6	9.3
55-65 years	7.5	(2.1)	5.9	9.1	6.6
65 years and above	10.9	*	8.8	10.8	9.1

( ) *Figures based on fewer than 100 cases in the cell.*
* *No figure given, because fewer than 30 cases in the cell.*

Source: Hauser and Becker (2001a), Tab 7.2.4.

Table 8.5   Proportion of people in the low-income and affluence bands
in West and East Germany 1973-1998 (in per cent)

Proportion with more/less than the mean equivalent net income	West Germany				East Germany	
	1973	1983	1993	1998	1993	1998
less than 50%	6.5	7.7	10.1	10.9	3.1	4.4
more than 200%	4.2	4.0	4.8	4.9	2.4	2.9
Mean - equivalent net income in DM	981	1,756	2,648	2,924	1,783	2,212

Source: Income and consumption survey database of the Faculty of Economics (distribution and social policy studies), Goethe University, Frankfurt am Main; author's own calculations.

Notes

1   Market income consists of gross wages, interest, rent, dividends and income from self-employment. Social security contributions of employers are not included.
2   Net income or disposable income is defined as market income minus social security contributions of employees and personal taxes plus social transfers.
3   For a detailed description of the limitations, cf. Hauser and Becker (2001a), pp. 46-60.
4   The German social security system consists of a mandatory pension system (gesetzliche Rentenversicherung), a mandatory sickness insurance (gesetzliche Krankenversicherung), a mandatory insurance for occupational accidents (gesetzliche Berufsunfallversicherung), a mandatory unemployment insurance (Arbeitslosenversicherung) and a mandatory insurance for the costs of nursing care (gesetzliche Pflegeversicherung).
5   The Theil measure rose from 0.188 (1973) to 0.222 (1998), i.e. by 18.1 per cent. The Atkinson Index with $\varepsilon = 2$ rose from 0.4071 to 0.5305, i.e. by 30.3 per cent (Hauser and Becker, 2001a). An explanation of these indicators can be found in Cowell (1995).
6   This distribution is artificial also because without the transfer and tax system, social adjustments would take place that cannot be estimated precisely.
7   Cf. Hauser and Becker (2001a), pp. 177
8   The Gini coefficients for personal distribution of equivalent net income for West Germany were 0.2670 in 1993 and 0.2696 in 1998; in East Germany the values were 0.1994 in 1993 and 0.2170 in 1998 (Hauser and Becker, 2001a, pp. 104) The Gini coefficients for personal distribution of total household net wealth for West Germany were 0.622 in 1993 and 0.640 in 1998; in East Germany the values of the Gini coefficient were 0.694 in 1993 and 0.676 in 1998 (Hauser and Stein 2001, pp. 124)
9   Calculated from Hauser and Becker (2001a), Tab 6.2.6, pp. 104
10   Hauser and Wagner (1996)
11   Cf. Wagner and Krause (2001), Tab. 3.1, pp. 29
12   Bundesministerium für Arbeit und Sozialordnung (2001), pp. 79
13   Wagner and Krause (2001), pp. 161
14   It should be pointed out that child benefit is only paid when the possible tax saving from the tax-free allowance for children is less than the child benefit amount. Taxpayers can theoretically choose between the two options, but the internal revenue service takes into account the more favourable solution for the taxpayer.

15 Hauser and Becker (2001b),
16 Micklewright and Stewart (2000), pp. 10; UNICEF (2000).

References

Bundesministerium für Arbeit und Sozialordnung (2001), *Lebenslagen in Deutschland. Der erste Armuts- und Reichtumsbericht der Bundesregierung*, Bonn.

Cowell, F. (1995), *Measuring Inequality*, 2nd ed., Prentice Hall, London.

Hanesch, W. (2001), *Einkommenslage bei Erwerbstätigkeit und Arbeitslosigkeit*, Studie im Auftrag des Bundesministeriums für Arbeit und Sozialordnung, Bonn.

Hauser, R. and Wagner, G. (1996), 'Die Einkommensverteilung in Ostdeutschland – Darstellung, Vergleich und Determinanten für die Jahre 1990 bis 1994', in R. Hauser (ed.), *Sozialpolitik im vereinten Deutschland III, Familienpolitik, Lohnpolitik und Verteilung*, Berlin, pp. 70-127.

Hauser, R. and Becker, I. (2001a), *Einkommensverteilung im Querschnitt und im Zeitverlauf 1973-1998*, Studie im Auftrag des Bundesministeriums für Arbeit und Sozialordnung, Bonn.

Hauser, R. and Becker, I. (2001b), 'Lohnsubventionen und verbesserter Familienlastenausgleich als Instrumente zur Verringerung von Sozialhilfeabhängigkeit', in H.-C. Mager, H. Schäfer and K. Schrüfer (eds), *Private Versicherung und Soziale Sicherung*, Metropolis, Marburg, pp. 293-312.

Hauser, R. and Stein, H. (2001), *Die Vermögensverteilung im vereinigten Deutschland*, Campus, Frankfurt am Main/New York.

Micklewright, J. and Stewart, K. (2000), 'Child Well-Being in the EU and Enlargement to the East', *UNICEF Innocenti Working Paper* (75), Florence.

UNICEF (2000), 'A League Table of Child Poverty in Rich Nations', *Innocenti Report Card* (1), June, Florence.

Wagner, G.G. and Krause, P. (2001), *Einkommensverteilung und Einkommensmobilität*, Studie im Auftrag des Bundesministeriums für Arbeit und Sozialordnung, Bonn.

Chapter 9

Social assistance between social protection and activation in Germany

Walter Hanesch

The changing role and basic functions of social assistance

In almost all European countries, the importance of social-assistance schemes has increased over the last two decades. Indicators for the expansion of the last safety net were increasing numbers of welfare recipients as well as increasing public expenditures on social assistance (see Eardley et al., 1996a). The increasing numbers of welfare recipients were and are primarily the result of rising poverty risks, which derived from a deep-rooted change in the economic, social, demographic and ethnic structure of European societies. But these trends have been and still are overlapped by changes in the availability of fiscal resources and shifts in the political concepts to overcome the increasing socio-economic problems. As a consequence of restructuring strategies in the primary safety nets, increasing numbers of people in need are falling outside of the framework of the social-insurance system. With the growing demand for assistance, scarce finances and new social policy concepts, there has been a general shift from insurance-based and earnings-related benefits to means-tested payments.

The increasing number of social-assistance recipients has raised new questions concerning the role, aims and tasks of this last-resort safety net in the member states of the European Union (European Commission, 1999). A common concern throughout Europe is how to prevent long-term dependency on social assistance and how to promote the activation of recipients, mainly through paid labour. Promoting 'active policies' instead of 'passive' reliance on income maintenance is one of the key concerns expressed in recent documents by the European Union. The fact that social-assistance schemes have been developed and changed continuously in a number of countries in the 1990s has emphasized the need for up-to-date research and evaluation. Important contributions to our knowledge on existing social-assistance schemes in Europe have come from such studies as Eardley et al., 1996a and 1996b; Guibentif and Bouget, 1997; Heikkilä and Keskitalo, 2001.

Generally there are two key aims for social assistance – the prevention of extreme material deprivation and the maintenance of integration by preventing social exclusion and marginalization (see Heikkilä et al., 2001, pp. 13-14): With regard to the first function, i.e. the prevention of extreme hardship among those with no other resources, we can recognize that almost all EU member states now have some kind of scheme that seeks to achieve this objective, the only exception being

Greece. Of course, there are still major problems in agreeing on an operational definition of what constitutes the minimum level to be guaranteed (Veit-Wilson, 1998). The second function of any minimum income arrangement is to prevent social marginalization and exclusion. During the 1990s, the concept of the 'activating welfare state' played a key role in the social policy discourse of the member states of the European Union. In current practice, the favoured form of activation policy involves programmes aimed at integrating unemployed social-assistance recipients into the labour market and improving their economic and social inclusion. The more activation has become a main topic of welfare reform, the more the question arises as to how far the social protection function is compatible with the activating function of the last safety net (see e.g. Loedemel and Trickey, 2000a; Hanesch and Balzter, 2001).

What is the role of social assistance in the – in Esping-Andersen's (1990) terms, 'corporatist' or 'conservative' – German welfare regime, how has this last safety net developed recently and in which direction do the current reform debates in Germany point? In my paper, I attempt to answer these questions. The essay starts with a short survey on the legal and institutional structure of social assistance in Germany. Against this background, I give an outline of the recent development of welfare receipt and welfare-dependency in Germany. A third section is dedicated to the role of social assistance as a means of activation. Finally, the essay summarizes the current reform debate about the last safety net in Germany.

The legal and institutional structure of social assistance in Germany

In the German welfare regime, the social-assistance scheme traditionally plays only a marginal role (see Hanesch, 2001). This is due to three characteristic elements of this regime type:

*   The German welfare regime is characterized by the fact that everyone who is of working age and is able to work has the obligation to make his living and to support his family by participating in the labour market. As a consequence of labour-market regulations and collective agreements, the participation of the (normally male) breadwinner in the labour market was based on what was known as the standard employment relationship (*Normalarbeitsverhältnis*). This means that there was unlimited full-time employment under the protection of labour and social laws, and that the level and structure of wages normally enabled every full-time worker to attain a standard of living above the poverty line.
*   In addition, there was and is a bundle of tax-financed means-tested and means-neutral benefits for certain specific needs such as child allowance, family allowance, housing allowance, grants for further education, etc. These benefits, in addition to wages and earnings, reduce the need for social assistance, even if there are children in the family or if housing costs are abnormally high.
*   But the core of the German welfare regime was and is a highly-developed social-insurance system: If general life risks occur like unemployment, old age,

invalidity, accident, illness or the need for assisted living, the social security system provides benefits for workers and employees and their family members on the basis of statutory contributions by employers and employees. These monetary benefits such as unemployment benefits, unemployment assistance, old-age pensions and disability cash benefits are determined by the individual's previous earnings and are intended to preserve his former relative income position within the community. Although there are no minimum income elements in the German social security system, until the beginning of the 1980s only a very small number of citizens either received social-insurance benefits that were so low that they had to claim supplementary social-assistance benefits, or did not receive any insurance benefits and were exclusively dependent upon social assistance.

Sozialhilfe, the German social-assistance scheme, was introduced in its present form at the beginning of the 1960s by the Federal Act on Social Assistance (Bundessozialhilfegesetz, BSHG), and was aimed to guarantee all citizens a minimum income and to help in special circumstances. The basic presumption was and is that this last safety net should provide help in temporary periods of crisis caused by atypical life risks. German *Sozialhilfe* includes two types of benefits, general assistance (Hilfe zum Lebensunterhalt) and assistance for people in difficult situations (Hilfe in besonderen Lebenslagen). While the second type covers special help for the blind and disabled, for older people, for people without health insurance or those with various other forms of special need, general assistance provides regular payments for an unlimited period, in order to guarantee a socio-culturally defined minimum level of subsistence.

General assistance benefits include regular benefit payments (a basic amount for every household member), supplements for certain groups of recipients, allowances for housing and heating, and, if necessary, exceptional benefit payments for clothing and other necessities. While allowances for housing and heating are paid according to their actual costs, the basic benefit, which varies according to the age and the beneficiary's position in the household, is generally calculated according to standard rates.[1] These have to be set by the states (Bundesländer) on the basis of what is called a 'statistical standard' (Statistik-Standard), which means that every five years the benefit level has to be derived from the statistically measured consumption expenditure of low-income groups; in the years in-between, the benefit level is adjusted by the cost-of-living price index. This statistical standard, which was introduced only in 1990, was suspended soon after its introduction and the adjustments were fixed in correspondence with political and fiscal expediency. As early as 1991, the increase in the level of general assistance benefits was capped by the introduction of a minimum gap (Abstandsgebot) between the level of household income of low-wage earners and the benefit level of general assistance; only households with several household members were allowed to receive a higher benefit level. The objective of this limitation on the development of the general assistance level was to preserve an incentive to work. Nevertheless, because of its stated aim of preserving a minimum level of subsistence, to date the level of general assistance is generally understood as an inofficial poverty line in Germany.

In principle, the Federal Act on Social Assistance provides an unlimited legal right to social assistance for any person in need. Since 1994, refugees and asylum claimants are excluded from social assistance and referred to a special form of assistance on the basis of the Act on Assistance for Asylum Claimants.[2] A main element of social assistance is the principle of subsidiarity; help is available only when a person can not provide for him – or herself, when no family support and no other benefits are available. Above all, those capable of working have to look for a job and must accept any job offered to them. Eligibility for assistance is restricted by the fact that the nature, form and extent of social assistance are governed by the special features of the individual case and by the person of the recipient. As a consequence of the extensive examination of personal and financial conditions this necessitates, welfare-dependency is perceived by many recipients as an extremely discriminatory situation. Although there is a broad range of reasons, the restrictive principles and conditions of entitlement are seen as a main cause for the fact that the non-take-up rate is estimated at between 50 and 60 per cent, which means that around half of all eligible persons renounce their claim to general assistance in Germany (see, e.g. Engels and Sellin, 2000).

While the legal competence for social assistance is located at the federal level, it is up to the municipalities[3] to offer monetary assistance as well as in-kind support[4] for people in need through their social service administration, and to carry the fiscal burden of general assistance and of services like, e.g. *Help Towards Work*. According to the principle of subsidiarity in the provision of social assistance in Germany, non-governmental organisations of voluntary welfare are closely involved with the provision of services. Compared with other benefit schemes, the provision of social assistance is characterized by a high degree of discretion, especially with regard to exceptional benefits and services.

Social-assistance receipt and welfare-dependency in Germany

Since the beginning of the 1980s, the role of social assistance has changed in Germany; the last safety net has become increasingly important for the functioning of the entire social protection system. The main indicator for this development is the fact that both the number of recipients of general assistance and the percentage of general assistance recipients in the total population increased constantly until the year 1997 (with the exception of the year 1994, due to the effect of the new Act on Assistance for Asylum Claimants). Only between 1998 and 2000 did the number of recipients decline slightly as a consequence of short-term improvement in the German labour market and the implementation of activation policies. But recently the increase of numbers has started again. Between 1980 and 2000 the number of recipients of general assistance (living outside of institutions) in West Germany increased by 165.1 per cent. Between 1992 and 2000 the number only rose from 2,050,000 to 2,256,000. In the same period of time, the number of recipients in East Germany rose much faster, from 289,000 to 421,000. Nevertheless, the proportion of the total population on social assistance has remained at a rather moderate level, at 3.3 per cent in total Germany (with 3.4 per cent in the West and 2.8 per cent in the East) in the year 2000 (Table 9.1).[5]

Table 9.1   Social assistance recipients in Germany 1984-2000

Year	Number of recipients in 1000*	Rate of recipients in population (in %)*
West Germany		
1980	922	1.4
1982	1,091	1.7
1984	1,287	2.0
1988	1,671	2.6
1992	2,108	3.1
1996	2,410	3.6
2000	2,268	3.4
East Germany		
1992	331	1.8
1996	314	2.0
2000	426	2.8
Total		
1992	2,438	2.9
1996	2,724	3.3
2000	2,694	3.3

*   *Recipients of general assistance living outside of institutions at the end of the year.*

Source: Database of the Social Assistance Statistics.

It may be astonishing to see that – although the income level is considerably lower than in the West – the number of social assistance recipients in East Germany was and is much lower than in West Germany.[6] The low number, at least at the beginning of the 1990s, can be explained by a very restrictive tradition of what was called *Sozialfürsorge* in the former GDR, and a presumably low take-up rate of general assistance in this part of unified Germany. Another reason is that, because of the traditionally high employment participation rate of men and women in the GDR, a relatively high proportion of east German households were eligible for transfers from the social-insurance system; therefore, to date they have been less dependent on social assistance. Finally, the unemployed in East Germany profit from a high volume of work-creation programmes (in part financed by the European Social Fund), which have been implemented to smoothen the negative employment effects of the transformation process in East Germany.

In addition to this increase in the number of people living on social assistance, the composition of the group of welfare recipients has changed as well. While typical recipients in the 1960s and 1970s were elderly women with low old-age or survivor pensions, homeless people and former prisoners, these groups of the 'traditionally poor' increasingly have been supplemented and overtaken by the group of the 'new poor'. Among this group the number of (German and foreign) immigrants experienced the highest growth rate. At the same time, children and youths have become the groups with the highest recipient rate; correspondingly, single-parent households and households with two or more children have shown a considerable increase in welfare receipt. Finally, ever more adults of working age have become welfare-dependent. While the number of 'working poor' living on additional social assistance is increasing but still of limited size (see my chapter on labour-market-related poverty in this volume), unemployment has become the main reason for social-assistance receipt in Germany.

In the German welfare regime, the function of social protection in the case of unemployment has to be fulfilled above all by the first safety net of unemployment insurance and unemployment allowance. Since the beginning of the 1980s, the last safety net of social assistance has become increasingly important for the social protection of the unemployed. While unemployment insurance and allowance are both aimed at income maintenance for the unemployed and their family members, the aim of poverty prevention does not play any role in this safety net. This is the task of the last safety net of social assistance, which provides additional or alternative assistance.

In the year 2000, 81.1 per cent of the 3.9 million unemployed registered received unemployment benefits or assistance (see Table 9.2). Most received unemployment benefits (43.6 per cent), while the number of those receiving unemployment assistance is increasing but as yet still lower (37.5 per cent). 18.9 per cent of the registered unemployed remained without unemployment benefits or assistance. Without benefit or assistance were also the 'hidden unemployed', who are not officially registered as unemployed. In principle, unemployed people without sufficient economic resources can apply for social-assistance benefits. But up to now, due to the restrictive conditions of eligibility in the German Act on Social Assistance, the number of welfare recipients among the unemployed has remained rather low. Of the 3.9 million unemployed persons registered in the year 2000, 644,000, or 16.6 per cent, received general assistance at the end of 2000. This amounted to 23.9 per cent of all recipients of social assistance in that year, or 39.8 per cent of all welfare recipients of working age. 417,000 (64.8 per cent) of the unemployed welfare recipients did not receive any unemployment benefits or assistance; 228,000 (35.2 per cent) received social assistance in addition to unemployment benefits or assistance (see Statistisches Bundesamt, 2002; Bundesanstalt für Arbeit, 2001).

In contrast to the rising number of recipients of social assistance, the proportion of the population defined as poor on the basis of a 50 per cent threshold has remained rather stable (see the chapter by Peter Krause). A recently published report on poverty in Germany (see Hanesch et al., 2000) documented that both the number and the proportion of social-assistance recipients in the population are lower than those of the poor. This results from the fact that major eligible groups do not claim social assistance.

It indicates furthermore that the level of general assistance, at least for some household types, is lower than the 50 per cent poverty threshold. But this still does not answer the question as to why the poverty rate has remained rather stable in Germany while the number of those living on social assistance has continued to rise.

Table 9.2   Social protection for the unemployed and responsibility for activation

	Social protection for registered unemployed							
	1993		1996		1998		2000	
	Absol. no. (in Tsd)	In % of all unemployed	Absol. no. (in Tsd)	In % of all unemployed	Absol. no. (in Tsd)	In % of all unemployed	Absol. no. (in Tsd)	In % of all unemployed
Registered unemployed*	3,419	100	3,965	100	4,279	100	3,889	100
among them:								
Social Code Book Three (SGB III)								
recipients of unemployment benefits*	1,887		1,989	50.2	1,987	46.4	1,695	43.6
recipients of unemployment assistance*	759		1,104	27.8	1,504	35.1	1,475	37.5
sum	2,646		3,093	78.0	3,491	81.5	3,152	81.1
Federal Law of Social Assistance (BSHG)								
total number of general assistance recipients**	2,529		2,724		2,903		2,694	
recipients of working age 15-65**	1,478		1,645		1,766		1,620	
registered unemployed receiving general assistance**	***	77.4	<u>581</u>	<u>14.7</u>	<u>709</u>	<u>16.6</u>	<u>644</u>	<u>16.6</u>
in addition to unemployment benefit/ assistance**	***	22.2	236	6.0	285	6.7	228	5.9
exclusively general assistance**	***	55.2	345	8.7	424	9.9	417	10.7

*   Average number of registered unemployed persons per year.
**   Number of recipients of general assistance living outside of institutions at the end of the year.
***   Numbers for the year are not available due to a reform of social-assistance statistics.

Source: Hanesch and Balzter, 2000.

The most realistic explanation assumes that ever more individuals and households have had to claim social assistance to fill the gap resulting from the reduction of social security benefits in the 1990s.

However, not only the number of recipients, but also the costs of social assistance have increased within the last two decades. The expanding costs of general assistance were due primarily to the increasing number of recipients; the costs per recipient showed only a modest increase. As a consequence of the dramatic increase in the number of recipients and, consequently, in the costs of social assistance, the local communities, which have to carry the brunt of the fiscal burden, are increasingly under pressure, both fiscal and administrative, and tend to be overextended. Nevertheless, the proportion of public expenditure for social assistance is still under five per cent of total social expenditure, which means that the last safety net is still of marginal fiscal importance in Germany.

Was and is the rise in claimants' numbers an indicator for increasing welfare-dependency in Germany? In both the scientific and the political debates on welfare reform, critics of social assistance take it for granted that long-term dependency has increased and that social assistance has become a permanent pension-like benefit for certain groups. Empirical research on the dynamics of welfare receipt undertaken in several municipalities during the 1990s has shown that the vast majority of claimants received social assistance for only brief periods of time, while the group of claimants receiving assistance for several consecutive years was surprisingly small. At the same time, most of the claimants claimed assistance for two or more spells. But even when the (gross or net) sum of periods of social-assistance receipt is considered, the short-term claimant is by far the most common type of social-assistance recipient (see, e.g. Leisering and Leibfried, 1999).

Furthermore, available data indicate that during the last two decades, the average time on social assistance has decreased continuously. It seems that the more social-assistance recipients have become predominated by the groups of the 'new poor', the less the assumption of rising long-term claims corresponds to reality. Finally, empirical findings on the reaction of the poor to their deprived income situation have shown that active coping strategies are more common than is generally expected (see Andreß, 1999). Thus the empirical proof for rising welfare-dependency, in the sense of an increasing 'underclass' of people who tend to prefer living on this last safety net, has yet to be delivered in Germany.

Activation policies for unemployed social-assistance recipients

Traditionally, social assistance as the last safety net in Germany not only has to guarantee the resources necessary to live in accordance with human dignity, but also to help the recipients reintegrate into economic and social life. Activation and integration policies can take the form of legal interventions, financial incentives, work integration services or social integration services and can be directed to the supply side (claimants/recipients) as well as to the demand side of the labour market (Hanesch and Balzter, 2001).

In principle, the municipalities, as local social-assistance agencies under Sections 18–20 BSHG, have an obligation to assist unemployed social-assistance claimants in breaking free of their need for social assistance and becoming integrated into the labour market. However, since *Help towards Work (Hilfe zur Arbeit)* is relatively unstandardized in the BSHG, the local authorities have extensive discretion in structuring the labour-market integration of unemployed social-assistance claimants in accordance with their own ideas of policy. Aims, instruments, use of resources and effects therefore differ from one local authority to another.

Conversely, clients who are of working age, have no job and no accepted reason to stay away from work (e.g., a child age three years or younger, or two or more children) have to be available for work and must actively look for a job. Furthermore, they have to accept any job offered to them by the public employment office or by the municipal social service administration. If a claimant for assistance refuses to comply with his obligation to co-operate or to accept a reasonable offer of a job or work opportunity, he must face a benefit reduction of at least 25 per cent.[7] As a consequence of repeated refusal to be available for work, the individual becomes ineligible for assistance, although payments to other family members must remain unchanged. However, in practice such consequences differ widely depending on the municipality.

In the case of unemployment, unemployment insurance acts in principle as an initial safety net, while social-assistance benefits are intended solely as a back-up measure in cases of unusual risk or special circumstances of need. Corresponding to the two safety nets, two different 'activating systems' are responsible for integrating unemployed social-assistance claimants into the labour market, as both systems of legislation and benefit have their own regulations and instruments. In this dual structure of activation and integration schemes in Germany, the main targets of local authorities' employment and labour-market policy strategies are unemployed social-assistance claimants, especially those who are solely dependent on general assistance. As a rule, this group has no access to the employment promotion schemes of the public employment office. Traditionally responsible for active labour-market policy, this office has proved increasingly overburdened and shows a limited ability to reintegrate the unemployed, particularly the target group of unemployed social-assistance claimants. As a result of the increasing demand for social assistance, the local authorities have been confronted with the need to develop their own initiatives in labour-market policy. At the end of the 1990s, virtually all local authorities were actively involved in efforts to come to grips with the problems of unemployment and the poverty created by the labour market.

As demonstrated by surveys conducted by the Federation of German Towns (most recently: Deutscher Städtetag, 2000), the volume of *Help towards Work* schemes and the numbers they assisted increased steadily throughout the 1990s (see Table 9.3).

Table 9.3 Number of participants in activation programmes

Groups of programmes with legal basis (SGB III/BSHG)	Number of participants in programmes in year							
	1993		**1996**		**1998**		**2000**	
	In Tsd	In %	In Tsd	In %	In Tsd	In %	In Tsd	In %
A Registered unemployed*	3,419	100	3,965	100	4,279	100	3,889	100
B Programmes of PEO (SGB III)** Programmes in total*	1,081	31.6	1,306	32.9	975	22.8	886	22.8
C Programmes §§ 19 and 20 BSHG. Programmes in total***	119	3.5 / 100	200	5.0 / 100	300	7 / 100	403	10.7 / 100
Single measures*** regular jobs (subsidized or non-subsidized)	13	11	46	23	48	16	77	19
created work opportunities with a contract	51	43	60	30	102	34	121	30
created work opportunities without a contract	46	39	84	42	132	44	185	46
special work opportunities without a contract	8	7	10	5	18	6	20	5

* Numbers of unemployed and of participants according to official statistics of the 'Bundesanstalt für Arbeit'.
** PEO = Public Employment Office, MSSD = Municipal Social Service Department.
*** Estimated numbers of participants according to surveys of the 'Deutsche Städtetag'.

Source: Hanesch and Balzter, 2000.

Whereas in 1993 the number of people accommodated in such schemes was no more than about 119,000, by 2000 the number of social-assistance claimants employed by schemes under Sections 19 and 20 BSHG alone had already risen to 403,000. In addition, nearly 100,000 job creation schemes of the public employment office (compared with about 90,000 in 1993) were co-financed by the local authorities. Although the number of unemployed general-assistance recipients (644,000) is hardly equivalent to the number of *Help towards Work* participants, the fact remains that at the end of the 1990s a significant proportion of benefit claimants were involved in labour-market integration schemes.

In the provision of work opportunities, the BSHG distinguishes between the 'remuneration' and 'additional expenditure' variants: Whereas the remuneration variant creates or offers opportunities for work on the basis of a regular contract of employment at the 'customary working wage', in the case of the additional expenditure variant, participants enter a public-law employment relationship in which they continue to draw general assistance and receive merely supplementary compensation for additional expenditures. In the year 2000, only around half of the *Help towards Work* employment relationships were of the 'remuneration' type (49 per cent), with an almost equal number of people employed under the 'additional expenditure' version (51 per cent). The proportion of those employed in the remuneration type had actually fallen slightly since 1993 (54 per cent). This can be seen as an indicator that many municipalities still primarily use the offer of *Help Towards Work* as an instrument to influence recipients' readiness to accept job offers.

If we consider the basic conceptual orientation of local authorities' employment promotion, we can see that the focus has shifted since the 1980s. Whereas at that time the primary emphasis was on the concept of the 'secondary employment market', by the 1990s the idea of the 'transitional employment market' had become dominant. The issue here is not so much the creation of a substitute employment market offering the kind of fixed-term and publicly subsidized jobs which traditionally dominated the *Arbeit statt Sozialhilfe* (Work Instead of Social Assistance) schemes. Rather, the focus in most municipalities today is on direct placement in the primary employment market, this direct-placement approach being more or less integrated into a wide range of preparatory and supplementary measures designed to improve the prospects of successful integration into the labour market. An important factor in making this reorientation possible was the relaxation of the placement monopoly of the public employment office in the mid-1990s.

Thus, ever more local authorities have come to adopt the concept of 'Work First', in which placement in the employment market takes absolute priority among the efforts made by social-assistance agencies. In numerous localities, the payment of social assistance has been made contingent upon recipients' willingness to participate in evaluation, advisory and placement schemes. In some cases, new applicants actually have to accept an 'on-the-job traineeship' without regular pay before their applications are processed. This arrangement undoubtedly owes much to the 1996 American model of social-assistance reform (Hanesch, 1997; Hanesch and Balzter, 2000; Voges et al., 2000).

A positive aspect that should be emphasized is that this approach broke up the social-assistance authorities' concentration on the need to make social assistance pay its way, and shifted the emphasis (back) toward the aspect of integration. Conversely, the risk is that, with this approach, integration into employment will be made an absolute condition, while the other functions laid down by the BSHG may be relegated to second place. The pressure to bring about employment is thus being increased, while the question of the kind of employment found and the future prospects it offers those affected is often left unanswered. To the extent that additional services are offered, their primary purpose is usually to eliminate obstacles to integration into the employment market.

The debate on reforms of the last safety net in Germany

Which are the main issues of the current debate on reforms of the last safety net; and what impact will the proposed reforms have on the future role of social assistance in Germany? In this last section, two main topics will be discussed which are dominating the current debate. A first topic is the controversial debate on the reasons and causes of the rising numbers of welfare recipients – above all of unemployed welfare claimants – and on the options for overcoming labour-market-related welfare-dependency. The key question here is whether the benefit scheme of social assistance should be restructured in a labour-market-friendlier way and whether the activation function would have to overlap the protection function of the last safety net (at least for claimants capable of working). A second topic, closely related to the first, concerns the question of how the activation and integration function of the last safety could be improved. Both reform debates include the question of whether and how the traditional division of labour between the primary and the last safety nets – again with special regard to the problem of labour-market-related welfare-dependency – should and could be redefined.

Causes of social-assistance receipt and options for welfare reform

In the political debate on increasing welfare-dependency in Germany, two approaches of welfare-reform proposals and activities can be distinguished: A first group of proposals is determined by the assumption that 'internal' deficits of the general assistance scheme are the main cause for increasing numbers of recipients and rising costs, and that only a fundamental reform of this safety net could overcome these problems. According to a second approach, the growing numbers of welfare recipients are caused primarily by the massive occurrence of economic and socials risks as well as by a neo-liberal oriented course of national social policy. As a consequence of these 'external' causes, the role and function of social assistance is changing dramatically.

The poverty trap and restructuring the last safety net Mainstream economists in Germany argue that there is not only an increase in the number of recipients, but also a shift in their behaviour in this last safety net. In this they echo public concerns that increasing numbers of social-assistance recipients and prolonged duration of receipt of social assistance could hamper employability and lead to long-term 'welfare-dependency'. This development is explained as an effect of what is known as the unemployment and/or poverty trap: On the one hand, too high a benefit level, which has risen faster than wages and earnings since the mid-1980s, is said to have reduced or even closed the gap between the level of social-assistance benefits and the household income of low-wage earners. On the other hand, the German social-assistance scheme is characterized by a lack of incentive to escape from welfare-dependency and to seek a job actively because of a withdrawal rate for job earnings which is close to 100 per cent (see, e.g. Institut für Weltwirtschaft, 1999; Schneider et al., 2002; IFO, 2002; critical comments by Hanesch, 1999). Thus, the thesis that the structure of social assistance – and the combined effect of unemployment benefits/assistance and social assistance – is the main cause for the increase of welfare-dependency has become a key issue in the recent reform debate.

Based on this approach, a series of welfare reforms were introduced by the former conservative federal governments between 1993 and 1998, which were intended to reduce the number of recipients and the costs of social assistance. These welfare reforms included a whole bundle of corrections to the legal framework of the Federal Act on Social Assistance: Among the elements included were the introduction of a benefit cap to slow down the growth rate of the benefit level, the widening of the minimum gap between the household income of low-wage earners and the benefit level of general assistance, the reduction of supplements for special groups of recipients (especially for the old and disabled), the enforcement of sanctions for unemployed welfare recipients who are not willing to accept a reasonable job (introducing an obligatory benefit reduction of at least 25 per cent as a first step), the introduction of additional instruments to increase the financial incentive to work, and the exclusion of asylum claimants and foreign refugees from social assistance (see Hanesch, 1996).

These reforms were not only designed to produce savings for municipal budgets; another even more important purpose of these reforms was the enforcement of economic pressure on welfare recipients. Although – as yet – empirical evidence is lacking, welfare reforms were instituted by the German federal government on the assumption that the main reasons for the welfare-dependency of the unemployed are a motivation deficit and insufficient readiness to accept any available job. These reform measures thus were aimed at overcoming labour-market-induced welfare-dependency by reducing the benefit level of social assistance and through the combination of financial incentives and enforced sanctions. In this way unemployed welfare recipients were to be brought back into the labour market and into the employment system. Up to now, with the exception of the Act on Assistance for Asylum Claimants, the above-mentioned reforms have had only little effect on the development of welfare recipient numbers and public welfare expenditure.

Because recent reforms are judged to be insufficient, a more fundamental welfare reform is being demanded. Such a reform should primarily include the restructuring of the benefit scheme. In the first half of the 1990s, this debate focused on the introduction of what was called *Bürgergeld* (citizens' pay), which was to replace not only general assistance, but also all other tax-financed benefits. It was to be integrated into the existing income tax scheme in the special form of a negative income tax. Based on a low withdrawal rate, the decisive advantage of this negative income tax was seen in its positive effect on the incentive to work. But because *Bürgergeld* was expected to become too expensive for public finance, the debate since has shifted to a rather small-scale reform. The current proposal is to transform social assistance into what is being designated a *Kombi-Lohn* (combined benefits-wages scheme). The incentive to move into low-paid jobs is to be increased through reduction of the withdrawal rate for earned income as well as reduction of the benefit level in the *Kombi-Lohn*, at least in real terms, by ending the existing adjustment to prices and consumption expenditure. New proposals have even demanded that the benefit levels be split and reduced by at least 25 per cent for claimants who can work (see IFO, 2002). It is hoped that through such a reform, benefit claimants would become more interested in actively seeking a job, the low-paid sector would become more acceptable for the unemployed population, and employers would offer more low-paid jobs.

Although the theoretical evidence of the poverty-trap hypothesis is controversial and its empirical importance has not yet been proved, it has become the predominant explanation for the development of social-assistance receipt in Germany. Critical objections, which have shown neither that the minimum income gap is closing (Engel and Sellin, 2001),[8] nor that an increase and/or a considerable volume of permanent welfare receipt can be observed (Leisering and Leibfried, 1999), nor that controls by the social-service departments have produced a significant number of moral hazard cases, have not yet attracted public notice (see, e.g. Hanesch, 1999; Gebauer et al., 2002).[9] If implemented, these reform proposals would reduce drastically the social protection function of the German social-assistance system.

As yet the new Federal Government has refused to opt for this reform approach rhetorically, but has in practice rejected reintroducing the *statistical standard*.[10] As a consequence, the benefit level of general assistance still lags behind increases in prices and consumption. Furthermore, in light of problems resulting from the existing double structure of social protection for unemployed people and the supposedly high benefit level of this protection system, the federal government is ready to transform unemployment assistance and general assistance into one uniform, means-tested benefit scheme. Among the options discussed for such a reform is the proposal to abolish unemployment assistance. Social assistance would be the only benefit available to the long-term unemployed. This would reduce considerably the level of social protection – especially for those who live exclusively from unemployment assistance – and the number of unemployed poor would be increased further (see my chapter on labour-market-related poverty in this volume).

Structural causes and the redefinition of the last safety net   Alternative explanations for the growing number of individuals and households living on social assistance for at least a certain period of time refer to changes in the economic and social structure of German society and the neo-liberal orientation of national economic and social policy. With ever more people falling below the poverty line, social assistance is being allocated the function of a basic income, which has to provide a minimum standard of living for a growing proportion of the German popu-

lation, at least for a short, transitional period. The problem is that the existing social-assistance scheme was not designed for this purpose and is therefore not the
instrument to fulfil this task in an adequate way.

While the dominance of financial calculations in the behaviour of welfare
claimants is questionable, the main causes for the rising number of welfare recipients are located outside rather than within the social-assistance scheme. Accordingly, strategies to prevent or to eliminate welfare-dependency must focus on two
levels: Above all, measures to improve access to employment and to sufficient
earnings must be developed in the context of employment, working-hours and labour-market policy as a prerequisite for the reduction of the volume of labour-
market-related poverty. In addition, reforms should be implemented in the social
protection system: For example, an increase in the levels of child, family, and
housing allowances is necessary. Even more important is the introduction of a
minimum income which more appropriately fulfils the task of guaranteeing a socially acceptable standard of living.

On the basis of this analysis, reform proposals for a basic income do not opt for
a radical change of the whole welfare system, but call for reform steps to introduce
a minimum-income scheme into the existing protection system (see, e.g. Hauser,
1996). Such a minimum-income scheme should be means-tested like social assistance and should cover the need for sufficient resources. Both aspects are included
in the term *Bedarfsorientierte Grundsicherung* (means-tested basic income
scheme), which has become the label for a whole bundle of reform proposals by
scientists, labour unions, non-profit organisations, and the socialist and the Green
parties. Compared with the existing general assistance scheme, the new minimum
income should be more standardized in its prerequisites, in the structure of benefits, and in the way in which means-tests are administered. The obligation to support other family members should be reduced. The obligation to participate in the
labour market would remain unchanged. The costs of the minimum income would
have to be carried by the federal government.

Such a minimum-income concept could be realized in a number of ways: A
first variation is the integration of a minimum-income scheme into the social-
insurance system, especially into unemployment benefits and in the old-age pension. The advantage of this form of a minimum income would be the guarantee
that these common life risks are covered by a special branch of the social security
system, which would provide insurance benefits as well as the minimum income in
the case of need.[11] A second variation would take the form of a separate, tax-
financed, nation-wide minimum income, which would replace general assistance
and would provide means-tested benefits for any citizen in need.

To prevent the need for claims to social assistance under normal conditions, the
introduction of the Bedarfsorientierten Grundsicherung would have to be supplemented by (or would have to include) a reform of the child benefit scheme. If child
benefits were increased up to a minimum income for all low-income households,
the social-assistance system would be relieved of this burden and the need for a
'minimum gap' between the level of household income of low-wage earners and
the benefit level of general assistance would be eliminated (see Hanesch et al.,
2000 and the chapters by Richard Hauser and by Gerhard Bäcker in this volume).

Redefining the role of social assistance as a means of activation

According to international comparative research (see Hanesch and Balzter, 2001, pp. 5-9), there are at the very least two options of activation in the context of so-cial-assistance schemes: While the 'soft' option emphasizes the expansion of chances and opportunities, the 'tough' option is focused on more restrictive condi-tions of access to social assistance. While the first option is normally based on the assumption that structural reasons are primarily responsible for welfare receipts by the unemployed population, the second option reflects a 'rational dependency' view of the welfare recipients: they themselves are held responsible for continuing receipt of social assistance. The main focus of the 'soft option' is on the introduc-tion of an individual's right of access to activation programmes, financial incen-tives and the improvement of the quality of activation services granted to unem-ployed welfare recipients to help them find work. Only this option focuses on the improvement of the conditions for the transition of the individual unemployed per-son into the labour market or in employment. The 'tough' option implies the use of financial pressure and/or legal obligations by reducing the level and duration of benefits or by tightening the conditions for entitlement to financial support. This plays a major role in the debate on disincentive effects and poverty or unemploy-ment traps. It also seems to be used in situations when the pressure on public budg-ets is high and expenditure on social assistance is to be reduced (in Germany above all for the municipalities).

Since the mid-1990s, the concept of the 'activating welfare state' has played a key role in the social policy discourse in Germany, as in most other EU states. There is a call for a paradigm shift in the debate on social policy: instead of merely 'passively' providing the marginalized groups in the labour market with benefit payments, it is argued, the focus of the welfare state's efforts should shift to the 'active' advancement of integration. The 'activation' of the unemployed can be seen here as a new guiding concept for active integration policy. This is especially true for the target group of the unemployed living on social assistance. In Germany as in many other countries, the debate on activation policies is focused on labour-market integration. With continuing employment problems in the Federal Republic of Germany, the (re-)integration of the unemployed into the employment system is one of the central tasks facing economic and social policy today.

Recent reforms during the 1990s – as already mentioned – opted for the 'tough option' by increasing the legal and administrative pressure on unemployed social-assistance claimants. But these reforms did not have a great impact, because, al-though *Help Towards Work* is regulated at national level, the local actors enjoy a high degree of discretion. As a consequence of the persisting pressure on case-load and costs, local authorities have improved their efforts in bringing the employable but unemployed recipients (back) into the labour market. Even if aims and pro-grammes of local activation policies are rather heterogeneous, more and more mu-nicipalities are opting for some kind of *'Workfare'* in the sense of tightening work requirements for recipients of social assistance recipients. The concept of 'Work First' or 'Work instead of Assistance' has become increasingly influential in the context of local labour-market policies (see Hanesch and Balzter, 2000; Voges et al., 2000).

Currently, the federal government is working on a proposal for a reform of general assistance by which local authorities would be obliged to offer activation programmes to their social-assistance claimants to a much higher degree than before. Following the calls for a new balance between passive and active measures and between the rights and duties of benefit claimants, the new legal order of the BSHG will focus on the social service administration's promoting employment and offering activation services to claimants who can work, whereas the provision of monetary or other in-kind-services will be of minor importance and will be primarily aimed at supporting integration into the labour market. It is still an open question as to which combination of legal, financial and service instruments and of 'soft' and 'tough' elements the new act will contain. Definitive is that it will not follow the reform proposals of the conservative opposition in the Bundestag and in the states, who – impressed by the results of the recent welfare reform in the US – have called for a total abolition of entitlement to monetary benefits and for its replacement by a right to be activated.

At the same time, the question has been raised, in which safety net activation policies for the long-term unemployed should be located. The current legal and political division of responsibility in the field of employment promotion for the target group of unemployed persons receiving social-assistance benefits is characterized by a dual structure, both in terms of the social-protection systems constituted by unemployment insurance and social assistance, and in terms of the activating systems consisting of active employment promotion by both the public employment offices and the municipal social-assistance administrations. Until recently there has been no systematic co-ordination between these two fields of legislation and action with a view to promoting employment. On the contrary, this dual structure encourages strategies through which the federal government and the local authorities indulge in a mutual delegation of political and financial responsibility for the social-welfare and labour-market integration of the (long-term) unemployed. Another perceived problem is the fact that the public employment offices and social-service departments have developed a dual structure of integration measures for the long-term unemployed at the local level, which has disadvantages for those receiving benefits, as it means they have to deal with two sets of benefit legislation and two different authorities (see Hanesch and Balzter, 2000).

In light of the problems and shortcomings in the interplay between unemployment insurance and social assistance, between public employment office and municipal service administration, and among the federal government, the states and local authorities, there has been a great deal of discussion about reform in Germany, and indeed practical initiatives towards reform already have been adopted. At present two main reform options are under discussion for resolving the dual activation responsibility of unemployment insurance and social assistance. First, it is proposed that all unemployed people should be brought within the jurisdiction of unemployment insurance, because this benefit scheme – in keeping with the logic of the German welfare state model – is responsible for covering the general risk of unemployment. In this case, the responsibility for activation would be directed only to the public employment office. The other option would mean the elimination of unemployment assistance and the transfer of all long-term unemployed to social assistance. In this second case, *Help towards Work* would become the only way for the long-term unemployed to become reintegrated.

While the reform debate is still under way, since 2000 public employment offices and social services administrations have been obliged by law to conclude and implement co-operation agreements exhausting every possibility of improving work placement, increasing the efficacy of help with integration into gainful employment, and designing the administrative procedure in a simple, citizen-friendly way. Furthermore, a federal programme has introduced a limited number of regional model projects. The intention is to promote three basic variants of a service for those claiming unemployment assistance and social assistance, in which overall services and payment of benefits is to be in the hands of one body (the one-stop-shop principle). In the first variation, the services are provided by the public employment office, in the second by the municipal social services administration, and in the third by an agency commissioned jointly by the public employment office and the social-assistance administration. These model measures are the subject of an academic evaluation and are being assessed with a view their possible implementation and generalization.

It is still an open question which of the mentioned reform options with regard to the benefit scheme, the activation policy and the division of labour between the first and the last safety nets will dominate the future perspective of social assistance. One reason for the difficult assessment of the outcome of this process is that there are at least three reform debates going on at the same time: the reform of social assistance, discussed in this essay, the reform of labour-market policy and labour-market services (see the contribution of Claudia Weinkopf in this volume), and the reform of the distribution of fiscal resources between the federal government, the states and municipalities. Each of these reforms will have enormous impacts on the other two reform projects. And each will contribute to an at least partial redefinition of the German welfare regime.

With the reform debate in full swing, it is all but impossible to predict the outcome of the reform process. Nevertheless, there is much to suggest that, in future, the local authorities will play a more important role than they have to date in social protection for the unemployed and in reintegrating the unemployed. Umbrella organizations lobbying for the interests of local authorities expect the burden of social welfare for the long-term unemployed to be passed on to them. A lack of financial compensation not only would have a detrimental effect on budgetary, social and labour-market policies for all local authorities, but also, given regional concentrations of labour-market and budgetary problems in structurally weak regions, would do nothing to close the gap in living standards between regions in the Federal Republic.

Even if, as the Hartz Commission (2002), a body established by the German government, has recently proposed, all workable social-assistance claimants were included in unemployment insurance by introducing a new means-tested minimum income, the so-called unemployment benefit 2, the consequences would be difficult to predict. Many experts expect that, step by step, groups with integration barriers will be classified by the public employment office as not available for the labour market and therefore not entitled to unemployment benefits. They would have to claim for general assistance, the double structure of social protection and activation would be resurrected, and again it would be the municipalities who would have to carry the financial responsibility.

Notes

1 Regular benefit payments of general assistance are based on the following equivalence scale: Head of household, 1.00; child under 7, 0.50; child under 7 in single-parent household, 0.55; child 7 to under 14, 0.65; child 14 to under 18, 0.90; every other adult 0.80.
2 This special safety net normally offers only in-kind support under very restrictive conditions.
3 Municipalities include kreisfreie Städte (cities with administrative- district status in their own right) and Landkreise (rural districts).
4 A wide range of services and in-kind support according to the specific kind of need has to be offered, e.g. in cases of unemployment, of indebtedness, of personal or family problems. Such services and in-kind support have to be offered in the case of need even if the client does not apply for them.
5 Since 1994, the number of social assistance recipients has to be corrected by those foreigners who have been excluded from social assistance because they were and are refugees or asylum claimants on the legal basis of the Act on Assistance to Asylum Claimants (Asylbewerberleistungsgesetz). If the number of recipients of this special assistance is added, the number of minimum-income recipients rose from 2,694 to around 3 million in the year 2000.
6 The benefit levels of general assistance in the eastern and the western states are almost the same with regard to regular benefit payments and supplements, but differ in accordance with the lower cost of housing in the East.
7 The penalty stipulated by Section 25 BSHG in such cases was stiffened in the mid-1990s.
8 That the benefit level of general assistance in Germany is rather modest is underlined by findings of both national (see Hanesch et al., 2000) and international comparative research (see, e.g. Eardley et al., 1996a; Kazepov and Sabatinelli, 2001).
9 Although empirical research on the dynamics of welfare receipt has not revealed any evidence for the empirical relevance of the dependency hypothesis, this concept has strongly influenced the debate on welfare reform and activation policies – not only in Germany, but in all OECD and EU member states (see, e.g. Leisering and Walker, 1998).
10 An important obstacle against the upgrading of general assistance is the fact that the basic federal income tax relief has been linked to the benefit level of this last safety net as a consequence of a decision of the Federal Constitution Court, according to which income necessary to cover basic needs may not be taxed.
11 In the year 2001, the federal government introduced a special form of Bedarfsorientierte Grundsicherung for the elderly and disabled population as a partial compensation for the reduction of the benefit level in the old-age pension system.

References

Andreß, H.-J. (1999), *Leben in Armut – Analysen der Verhaltensweisen armer Haushalte mit Umfragedaten*, Westdeutscher Verlag, Opladen/Wiesbaden.

Breuer, W and Engels, D. (1999), *Der Abstand zwischen der Sozialhilfe und unteren Arbeitnehmereinkommen*, Forschungsbericht des Bundesministeriums für Arbeit und Sozialordnung 276, Bonn.

Bundesanstalt für Arbeit (2001), *Arbeitsmarkt 2000*, Nuernberg.

Commission of the European Communities (1999), *Report from the Commission to the Council on the Implementation of the Recommendation 92/441/EEC of June 1992 on Common Criteria Concerning Sufficient Resources and Social Assistance in Social Protection Systems*, Brussels.

Deutscher Städtetag (2000), *Kommunale Beschäftigungsförderung. Ergebnisse einer Umfrage über Hilfe zur Arbeit nach BSHG und Arbeitsbeschaffungsmaßnahmen nach SGB III im Jahr 2000*, Köln.

Eardley, T., Bradshaw, J., Ditch, J. and Whiteford, P. (1996a), *Social Assistance in OECD Countries: Volume I Synthesis Reports*, DSS 1274 Social Policy Research Unit, University of York.

Eardley, T., Bradshaw, J., Ditch, J. and Whiteford, P. (1996b), *Social Assistance in OECD Countries: Volume II Country Reports*, DSS 1274 Social Policy Research Unit, University of York.

Engels, D. and Sellin, C. (2002), *Vorstudie zur Nichtinanspruchnahme zustehender Sozialhilfeleistungen,* Forschungsprojekt zum Ersten Armuts- und Reichtumsbericht der Bundesregierung, Bonn.

Esping-Andersen, G. (1990), *The Three Worlds of Welfare Capitalism*, The Polity Press, Cambridge.

European Foundation (for the Improvement of Living and Working Conditions) (ed.) (1999), *Linking Welfare and Work*, Office for Official Publications of the European Communities, Luxembourg.

Gesetz zur Verbesserung der Zusammenarbeit von Arbeitsämtern und Trägern der Sozialhilfe 2000, Bonn.

Gebauer, R., Petschauer, H. and Vobruba, G. (2002), *Wer sitzt in der Armutsfalle? Selbstbehauptung zwischen Sozialhilfe und Arbeitsmarkt*, edition sigma, Berlin.

Hanesch, W. (1996), *Reform der Sozialhilfe*, Düsseldorf.

Hanesch, W. (1997), 'Armut und Sozialhilfereform in den USA', in *WSI-Mitteilungen* (4), Köln.

Hanesch, W. (1999), 'Welfare and Work. The Debate about Reforms of Social Assistance in Western Europe', in European Foundation (1999).

Hanesch, W. (2001a), 'From Welfare to Work. Neue Reformkonzepte in der Sozialhilfe', in Stelzer-Orthofer (2001).

Hanesch, W. (2001b), *Flexibilisierung und Soziale Sicherung in Deutschland: Reformbedarf und Reformoptionen für die Sozialhilfe*, Expertise für das Wirtschafts- und Sozialwissenschaftliche Institut in der HansBöcklerStiftung, Düsseldorf.

Hanesch, W., Krause, P., Bäcker, G., Maschke, G. and Otto, B. (2000), *Armut und Ungleichheit in Deutschland,* Der neue Armutsbericht der Hans Böckler Stiftung, des DGB und des Paritätischen Wohlfahrtsverbandes, Rowohlt, Reinbek.

Hanesch, W. and Balzter, N. (2000), *Integrated approaches to active welfare and employment policies – Coordination of activation policies for unemployed social assistance claimants*, National study on the Federal Republic of Germany for the European Foundation for the Improvement of Living and Working Conditions, Darmstadt.

Hanesch, W. and Balzter, N. (2001), *Activation Policies in the Context of Social Assistance. The Role of Social Assistance as Means of Social Inclusion and Activation*, Report 4, Helsinki.

Hartz-Kommission (2002), *Moderne Dienstleistungen am Arbeitsmarkt*, Vorschläge der Kommission zum Abbau der Arbeitslosigkeit und zur Umstrukturierung der Bundesanstalt für Arbeit, 16 August 2002, no location.

Hauser, R. (1996), *Ziele und Möglichkeiten einer sozialen Grundsicherung*, Nomos, Baden Baden.

Heikkila, M. and Keskitalo, E. (eds) (2001), *Social Assistance in Europe. A comparative study on minimum income in seven European countries*, Synthesis report, STAKES, Helsinki.

Heikkilä, M., Fridberg, T. and Keskitalo (2001), 'Guaranteed Minimum Income – Recent Trends and a Socio-political Discussion', in Heikkila and Keskitalo (2001).

IFO (Institut für Wirtschaftsforschung) (2002), 'Aktivierende Sozialhilfe. Ein Weg zu mehr Beschäftigung und Wachstum', *IFO-Schnelldienst* (9), Munich.

Institut für Weltwirtschaft (1999), *Würdigung der Sozialhilfe in einem gesamtwirtschaftlichen Kontext*, Forschungsbericht für das Bundesministerium für Gesundheit, Kiel.

Kazepov, Y. and Sabatinelli, S. (2001), 'How generous are Social Assistance schemes?', in Heikkila and Keskitalo (2001).

Leisering, L. and Walker, R. (1998), *The Dynamics of Modern Society: Poverty, Policy and Welfare*, The Policy Press, Bristol.

Leisering, L. and Leibfried, S. (1999), *Time and Poverty in Western Welfare States. United Germany in Perspective*, Cambridge University Press, Cambridge.

Loedemel, I. and Trickey, H. (2000a), 'A new contract for social assistance', in Loedemel and Trickey (2000).

Loedemel, I. and Trickey, H. (eds) (2000b), *An offer you cant refuse. Workfare in international perspective*, The Policy Press, Bristol.

Schneider, H. et al. (2002), '*Anreizwirkungen der Sozialhilfe auf das Arbeitsangebot im Niedriglohnbereich*', Schriften des Instituts für Wirtschaftsforschung Halle 12, Nomos, Baden Baden.

Statistisches Bundesamt (2002), *Statistik der Sozialhilfe. Empfänger/-innen von laufender Hilfe zum Lebensunterhalt am 31.12.2000*, Wiesbaden.

Stelzer-Orthofer, C. (ed.) (2001), *Zwischen Welfare und Workfare. Soziale Leistungen in der Diskussion*, Institut für Gesellshafts- und Sozialpolitik der Johannes Kepler Universität, Linz.

Veit-Wilson, J. (1998), *Setting adequacy standards. How governments define minimum incomes*, The Polity Press, Chippenham.

Voges, W., Jacobs, H. and Trickey, H. (2000), 'Uneven development – local authorities and workfare in Germany', in Loedemel and Trickey (2000b).

Chapter 10

Income distribution and poverty in the OECD area: Trends and driving forces*

Michael F. Förster and Mark Pearson**

Introduction

There have been rising concerns that economic forces are causing income inequality to rise, creating a difficult challenge for policy makers. However, policy mistakes can be avoided only if trends in income distribution are well understood and that has not been the case for the OECD area since few comparative statistics have been available. Furthermore, the distribution of income is affected by many factors and the trends driving changes in e.g. joblessness, earnings, capital income and family size are complex and sometimes off-setting. However, some idea of which factors may be key can be gleaned by comparing country experiences in order to see which trends are truly global, which affect only economies and societies of a particular type, and which are country specific, perhaps reflecting contingent policy choices.

There is an increasing literature of *national* empirical analyses of income distribution and poverty trends in OECD Member countries. The main impression gained from these studies is that of a broad stability during the decade of the 1970s and increasing polarization since the 1980s, starting in the Anglo-Saxon countries and followed by many continental European countries in the 1990s. Those studies, however, make use of different definitions and concepts of income and inequality and often focus particularly on earnings rather than other components of household income. The final distribution of income (disposable incomes) is the result of a complex set of relationships, including family formation and dissolution, longevity and fertility, as well as the more obvious trends in earnings, taxes and the returns on capital.

The present article uses comparable data and definitions to look at over 20 OECD countries, a coverage sufficient to determine whether one can truly speak of 'OECD-wide' trends, rather than a few country-specific tendencies.[1] Unlike previous comparative studies, inequality trends are examined for a majority of OECD countries and this study also considers the working-age population separately from the retirement-age population, looks in more detail at the distribution of different cash transfers, and analyses both relative and 'absolute' poverty.[2] The second section documents recent trends in the overall distribution of disposable income in OECD countries, as well as identifying population groups who were among the winners and losers. The third section analyses the driving forces underlying these trends, including the frequently off-setting trends in the distribution of market-based incomes and the redistributive impact of taxes and transfers. The conclusion assembles 12 stylized facts that emerge from this analysis and provide important context for making policy choices in this difficult area.

Main trends in the distribution of disposable incomes and poverty

Overall trends in income distribution

Over a longer time-span, there has been no clear general trend in final income inequality. Table 10.1 summarizes the evidence on trends in the distribution of income, based on the movements in the value of the Gini concentration coefficient of income (see the box on the definition of income for an explanation of the methodology followed).

Table 10.1   Overall trends in income inequality: summary results for the entire population[3]

	Down a lot	Down	Down a bit	No change	Up a bit	Up	Up a lot
Mid-70s to mid-90s	Greece		Canada Finland	Japan Mexico Sweden	Australia	Netherlands United States	United Kingdom
Mid-70s to mid-80s	Greece	Finland	Canada Japan Mexico Sweden		Netherlands	Australia United States	United Kingdom
Mid-80s to mid-90s			Australia Denmark Hungary Ireland	Austria Canada France Greece United States	Belgium Germany Japan Mexico Sweden	Finland Netherlands Norway United Kingdom	Italy Turkey

Notes: No comparable data is available for countries not included. The results are based on the values of the Gini coefficient for all countries in three reference years which may vary among countries. For Hungary the period refers to 1991-1997.
Source: OECD questionnaire on distribution of household incomes (2000).

In the ten countries for which a relatively long time span can be considered, from the mid-1970s to the mid-1990s, there are four countries where the income distribution widened, three countries where it narrowed, and it remained stable in the remaining three. In five of the ten countries, movements in the first decade (declines in Finland, Japan, Mexico and Sweden; increase in Australia) tended to be offset by opposite movements in the second. However, there *are* signs of a more general trend across OECD countries in more recent times. According to the Gini coefficient, from the mid-1980s to the mid-1990s[4] inequalities decreased only slightly in four of the 20 countries for which trend data are available, remained stable in another five, but increased in the other 11 countries, in half of them by considerable amounts.

The income concept used in this paper is that of *equivalent disposable household income per individual*. The income unit is the household, defined as a group of persons sharing a set of common resources. Incomes are recorded on an annual basis and all possible types of cash income have been grouped into four categories:

1. Gross earnings: the salary income of the household from dependent employment (excluding employers' contributions to social security, but including sick pay paid by social security);
2. Gross capital and self-employment incomes: financial gains, real estate rents, occupational pensions and all kinds of private transfers as well as self-employment incomes (but not including imputed income from owner occupation);
3. Social security transfers: all kinds of cash transfers from public sources;
4. Taxes: direct income taxes and employee social security contributions paid by households.

Household disposable income is defined as total market income (1 + 2) plus transfers from general government (3), less income taxes and social security contributions (4).

The analysis has been conducted for individuals rather than households and their personal income has been defined as equivalent disposable income and calculated as follows: First, the sum of the disposable incomes of all household members equals household disposable income. Household disposable income then is adjusted for differences in household size to obtain *equivalent household disposable income*. This adjustment recognizes some 'economies of scale' of consumption within the household. In particular, household disposable income is divided by the square-root of the number of persons in the household: for example, the equivalent income of a four-person household is household income divided by two. (This is usually referred to as 'equivalence-scale elasticity' of 0.5. A higher elasticity value assumes less economies of scale in consumption, until the elasticity value of 1.0 which assumes no economies of scale). Third, equivalent household income is attributed equally to all individuals in the household, even though the incomes they receive as individuals may be different. Children and spouses are assumed to benefit equally from household income. Finally, individuals are ranked by the (ascending) levels of their *equivalent disposable income* (Atkinson et al., 1995).

Different measures of inequality. can give different results, and a careful reading of the Table 10.8 in the Annex shows that during the mid-1980s to the mid-1990s, inequality among the entire population increased unambiguously –

i.e. four different indicators of inequality pointed to a rise – in just eight of the 20 countries for which multiple trend data are available.

Table 10.2   Gains and losses of income share by income quintile: entire population, mid-1980s to mid-1990s

	Bottom quintile	Middle quintiles	Top quintile
Australia	=	=	=
Austria	=	=	=
Belgium	=	---	+++
Canada	=	=	=
Denmark	+	=	-
Finland	=	---	+++
France	=	-	+
Germany	-	=	+
Greece	=	=	=
Hungary	+	=	=
Ireland	+	=	=
Italy	---	-	+++
Japan	-	=	+
Mexico	=	---	+++
Netherlands	-	=	+
Norway	-	-	+++
Sweden	-	=	+
Turkey	-	---	+++
United Kingdom	-	-	+
United States	=	-	+

Notes: +++: increase of more than 1.5 percentage points in the share of final disposable income, received by the decile group, +: increase of between half and 1.5 percentage point, =: -0.5 to +0.5 percentage point change, -: decrease of between half and 1.5 percentage point, ---: decrease of more than 1.5 percentage points.
The results are based on percentage point changes of quintile shares in disposable income.

Source: Calculations from OECD questionnaire on distribution of household incomes (2000).

In all other countries, inequality indicators moved in different directions. This implies that in no country an unambiguous trend towards greater income *equality* was recorded (see annex). Of course, real incomes have grown in most countries. In 15 of the 21 countries considered, the mean income of each decile in the most recent year lies above that for earlier years. In other words, the bottom 10 per cent in the mid-1990s are better off *on average* than the bottom 10 per cent in the mid-1980s; the second 10 per cent in the mid-1990s have higher average incomes than their counterparts in the mid-1980s, and so on up the income distribution. There are relatively few exceptions – Australia, Canada, Italy, Norway and Turkey and, in particular, Hungary.[5] This does not mean that all parts of the income distribution gained in overall prosperity to the same extent.

In particular, the general pattern has been that the three lower deciles did not share in overall growth to the same extent as higher decile groups. In Germany, Greece, Mexico, the Netherlands, the United Kingdom and the United States, the average incomes of the bottom deciles were just about the same in the mid-1990s as they had been in the mid-1980s. A more significant increase of real mean incomes for the lower three income deciles (15 per cent or more) took place in Austria, Belgium, Denmark, France, Ireland and Japan.

Changes in aggregate inequality can hide other trends. If, for instance, groups in the middle deciles lose ground whilst both bottom and top incomes increase their shares, one can speak of a 'hollowing out' of the distribution. Table 10.2 shows that this was generally not the case during the past decade, with a 'hollowing out' occurring only in Belgium and, very marginally, in France and the United States. A widening of the income distribution could happen if the poor become relatively poorer; the rich have relatively more; or a combination of the two. Table 10.2 suggests that the second of these possibilities has predominated: there has been a trend for those at the top of the income distribution to receive a greater proportion of household income. In 13 of the 20 countries the top income quintile now has a greater proportion of household income than in the mid-1980s, substantially so in Belgium, Finland, Italy, Mexico, Norway and Turkey. Persons at the bottom of the income ladder lost ground relative to the average in eight countries, these losses being largest in Italy.

Overall trends in poverty

The changes in the distribution of income are reflected in changes in poverty in the countries concerned. 'Poverty' is very difficult to define and measure, particularly when making comparisons across countries. People in different countries have different needs, social and family networks, and governments may provide some services without charge which in other countries would require purchase. A given level of income may support very different standards of living in different countries. But much is nevertheless revealed even if all we do is to look at those households which have low incomes.[6] Although no-one could pretend that such a measure is ideal, we can at least reconcile ourselves to using such a measure on the grounds that low income in itself may not be sufficient to cause hardship, but it is at least a necessary element of poverty.

The most common measure of income poverty. is the number of people with incomes below a given threshold. Figure 1 defines this threshold using a relative measure ('relative' means that the poverty thresholds in each country refer to a percentage of the median with regard to each country *and each year*). People are said to be in income poverty if their incomes are below 50 per cent of the median disposable income of households, after adjusting for household size.

There has been, on average, little change in poverty levels over time (Figure 10.1). From the mid-1980s to the mid-1990s, income poverty at the 50 per cent level fell in six countries, rose in five, and stayed approximately the same in nine.

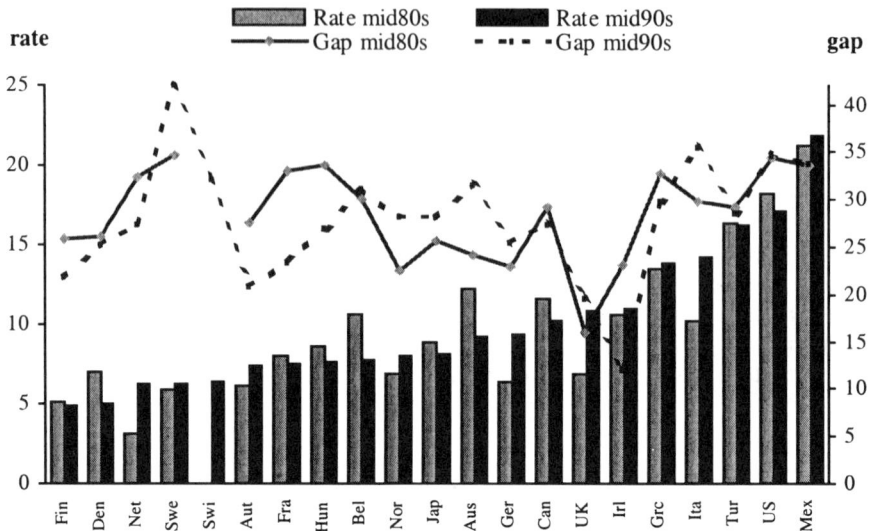

Figure 10.1   Income poverty rates and poverty gaps in 22 OECD countries, mid-1980s and mid-1990s

Notes: Poverty thresholds are defined as 50 per cent of median adjusted disposable income in each period in each country. Poverty rates defined as number of persons in households below the threshold in per cent of the total population. Poverty gap defined as average shortfall of low incomes in per cent of the poverty threshold.

Source: OECD questionnaire on distribution of household incomes (2000).

However, opinion varies as to what level of income should be considered 'poor', and poverty estimates can be very sensitive to the particular threshold chosen. Förster and Pellizzari (2000) present results for three alternative poverty lines: the number of persons living in households below 40 per cent, 50 per cent and 60 per cent of the median disposable income in each country, with much smaller declines in the number of 'very poor' with incomes less than 40 per cent of the median – only in France and Ireland were reductions in poverty mainly in the number of 'very poor'. Looking at the global picture, however, the basic pattern of changes shown in the table is not misleading: falls in poverty at the 50 per cent level are usually accompanied by falls in poverty at both the 40 per cent and 60 per cent level (exceptions being Ireland and the United States, where reductions in the number of 'very poor' have taken place at the same time as the number of those below the 60 per cent threshold stayed constant (the United States) or even increased (Ireland)).

The *number* of people with a low income. is only one way of measuring poverty. It says nothing as to the average income level of the poor which could be very close or far beyond a given threshold. Another relevant measure is therefore the intensity of poverty – the income gap ratio – which measures how far below the poverty line is the average poor person, in per cent of the poverty line. This is shown in the lines in Figure 10.1. On average across 21 OECD countries, the incomes of the poor are some 28 per cent below the poverty threshold of 50 per cent of the median in the mid-1990s, with lower ratios in Austria, Finland, the United Kingdom and, in particular, Ireland and higher ratios in Italy, Mexico, Sweden and the United States. In general, income gap ratios have followed the movements of the poverty head-count rates. This means that in countries in which the proportion of the poor in the population decreased, the average income as a proportion of the poverty line of the remaining poor decreased, and *vice versa*. A few exceptions are noteworthy: in Australia and, to a lesser extent, Belgium and the United States, the income gap widened although poverty rates fell (in other words, fewer people are 'poor', but those who remain have particularly low incomes) and in Austria and the Netherlands, the inverse was the case. Apart from Australia, poverty intensity increased significantly in Italy, Norway and Sweden. On the other hand, a large reduction of the income gap ratio occurred in Ireland.

These poverty estimates refer to percentages of the median income in each of the years considered. Of course, in many countries there have been large increases in average incomes (and in a few others, average household incomes have fallen). Because in most countries incomes have been increasing, poverty rates compared with a fixed level of income have generally fallen. Poverty below constant thresholds – i.e. fixed in real terms at the beginning of the period – increased from the mid-1980s to the mid-1990s in only a few countries (Hungary, Italy and Turkey – in Hungary and Turkey, because real mean incomes fell over the period). The most striking case is Hungary: against the background of a deep recession at the beginning of the transition restructuring (1990 to 1993/94), real median income and, hence, the relative poverty threshold fell by one-third. As a consequence, relative poverty rates remained broadly stable while poverty rates under a constant threshold tripled. In all other countries, real incomes increased over the period and poverty below constant thresholds stayed the same or fell, particularly so in Finland and Greece (between the mid-1970s and the mid-1980s) and Ireland (from the mid-1980s onwards).

The trouble with comparing 'how many people are poor and to what extent' in different years is that we are not comparing the same people. These results have to be put in the context of income dynamics. Talk of there being fewer people in poverty in the mid-1990s compared with the mid-1980s implies that a few of those who were poor have clawed their way above the threshold. In fact, of course, it is perfectly possible that *none* of those who were poor in the mid-1980s remained so ten years later, because as people's circumstances change, so they move up and down the income distribution. To some extent, comparisons of 'head-counts' of low incomes at a point in time depersonalizes the concept of poverty. Poverty is, however, a very personal state, and the amount of time that people spend below an income threshold is very important in determining living standards.

Low income head-counts both massively underestimate and at the same time overestimate the problem of poverty. Oxley et al. (2000) and OECD (2001) take the same concept of low incomes – 50 per cent of median household income after adjusting for family size – and follow the same people over a period of six years, or more for a restricted sample of countries. These studies show that:

- On average, at any moment in time, between 6 and 20 per cent of the population in the countries considered have low incomes.
- A larger part of the population than suggested by 'static' poverty rates is touched by income poverty over a six-year period, namely between 12 and 40 per cent.
- Only around 1-2 per cent of the population is continuously poor throughout the six years in Canada, Germany, the Netherlands and Sweden. The proportion in the United Kingdom and the United States is significantly higher.
- This means that between 2/3 (in the United States and the United Kingdom) and 6/7 (in the Netherlands) of all those who have low incomes at any point in time, will not be poor at some other time in the six years.
- Even in Sweden, nearly 12 per cent of the population will have low incomes at some point during the six years. In the United Kingdom, this ratio reaches nearly 40 per cent of the sample.
- Persistent poverty is closely associated with the lack of earned income.

'Winners' and 'losers' of relative income changes

The classical life-cycle pattern would predict that income increases when individuals enter working life; continues to rise as individuals gain experience in the labour market and accumulate capital assets and declines when moving into retirement. Broadly speaking, this is indeed the pattern found in most countries. Table 10.3 shows that children are, on average, a little under 10 per cent poorer than the population average. The richest age group are individuals aged 41 to 50 (and indeed this is true within every country, other than the United States and Sweden). Beyond 65, average incomes are 10 per cent below the population average, falling to 20 per cent below average for those aged over 75.

However, the changes in this distribution have been significant. In nearly all countries people aged 41-50 have seen an increase in incomes relative to the average of all age groups between the mid-1980s and mid-1990s. Even more strikingly, in most countries, elderly age groups also benefited from changes in the income distribution, in particular those just before or just after retirement: relative incomes of those aged 51 to 65 increased by 3 percentage points on average, and relative incomes of those aged 66 to 74 increased 2 percentage points (falls in incomes beyond the age of 65 being found in Australia, Greece, Ireland, Mexico, the Netherlands and Turkey). However, relative incomes of those aged 75 and over increased by less, if at all.

In stark contrast, younger age groups lost ground during the past ten years: relative incomes of children decreased by approximately 1 percentage point, on average, and those of persons aged 18 to 25 by 5 percentage points. This latter

Table 10.3 **Relative disposable incomes, by age group (average income of entire population = 100)**

	Children	Young Adults	Young Adults	Adults	Older Adults	Younger Senior Citizens	Older Senior Citizens
	Age 0-17	Age 18-25	Age 26-40	Age 41-50	Age 51-65	Age 65-75	Age 75+
Australia, 1984	87	130	..	107	..	72	..
Australia, 1994	86	122	..	112	..	68	..
Austria, 1983	90	110	104	117	109	82	79
Austria, 1993	90	109	101	116	108	91	80
Belgium, 1983	..	..	..	..	..	..	..
Belgium, 1995	105	83	102	118	108	83	71
Canada, 1985	88	102	103	116	110	91	84
Canada, 1995	88	100	100	114	114	99	95
Denmark, 1983	100	105	109	114	103	74	60
Denmark, 1994	97	97	104	119	113	79	65
Finland, 1986	98	97	103	116	103	80	74
Finland, 1995	101	88	102	114	108	82	75
France, 1984	95	102	106	112	103	86	82
France, 1994	95	97	100	115	109	94	82
Germany, 1984	93	98	102	113	109	85	81
Germany, 1994	91	96	99	118	110	93	77
Greece, 1988	94	104	108	111	102	84	79
Greece, 1994	98	104	110	113	100	80	72
Hungary, 1991	99	109	103	119	96	81	77
Hungary, 1997	93	111	104	109	104	88	81
Ireland, 1987	87	130	105	103	112	85	83
Ireland, 1994	89	117	109	112	111	77	71
Italy, 1984	90	107	106	106	108	82	78
Italy, 1993	89	103	105	109	108	85	82
Mexico, 1989	84	119	113	114	115	99	78
Mexico, 1994	83	113	114	128	121	91	75
Netherlands, 1984	89	104	102	109	112	93	84
Netherlands, 1995	89	97	105	114	112	90	79
Norway, 1986	96	105	104	118	109	78	60
Norway, 1995	98	94	101	120	117	84	61
Sweden, 1983	101	71	105	119	119	91	70
Sweden, 1995	99	60	100	120	127	96	78
Turkey, 1987	89	109	100	117	116	103	106
Turkey, 1994	85	111	103	127	119	89	102

Table 10.3 (cont)

	Children	Young	Young Adults	Adults	Older Adults	Younger Senior Citizens	Older Senior Citizens
	Age 0-17	Age 18-25	Age 26-40	Age 41-50	Age 51-65	Age 65-75	Age 75+
United Kingdom, 1985	90	114	105	124	105	74	72
United Kingdom, 1995	86	112	106	123	108	80	74
United States, 1985	82	99	104	118	121	99	84
United States, 1995	84	94	102	118	124	99	82
Average 17, mid-1980s	92	105	105	114	109	86	78
Average 17, mid-1990s	91	100	104	117	112	88	78

Notes: For Australia, the group 'adults' refers to age 26-65, and the group 'younger senior citizens' to age above 65. For calculating relative income changes, population shares have been kept constant at the beginning of the period.

Source: OECD questionnaire on distribution of household incomes (2000).

development is linked to delayed labour market entry of younger people due to longer education periods and/or unemployment.

There are large differences in standards of living across different family types. Persons living in households with only one adult generally have lower relative incomes than those living in households with two or more adults (Table 10.4). The gap between the incomes of the two types of households has not become smaller over time. Lone parents have – by far – the lowest relative incomes, usually between half to two-thirds the level of the average income of the entire working-age population. Only in three Nordic countries, Austria and Greece did they have relative incomes above two-thirds of the average. Their income position relative to the rest of the population has declined in recent years in half the countries. Relative incomes of persons living in two-adult households with children did not move very much (except in Austria and Greece where they increased and in Mexico where they decreased). Those living in two or more adult households without children improved their income position in six countries, particularly in Mexico but lost ground in another four countries, particularly in Austria.

These patterns in the distribution of income are replicated to some extent when looking at poverty rates. Taking the average of all countries, people aged under 25 and over 65 have higher than average poverty rates. The only two countries in which poverty rates of *all* ages increased were the Netherlands and the United Kingdom, and relative poverty declined across all age groups in Australia. Elsewhere, the age profile of poverty has shifted. Overall, whereas the probability of the younger age groups being poor has been rising relative to the average since the mid-1980s, for the older age groups it has generally been declining (particularly in Canada, Denmark and France). At the same time, as already described, the number of people in the younger age groups has been declining and the number of older persons has been rising. As a result, despite a higher proportion of young people having low incomes, the proportion of poor people who are young has not changed much.

Table 10.4   Relative disposable incomes, by family types (average income of working-age population = 100)

	Single adult, with children	Single adult, no children	Two adults, with children	Two adults, no children
Australia, 1984	53	99	92	131
Australia, 1994	57	92	93	129
Austria, 1983	63	93	95	121
Austria, 1993	87	85	98	110
Belgium, 1995	69	126	85	125
Canada, 1985	50	90	94	121
Canada, 1995	57	85	94	120
Denmark, 1983	61	77	101	113
Denmark, 1994	59	75	100	115
Finland, 1986	75	75	100	113
Finland, 1995	76	75	100	112
France, 1984	73	95	96	113
France, 1994	66	94	97	113
Germany, 1984	55	87	95	113
Germany, 1994	57	90	95	112
Greece, 1988	68	104	95	112
Greece, 1994	82	98	97	107
Italy, 1984	57	97	91	118
Italy, 1993	52	93	91	118
Mexico, 1989	75	133	87	151
Mexico, 1994	62	124	85	161
Netherlands, 1984	60	90	92	121
Netherlands, 1995	55	80	93	123
Norway, 1986	65	81	99	115
Norway, 1995	67	73	99	117
Sweden, 1983	76	77	101	126
Sweden, 1995	72	74	101	131
Turkey, 1994	65	107	91	169
United Kingdom, 1985	59	87	94	124
United Kingdom, 1995	51	92	93	127
United States, 1985	46	100	92	130
United States, 1995	49	99	93	127
Average 15 mid-1980s	62	92	95	122
Average 15, mid-1990s	63	89	95	121

Notes: Two adults refer to two and more adults. For calculating relative income changes, population shares have been kept constant at the beginning of the period.
Source: OECD questionnaire on distribution of household incomes (2000).

Child poverty has risen in about half of all countries, and declined in half. Child poverty has moved sharply up the political agenda in many countries, reflecting much greater concern about the effects of poverty in childhood on future life-chances. It is becoming relatively common for countries to set targets for reducing child poverty. Children are, in general, represented in the poor population as much as in the entire population. The exceptions are the four Nordic countries, with child poverty rates well below the average for the population, and Canada, Hungary, the Netherlands, the United Kingdom and the United States, where child poverty exceeds the average (Oxley et al., 2001). There are some remarkable differences between countries. In Hungary, Italy, Mexico, Turkey, the United Kingdom and the United States persons in families with children have a considerably higher poverty risk than those families without children. The other extreme is Belgium and the four Nordic countries where *childless* families are more likely to experience poverty than families with children.

On average, single parents are represented three times as often in the poor population than in the working-age population as a whole. This over-representation has however been decreasing over time in about half the countries and this decline was especially notable in Australia, Canada, Germany and the four Nordic countries. Poverty rates of lone parents, however, remain high in almost all countries studied. In some countries (Canada, Denmark, Germany, Netherlands, United Kingdom) their poverty rates are as much as four times higher than for the total working age population. A remarkable exception is Sweden. In this country, poverty rates for persons living in single parent households fell significantly during the past 10 to 20 years, and are today at the same low level as for the entire population, and slightly lower than for the working-age population.

Whilst the *chance* of being poor varies sharply across groups, this information is not enough to give a full picture of poverty. Lone parents are particularly likely to be poor, but they remain a relatively small part of the poor population. Persons in families with children made up around one-third or less of the poor population in the four Nordic countries and Belgium, but a majority in the other countries, and more than 70 per cent in Hungary, Italy, Mexico, Turkey, the United Kingdom and the United States. Single parents account for 20 per cent to 25 per cent of the poor population in Australia, Canada, Denmark, the Netherlands, Norway and the United States, and over one-third of those with low incomes in the United Kingdom. On the other hand their share is below 5 per cent in Greece, Italy and Mexico and negligible in Turkey.

Driving factors of changing income distributions

The distribution of income and the level of poverty can best be understood as being determined by two factors: differences in market income and the redistributive impact of fiscal and social policy. In policy discussions, most attention is given to the effects of taxes and transfers, i.e. how much governments take from one group and give to another. This is indeed of great importance, and there are large differences in the extent of this redistribution of income across countries. However, before looking at how government redistributes income, it is important to understand why it is that some groups have little income other than income transfers, and why others have sufficient incomes for governments to tax them for redistribution.

The analysis in the following two sections is confined to the working-age population, in order to abstract from changes that took place in shares of public and private pensions.[7] These sections explore the extent to which shifts in components of disposable income (market income, transfers and taxes) and trends in employment concentration within and across households contributed to changes in income inequality. What is particularly interesting is that whereas governments have taken different approaches to redistribution over the past ten or 20 years (in some countries redistribution has increased, in others it has not), there is a common, underlying trend in the distribution of income *before* taxes and transfers towards increasing inequality.

Driving factors: Market incomes

Market income distribution In many national studies, the distribution of market income has been described as widening, and gross earnings have been identified as the main contributor to increased overall income inequality. Table 10.5 confirms this picture. It shows the allocation market income and its two components – gross earnings and capital/self-employment income – across three income groups: the bottom three deciles (lower incomes), the four middle deciles (middle incomes), and the top three deciles (higher incomes). The shares of earnings and other market incomes going to the lower incomes are small: the poorest 30 per cent of the population receive between 6 and 12 per cent of total market income in most countries. While it should not be surprising that very few people in the bottom deciles have much income from capital, it is striking that nearly one-third of the working-age population has so little income from labour. This suggests that barriers to working play a critical role in explaining low incomes, a linkage that is examined in greater detail below. In contrast, the richest 30 per cent of the population have something between 50 per cent and 60 per cent of all market income, the exceptions being Mexico and Turkey, where the richer part of the population commands an even greater share of market income.

Furthermore, the trend has been for the top 30 per cent of the population to receive an ever larger proportion of capital and labour income, the only exception being Ireland. At the same time, those with incomes at the bottom of the distribution have seen a relative decline in market income in all countries; and those in the middle of the distribution in most countries, as well. Among market incomes, the dispersion of capital and self-employment incomes increased particularly rapidly, although country patterns are much more diversified than for earnings.

This pattern of a widening distribution of market income predates the mid-1980s, going back to the 1970s in many, albeit not all, countries. The *underlying* trend in the distribution of market income has been towards a widening. Whatever governments have been doing to taxes and transfers in order to make economies and societies more or less equal according to political preferences[8] has been happening against this backgrounds of the richer groups getting relatively richer, and the poorer groups receiving relatively less income from their efforts in working or saving.

Table 10.5   **Distribution of market income: Proportion of different sources of income received by different income groups of the working-age population**

	Share of earnings, mid-1990s			Share of capital and self-employment income, mid-1990s			Share of total market income, mid-1990s		
	Poorest 30%	Middle 40%	Richest 30%	Poorest 30%	Middle 40%	Richest 30%	Poorest 30%	Middle 40%	Richest 30%
Australia	6.3	36.7	57.0	13.8	32.3	53.9	7.4	36.0	56.6
Belgium	7.4	38.8	53.8	7.2	16.0	76.7	7.4	33.8	58.8
Canada	9.2	36.7	54.1	11.2	29.3	59.5	9.6	35.5	54.9
Denmark	11.1	39.0	49.9	13.5	27.3	59.2	11.4	37.8	50.8
Finland	7.5	36.8	55.7	18.4	31.9	49.7	10.2	35.6	54.2
France	10.7	35.7	53.6	12.1	20.8	67.1	10.9	33.5	55.6
Germany	12.2	37.4	50.4	9.2	28.3	62.5	11.9	36.3	51.8
Greece	9.6	36.7	53.6	14.2	31.4	54.4	11.7	34.3	54.0
Hungary	8.5	34.0	57.5	8.8	22.6	68.6	8.6	32.0	59.4
Ireland	4.8	34.9	60.3	8.9	27.1	63.9	5.7	33.2	61.1
Italy	10.4	37.2	52.4	5.9	20.3	73.8	9.0	31.9	59.1
Mexico	5.3	24.8	69.9	9.1	22.7	68.2	6.4	24.1	69.4
Netherlands	9.9	38.3	51.8	10.8	30.7	58.6	10.0	37.1	52.8
Norway	11.6	41.0	47.4	8.7	21.2	70.1	11.0	37.3	51.7
Sweden	8.8	37.3	53.9	16.1	30.0	53.9	9.3	36.9	53.9
Turkey	12.3	35.5	52.2	6.0	18.2	75.8	8.0	23.9	68.1
United Kingdom	6.9	36.3	56.7	11.3	28.6	60.0	7.8	34.9	57.4
United States	8.9	35.1	56.0	9.2	26.2	64.6	8.9	33.9	57.1
Average (13)	9.0	37.2	53.8	11.2	26.4	62.4	9.3	35.3	55.4
Change mid-80s to mid-90s	-1.7	-0.5	2.2	-2.8	-0.7	3.5	-1.7	-0.6	2.3

Notes: Data for Greece, Hungary, Mexico and Turkey refer to market incomes net of taxes and are therefore not entirely comparable with the results from the other countries. They are excluded from the average. For calculating the average of percentage point changes, Belgium has also been excluded due to lack of mid-1980s data. Income groups were built on the basis of final disposable adjusted income.

Source: OECD questionnaire on distribution of household incomes (2000).

There have been some recent trends in the economy which have widened the distribution of market incomes. Unemployment was higher in most countries in the mid-1990s than in the mid-1980s and 1970s. Those with particularly valuable skills in the new economy have been able to command very high rates of remuneration. The rate of return on capital has been high in the 1990s. But these 'explanations' are only part of the story. After all, unemployment may have been high, but because female employment had continued to rise, employment rates were nearly as high as they had ever been.

The main contributor to increased overall income inequality has been the distribution of gross earnings across households. The shares of earnings going to the lower income groups has fallen in practically all countries. In addition, capital and self-employment income has also become more unequally distributed, although because such income is small in comparison with earnings, the overall effects are less important.

'Work' is becoming more concentrated in some households. In other words, there are more households where all adults are working, more households where no adults are working, and fewer households where there is at least one adult working and one adult not working. This process – the simultaneous increase in both workless and fully employed households – has been described as a process of 'employment polarization' by Gregg and Wadsworth (1996). OECD (1998) found this process being at work in nine of 11 European OECD Member countries.

Table 10.6 divides the population where the head of the household is still of working-age into three groups: those where every adult who is present in the household is working; those where no adult in the household is working, and 'mixed' households where one adult is working and the other adult(s) is (are) not. The share of those living in households where there is full employment increased in all but three of the 15 countries. The share of people in workless households also increased in most countries, and the share of persons in 'mixed' households (those with two or more adult households with only one earner) declined in all 15 countries during the ten-year period. Overall, the evidence suggests that employment polarization took place in ten countries. Exceptions are the Nordic countries, where the share of persons in fully-employed households slightly decreased and Greece and the United States, where the proportion of those in workless households decreased.

Of course, the *quantity* of work across households is only part of the story. The *wage rates* that people get when they work must be added to the equation in order to explain changes in earnings distribution. Here the story varies across countries. As described in OECD (1996), there has been little common trend across countries in wage rates of those in full time work. Large increases in earnings dispersion certainly have taken place in some countries (the United Kingdom, the United States), but not in others (Canada, Finland, Germany). But of course trends in earnings are inextricably related to trends in employment. Low-skilled (low-wage) workers are much more likely to be without work than higher-skilled (high-wage) workers.

In order to assess the possible effects of employment concentration for trends in income distribution, aggregate changes in inequality can be decomposed into three parts,[9] on the basis of the three employment groups (persons in fully employed, workless and 'mixed' households):

1. first, a 'within group' inequality effect: if inequality in one of the three groups increases, overall inequality would increase, population shares held constant;
2. second, a 'between group' effect: if two groups had the same internal distribution, but the difference between the average incomes of the groups widens, overall inequality would increase, population shares held constant;
3. finally, a 'structural' effect, brought by the changing shares of each of the three groups in the population.

Table 10.6   Changes in households' employment concentration (percentage point change in the distribution of working-age households)

	Population shares		
	Fully employed	**Workless**	**'Mixed'**
Australia, 1984-1994	5.2	1.7	-7.0
Austria, 1983-1993	13.7	0.6	-14.4
Canada, 1985-1995	1.9	1.9	-3.8
Denmark, 1983-1994	-0.4	2.5	-2.0
Finland, 1986-1995	-0.8	4.1	-3.3
France, 1984-1994	4.1	1.1	-5.2
Germany, 1984-1994	0.1	1.4	-1.5
Greece, 1988-1994	8.4	-1.3	-7.1
Italy, 1984-1993	0.2	4.7	-4.9
Mexico, 1989-1994	5.7	0.8	-6.5
Netherlands, 1984-1995	14.4	1.6	-16.1
Norway, 1986-1995	2.0	4.8	-6.8
Sweden, 1983-1995	-1.2	3.4	-2.2
United Kingdom, 1985-1995	4.8	0.6	-5.4
United States, 1985-1995	3.1	-0.6	-2.5
Average change	4.1	1.8	-5.9
Average levels mid-1990s	64.7	9.8	25.5

Notes: 'Fully employed households' are households in which all adult persons have an employment; 'workless households' households in which no person has an employment; and 'mixed households' two or more adult households with only one earner. Data refer to households with a head of working-age. Changes are percentage point changes.

Source: OECD questionnaire on distribution of household incomes (2000).

In ten of the 15 countries considered, the 'within group' effect was the main contributor to changes in overall inequality, both up and downwards: Austria, Canada and Denmark for decreases in inequality, and Australia, Finland, Italy, Mexico, the Netherlands, Norway and the United Kingdom for increases. This means that in a majority of countries, changes in overall inequality were driven by increased (or decreased) income dispersion *within* different households' employment categories. The effect of growing disparities *between* the three employment categories played a major role only in Germany and the United States, pushing overall inequality up. The structural effect, *i.e. changing shares* among the three employment categories, made a significant contribution to inequality reduction in France and Greece. This effect was also somewhat important in the Nordic countries, but playing an inequality-increasing role there.

Poverty rates for those living in households with two or more earners are very low (under 1 per cent of two-earner households in Austria, Belgium, Denmark, Germany, Norway and Sweden and under 6 per cent in all countries other than Mexico and Turkey, where the poverty rate exceeds 13 per cent) and these rates have been on a downward trend since the 1980s. On the other hand, poverty rates for those in workless households are very high – over 18 per cent in all countries other than Belgium and Denmark, and over 40 per cent in Canada, Germany, Ireland and the United States. The poverty rate of workless households has generally been increasing (but did actually decrease considerably in Australia, Denmark, Norway and Sweden). In most countries, people in workless households are represented three to five times as often in the poor population than they are in the total working-age population.

The importance of work in explaining income distribution and poverty changes can be seen as the primary cause of many changes in the relative income of particular groups. Why has the position of youths declined? At least in part because employment rates have declined. What explains the very low income of lone parents? The very low employment rates are often the key factor. Hence the striking result referred to above that lone parents in Sweden are not at greater risk of poverty than others in the population is explained mainly by the fact that a large majority of Swedish single parents are working: almost nine out of ten, whereas in most other countries the share of single parents who are working is between 50 and 70 per cent. Poverty rates for single parents who do not work are very high in all countries and, with the exception of Mexico, are at least twice as high as those for working single parents. In Canada, Germany, Italy, the United Kingdom and the United States, more than 60 per cent of non-working single parents are poor.

Driving factors: Transfers and taxes

Across the income distribution, most household income is market income – income which comes from work, or from the returns to investment. However, governments tax that income and distribute cash transfers, so altering *disposable* income. This is illustrated in Figure 10.2, which compares changes in the distribution of market incomes over the past ten years with changes in the distribution of disposable incomes. When juxtaposing these trends, it can be seen that in almost all countries the gains of the highest income quintile are substantially higher for market income than for disposable income. By contrast, market income shares for the lowest quintile (and most often for both lowest quintiles) declined substantially (exceptions being Ireland and, to a lesser extent, the United States). In a great majority of countries, the workings of tax/transfer systems resulted in disposable household incomes falling by less than the fall in market incomes for the lower quintiles, and in four countries the falling trend of market incomes actually was reversed (Australia, Canada, Denmark and France). However, in Italy and the Netherlands, both market and disposable income fell by the same amount for the lowest quintile and in Germany the income losses of the lowest quintile were higher after than before taxes and transfers.

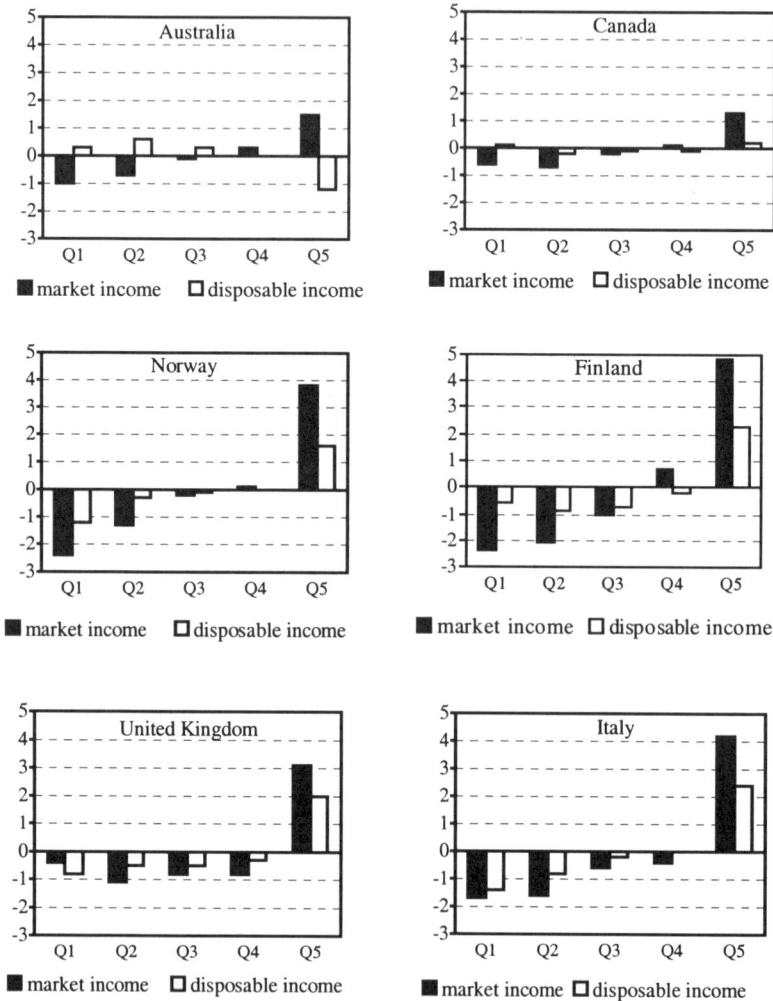

Figure 10.2 Gains and losses by income quintiles: market and disposable income. Working-age population, mid-1980s to mid-1990s

Note: Q1 corresponds to the lowest income quintile, Q5 to the highest income quintile. Quintiles were built on the basis of final disposable adjusted income. Changes are in percentage points and sum up to 0.

Source: OECD questionnaire on distribution of household incomes (2000).

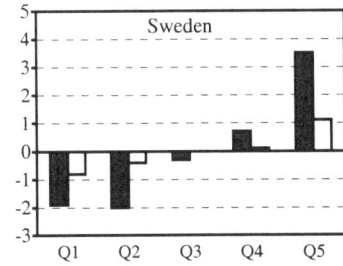

market income ☐ disposable income

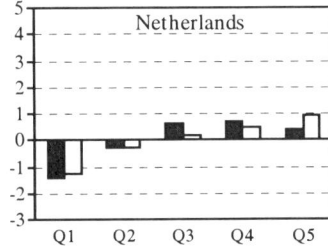

market income ☐ disposable income

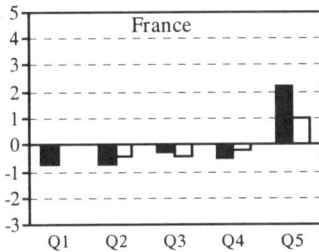

market income ☐ disposable income

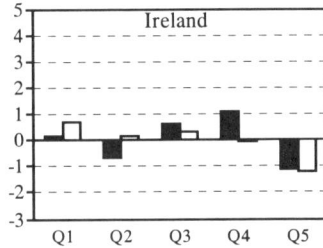

market income ☐ disposable income

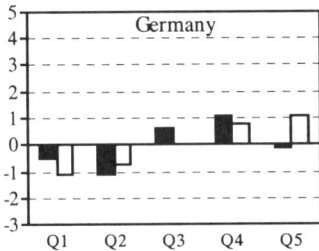

market income ☐ disposable income

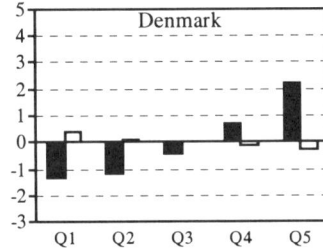

market income ☐ disposable income

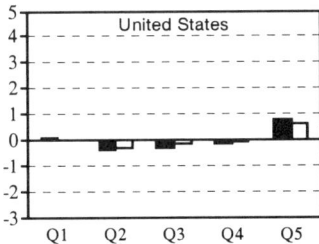

market income ☐ disposable income

Figure 10.2 (cont)

Benefit systems redistribute income. But they do not primarily redistribute from rich to poor. Rather, they redistribute from young to old, from those who work to those who do not, and from childless families to families with children. In most countries (Australia and New Zealand being exceptions), most benefits are based not on the income of the individual or family, but on the circumstances of the family and the individuals that make up the family more generally.

(Re)distributive patterns of family and unemployment benefits

Even so, the distribution of non-pension transfers altogether was slightly progressive in all OECD countries studied in the mid-1990s – progressive in the sense that higher transfer shares are going to poorer than to richer income groups. In most countries, between one-third and 40 per cent of those transfers went to the lower income groups in the working-age population (bottom three deciles), and between 20 per cent and 25 per cent to the higher income groups (top three deciles). The progressive pattern was stronger in Australia, Ireland, the United Kingdom and the United States where 50 to 60 per cent went to the lower income groups, and only 10 to 20 per cent to the higher incomes. All these countries rely on means-tested benefits to a greater extent than most other countries, so this pattern is not surprising – it simply confirms the effect of these policies in restricting benefit entitlements of higher-income groups.

Non-pension transfers in particular have become more progressively distributed over the past ten years: this has happened in 12 of the 16 countries where such data are available. In ten of those countries, the lower three deciles of the income distribution were the sole beneficiaries of this trend, and in two Nordic countries – Finland and especially Sweden – middle-income groups also benefited from this trend in distribution. In two Southern European countries – Greece and Italy – the middle-income classes benefited considerably from these changes at the expense of both lower- and higher-income groups. Canada and, in particular, the United States stand apart. In these countries a change towards a less progressive distribution of non-pension transfers among the working-age population took place.

Förster and Pellizzari (2000) compared the distributional patterns of two of the most important benefits among non-pension transfers: family cash benefits, and unemployment benefits.[10] For *family cash benefits*, two groups of countries emerge:

- Australia, Canada, Denmark, France, Ireland, the Netherlands, the United Kingdom and the United States all show a progressive distribution of family cash benefits; moreover, most of these countries (the exceptions being Denmark, the Netherlands and the United States) also clearly moved towards a more progressive distribution during the last decade.
- In Austria, Belgium (data for 1995 only), Finland, Hungary, Norway and Sweden in the mid-1980s, family cash benefits seemed to be distributed more equally across the income distribution with an emphasis on the middle class; a distributional pattern sometimes described as 'targeted to the middle classes'. However, Hungary moved towards a progressive pattern in the 1990s.

By 1995, in all countries considered except Belgium, the proportion of family benefits going to the bottom three deciles was higher than the proportion going to the top three income deciles. Family benefits, therefore, played a role in the redistribution of incomes to lower segments among the working-age population.

As to *unemployment benefits*, the country patterns are different:

- Unemployment benefits show a clear progressive pattern in seven countries: Australia, Austria, Belgium, Finland, Hungary, Ireland and the United Kingdom. In Hungary, they became considerably more progressively distributed over the years, while their distribution became somewhat less progressive in the United Kingdom. In Ireland, changes favoured lower middle and middle income groups and in Australia and Finland, no significant change occurred.
- In the remaining seven countries, unemployment benefits are almost equally distributed across income groups of the working-age population. This is particularly the case in the Netherlands. In Canada, Norway, Sweden and, to a lesser degree, Denmark, the distribution of unemployment benefits showed some signs of a 'targeting to the middle class'. And in France and the United States, the distribution of these benefits moved from such a pattern to a slightly regressive one.

Taken together, family cash benefits seemed to be a more important tool for redistributing incomes from higher to lower segments than unemployment benefits in Canada, Denmark, France, the Netherlands and the United States, whereas the inverse was the case in Austria, Belgium, Finland and Hungary. In Australia, Ireland and the United Kingdom, both benefits played an important redistributive role. Only in Norway and Sweden were both benefits more middle-income class oriented. This has to be seen against the background that, in a majority of the countries considered here, the prime aim of those benefits is not a redistribution of incomes towards lower income groups but the maintenance of the income status in case of child rearing and compensation for loss of employment, regardless of income status.

Overall effects of tax/transfers among the working-age population

Just because a benefit system is proportional (in the sense that benefits are equally distributed across the population) does not mean that it plays no role in redistributing income. Poor households (by definition) have less other income than richer ones, so the higher is the level of a benefit, the greater will be the reduction in inequality, even if everyone receives exactly the same amount of benefit. It follows that just because a benefit system is not particularly targeted on the poor, it cannot be concluded that the effects on poverty are necessarily small.

Table 10.7 summarizes the distribution of all benefit payments taken together, together with tax payments and social security contributions of employees across the income distribution of the working-age population. *On average* the bottom

30 per cent of the population do get more than 30 per cent of total benefit payments, but not by much. The top 30 per cent of the population get, on average, over 25 per cent of all benefits. In other words, the benefit system does not have a very different effect on final income inequality from paying everyone in the population a fixed amount of benefit, regardless of income level.

Table 10.7   Redistribution by government: proportion of total transfers (taxes) received (paid) by different income deciles of the working-age population

	General government transfers			Taxes		
	Poorest 30%	Middle 40%	Richest 30%	Poorest 30%	Middle 40%	Richest 30%
Panel A: distribution of benefits received and taxes paid						
Australia, 1994	62.3	31.1	6.5	3.7	31.1	65.1
Austria, 1993	26.8	40.9	32.3	..	..	..
Belgium, 1995	36.0	41.6	22.5	3.9	32.6	63.5
Canada, 1995	41.5	37.7	20.8	6.2	33.4	60.4
Denmark, 1994	43.4	38.9	17.7	14.1	37.2	48.7
Finland, 1995	43.2	40.4	16.4	9.8	33.4	56.8
France, 1994	35.6	39.3	25.1	8.7	23.5	67.9
Germany, 1994	31.7	37.6	30.7	10.0	36.5	53.6
Greece, 1994	20.9	37.7	41.5	..	..	..
Hungary, 1997	28.7	42.8	28.5	..	..	..
Ireland, 1994	47.1	38.1	14.8	3.3	30.3	66.4
Italy, 1993	20.5	45.0	34.5	6.7	31.0	62.3
Mexico, 1994	13.7	27.2	59.1	..	..	..
Netherlands, 1995	45.8	36.1	18.1	11.7	36.1	52.2
Norway, 1995	45.1	36.6	18.3	10.2	36.1	53.8
Sweden, 1995	33.7	40.5	25.8	11.0	35.8	53.3
Turkey, 1994	15.2	40.2	44.6	..	..	..
United Kingdom, 1995	54.5	33.9	11.7	6.0	32.0	62.0
United States, 1995	41.4	35.5	23.0	6.3	28.4	65.3
Average level	36.2	37.9	25.9	8.0	32.7	59.4
Panel B: Changes in redistribution, mid-1980s to mid-1990s, percentage points						
Australia, 1984-1994	4.2	-0.3	-4.0	-6.6	-3.1	9.8
Austria, 1983-1993	2.3	-0.3	-2.0	..	..	..
Canada, 1983-1994	-0.3	-0.6	0.9	-0.8	-0.7	1.4
Denmark, 1983-1994	5.1	-1.4	-3.7	0.2	-2.2	2.0
Finland, 1986-1995	2.2	1.5	-3.8	-1.1	-1.0	2.1
France, 1984-1994	2.3	0.8	-3.1	-3.8	-2.3	6.1
Germany, 1984-1994	-2.2	0.9	1.3	-1.1	2.9	-1.9
Greece, 1988-1994	4.1	1.8	-5.9	..	..	..
Hungary, 1991-1997	-1.4	0.7	0.7	..	..	..
Ireland, 1987-1994	4.8	-2.9	-1.9	-0.5	-0.5	1.0
Italy, 1984-1993	-5.4	3.3	2.1	-4.1	-1.1	5.2
Mexico, 1989-1994	8.7	-0.5	-8.2	..	..	..

Table 10.7 (cont)

	General government transfers			Taxes		
	Poorest 30%	Middle 40%	Richest 30%	Poorest 30%	Middle 40%	Richest 30%
Netherlands, 1985-1995	5.0	-2.2	-2.8	-1.7	0.6	1.1
Norway, 1986-1995	3.2	-1.3	-2.0	-2.9	-1.8	4.6
Sweden, 1983-1995	1.3	0.6	-1.9	-1.3	-0.7	2.0
Turkey, 1987-1994	1.2	-1.6	0.4	..	..	..
United Kingdom, 1985-1995	0.4	1.3	-1.7	-1.3	-3.7	5.0
United States, 1985-1995	-2.0	-0.6	2.6	1.0	-1.4	0.4
Average change	1.8	0.0	-1.7	-1.7	-1.1	2.8

Notes: General government transfers include all public cash transfer benefits. Taxes include all direct income taxes, including employees social security contributions. Income groups were built on the basis of final disposable adjusted income.

Source: OECD questionnaire on distribution of household incomes (2000).

Of course, averages hide a lot of cross-country variation. Australia, the United Kingdom, the Netherlands, Ireland and some of the Nordic countries target payments towards the poorer end of the distribution to a much greater extent than Austria, Hungary, Italy and Greece, where the poorest 30 per cent of the population receive less than 30 per cent of all benefit payments. In Turkey and Mexico, benefits are even more likely to be targeted towards richer groups, reflecting 'dual' labour markets – individuals have to be in the 'modern' sectors of the economy to qualify for social insurance.

Taxes, on the other hand, are very strongly related to income. Of course, this is not the full story as regards taxes – the figures in the table exclude consumption taxes and social security contributions paid by employers, both of which bear much more heavily on lower income groups than the personal income taxes and employee social security contributions which are included. But nevertheless, it is readily apparent that taxes have a great effect in equalizing incomes across households.

The trend has been towards a greater share of taxation being paid by higher income groups. This is *not* the same as saying that there is greater progressivity in the tax system than previously. In fact, if compared with changes in the distribution of market income, only in Australia, France, Ireland and the United Kingdom has the share of taxes paid by the top 30 per cent gone up significantly *more* rapidly than market income. In the Nordic countries, the increases in taxes paid by the upper income groups was less than the increase in their market incomes – in other words, their average tax rate fell relative to lower income groups.

The analysis above referred to the distribution of a given overall level of non-pension transfers among the working-age population. However, although a specific transfer might be distributed more progressively in one country than in another, its weight for the lower income groups might be higher in another country because of a higher overall level of this transfer. An equally important question therefore concerns the relative importance of those transfer payments in the disposable incomes of lower, middle and higher income groups. Förster and Pellizzari (2000) analysed non-pension transfer shares in the disposable income of income groups. Those shares rose for the working-age population as a whole in the last ten years, from below 10 per cent on average, to 11.4 per cent. The increase for the lower income groups, however, was much stronger: it varied on average across the countries from around one-quarter of their disposable income to around one-third. Those increases were recorded in *all* countries but were strongest in the four Nordic countries (where more than 10 percentage point increases were recorded). This underlines the growing importance of non-pension transfers for lower income groups of the working-age population.

Poverty alleviation through taxes and transfers

Results from earlier analysis based on a smaller sample of five OECD countries (Burniaux et al., 1998, Oxley et al., 1999) showed that tax/transfer systems reduced substantially aggregate poverty rates in those countries.

This is confirmed by the results from the present analysis, which are available for 14 countries and which consider poverty among the working-age population. Whereas poverty rates based on pre-tax and transfer incomes amounted to between 14 and 26 per cent in the countries studied, post-tax and transfer rates were considerably lower – between 4 and 17 per cent. Furthermore, this effectiveness tended to strengthen in a majority of countries as is shown in Figure 10.3. While pre-tax/transfer poverty rates rose in all countries, on average by more than 3 percentage points, post-tax/transfer poverty rates fell in half the countries and decreased by less than the pre-tax/transfer poverty rate in the others, except in Germany and the Netherlands. Absolute rates of reduction in poverty were higher in Australia, Belgium, France, Ireland and the Nordic countries (Norway excepted), and lower in Canada, Germany, Italy and the United States (Figure 10.4).

Driving factors: Underlying demographic changes

Putting the two pieces of the equation together – trends in market income and trends in government tax and transfer policy – gives most of the information necessary to understand the overall picture of income distribution. One last piece of the jigsaw puzzle remains to be inserted: changes in the demographic structure of the population.

There are considerable differences between countries and country groups as to the *levels* of these shares: in the Nordic and the Continental European countries, children are 20 per cent of the population; in the Anglo-Saxon countries, they account for around 25 per cent, and in Mexico and Turkey the share of children in the population is much higher, around 40 per cent.

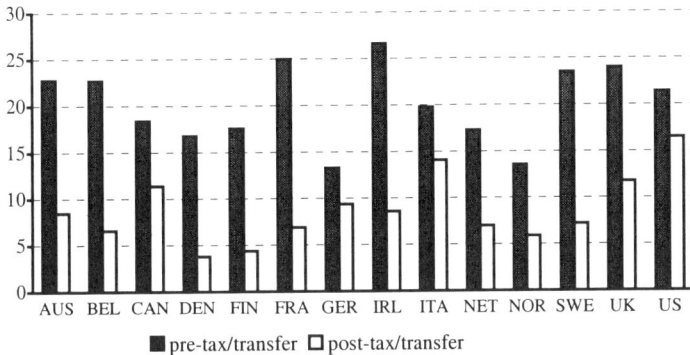

Figure 10.3 Poverty rates before and after taxes and transfers, working-age population - Poverty rates mid-1990s

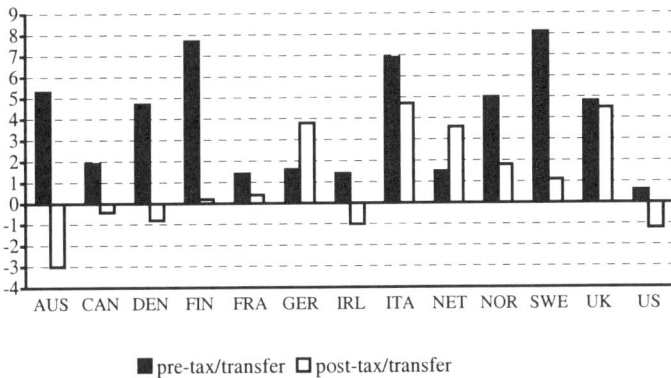

Figure 10.4 Poverty rates before and after taxes and transfers, working-age population – Percentage point changes mid-1980s to mid-1990s

At the same time, there have been very large changes in the structure of populations in OECD countries. In nearly all countries, the proportion of children in the total population decreased from the mid-1980s to the mid-1990s, on average by some 2 percentage points.[11] Similarly, the share of young people – those aged 18 to 25 – fell in most countries, on average by 1 percentage point. On the other hand, the proportion of persons aged 65 and over increased in all countries but Sweden, on average by over 1 percentage point (Förster and Pearson, 2000).

The changes do not stop there. The fewer children are much more likely to be in households where there is only one adult – the proportion of lone parent families has been increasing. In the Anglo-Saxon countries and the Nordic countries, between 10 and 20 per cent of those in households with children live in lone parent households. In the Continental European countries their share is just below 10 per cent, and in the Southern European countries, Turkey and Mexico, below 5 per cent. The proportion of children who are in lone parent households rather than households with two or more adults has also been rising, and is around 25 per cent of the total in Sweden. Within the working-age population, fewer people live in households without children than in households with children, but their share increased from one-third to almost 40 per cent in the ten years from the mid-1980s to the mid-1990s.

Furthermore, mainly as a consequence of population ageing (but also reflecting an increased preference for living alone among younger age groups), the average household size has also been falling for the last ten to 20 years throughout the OECD area, and is close to being just two people in some of the Nordic and Continental European countries. The average household size is closer to three in the Southern European countries and still above four in Mexico and Turkey.

Such changes may not sound very significant. In fact, taken together they amount to a huge change in the structure of the population, in many countries to an extent unprecedented in recent times outside of war, famine or epidemic. Here, it is worth noting simply that these demographic trends *directly* affect trends in inequality. If older people have less income than younger people, then as there are more of them in the population, so income distribution will apparently widen. Similarly, if small households are poorer than large ones, so will the trends described above lead to a stretching out of the income distribution, regardless of whether the average income of small households is changing relative to larger ones.

Conclusions: 12 stylized facts on trends in income inequality and poverty

Overall distributional trends and movements at the bottom

- There has been no generalized long-term trend in the distribution of disposable household incomes since the mid-1970s. However, during the more recent period (mid-1980s to mid-1990s), income inequality has increased in at least half the countries, while none of the remaining countries recorded an unambiguous decrease in inequality.
- There is no trend towards a 'hollowing out' of the income distribution at the expense of the middle-income class. Simultaneous gains of both the lower and higher incomes relative to the middle incomes occurred in only a few countries (Belgium and, marginally, France and the United States during the past decade, and Canada and Finland over the last 20 years).
- Relative poverty rates have remained broadly stable over the last ten years. Some countries have, however, experienced declines (in particular Belgium and Denmark) and some others increases (in particular Italy and the United Kingdom). Poverty rates based on constant thresholds fell in most of the countries in which real incomes increased.

Changes in relative positions of specific social groups

- In those countries where inequalities increased, this happened mostly among the working-age population, whilst there were fewer changes among the retirement-age population.
- Changes in income distribution in the past ten years generally favoured the prime-age and elderly age groups, particularly those around retirement age. Younger age groups lost ground, in particular those aged 18 to 25, reflecting delayed labour market entry. Similarly, poverty rates for the elderly fell in all but four countries, youth poverty rates increased, and child poverty rates increased slightly in a number of countries.
- Relative income levels of single parents and persons in workless households are very low and have worsened in a number of countries.

Driving factors

- Market income inequality has widened in every country. The increased dispersion from gross earnings has been the main cause. A variety of factors have explained this, in turn, increased inequality in earnings themselves and a trend towards 'employment polarization' in many countries, leading to a simultaneous increase in 'work-rich' and 'work-poor' shares of households.
- Capital and self-employment incomes are distributed more unequally than earnings. However, as their share in total disposable income is lower, their contribution to levels and, in most cases, changes in overall inequality is less important than that of earnings (with the notable exception of Italy).
- Joblessness is the main cause of poverty.

Distributional effects of public transfers and taxes

- The effectiveness of taxes and transfers in reducing inequality and poverty has increased. As a result, the increase in market income inequality was not, or not entirely, translated into higher inequality of disposable incomes for the working-age population.
- Targeting of benefits has increased. The shares of family cash benefits and/or unemployment benefits going to lower income groups among the working-age population increased in a majority of countries.
- Non-pension transfers form an increasingly large part of the income of low-income households among the working-age population in all countries.

Annex

Table 10.8　Trends in four income inequality indicators for the entire population

| | Levels | | Absolute change[*] | | | | | | | |
| | Gini coefficient mid-90s | P90/P10 Decile ratio mid-90s | Gini | | Decile ratio | | SCV | | MLD | |
			A	B	A	B	A	B	A	B
Australia	30.5	3.9	2.1	-0.7	0.2	-0.4	3.2	1.2	1.8	0.5
Austria	23.8	3.0	..	0.2	..	0.1	..	1.4	..	-0.2
Belgium	27.2	3.2	..	1.2	..	0.0	..	9.1	..	0.4
Canada	28.5	3.7	-0.8	-0.4	-0.6	-0.2	4.0	0.7	-2.5	-1.0
Denmark	21.7	2.7	..	-1.1	..	-0.2	..	0.4	..	-1.5
Finland	22.8	2.8	-2.8	2.1	-0.5	0.1	-3.7	7.8	-3.0	1.2
France	27.8	3.4	..	0.3	..	0.1	..	6.9	..	-0.8
Germany	28.2	3.7	..	1.7	..	0.4	..	-2.2	..	1.6
Greece	33.6	4.7	-7.7	0.0	-2.1	-0.2	-47.9	1.1	-11.5	-0.4
Hungary	28.3	3.4	..	-0.9	..	-0.2	..	1.2	..	-2.9
Ireland	32.4	4.2	..	-0.6	..	-0.1	..	32.0	..	-3.0
Italy	34.5	4.6	..	3.9	..	0.8	..	18.1	..	6.7
Japan	26.5	3.3	-1.4	1.2	-0.1	0.2	-5.8	5.3	-1.0	1.5
Mexico	52.6	11.3	-2.0	2.3	-3.9	1.8	20.8	-28.9	-5.0	-6.4
Netherlands	25.5	3.2	0.7	2.1	0.1	0.4	2.7	2.5	0.6	2.3
Norway	25.6	3.0	..	2.2	..	0.1	..	2.3	..	3.1
Sweden	23.0	2.7	-1.6	1.4	-0.2	0.1	-2.1	8.0	-1.8	2.0
Switzerland	26.9	3.1	..	..	..	..	..	..	..	..
Turkey	49.1	6.8	..	5.6	..	0.3	..	..	..	..
United Kingdom	31.2	4.1	3.8	2.5	0.5	0.5	10.3	8.6	3.1	3.0
United States	34.4	5.5	2.7	0.4	0.8	-0.2	7.7	1.2	3.2	0.5

[*] *Absolute change is the difference in the value of the index.*

Notes:　A = Mid-70s-mid-80s, B = Mid-80s-mid-90s. For Hungary, the period refers to 1991-1997.

Source :　OECD questionnaire on distribution of household incomes (2000).

Notes

* 　 The authors, both from the Directorate for Education, Employment, Labour and Social Affairs, wish to thank Sveinbjörn Blöndal, Thai-Thanh Dang, Howard Oxley, Peter Scherer, Paul Swaim and, in particular, Michele Pellizzari for their comments and help in this project. The opinions expressed in the paper are those of the authors and do not engage the OECD or its Member countries. Errors are the sole responsibility of the authors.

** This article previously appeared in *OECD Economic Studies* (34), 2002/1

1. The full analysis upon which this article is based is reported in Förster and Pellizzari (2000).

2. 'Household income' is often used synonymously with 'household resources'. It is not: households have access to goods and services provided to them at no cost by the state; indirect taxes affect the purchasing power of a given amount of resources; barter, charity and mutual exchange between and within families play a greater or lesser role in different countries. The absolute level of measured income inequality or poverty, however interesting, cannot be used to make reliable cross-country comparisons. But trends in income distribution and poverty, if measured on a comparable basis, do permit a number of key findings to be drawn from the analysis.

3. Up a lot: significant rise in income inequality (more than 12 per cent increase).
   Up: rise in income inequality (7 to 12 per cent increase).
   Up a bit: modest rise in income inequality (2 to 6 per cent increase).
   No change: -1 to +1 per cent change.
   Down a bit: modest decrease in income inequality (2 to 6 per cent decrease).
   Down: decrease in income inequality (7 to 12 per cent decrease).
   Down a lot: significant decrease in income inequality (more than 12 per cent decrease).

4. The data for Hungary refer to the period 1991 to 1997.

5. This country experienced a deep recession at the beginning of its economic transition (between 1990 and 1993/94) during which real incomes fell for the population as a whole. At the same time, the distribution of those incomes flattened slightly.

6. This means that other dimensions, such as benefits in-kind, consumption, wealth, deprivation or social exclusion have not been taken into account for the analysis (for a conceptual discussion of using different criteria and methods in the frame of international comparisons, see Förster, 1994).

7. As public transfers are the main component of income for retired persons in most OECD countries, an increasing transfer share in the incomes of the entire population, and effects on inequality, might simply reflect the increased share of pensioners in the population.

8. It should be noted that governments' redistribution is not only confined to taxes and transfers but also influences market distribution directly, e.g. via minimum wage policies.

9. Förster and Pellizzari (2000) used the MLD as the summary inequality index which allows for this decomposition. Overall trends on the basis of the MLD differ somewhat with respect to results obtained from other indicators (see annex). For the methodology of the decomposition, see Burniaux et al. (1998).

10. Other cash transfers going to the working-age population, such as housing benefits or social assistance payments have not been included in the detailed analysis because information was often not available separately; lumped together, these 'other' transfers constitute approximately 10 to 20 per cent of all non-pension transfers in most countries (30 per cent in Sweden and the United Kingdom).

11. Exceptions were Germany, Sweden, the United Kingdom and the United States.

References

Atkinson, A.B., Rainwater, L. and Smeeding, T.M. (1995), 'Income distribution in OECD countries, Evidence from the Luxembourg Income Study', Income Distribution in OECD Countries, *OECD Social Policy Studies* (18), Paris.

Burniaux, J.-M., Dang, T.-T., Fore, D., Förster, M.F., Mira d'Ercole, M. and Oxley, H. (1998), 'Income Distribution and Poverty in Selected OECD Countries', *Economics Department Working Paper* (189), Paris.

Förster, M.F. (1994), 'Measurement of poverty and low incomes in a perspective of international comparisons, *OECD Labour Market and Social Policy Occasional Paper* (14), Paris.

Förster, M.F. assisted by Pellizzari, M. (2000), 'Trends and driving factors in income inequality and poverty in the OECD area', *OECD Labour Market and Social Policy Occasional Papers* (42), Paris.

Förster, M.F. and Pearson, M. (2000), *Income distribution in OECD countries. OECD Development Centre Conference on Poverty and Income Inequality in Developing Countries: A Policy Dialogue on the Effects of Globalization*, Paris November/December.

Gregg, P. and Wadsworth, J. (1996), 'It takes two: employment polarization in the OECD', *Centre for Economic Performance Discussion Papers* (304), London.

OECD (1996), *Employment Outlook*, June, Paris.

OECD (1998), *Employment Outlook*, June, Paris.

OECD (1999), *A Caring World – The New Social Policy Agenda*, Chapter 3: 'The distribution of income*, Paris, pp. 65-80.

OECD (2001), *Employment Outlook*, June, Paris.

Oxley, H., Burniaux, J.-M., Dang, T.-T and Mira d'Ercole, M. (1999), 'Income distribution and poverty in 13 OECD countries', *OECD Economic Studies* (29), Paris, pp. 55-94.

Oxley, H., Dang, T.-T and Antolin, P. (2000), 'Poverty dynamics in six OECD countries', *OECD Economic Studies* (30), Paris, pp. 7-52.

Oxley, H., Dang, T.-T, Förster, M.F. and Pellizzari, M. (2001), 'Income inequality and poverty among children and households with children in selected OECD countries: trends and determinants', in *Child Well-being, Child Poverty and Child Policy in Modern Nations: What Do We Know?*, Smeeding and Vleminckx (eds), The Policy Press, Bristol, pp. 371-405.

PART III

LABOUR MARKET RELATED POVERTY
A CHALLENGE FOR SOCIAL PROTECTION AND INTEGRATION STRATEGIES

Chapter 11

Labour market related poverty in Germany

Walter Hanesch

Introduction

All studies on national income levels are in agreement that the poverty rate in Germany is traditionally lower than the average for the European Union as a whole. This applies to poverty both before and after state redistribution. The comparatively low rate of poverty among those not participating in the labour market in Germany is a decisive factor underlying this healthy socio-political image. A rather different impression is gained if one considers the income levels of those able to work and their families and then proceeds to analyze the extent of labour market related poverty.

The 2002 European Commission report on social conditions in the European Union shows that rates of poverty in Germany reached a European high in 1998, in households which included persons able to work but not in gainful employment (56 per cent as opposed to an EU average of 51 per cent); only the Republic of Ireland has a higher rate of poverty than Germany, measured by these criteria. However, the rate of poverty is still slightly above the European average (23 per cent as opposed to 22 per cent) in households where only some of those able to work are gainfully employed. It is only if all of those able to work are gainfully employed that the rate of poverty is below the European average (3 per cent as opposed to 5 per cent). A European Commission report of 2000 reveals similar findings.

What form does labour market related poverty in Germany take, how has it developed, how is this problem being discussed at present and what is being proposed to redress this problem? These are some of the questions which this report seeks to answer. The following investigation into the material circumstances of the gainfully employed and the unemployed focuses on households occupied by the gainfully employed and the unemployed, and on those who form part of those households, and considers the income levels, at certain points in time and during certain periods of time, of the gainfully employed and unemployed, as well as the incomes of those who share the same households as the gainfully employed and unemployed. The empirical findings presented below are taken from a survey produced by the SOEP[1] on the basis of a study on 'Poverty and Inequality in Germany', which was carried out on behalf of the Federation of German Trade Unions (DGB), the Joint Welfare Association and the Hans-Böckler Foundation (Hanesch et al., 2000), and of a further study which was undertaken for the

Government of the Federal Republic of Germany's First Report on Poverty and Wealth (Hanesch and Hölzle, 2001).

The article below begins by examining various findings on poverty due to unemployment and in households that include unemployed people. The report considers the extent to which unemployment related poverty exists in the Federal Republic of Germany and examines those groups in which such poverty manifests itself. The way in which poverty develops over the course of time is also investigated. The second part examines the development of poverty in spite of gainful employment. Here, too, the research looks at poverty among all household members, including those who are gainfully employed, rather than simply focussing exclusively on poverty among the gainfully employed. The article ends by presenting the current socio-political debate on this topic and with a number of conclusions and recommendations for the prevention or elimination of labour market related poverty.

Poverty in the event of unemployment

On an individual level, the risk of unemployed people suffering poverty is governed by whether, and to what extent, temporary state benefits (in particular wage compensation payments under unemployment insurance) compensate for the earnings lost as a consequence of a person becoming unemployed. In the context of the household, however, other factors may absorb or compensate for an individual's loss of earnings. The incidence of income poverty will therefore also depend on the existence and level of other earned income within the household, on the existence and level of other forms of income (unearned income, private allowances), and also on the level of household-specific consumption, which is in turn determined by the size and composition of the household.

Since notional or actual poverty among the unemployed affects not just the individual concerned but also those people with whom he/she lives, it would be inadequate for the purposes of this study to consider the unemployed in isolation. The household context of the population group under review must therefore constitute the central theme. Hereinafter, all households in which the breadwinner or his/her partner is unemployed are regarded as unemployed households. Unemployed children or other members of the household are to be disregarded, provided that they live in households in which none of the breadwinners is unemployed. In this way, the breadwinner and his/her partner are regarded as having an equally important part to play in making the decisions which affect the standard of living of all members of the household. Only those persons who have indicated they are registered as unemployed at the employment office are to be regarded as unemployed. The poverty threshold is set at one half (50 per cent) of the average disposable, consumption-weighted per capita income. The consumption weighting is based on an equivalence scale in which the first adult is assigned an equivalence weighting of 1, each additional person of 15 years of age and over is assigned a value of 0.7 and each additional person below 15 years of age is assigned a value of 0.5.

Table 11.1   Rates of poverty in unemployed households

People in...	Former West Germany			New federal states	
	1985	**1991**	**1998**	**1991**	**1998**
All households	11.2	8.8	9.5	4.1	4.6
Unemployed households	29.8	26.3	31.6	9.6	12.5
Unemployed households					
- With one unemployed breadwinner, single	33.9	30.3	25.8	35.2	22.6
- With two unemployed bread-winners	38.1	(45.9)	(42.5)	28.8	20.5
- With one breadwinner gainfully employed and one breadwinner unemployed	14.0	18.6	32.4	3.2	7.6
- With one breadwinner unemployed and one bread-winner not participating in the labour market	54.2	35.5	34.2	17.0	4.0
- Single-person households	21.5	(17.3)	29.9	( )	23.3
- Households made up of couple without children	19.4	10.0	19.4	7.0	7.1
- Households made up of couple with minors	35.8	35.9	42.4	6.8	13.0
- Single-parent households with minors	46.9	(68.6)	31.9	( )	25.6
- Families with adult children	15.9	19.2	21.6	4.4	6.4

Source: Hanesch and Hölzle, 2001.

According to Table 11.1, the level of income poverty among people living in unemployed households in 1998 was some three times the level of that for the population of the Federal Republic of Germany as a whole (West: 31.6 as opposed to 9.5 per cent and East: 12.5 as opposed to 4.6 per cent). An examination of the trend over time reveals that poverty increased slightly in this sector of the population in the former West Germany during the period between 1985 and 1998, whereas it fell in the population as a whole. In comparison with the former West Germany, poverty among the unemployed population in the new federal states was relatively low, at 12.5 per cent, although here the ratio to poverty in the population as a whole is similar to that in the former West Germany. The proportion of people in unemployed households falling into the category of 'precarious prosperity', which covers those situated between 51 and 75 per cent of the mean, was also significantly higher than the figure for all households. This applies both to the states of the former West Germany, with 29.4 as opposed to 24.3 per cent and even more so to the new federal states, with 41.7 as opposed to 23.0 per cent.

If the population residing in unemployed households is considered on the basis of the status of the breadwinners in terms of gainful employment, then households with two unemployed breadwinners were found to be the most susceptible to poverty (1998: 42.5 per cent). Next most likely to suffer the effects of poverty were people in households where one breadwinner was unemployed and one breadwinner was not participating in the labour market (34.2 per cent). By comparison, the rate of poverty among households comprising a single unemployed breadwinner was significantly lower (25.8 per cent). The rate of poverty where one breadwinner was unemployed and one breadwinner was gainfully employed was only slightly lower (32.4 per cent), while in households which included one full-time employee the poverty rate was very low (17.3 per cent). In the new federal states, the highest levels of poverty were to be found in households containing one single unemployed breadwinner (22.6 per cent) or two unemployed breadwinners (20.5 per cent).

Table 11.2   Mobility into and out of low incomes for those registered unemployed, 1991 to 1997

Income status of those registered unemployed in 1991 as % of the mean	Income status in 1997 of those registered unemployed in 1991 as % of the mean		
	Up to 0.75	0.76 and over	All
Former West Germany			
Up to 0.75	29.9	17.0	46.9
0.76 and over	18.5	34.7	53.1
All	48.4	51.7	100
New federal states			
Up to 0.75	17.2	20.5	37.7
0.76 and over	17.4	44.9	62.3
All	34.6	65.4	100

Source: Hanesch and Hölzle, 2001.

If poverty levels in unemployed households are examined on the basis of the types of household as defined by the form of cohabitation, the highest levels of poverty in the former West Germany were to be found in households made up of couples with minors (1998: 42.4 per cent), followed by single-parent households with minors (31.9 per cent), single-person households (29.9 per cent) and family households with adult children (21.6 per cent), whereas households made up of couples without children (19.4 per cent) were the least susceptible to poverty. What is striking about this finding is that the household pattern exhibiting the highest rate of poverty was also the most significant in numerical terms. In the new federal states, the levels of poverty in unemployed households made up of couples with minors were considerably lower (13 per cent) than those in the former West Germany, although in numerical terms the figures were comparable. This is probably due to the fact that in the new federal states those cohabiting in this way are traditionally more likely to be gainfully employed than their counterparts in the West. In the new federal states, therefore, poverty was found to be particularly prominent in single-parent households (25.6 per cent) and in single-person households (23.3 per cent), in which it is not possible to offset the loss of earnings suffered in the event of unemployment.

This 'snap-shot' assessment of poverty due to unemployment, which has been the basis of the study so far, has to be supplemented by incorporating the dynamic aspects of the correlation between unemployment and income status. Various research projects have revealed that in the Federal Republic of Germany the population group classified as 'the unemployed' is notable for its volatility. The questions which arise in this context are: how long does poverty last among the registered unemployed and to what extent is it possible (particularly by changing a person's earning status) to improve the income situation? To find answers to these questions we need to examine the changes in the income status of those registered unemployed in the six-year period between 1991 and 1997.

Table 11.3   Labour market mobility and low income status of the registered unemployed during the period 1991 to 1997

	Employment status and income status in 1997 of those registered unemployed in 1991			
	Total	Registered unemployed	Non-registered unemployed	Gainfully employed	Not participating-in the labour market
Former West Germany					
All of which, with incomes of up	100	23.0	( )	38.6	30.8
to 0.75	48.4	86.1	( )	29.5	43.5
New federal states					
All of which, with incomes of up	100	23.5	( )	48.4	25.2
to 0.75	37.7	( )	( )	( )	( )

Source: Hanesch and Hölzle, 2001.

In the former West Germany, the trend for income distribution among those registered unemployed in 1991 deteriorated slightly during the period under review (see Table 11.2). While in 1991, 46.9 per cent of the unemployed were of low-income status, this figure had increased to 48.4 per cent by 1997. Conversely, the proportion of the population enjoying a secure standard of living fell from 53.1 per cent to 51.7 per cent. In 1991 the new federal states exhibited a much more favourable initial income spread among the registered unemployed, since the proportion of these receiving low incomes was just 37.7 per cent. What is more, by 1977 this figure had declined even further to 34.6 per cent. However, this relative stability in income distribution in both the western and eastern parts of the country conceals the significant capacity for mobility among the registered unemployed. In the former West Germany, for example, more than one third of those formerly receiving low incomes in the unemployed category still went on to achieve a secure standard of living (36.1 per cent). In the new federal states, more than one in two of those formerly receiving a low income were able to improve his/her income status (54.5 per cent).

What is the connection between these changes in income status and the changes in the employment status of those formerly unemployed? Table 11.3 shows that, by the end of this seven-year period, 23.0 per cent of those formerly registered as unemployed in the former West Germany had remained in this employment status (or had returned to it), while 38.6 per cent had taken up gainful employment and 30.8 per cent did no more participated in the labour market. A similar number of unemployed people remained on the unemployment register in the new federal states (23.5 per cent); here the number moving out of the labour market was significantly lower (25.2 per cent), whereas considerably more formerly unemployed people had succeeded in finding employment (48.8 per cent). So, even though the unemployment figures and ratios for the new federal states are much less impressive than those for the former West Germany, a significantly higher number of unemployed people were able to make the transition into the employed sector. The concentration of active employment policy measures in the new federal states has presumably contributed to this relatively favourable result.

Because of the size of the sample, a study of income distribution for the various employment situations has to be restricted to the former West Germany. Here it is evident that the highest proportion of those receiving a low income was to be found among those remaining on the unemployment register (86.1 per cent), that this proportion fell significantly among those moving out of the labour market (43.5 per cent) and that the lowest proportion of people receiving a low income (at 29.5 per cent) was to be found among those making the move into gainful employment. Although no definitive figures are available for the new federal states, it is likely that here too the transition to gainful employment, relatively frequent in comparison with the West, contributed to the positive image of income mobility. All in all, these findings show that the transition to gainful employment has made the most significant contribution to the substantial improvement in income levels. The other options not only perpetuate exclusion from the labour market but also sustain the difficult income situation.

The final aspect to be considered is the effect of state redistribution on poverty levels among the unemployed. State services and redistribution measures significantly reduce the levels of poverty among the unemployed: in 1997 poverty rates in the former West Germany fell from 42.4 per cent prior to redistribution to 22.6 per cent after redistribution, while in the new federal states they fell from 45.0 per cent to 14.0 per cent. However, State redistribution was unable to eliminate the problem of increasing dependency as the period of unemployment continues, this being expressed in the form of increasing rates of poverty, even after redistribution.

Poverty in spite of gainful employment

To what extent are people living in households that include the gainfully employed susceptible to income poverty? A household that includes the gainfully employed is defined hereinafter as a household in which at least one breadwinner is in gainful employment, irrespective of the nature and scope of the gainful employment.

If we take as a basis the concept of poverty already defined in the previous section, then it can be seen that in 1998, in both the old and in the new federal states, the proportion of people in poverty in households that included the gainfully employed was lower than for the population as a whole. Rates of poverty were 8.6 per cent in the West, as opposed to 9.5 per cent in all households, and 3.5 per cent in the East, as opposed to 4.6 per cent (Table 11.4). In Germany the proportion of people in poverty in spite of gainful employment – known as the 'working poor' – has not changed significantly since the mid 1980s or early 1990s. At the same time, the rates of poverty in these households are just one or two percentage points below the general rate of poverty. People living in households that include the gainfully employed do not of course belong to the 'problem groups' for poverty in the strict sense of the meaning. However, even in the Federal Republic of Germany poverty does not just affect households that are without gainful employment. In fact, poverty in households where there is gainful employment is much higher than is usually assumed in the public debate.

The same applies to the risk of being dependent upon a low household income in that income bracket referred to as a 'precarious standard of living' (between 51 and 75 per cent of the mean). However, taking 1998 as an example, in the former West Germany 24.6 per cent of those living in households that included gainfully employed persons (as opposed to 25.4 per cent of all households) and 21.9 per cent of the people living in households that included the gainfully employed in the new federal states (as opposed to 22.3 per cent), were living on an income of this kind, where there is a high risk of falling into poverty, e.g. in the event of a critical life event occurring.

A more complex picture results if households that include gainfully employed persons are broken down on the basis of various criteria. Specific features of significance are, on the one hand, the patterns of gainful employment in the household and the nature of the household based on the form of cohabitation and, on the other, those criteria that relate to the individual employment relationship, such as the type of employment and the level of earnings.

As far as patterns of gainful employment in the household are concerned, those households where one breadwinner is in gainful employment and one breadwinner is unemployed are most susceptible to poverty in the former West Germany (1998: 32.4 per cent). Rates of poverty among households where one breadwinner is in gainful employment and one breadwinner is in non-gainful employment are significantly lower, but remain above average (1998: 11.0 per cent). On the other hand, poverty rates in the other two scenarios are at a considerably lower level. In the new federal states, too, the rates of poverty in households that include the gainfully employed are at their highest in households where one breadwinner is in gainful employment and one breadwinner is unemployed (1998 7.6 per cent). Next come households with one single person in gainful employment (1998 5.2 per cent) and households that include one breadwinner in gainful employment and one breadwinner in non-gainful employment (5.1 per cent). It is interesting to note that the effects of poverty always increase rapidly in households that include two breadwinners in gainful employment where no conventional employment relationship is involved (Table 11.4).

Table 11.4   Rates of poverty in gainfully employed households

People in...	Former West Germany			New federal states	
	1985	**1991**	**1998**	**1991**	**1998**
All households	11.2	8.8	9.5	4.1	4.6
Gainfully employed households	9.4	7.9	8.6	3.2	3.5
Gainfully employed households					
-　with full-time contracts of employment	6.5	6.2	5.7	2.1	2.1
-　without full-time contracts of employment	16.4	15.0	17.2	6.1	11.0
-　with self-employed people	20.4	12.3	13.6	6.1	5.3
Gainfully employed households					
-　with one gainfully employed breadwinner, single	10.9	9.4	6.2	6.3	5.2
-　with two gainfully employed breadwinners	5.2	4.4	4.8	2.3	1.5
-　with one breadwinner gainfully employed and one breadwinner unemployed	14.0	18.6	32.4	3.2	7.6
-　with one breadwinner unemployed and one breadwinner not participating in the labour market	12.5	11.2	11.0	5.0	5.1
-　Single-person households	8.1	2.8	3.7	3.2	6.0
-　Households made up of couple without children	1.3	1.7	2.6	1.7	1.9
-　Households made up of couple with minors	12.8	10.4	11.9	3.3	3.8
-　Single-parent households with minors	20.6	29.5	14.6	8.9	6.5
-　Families with adult children	5.4	6.1	6.7	1.6	2.0

Source:　Hanesch and Hölzle, 2001.

If rates of poverty are considered by type of household, in 1998 just 3.3 per cent of those deemed to be living in poverty in the West, and 4.2 per cent in the East, were living in single-parent households with minors; however, this type of household is the most susceptible to poverty (West 14.6 per cent and East 6.5 per cent). In the West, households made up of couples with minors also exhibited above-average rates of poverty (11.9 per cent), whereas in the East it was the single-person households which did so (6.0 per cent).

As far as the type of employment is concerned, the lowest rates of poverty in the West and East are to be found among households where (at least one) breadwinner is in full-time employment. By comparison, rates of poverty are above average in households that include self-employed persons (West: 13.6 per cent and East: 5.3 per cent) and households made up of part-time employees only (West: 17.2 per cent and East: 11.0 per cent). The risk of poverty in households that include gainfully employed persons therefore centres on households that include self-employed persons and part-time employees, whereas, on average, there is comparatively little risk to those households that include breadwinners in conventional employment.

Here the part played by low earnings requires further explanation: as far as the relative proportion of low monthly earnings is concerned, the Federal Republic comes in third in comparison with the rest of the EU, with 17 per cent, just behind the United Kingdom (21 per cent) and the Republic of Ireland (18 per cent).[2] The is therefore no truth in the kind of statement often made in debates on employment policy that the 'low-income sector' in Germany is either underdeveloped or non-existent. SOEP figures show that in 1998, for example, 18.9 per cent of all of those gainfully employed in the former West Germany, and 13.7 per cent of all of those gainfully employed in the new federal states, were on low income. The proportion of low earnings has declined slightly in the West since the mid-1980s, whereas it has been increasing slightly in eastern Germany since 1991. At the same time the proportion of jobs offering low hourly rates of pay is declining, while the number of part-time jobs is on an upward trend.

As regards the connection between private earned income from gainful employment and household income, Table 11.5 shows that there is clear evidence of the effect produced by low earnings, although the size of this effect varies according to the respective household and earnings patterns. In 1998, for example, the rates of poverty among single breadwinners in gainful employment increased progressively down the earnings hierarchy. Classification in the lowest earnings category is reflected by a poverty rate of 25.9 per cent. The effects of poverty also decline rapidly in the higher private-income brackets. Similarly, a low income status in households where one breadwinner is in gainful employment and one breadwinner is not participating in the labour market is accompanied by a higher than average rate of poverty. The poverty rate among those whose earnings fell into the lowest earnings category was 26.1 per cent. Even if earnings were in the next higher income category the poverty rate (27.5 per cent) was still above average, while for those whose earnings were in the third of the total of four categories the poverty rate was astonishingly high (18.5 per cent). Furthermore, rates of poverty remain above average in those households with one breadwinner gainfully employed and one unemployed where earnings fall within the lowest or second lowest income category (42.1 and 43.5 per cent). The risk of poverty is therefore generally higher in households in which one breadwinner is gainfully employed and one is not participating in the labour market, or is unemployed, even if their earnings are mid-range. Since these households tend to be larger than those with single breadwinners (although there may be one or more children living in the latter as well), earnings are often insufficient to pay for more than the basic necessities.

Combating poverty in Europe

The lowest risk of poverty was to be found in those cases where there were two breadwinners, both gainfully employed. Here too, however, there was evidence of a higher than average susceptibility to poverty where both breadwinners' earnings fell within the lowest income category (48.3 per cent) or within a combination of the lowest and second lowest categories (16.8 per cent). This shows that the existence of a dual income by no means guarantees freedom from poverty. In this pattern of gainful employment, too, such a condition will depend on the level of these two incomes. There is evidence of a similar link in the new federal states – in as far as the size of the sample is sufficient for a conclusion to be drawn.

Table 11.5   Rates of poverty in gainfully employed households according to pattern of gainful employment and level of gross earnings* (1998)

People in...	Gross earnings as % of average full-time earnings		
	Up to 0.5	0.51-0.75	0.76-1
Former West Germany			
All gainfully employed households with one wage	28.5	24.5	12.4
In gainfully employed households			
- with one gainfully employed breadwinner, single	25.9	9.7	2.7
- with one breadwinner gainfully employed and one breadwinner unemployed	42.1	43.5	6.8
- with one breadwinner gainfully employed and one breadwinner not participating in the labour market	26.1	27.5	18.5
	Up to 0.5 Up to 0.5	Up to 0.5 0.51-0.75	Up to 0.5 0.76-1
- with two breadwinners gainfully employed	48.3	16.8	3.2
New federal states	Up to 0.5	0.51-0.75	0.76-1
All gainfully employed households with one wage	31.3	5.0	1.6
In gainfully employed households			
- with one gainfully employed breadwinner, single	( )	5.1	0.0
- with one breadwinner gainfully employed and one breadwinner unemployed	(33.8)	1.9	0.0
- with one breadwinner gainfully employed and one breadwinner not participating in the labour market	( )	10.8	4.2
	Up to 0.5 Up to 0.5	Up to 0.5 0.51-0.75	Up to 0.5 0.76-1
- with two gainfully employed breadwinners	31.3	5.0	1.6

*   Gross earnings above 100 per cent of average earnings are not shown here.

Source: Hanesch and Hölzle, 2001.

These findings demonstrate that an individual's earnings status has but a limited impact on the income level of the household as a whole. What is much more important here is the nature of the consumption pattern, which is a factor of the size and composition of the household and the number of wage earners it contains. This may be regarded as due cause to downgrade the income level as being less significant in socio-political terms and to hold more tenable the employment-policy based calls for a reduction in income levels coupled with an expansion of the low-wage sector. In actual fact, however, low income levels – regardless of the respective household configuration – are associated with significant risks for the individual's lifetime income, since wage compensation payments made under the social security system mean that the low-income status is maintained both during interruptions to, and after termination of, the person's working life. This is made all the more serious because those jobs that pay low wages are often associated with increased risks of unemployment. In such cases, an increased probability of the life contingency of unemployment is combined with a comparatively low level of material security. Furthermore, it cannot necessarily be assumed that a low earned income will be compensated for within the context of the household, e.g. by the existence of other earned income. Compensation of this kind can be compromized, for example, if one of the partners becomes unemployed – particularly if the said unemployment lasts for a considerable period and if the person concerned is only receiving the reduced rate of means-tested unemployment assistance. However, this also applies if the composition of the existing household is altered or even broken up, for example as a result of separation or divorce.

Table 11.6   Change in equivalent household income status in gainfully employed households between 1991 and 1997

Equivalent household income status 1991, as % of the mean	Equivalent household income status 1997, as % of the mean			
	Under 50	51-75	Over 75	Total
Former West Germany				
Under 50	2.7	3.0	1.7	7.4
51-75	3.5	13.1	10.3	27.0
Over75	1.8	9.8	54.1	65.6
Total	8.0	25.9	66.1	100
New federal states				
Under 50	0.3	1.9	0.6	3.3
51-75	1.8	7.3	5.6	18.2
Over 75	2.7	12.9	62.8	78.5
Total	4.8	22.1	73.1	100

Source: Hanesch and Hölzle, 2001.

How pronounced is income mobility in gainfully employed households? A comparison of income status over a six-year period (see Table 11.6) reveals that the spread of equivalent household income status in gainfully employed households hardly changed during the period from 1991 to 1997: while in 1991 some 7.4 per cent of the population in the former West Germany was still affected by income poverty, the corresponding poverty rate for 1997 was 8.0 per cent – an insignificant increase. Neither was there any significant change in the proportion of people in the precarious income bracket (51-75 per cent), the figures being 27.0 per cent for 1991 and 25.9 per cent for 1997. An examination of the mobility processes reveals that, in spite of the fact that the structure of the spread remained unchanged during the period under review, a significant amount of regrouping did take place among the gainfully employed poor. Even though the number of poor people in 1997 was similar to that in 1991, a number of those living under difficult income circumstances during this period did in fact leave this group and were replaced by others. An examination of those in income poverty in 1991 reveals that just 36.0 per cent remained in this lowest income class, while 40.5 per cent rose into the next category up and 23.5 per cent even managed to move into higher income brackets. Conversely, just 33.2 per cent of those classified as income poor in 1997 had been so in 1991, whereas 44.0 per cent had previously been in the next class up and 22.9 had been in the top categories. This means that while slightly fewer than 40 per cent remained in poverty (or found themselves in poverty once again), over 60 per cent of those formerly in poverty managed to escape this income bracket and improve their situation. A similar number of persons from higher income categories had to accept being consigned to the ranks of the poor, while a third of the new poor had already been poor before. The picture in the new federal states is much the same: here, too, the number of people in the two lowest income classes remained at similarly low levels (4.8 as opposed to 3.3 per cent and 22.1 as opposed to 18.2 per cent), the problem of poverty among this group having become a much more relevant issue during the period under review. There was also a certain amount of regrouping among those affected, in the same way as in the West. However, because of the size of the sample group it has not been possible to determine the precise extent of this movement.

To what extent does government redistribution help prevent poverty among the gainfully employed? By comparison with poverty due to unemployment, there is evidence that here the impact is relatively small. In 1997, for example, government redistribution only made a comparatively small contribution to reducing poverty rates in the former West Germany (from 9.7 to 8.3 per cent). The low rates of poverty before and after the slight reduction due to State redistribution indicate that, even before redistribution, the majority of gainfully employed households had sufficient income at their disposal to be able to enjoy a life free of poverty. In terms of individual gainful employment patterns there was even evidence of a negative effect in the former West Germany, since the sums paid into the contributions system outweighed the topping-up effect of the benefits system and the rate of poverty was in fact higher after redistribution than before (two-earner households: 5.6 as opposed to 4.6 per cent). However, in the new federal states there was evidence of a much more pronounced effect on poverty reduction. Here, the poverty rate of 13.0 per cent prior to redistribution fell to a level of 6.0 per cent after redistribution. One consequence of the ongoing structural and adjustment crisis in the employment system is that the gainfully employed and their relatives continue to remain much more dependent on supplementary state benefits than their counterparts in the former West Germany.

Proposals for the resolution of labour market related poverty

Labour market related poverty in the current poverty debate

In so far as the problem of poverty in the Federal Republic of Germany has been acknowledged to date, it has generally been associated with non-participation in the labour market. The link between unemployment and income poverty has been the main issue at the heart of current discussions on the cause and effect of poverty. Questions on the extent of the poverty problem, and its underlying causes, were first raised as far back as the early 1980s – as part of the debate on 'new poverty'. It is now generally agreed that the problem of unemployment has become the main cause of poverty and the reason for dependency on welfare benefits. However, there is much dispute about the reasons for poverty among the unemployed and about how this problem might be solved.

At the same time, the debate on poverty policy has been increasingly supplemented and masked in recent years by an approach that is primarily employment policy based. In this context the issue of income levels in the event of unemployment has been, and continues to be discussed less from the point of view of the adequacy of the socio-political protection and more with regard to whether or not the protection measures themselves are to be seen as the reason why unemployment levels in Germany are undiminished (see e.g. Siebert, 1994; Schneider et al., 2001; IFO, 2002). The focus has therefore been placed on the impact of economic incentives associated with the income protection, rather than on income support and the safeguarding of a person's livelihood. Considering the relevance of this subject matter, however, there has been comparatively little research done to date into actual income levels in the event of unemployment (see e.g. Bosch et al., 1998; Gilberg et al., 1999; Hanesch et al., 2000; Büchel, Frick and Krause, 2000) and above all into the risk of poverty associated with unemployment

The phenomenon of the 'working poor', that is to say those who remain in poverty in spite of gainful employment, has not really been part of the debate on poverty in Germany, apart from coverage in a few specialist articles. Where there has been a discussion, it has centred mainly on the Anglo-Saxon countries. The common assumption in expert and political circles is that in the German welfare state model, the legal regulation of employment relationships and collectively-agreed minimum wage levels, on the one hand, and supplementary welfare state benefits to cover special needs, such as child benefits, housing benefits, etc., on the other, should virtually exclude the possibility of poverty among gainfully employed persons. It is only in recent times that the thinking on this matter has changed. However, even though empirical findings on this subject have been presented and empirical proof has been provided of the existence of 'poverty in spite of gainful employment' in the Federal Republic of Germany (see e.g. Bäcker and Hanesch, 1998; Hanesch et al., 2000; Krause, Hanesch and Bäcker, 2000; Strengmann-Kuhn, 2000), such reports have met with very little response in political and public circles. Instead, the increased interest in this subject matter has stemmed from the fact that institutionalized economic experts have deemed a 'low wage strategy' either necessary or appropriate to overcome the problem of continuing mass unemployment in the Federal Republic of Germany (see e.g. Schmidt et al., 2001; IFO, 2002; Der Wissenschaftliche Beirat beim BMWT, 2002).

The official policy on poverty has been modified since the change of national government in 1998. However, this reorientation has not included the problem of labour market related poverty. Although a special report on income levels among the gainfully employed and the unemployed was actually commissioned for the Government of the Federal Republic of Germany's 'First report on poverty and wealth' (see Hanesch and Hölzle, 2001), the 'National Action Plan against poverty and social exclusion' failed to include this subject, showing just how little attention even current policy pays to the subject of labour market related poverty (see Bundesrepublik Deutschland, 2001).

Instead of differentiating between the nuances and controversies surrounding the current debate, the essay will conclude by attempting to outline – against the legal and institutional background of the German welfare state model – various starting points for avoiding and/or overcoming labour market related poverty.

Overcoming poverty in the event of unemployment

The legal and institutional structure of the German system of social security and unemployment support can be described as follows:

(1) Social protection in the event of unemployment: In the German welfare state system, income support in the event of unemployment is provided primarily by way of unemployment insurance (especially through unemployment benefit and unemployment assistance), which is the safety net with prime responsibility. This is backed up by the additional safety-net of social assistance. A characteristic feature of the wage compensation payments made by the unemployment insurance scheme is that such welfare benefits are intended solely to stabilize the standard of living of those affected and their families. The fact remains that it is not the purpose of unemployment insurance to avert poverty. This is essentially the objective of the supplementary or sole-payment allowances provided by the social assistance system.

Unemployment insurance is therefore simply unable to protect all jobless persons from the material consequences of unemployment. The design faults arising from its insurance-type structure have been aggravated over the course of the employment crisis as a result of repeated political interference in benefits legislation. However, the social assistance system also suffers from shortcomings when it comes to poverty prevention and these failings have been compounded by the reforms made over the last two decades. There is therefore no guarantee whatsoever that a supplementary or exclusive right to social assistance will provide effective protection against poverty in the event of unemployment.

Although most registered unemployed persons receive wage compensation benefits under unemployment insurance, there has been a steady rise in the proportion of unemployed people who are dependent on social assistance either as their sole or supplementary income. In this sense, social assistance now serves as a basic material safeguard for an ever-increasing number of unemployed persons – a role which was not anticipated when the Federal Act on Social Assistance (BSHG) was introduced and is not consistent in the long term with the purposes for which social assistance was intended (see e.g. Hanesch and Balzter, 2000; see my contribution on social assistance in this volume).

(2) Active labour market policy and employment promotion: In principle, the task of avoiding or overcoming unemployment and the material problems associated with it is an employment policy matter and therefore primarily the responsibility of the Government of the Federal Republic of Germany. While the function of employment policy is to achieve levels of employment and unemployment that are appropriate for the welfare state, the primary objective of the range of measures taken under labour market policy is to offer specific target groups in the labour market special assistance for personal development and integration in order to make up for the disadvantages which these groups have to face in the labour market.

The dual structure of social protection for the unemployed has its counterpart in the responsibility which is held for measures and instruments aimed at (re)integrating the unemployed into the labour market and employment system:

- Firstly, according to the Section III of the Social Security Code (SGB III), employment protection is a statutory obligation of the Federal German Employment Office (Bundesanstalt für Arbeit), as the provider of unemployment insurance, and is implemented by the local employment offices.
- However, since the 1980s, employment promotion has increasingly developed into an area of responsibility and operation for local economic and social policy, with municipality efforts being focussed on unemployed social assistance claimants.

The empirical findings presented in this essay show that the unemployed population is particularly susceptible to income poverty and precarious income levels. This applies to the unemployed themselves as well as to those living in the same household as unemployed persons. We now have to examine what the current prospects are of finding solutions to the problem of unemployment poverty.

The current debate on reducing the scale of the unemployment problem in general, and of long-term unemployment in particular, focuses firstly on the incentive-oriented reorganization of social protection benefits for the unemployed and, secondly, on extending aid for integration as part of a policy of realignment geared towards an 'activating welfare state'. Taking as a starting point the theory of an 'unemployment and poverty trap' (see Hanesch, 1999, for a critical view thereof), there is a call for the level of benefits provided in the form of unemployment assistance and social assistance payments to be reduced, for the period for which benefits are payable under unemployment insurance to be curtailed and for the incentives associated with social assistance benefits to be increased. The implementation of these proposed reforms would continue the policy of benefit cuts so typical of the 1990s and would therefore further reduce the level of protection against the material consequences of unemployment provided under the social protection system. Instead of reducing poverty in the event of unemployment, such measures would only aggravate the situation. As far as poverty policy is concerned, any extension of the incentives policy also has to be looked at with a measure of ambivalence, since as well as creating a better advisory and mediation service such a set-up would also result in a stronger system of controls and penalties (see e.g. the proposed reforms put forward by the 'Hartz Commission' (2002) appointed by the Government of the Federal Republic of Germany).

On the other hand, what would be the format of a new set of reforms designed primarily to reduce the poverty risk associated with unemployment (see Hanesch et al., 2000)?

(1) Since poverty rates are determined largely by the duration and frequency of periods of unemployment, there is a need for employment promotion measures to be introduced in an attempt, if not to reduce the extent of the unemployment problem, at least to shorten the periods of time for which an individual remains unemployed. Strategies that are aimed at (re)integrating the unemployed permanently into the labour market are most likely to prove successful in improving income levels. What is required here above all, in addition to employment and working-time strategies, is an extension of those instruments that are geared towards active employment promotion. However, this must not mean forcing reintegration at any price as part of a 'workfare concept', since any transfer into an (extremely) low earnings category, for example, would not eliminate the risk of poverty – as demonstrated by the results of the study on the 'working poor' There are significant employment policy and poverty policy risks attached to a strategy that is aimed at increasing the size of the low-income group – possibly supplemented by top-up benefits under a 'combined benefits-wages scheme'.

(2) It has to be remembered here that specific measures aimed at integrating into the labour market those problem groups which on the verge of poverty are only likely to achieve lasting success if they pegged into a macroeconomic strategy for innovation, growth and work-time structuring; this would result in a general revival of the labour market and create new jobs and, by way of chain reactions and trickledown, would also help improve the employment prospects of job-seekers with placement problems and the long-term unemployed.

(3) Although the unemployed should preferably be placed in the primary labour market, target group-specific jobs must also be provided in the 'secondary labour market' in order to build 'bridges', develop training and development measures and put non-marketable public-service requirements to work for the labour market. Depending on specific circumstances, the training measures must also be associated with actions aimed at socio-educational integration (counselling and psycho-social assistance).

(4) Although motivation and integration strategies have to take precedence, the social protection for the newly and long-term unemployed need to be improved in such a way that the risk of poverty in the event of unemployment is averted. Measures aimed at reducing the level of social protection given to the unemployed, as are being discussed at present in the form of proposals for converting unemployment assistance into social assistance, would in fact only worsen the material circumstances of the long-term unemployed. What is required instead is a 'ring-fencing' of the social protection function of unemployment insurance – especially for those who are particularly dependent on this benefits system. This could best be achieved by way of a 'means-tested minimum income system' in the event of unemployment.

(5) Reforms are also needed in other sectors of the social protection system, in order to provide help in cases of special need and to avert the risks of poverty associated with such circumstances. This applies in particular to those with housing and child related needs, where support has to be provided as part of a reorganization of the housing and child benefits scheme. Finally, measures designed to ease the problems of combining family and career may also serve to improve the prospects of households with children enjoying greater participation in the labour market and supplementing their income by means of additional earnings.

Overcoming poverty which exists in spite of gainful employment

The German welfare state model is based on the assumption that every person capable of working is willing and able, by deploying his/her labour, to earn a living for themselves and their families. At the same time, interventions by the welfare state provide framework conditions that are intended to facilitate and safeguard the implementation of this model. A distinctive feature of this system is the close interaction between employment policy and social policy:

(1) Using the legal framework in place for the employment market, employment policy therefore pursues the objective of guaranteeing every person in gainful employment a secure employee's livelihood. This regulation of the labour market is aimed at achieving a 'standard employment relationship', whereby it is possible for a person to secure a reasonable standard of living by way of earned income. However, it is also the role of employment policy to ensure that a sufficient number and quality of employment opportunities are available for all those who are able to work. Finally, the adjustment processes required within the labour market have to be supported by relevant labour market policies.

(2) By contrast, the function of social policy is to provide preventive and/or compensatory benefits in the event that income from gainful employment is lost or does not reach an adequate level, or in the event of other need scenarios arising. Those receiving low net incomes are generally entitled to benefits such as family allowances, housing benefits, educational allowances and training grants. The aim of these benefits, which are financed through taxation, is to supplement inadequate market income in cases of special need. Within the social protection system, social assistance is assigned the role of a basic safety net, which is only used if all the preceding benefits prove insufficient to guarantee a minimum subsistence level. In

the case of the gainfully employed, low household incomes can be topped up by supplementary payments, although here a series of very restrictive conditions make it more difficult to access this last line of social protection.

As already stated, the amount of earned income cannot alone be used as a basis for drawing direct conclusions about a person's income and subsistence level. The decisive factor here is the household's disposable income. This is the only criterion which indicates whether and to what extent (low) earned income is supplemented by other personal income or by the income of other family members (spouses, children) and whether the household's income is supplemented by welfare benefits, such as family allowance payments and/or housing benefit. Since these benefits (other than family allowance) are means tested, they are reduced and ultimately cease altogether as the income level increases.

Whether the combined net income (considering the number and ages of the members of the household) is sufficient to meet the socio-cultural subsistence requirements, can only be seen at household level. If the income is inadequate, social assistance is provided by the *welfare state* under the social protection system. Low individual wages and the resulting claims to social protection benefits therefore establish a state of 'potential' or 'latent' need for social assistance, since individual employees are unable to foresee with certainty whether or not, at household level, a particular risk can be offset or whether a problem will intensify.

In this context, what measures could be taken to reduce the problem of poverty among the gainfully employed? What is required here is an overall concept for an integrated poverty policy, which is both preventive – in that it arrests the downward slide into poverty – and also compensatory – in that it helps those who have become poor to escape their poverty. Such a system would essentially have to include employment-policy, taxation-policy and social-policy instruments (for more details see Bäcker and Hanesch, 1998; Hanesch et al., 2000):

- Even though atypical employment relationships – in terms of the economy as a whole – were once seen as additional to, rather than as a replacement for, 'standard employment relationships', they are becoming increasingly important in the labour market. Not all forms of atypical employment incorporate the same type of risk of such an employment scenario being unable to guarantee a secure livelihood. However, in order to ensure a minimum income during employment and to provide social protection in the event of employment of this kind being interrupted or terminated, a minimum requirement should be put in place to the effect that such employment must not be excluded from the protection provided by employment law, collective bargaining agreements and by social legislation.
- Although the earnings structure remained relatively consistent during the period under review, the risk of poverty associated with current low earnings indicates a need for action in terms of employment and social policy. Where minimum wages are agreed upon by parties to collective agreements, it is increasingly difficult to guarantee that the level of individual earnings for gainfully employed people will provide an adequate standard of living. In

view of the fact that collective agreements are having less of an impact on actual earnings, there is now a growing need for statutory regulations. However – as experience in other countries has demonstrated – even a statutory minimum wage is no guarantee for a secure livelihood.

- Improving the relationship between gross salaries and net salaries constitutes a further approach – whether this is done by reducing the income tax or the social security contributions payable by low earners. The current debate on employment policy seems to favour the latter method as a means of cushioning the social consequences of a reduction in the gross earnings of those in the lowest income bracket. Other proposals, such as the introduction of negative taxation, a 'combined benefits-wages scheme' or a different system for the deduction of earned income under social assistance rules, have been put forward with the same objective in mind. What is common to all these models is that they would involve high fiscal expenditure, that their impact on employment policy would be quite unpredictable and that their effect on the poverty situation would most likely be counterproductive.

- If families with low earnings are also to achieve an adequate standard of living, it is important that they are provided with the opportunity to improve the household's involvement in gainful employment. This requires not only a more family-oriented arrangement of the working environment (particularly with regard to working hours), but also the provision of more widely available and better-quality family friendly facilities and services (with a focus on care for children of all age groups).

- The fact that there is poverty among persons in gainful employment, especially in families with children, indicates that the German state welfare system has so far proved inadequate when it comes to compensating for special needs and alleviating hardship. This applies not only to housing benefits, whose purpose is to offset the burden of housing costs, but also to family compensation benefits, whose function is to alleviate the financial burden associated with having children in the household. Since neither housing benefits nor child benefits cover the actual costs incurred, the existing system has sought to supplement low household incomes – in order to cover thc cssential costs of living – by providing social assistance under the Federal Act on Social Assistance. In order to prevent poverty, housing benefit and child benefit in the low-income range would have to be supplemented in such a way as to produce – in conjunction with net earnings – an income capable of ensuring a secure standard of living. In the case of child benefit, therefore, the non-means-tested basic sum used to date could be supplemented by a means-tested allowance to cover the minimum standard of living required for children. Such a reorganization of the child-burden equalization system would, in most cases, avert the need for supplementary social assistance.

Notes

1   The SOEP takes the form of a representative panel survey, in which the same people in private households are questioned every year on demographic, social, economic and attitude matters. For more details, see Peter Krause's article in this volume.
2   For the purposes of the present analysis, 50 per cent of average full-time monthly earnings has been used as a basis for the low earnings threshold. The information on the EU, as provided by Marlier and Ponthieux (2000) for 1996 on the basis of the European household panel, uses a low earnings threshold of 60 per cent of the mean value of all monthly earnings from working weeks of at least 15 hours in duration.

References

Andreß, H.-J. (1999), *Leben in Armut. Analysen der Verhaltensweisen armer Haushalte mit Umfragedaten*, Westdeutscher Verlag, Opladen/Wiesbaden.
Andreß, H.-J. and Strengmann-Kuhn, W. (1997), 'Warum arbeiten wenn der Staat zahlt? Über das Arbeitsangebot unterer Einkommensschichten', *Zeitschrift für Sozialreform* (7).
Bäcker, G. and Hanesch, W. (in collaboration with P. Krause, J. Hilzendegen, M. Koller, W. Schiebel and R. Bispinck) (1998), 'Arbeitnehmer und Arbeitnehmerhaushalte mit Niedrigeinkommen in Nordrhein-Westfalen', *Landessozialbericht* 7, Ministerium für Arbeit, Gesundheit und Soziales des Landes NRW (ed.), Düsseldorf.
Bosch, G. et al. (1998), *Arbeitslose, Langzeitarbeitslose und ihre Familie*, Landessozialbericht Band 8 des Landes NRW, Ministerium für Arbeit, Gesundheit und Soziales des Landes NRW (ed.), Düsseldorf.
Büchel, F., Frick, J. and Krause, P. (2000), 'Arbeitslosigkeit, öffentliche Transferzahlungen und Armut – Eine Mikro-Simulation für West- und Ostdeutschland', in F. Büchel et al. (eds)(2000).
Büchel, F. et al. (eds) (2000), *Zwischen drinnen und draußen. Arbeitsmarktchancen und soziale Ausgrenzung in Deutschland*, Leske und Budrich, Opladen.
Bundesrepublik Deutschland (2001), *Nationaler Aktionsplan zur Bekämpfung von Armut und sozialer Ausgrenzung 2001 – 2003*, Berlin.
Der Wissenschaftliche Beirat beim BMWT (Bundesministerium für Wirtschaft und Technik) (2002), *Reform des Sozialstaats für mehr Beschäftigung im Bereich gering qualifizierter Arbeit*, Bonn/Berlin.
European Commission (2000), *European social statistics – Income, poverty and social exclusion*, Luxembourg.
European Commission (2002), *Die soziale Lage in der Europäischen Union*, Luxembourg.
European Foundation (for the Improvement of Living and Working Conditions) (ed.), (1999), *Linking Welfare and Work*, Luxembourg.
Gilberg, R. et al. (1999), 'Arbeitslosenhilfe als Teil des sozialen Sicherungssystems', *IAB-Werkstattbericht* (11).
Hanesch, W. (1999), 'Welfare and Work. The Debate about Reforms of Social Assistance in Western Europe', in European Foundation (ed) (1999).
Hanesch, W., Krause, P., Bäcker, G., Maschke, M. and Otto, B. (2000), *Armut und Ungleichheit in Deutschland*. Der neue Armutsbericht der Hans Böckler Stiftung, des DGB und des Paritätischen Wohlfahrtsverbandes, Rowohlt, Reinbek.

Hanesch, W. and Hölzle, T. (2001), 'Einkommenslage bei Erwerbstätigkeit und Arbeitslosigkeit', *Gutachten für den Armuts- und Reichtumsbericht der Bundesregierung*, Bonn.

Hanesch, W. and Balzter, N. (2000), *Integrated approaches to active welfare and employment policies – Coordination of activation policies for unemployed social assistance claimants*, National study on the Federal Republic of Germany for the European Foundation for the Improvement of Living and Working Conditions, Darmstadt.

Hanesch, W. (2002), 'Reformbedarf und Reformoptionen für die Sozialhilfe', in Ministerium für Arbeit und Soziales, Qualifikation und Technologie des Landes NRW (eds), *Flexicurity – Soziale Sicherung und Flexibilisierung der Arbeits- und Lebensverhältnisse*, Düsseldorf.

Hartz-Kommission (2002), *Moderne Dienstleistungen am Arbeitsmarkt. Vorschläge der Kommission zum Abbau der Arbeitslosigkeit und zur Umstrukturierung der Bundesanstalt für Arbeit*, 16 August 2002, no location.

IFO (Institut für Wirtschaftsforschung) (2002), 'Aktivierende Sozialhilfe. Ein Weg zu mehr Beschäftigung und Wachstum', *IFO-Schnelldienst* (9).

IFW (Institut für Weltwirtschaft) (1999), *Würdigung der Sozialhilfe in einem gesamtwirtschaftlichen Kontext*, Forschungsbericht für das Bundesministerium für Gesundheit, Kiel.

Krause, P., Hanesch, W. and Bäcker, G. (2000), 'Normalarbeitsverhältnisse, niedrige Erwerbseinkommen und Armut', in F. Büchel et al. (eds) (2000).

Marlier, E. and Ponthieux, S. (2000), 'Niedriglöhne in den Ländern der EU', in *Statistik kurzgefasst* (11), Thema 3, Eurostat.

Marlier, E. and Sohen-Solat, M. (2000), 'Sozialleistungen und ihre Umverteilungseffekte in der EU', in *Statistik kurzgefasst* (9), Thema 3, Eurostat.

Mejer, L. (2000), 'Soziale Ausgrenzung in den EU-Mitgliedsstaaten', in *Statistik kurzgefasst* (1), Thema 3, Eurostat.

Schäfer, C. (ed.) (2000), *Geringe Löhne – mehr Beschäftigung? Niedriglohn-Politik*, VSA, Hamburg.

Schmidt, C., Zimmermann, F.K., Fertig, M. and Kluve, J. (2001), *Perspektiven der Arbeitsmarktpolitik. Internationaler Vergleich und Empfehlungen für Deutschland*, Springer, Berlin et al.

Schneider, H., Lange, C., Rosenfeld, M.T., Kempe, W. and Kolb, J. (2002), *Anreizwirkungen der Sozialhilfe auf das Arbeitsangebot im Niedriglohnbereich*, Nomos, Baden-Baden.

Siebert, Herbert (1994), *Geht den Deutschen die Arbeit aus? Neue Wege zu mehr Beschäftigung*, Beck, München.

Strengmann-Kuhn, W. (2000), 'Erwerbstätigkeit und Einkommenarmut, Armut trotz Erwerbstätigkeit?', in F. Büchel et al. (eds) (2000).

Chapter 12

Immigrants between labour market and poverty

Michael Maschke

'We called for workers, and
people came. They do not eat
away at our prosperity on the
contrary, they are essential
for prosperity.' Max Frisch

Migration in the European Union

Migration is a European theme with specific national features. Viewing the issue of migration in purely national terms neglects the fact that migration policy was incorporated into the European Union's institutional framework with the Maastricht Treaty, and that with the entry into force of the Amsterdam Treaty on 1 May 1999, core areas of asylum and immigration policy have become Community responsibilities. By 2004, the Council of the European Union will adopt initial measures which are intended to facilitate free movement of persons and approximate the rules governing the crossing of the EU's external borders as well as asylum and immigration policy within the European Union. At a special meeting of the European Council in Tampere in October 1999, the political guidelines for this process were elaborated and the European Commission was authorized to draft a package of directives harmonizing asylum and immigration policy in the European Union. Beyond 2004, common rules are to be introduced concerning conditions of entry and stay of third-country nationals and procedures on the issuing of long-term visas, including for family reunification purposes. The development of these measures and rules and the approximation of national laws and regulations will continue to necessitate many discussions and compromises, as there have traditionally been major national differences across the EU countries with respect to the scale of migration and the legal, economic and social status of migrants. Critical observers of this process emphasize that harmonizing asylum and immigration policy in the EU could result either in a considerable improvement of the migration policies of the Member States, or just in the reinforcement of 'Fortress Europe' (European Network Against Racism, 2001).

The situation of migrants and the political and administrative approach to migration are already the subject of political disputes at national level in virtually all the EU Member States today. With regard to the social status of migrants, the Council of the European Union, in a joint report analyzing all the National Action Plans against poverty and social exclusion, pointed out that in most Member States, migrants are one of the groups facing a high risk of social exclusion. Access to the labour market is often linked with particular obstacles for migrants and members of ethnic minorities (Rat der Europäischen Union, 2002). It is the political and administrative approach to the issue of migration, however, which casts national differences into sharper relief. In many countries, there is obvious ambivalence surrounding the issue of migration: due to falling birth rates throughout the European Union and the associated prospect of demographic deficits in future, the need for immigration is underlined and immigration is called for at political level. Yet at the same time, fears of rising unemployment and growing alienation as a result of immigration are exploited in election campaigns in a bid to win votes, with the result that migration has become a highly emotive issue.

Overall, since the start of the 1990s, the population of the European Union has steadily increased, primarily due to positive net migration. For the individual Member States, however, no uniform migration trends have been noted, since both the immigration of persons from third states and internal migration vary widely across the European Union states. From 1985 to 1994, immigration into Germany was the main cause of the European Union's positive net migration. During this period, some Member States, notably Ireland and Portugal, still had negative net migration. During the second half of the 1990s, all Member States then had positive net migration, and Germany's significance in the overall European migratory balance decreased (cf. Eurostat, 2002a). In 2000, the major territorial states – Italy, Great Britain and Germany – were the key target countries for immigration. Setting aside the size of the country and viewing net migration solely in relation to population size, Luxembourg (8.3), Ireland (5.3) and the Netherlands (3.3) had the highest increases that year. With 1.3 migrants per 1000 inhabitants, Germany fell well below the EU average of 1.8 in 2000 (cf. Eurostat, 2002b).

Germany – an immigration country

The Federal Republic's history of migration differs from that of other European countries. Unlike countries with a long colonial tradition of migration, such as England, Netherlands or France, Germany has no commitments to immigrants from former colonial states. Yet at the same time, not all its immigrants are foreign nationals, unlike the Scandinavian countries, for example. For the Federal Republic, the distinction between German and foreign immigrants is therefore especially significant. Out of a total of 30 million people who immigrated into Germany during the second half of the 20th century, around 20 per cent were legally German. Alongside expellees after the Second World War and resettlers from the former GDR, the German immigrants also included, and continue to include, (*Spät-*) *Aussiedler* – migrants of German origin from Eastern Europe and the former Soviet Union.[1] The remaining 80 per cent of immigrants were foreign migrants (guest workers (Gastarbeiter) in the 1960s and 1970s, new economic migrants, asylum seekers, and war/civil war refugees). Due to the specific phenomenon of the immigration of migrants of German origin and the high level of out-migration by foreign nationals, Germany – in contrast to all other European countries – had more of its own nationals among its immigrants than among its out-migrants (cf. Eurostat, 2002b). Today, there are 7.3 million people living in Germany who do not hold a German passport. In reality, Germany has become Europe's largest immigration country. In 2001, Germany had a higher percentage – 8.9 per cent – of non-nationals in its total population than any other major European territorial state.

Although the large number of German and foreign migrants[2] is statistically proven, the policy pursued by successive Federal Governments for many years was to deny its existence in stereotypical terms. In contrast to other European states such as France, Netherlands or Great Britain, the Federal Republic did not – and does not – regard itself as a country of immigration but as a 'community of descent and culture' (Abstammungs- und Kulturgemeinschaft). The entry of large numbers of (foreign) migrants into the country was permitted solely in the interests of the economy. During the 'economic miracle', there were labour shortages in some economic sectors as early as the mid 1950s, which rapidly became a problem, especially after the GDR's borders were closed. For this reason, Germany signed bilateral agreements with most Mediterranean countries on the recruitment of workers, which continued until the 1970s. In accordance with the rotation principle, however, this was only supposed to involve temporary residence for a few years, not immigration on a permanent basis. However, the ideological construct of the 'community of descent and culture' collapsed when faced with reality, for while Germany had called for workers, people came. Many of the immigrants settled permanently, their families joined them, and 'foreigners' became a integral feature of West German society. In the late 1980s and early 1990s, following the collapse of the Eastern bloc, there was substantial immigration by resettlers from the GDR and ethnic Germans (Aussiedler) from the Soviet Union and Eastern Europe. In parallel, there was an increase in the number of asylum seekers and refugees fleeing to Germany from war, civil war and persecution on ethnic grounds, as well as from hunger and poverty (for the history of migration in the Federal Republic, cf. Münz, Seifert and Ulrich, 1999).

Against this background, what developed – at least for foreign migrants – was not a well-regulated immigration system with targeted integration measures and agreements to ensure that migrants were integrated into the workplace and became recognized members of society, but something more akin to a defensive system. To regulate immigration and protect German workers in the labour market, a dual permit procedure for residence and employment was established. This means that foreign migrants, having passed the first hurdle, i.e. immigration, and having acquired a residence status, still face a second hurdle, namely securing the right of access to the German labour market. The outcome of these regulations was – and is – legal, economic and social discrimination.

The analysis, presented in this article, of the income position of German and foreign migrants therefore begins with an overview of the hierarchy of the legal residence titles currently in force. The following section shows how access to earned income and social income is restricted through legal discrimination, and how unemployment and welfare recipiency among foreign migrants have developed over the last 20 years. Against this background, income distribution and income poverty among migrants is explored. Here, alongside key statements drawn from the Federal Government's first Poverty and Wealth Report (Armuts- und Reichtumsbericht) (cf. Bundesministerium für Arbeit und Sozialordnung, 2001a) on income poverty among migrants, the findings of a study undertaken as part of the Poverty Report (Armutsbericht) published by the Hans Böckler Foundation, the Non-Denominational German Welfare Association (Paritätischer Wohlfahrts-verband) and the German Labour Union Federation (DGB) (Hanesch, Krause, Bäcker, Maschke and Otto, 2000) are presented. The conclusions, set out at the end of this article, take the form of a socio-political perspective on how the changes introduced through the Immigration Act (Zuwanderungsgesetz), due to enter into force at the start of 2003, will affect legal discrimination and the income position of foreign migrants.

The legal status of German and foreign migrants

Not every person living in Germany has the same rights in law. While German migrants have the right to naturalization, which confers all the privileges and obligations of citizenship and the right to claim specific benefits promoting integration, foreign migrants are subject to various types of special status in law. Depending on their residence status and nationality, foreign migrants have different types of status in labour and in social law. The law in force in the Federal Republic defines the following four types of residence authorization for foreign migrants (on this point, cf. Lederer, 1997; Brand, 1999; Heinhold, 2000):

- Right of residence (Aufenthaltsberechtigung) under Article 27 of the Aliens Act (Ausländergesetz – AuslG): the most secure residence status conferred by the Aliens Act (the second stage in consolidating permanent residence).
- Residence permit (Aufenthaltserlaubnis) under Articles 15-26 and Article 35 of the Aliens Act: the basis for permanent residence and the first stage in consolidating residence. A limited residence permit is issued initially (Articles 15-23 of the Aliens Act); after a five-year period and fulfilment of further conditions (Articles 24 and 26 of the Aliens Act), it is converted into an unlimited residence permit.
- Residence title for special purposes (Aufenthaltsbewilligung) (Articles 28-29 of the Aliens Act): Residence status for a limited period, whose duration is strictly dependent on the purpose of the stay. Should this purpose no longer apply, the 'foreigner' in question (e.g. contract workers, students) must leave the Federal Republic forthwith.
- Residence title for exceptional purposes (Aufenthaltsbefugnis) (Articles 30–34 of the Aliens Act and Article 70 of the Asylum Procedure Act (Asylverfahrensgesetz – AsylVerfG)): status for persons permitted to enter and remain in the Federal Republic for reasons relating to international law or for compelling humanitarian or political reasons, or for persons who, under the Geneva Convention on Refugees, may not be deported (Article 51 (1) of the Aliens Act – 'minor' asylum), for war and civil war refugees (Article 32a of

the Aliens Act) and for asylum seekers whose asylum applications have been rejected or who have been granted a temporary suspension of deportation (Duldung) (after two years).

Alongside these regulations, special provisions apply to nationals of EU Member States and Turkish workers:

- EC residence permit (Article 1 ff. of the Act on the Entry and Residence of Nationals of Member States of the European Economic Community, known as the Residence Act/EEC (Aufenthaltsgesetz/*EWG*)): This Act grants free movement of persons to workers, service providers and the self-employed in particular. With the EC residence permit, EU citizens enjoy legal status equal to that of German nationals in broad areas.
- Special status of Turkish workers and their families in accordance with Association Council Decision No 2/76 and Decision No 1/80: These decisions provide for the gradual introduction of freedom of movement for Turkish workers in the contracting EU states from 1963, as well as for the preparation of Turkey's accession to the EU over the long term.

In addition to these residence authorizations, Germany's laws on foreign nationals and on asylum also provide for the following residence titles:

- Temporary suspension of deportation (Duldung) (Article 55 of the Aliens Act) for persons facing danger to life, limb and liberty, the threat of torture or the death penalty, or due to the home country's refusal to re-admit the foreign national, etc.
- Permission to stay (Aufenthaltsgestattung) (Articles 55-67 of the Asylum Procedure Act) for asylum seekers for the duration of the asylum procedure.

Persons residing in Germany without any of the above-mentioned residence titles have no legal status under aliens law, but that does not mean that their presence in Germany is illegal. As well as persons who have entered the country illegally or whose residence status has expired, some migrants, for example – such as those who have applied for residence authorization – also have no residence title. The situation of migrants who have no legal status under aliens law is notable in that possible entitlements are often not claimed as they would jeopardize residence (on this point, cf. Bundesarbeitsgemeinschaft der Freien Wohlfahrtspflege, 1999; Beauftragte der Bundesregierung für Ausländerfragen, 2000; Alt and Cyrus, 2002).

As residence status determines foreign migrants' access opportunities and thus their life chances, the granting of residence titles to foreign migrant groups plays a key role in determining the extent of discrimination. Of the 7.3 million people registered in the Central Register for Foreigners at the end of 1999, 10.3 per cent held an EC residence permit, 11.2 per cent held a right of residence, 27.6 per cent an unlimited and 23.9 per cent a limited residence permit. The remaining 27.0 per cent had one of the other time-limited and conditional residence titles.

Restrictions on access to earned and social income

German migrants have unlimited access to the labour market and to other forms of specific assistance to promote their integration into the workplace, and are also able to claim all welfare benefits to the full extent. For foreign migrants, however, access to the labour market and welfare entitlements is restricted. This legal discrimination impedes access to earned and social income. The following section describes, firstly, the extent of this discrimination for the various types of residence status. Secondly, it examines trends in unemployment and welfare recipiency among foreign migrants over the last 20 years.

Access to the labour market

For foreign migrants, access to the labour market is regulated according to the principle of 'prohibition with the reservation of permission' (Verbot mit Erlaubnisvorbehalt) and is dependent on their residence status. In general, foreign migrants require permission from the Employment Office (Arbeitsamt) to practise an occupation. Under Article 284 of Section III of the Social Security Code (Sozialgesetzbuch – SGB), only EU citizens and persons from third states holding a right of residence or an unlimited residence permit, or whose residence is regulated by intergovernmental agreements (Articles 28-29 of the Aliens Act, e.g. contract workers) are exempt from this requirement. Turkish workers and their families have special status. In accordance with Decision No 1/80 adopted by the EEC-Turkey Association Council, they have equal status in the labour market with Germans and workers who are nationals of EU states. All other foreign migrants from third states may be granted two types of work permit – depending on their residence status – by the Employment Offices, if labour market developments and conditions so permit, in accordance with Article 1 of the Regulation Pertaining to Work Permits (Arbeitserlaubnisverordnung). These are the work permit (Arbeitserlaubnis), and the certificate of permission to work (Arbeitsberechtigung).

In contrast to a work permit, which is time-limited and can be restricted to specific companies, occupation groups, economic sectors or districts, a certificate of permission to work is unlimited and is granted unconditionally. Whereas persons who comply with the conditions and have fulfilled the waiting times for the granting of a certificate of permission to work have a legal entitlement to enter the labour market, migrants who hold a residence title for exceptional purposes (Aufenthaltsbefugnis), permission to stay (Aufenthaltsgestattung) or a temporary suspension of deportation (Duldung) may only be granted a work permit after consideration of their individual circumstances and labour market conditions. They thus have no legal entitlement to a general work permit. This is granted only for one year and is then reviewed, again taking labour market conditions into account. For some groups of foreign migrants, it has now become almost impossible, under the current administrative practice, to obtain permission to work. In line with a directive issued by the former conservative-liberal Federal Government, no work permits were issued to asylum seekers., foreign nationals granted a temporary suspension of deportation or refugees until the end of 2000. Persons living in the Federal Republic with no legal residence status do not have any legally safeguarded access to the labour market (cf. Brand, 1999; Lederer, 1997).

Unemployment trends

After recruitment was halted in 1973, there was a shift in demographic composition, resulting in a steadily declining rate of employment among migrants. In 2001, the employment rate among migrants – once far higher than among the population with German nationality – stood at just 53 per cent, whereas the rate for German nationals stood at 67 per cent (Unabhängige Kommission 'Zuwanderung', 2001). This development occurred because the labour supply potential of foreign migrants increased during this period, whereas between 1975 and 1985, the number of employed foreign migrants liable to pay social insurance contributions decreased by around one-quarter, and has only just returned to the approximate level reached after recruitment was halted in 1973, i.e. 2 million workers.

In parallel to this development, there has been a substantial rise, over the last 20 years, in unemployment among foreign migrants who do have access to the labour market.. Until the 1970s, there was no significant unemployment among foreign migrants. Migrant workers were employed primarily in mass production and heavy industry. As job loss generally resulted in the loss of residence rights and mainly young workers had been recruited, the rate of employment among migrants was markedly higher, and the rate of unemployment lower, than among Germans. Since then, with the general rise in unemployment, the number of jobless migrants had also increased sharply. As shown in Figure 12.1, since the 1980s, the unemployment rate among foreign migrants has stood at consistently higher levels than among the West German population overall. In the early 1990s in particular, the labour supply expanded dramatically as a result of migration, whereas the demand for workers decreased overall, especially in industrial production, with the result that the unemployment rate continued to rise. In 2000, according to statistics from the Federal Institute for Employment (Bundesanstalt für Arbeit), the unemployment rate among foreign migrants in West Germany stood at 16.4 per cent, i.e. more than twice the rate among the West German population overall (7.8 per cent) (cf. Bundesanstalt für Arbeit, 2002). The real unemployment rate among foreign migrants is probably even higher, for two reasons: firstly, since August 1992, asylum seekers who are registered as unemployed are no longer included in the unemployment statistics if they are not entitled to claim unemployment benefit or unemployment assistance.; secondly, foreign nationals who lose their jobs often do not register with the job centres for fear of being deported (cf. Bundesanstalt für Arbeit, 2001; Lederer, 1997; Schulz, 1999).

In contrast to the migrant groups mentioned above, who have no access to the labour market, the foreign migrants who are registered as 'unemployed' do have access to the labour market, albeit restricted in some cases. In addition to possible legal uncertainties, the above-average rates of unemployment among these foreign migrants with access rights are probably due to their lack of education and training, for a key feature of this group is their far lower level of formal qualifications and poorer skills (on this point, cf. Artelt et al., 2001; German Institute for Economic Research (DIW), 1999a and 1999b; Zimmermann, 1999). A further reason is the imbalance in the employment structure among foreign migrants, reflected in the high proportion of foreign migrants employed as manual and unskilled workers in vulnerable economic sectors and industrial production, and in jobs for which they are over-qualified (on this point, cf. Beauftragte der Bundesregierung für Ausländerfragen, 2000; Bender, Rürup, Seifert and Sesselmeier, 2000). German migrants, such as the *Spätaussiedler*, also have difficulties integrating into the labour market, although by law, they have unrestricted access to the labour market, receive state support for language training, schooling and vocational training, and generally have better formal qualifications. The Federal Institute for Employment keeps a separate record of ethnic German *Spätaussiedler* who entered Germany no more than five years ago, but does not show any group-specific unemployment rate in its statistics. The average unemployment rate among ethnic German immigrants in 1998 is estimated to have stood at over 20 per cent (cf. Bundesanstalt für Arbeit, 2001). It is apparent from this that even when efforts are made to promote political, legal and social inclusion, exclusion mechanisms continue to exist in the labour market (cf. Seifert, 1996a; Bender, Rürup, Seifert and Sesselmeier, 2000).

Access to and claiming welfare benefits

The contributory social insurance schemes which are typical of the German social welfare model safeguard against the major risks which lead to loss of income (accident, sickness, dependency on care, old age, unemployment) for working people. Other specific risks are covered by special transfer payments funded from taxation, notably welfare. Whereas social insurance benefit entitlements are generally dependent on the contributions paid, every German citizen has a statutory right to welfare, should the need arise. For German migrants, the principle of equivalence between contributions and benefits does not apply. They are granted direct membership of all the social insurance schemes and their periods of employment in other countries are recognized and credited to them as contributory periods (cf. Bundesministerium für Arbeit und Sozialordnung, 1998). In general, they have the same entitlements to all other welfare benefits as the German population.

For foreign migrants, on the other hand, access to welfare benefits is dependent on residence status. In principle, foreign migrants are able to claim welfare, but this is restricted by Article 120 of the Federal Act on Social Assistance (Bundessozialhilfegesetz – BSHG) which applies solely to 'foreigners'. Under this legislation, only foreigners who are actually resident in the Federal Republic can claim support for living costs, medical aid, maternity benefits, and assistance with care. Similarly, foreign nationals who have entered the Federal Republic to claim welfare or medical aid have no entitlements. In the event of illness, medical aid may only be provided to alleviate an acute and life-threatening condition or a serious or infectious disease requiring immediate treatment. Furthermore, persons entitled to receive benefits under Article 1 of the Act on Assistance to Asylum Claimants (Asylbewerberleistungsgesetz – AsylbLG) are not entitled to claim any welfare benefits. Indeed, Article 120 of the Federal Social Assistance Act exhorts the authorities concerned, when granting welfare benefits to 'foreigners', to draw attention to the benefits provided under existing return and onward migration programmes and, in appropriate cases, 'to encourage recourse to such programmes'. For foreign migrants whose residence status is not secure (residence title for special purposes (Aufenthaltsbewilligung) and limited residence permit (befristete Aufenthaltserlaubnis)), this means that their residence may be jeopardized in law if they claim benefits such as welfare.

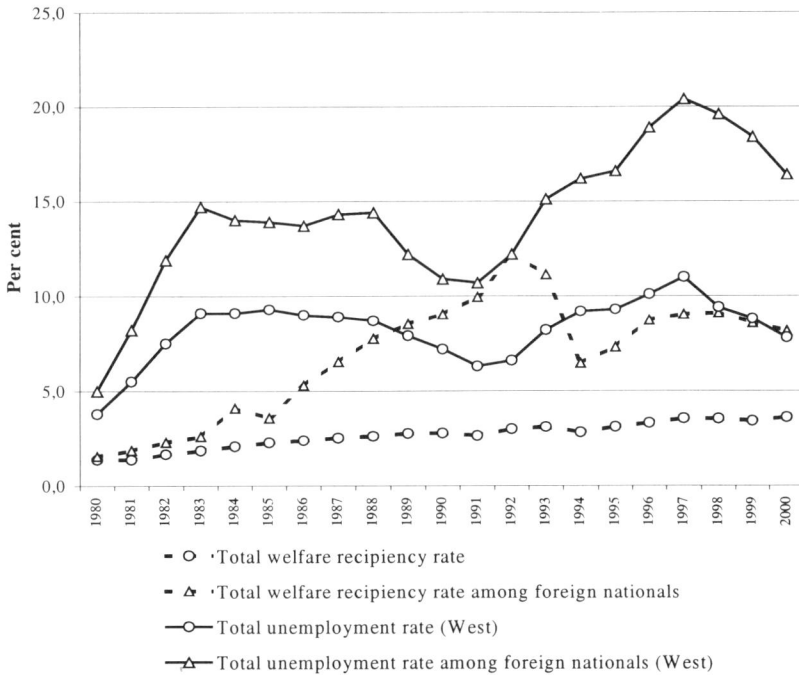

Figure 12.1   Development of welfare recipiency rates (General Assistance (Hilfe zum Lebensunterhalt – HLU)) and unemployment rates in West Germany

Source: Data from the Federal Statistical Office 2001 and the Federal Institute for Employment 2002. Welfare recipiency rates up to 1990 relate to the former federal territory, and from 1991 to Germany.

With the entry into force of the Act on Assistance to Asylum Claimants on 1 November 1993, some foreign migrants were excluded from claiming welfare by means of a separate Act applicable solely to them. In 1997, the scope of the Act was expanded; now, persons who hold a residence title for exceptional purposes (Aufenthaltsbefugnis) under Articles 32/32a of the Aliens Act, or who have been granted permission to stay (Aufenthaltsgestattung) or a temporary suspension of deportation (Duldung), or persons wishing to entry Germany via an airport and whose entry has not (yet) been granted (asylum seekers and refugees), are no longer entitled to claim welfare.

Due to the declining share of workers liable to pay social insurance contributions and the rise in unemployment among foreign migrants, the risk of becoming reliant on the welfare safety net (Regular Support for Living Costs (Laufende Hilfe zum Lebensunterhalt)) has increased substantially for foreign migrants. Foreign migrants of retirement age, in particular, but also migrants who have only lived in the Federal Republic for a short time and who are not yet integrated into the labour market tend to have a higher risk of welfare dependency (cf. Stubig, 1998; Büchel, Frick and Voges, 1997).

As shown in Figure 12.1, the welfare recipiency rate (general assistance) among 'foreigners' soared between 1980 and 2000. In 2000, 3.6 per cent of the total West German population received general assistance, whereas among 'foreigners', the figure was 8.6 per cent (cf. Bundesanstalt für Arbeit, 2002). The sharp fall in the welfare recipiency rate in 1993/1994 was due to the introduction of the Act on Assistance to Asylum Claimants (Asylbewerberleistungsgesetz – AsylbLG)). Without the introduction of this Act, the welfare recipiency rate among foreign migrants would therefore be even higher. The Federal Statistical Office does not keep separate records on migrants with German nationality, but here too, it may be assumed that the welfare recipiency rates are higher (cf. Seewald, 1999; Engels, Sellin, Hägele and Machalkowski, 2000).[3]

Income position and income poverty among migrants

As early as the late 1960s, various studies have repeatedly highlighted the poor socio-economic status of foreign migrants who came to Germany through the recruitment process and associated family reunion. Due to the radical changes since the end of the 1980s in the composition of migrants permanently resident in Germany, this research has been supplemented by further studies on the socio-economic status of new migrant groups – such as asylum seekers and refugees, but also German immigrants (cf. Frick and Wagner, 1996). These studies reveal, yet again, the poor economic status of migrants, which has been attributed primarily to the accumulation of general risk factors, such as poorer educational qualifications and training, lower occupational status, or large numbers of children in the household, but also to discrimination in the labour market (cf. Seifert, 1994). The failure to focus on the economic position of foreigners in the public debate, despite these findings, was also due for a long time to the lack of visible signs of poverty – such as increased public transfers. Only in the last 20 years has the disproportionately sharp increase in the number of 'foreign' welfare recipients and jobless 'foreigners' brought to light the poor economic position of migrants. In its Poverty and Wealth Report, the Federal Government has taken account of this fact, devoting a separate chapter to the situation of migrants. In the following section, the core statements contained in this chapter of the Report, which focusses on income poverty among migrants, are presented and then supplemented with the findings of a study carried out as part of the Poverty Report (Armutsbericht) published by the Non-Denominational German Welfare Association (Paritätischer Wohlfahrtsverband) and the German Trade Union Federation (DGB).

Findings of the Federal Government's Report on poverty among migrants

Unlike previous governments, which consistently denied the existence of poverty in the Federal Republic by referring to the availability of welfare, the Red-Green Federal Government officially acknowledged that poverty exists in our affluent society with the publication of its first Poverty and Wealth Report (cf. Bundesministerium für Arbeit und Sozialordnung, 2001a). The separate chapter on immigration in the Government's Report thus breaks two political taboos. Firstly, the chapter on 'Immigration' in Part A of the Report explores the extent to which social problems in the fields of education, employment, housing and health impede the integration of German and foreign migrants or even result in social exclusion. Yet no separate expert analysis was commissioned for this chapter – an omission which conflicts with the fundamental concept of the Report. Instead, the findings referred to in the Report are based almost exclusively on official statistics or are taken from the expert analyzes on other topics.[4]

On the issue of poverty among German migrants, the Report provides very little information, ascribing this to the poor availability of data. On the situation of foreign migrants, the Report contains a brief overview of specific areas of life and access to services: education and training, work and unemployment, housing, health and economic status. The Report's core findings on poverty among foreign migrants are as follows:

- The average net equivalent income of foreign migrants stood at 73 per cent of the West German resident population average in 1998. As well as this difference in levels, the income spread was also less pronounced.
- The poverty rate (based on the poverty threshold of 50 per cent of average net equivalent income) of foreign migrant households has risen since the early 1980s, reaching 26.4 per cent in 1998, i.e. twice the rate of all households. The proportion of affluent households, on the other hand, was only 1 per cent: about one-fifth of the share for the population as a whole.
- The savings behaviour of foreign migrants has come into line with that of the German population stock and the scale of financial transfers to the country of origin has declined.
- Foreign migrant households have a higher risk of being reliant on benefits from welfare or the Act on Assistance to Asylum Claimants. The reasons for this are higher unemployment due to lower participation in education and training, and restrictions on labour market access. The percentage of 'foreigners' – 23.1 per cent – among the 2.9 million welfare recipients (Support for Living Costs) was much higher than the percentage of the total

population. Furthermore, in 1998, around 450,000 people were receiving benefits under the Act on Assistance to Asylum Claimants. These benefits are 14-28 per cent below the level of benefits provided through welfare (Support for Living Costs), i.e. well below the socio-cultural poverty line.

Furthermore, the separate volume containing background material (cf. Bundesministerium für Arbeit und Sozialordnung, 2001b) contains two tables which are not discussed in detail in the Report itself and are incomprehensible without prior empirical knowledge. Using the data presented in these tables, it can be shown that despite their higher rates of welfare dependency and unemployment, foreign migrants benefit to a far lesser extent from income redistribution via the welfare state than Germans do. Thus before this redistribution, 32.2 per cent of all Germans and 31.2 per cent of all 'foreigners' fell below the poverty line with their market equivalent income (50 per cent of the arithmetical mean based on the old OECD scale). After redistribution (after deduction of taxes and social insurance contributions, and including public transfers), the net equivalent income of just 13.2 per cent of all Germans fell below the poverty line. Among 'foreigners', however, the corresponding share was 26.4 per cent. An increase in market income in the lower income brackets thus occurs to a far lesser extent among migrants than among the general population. These findings correspond with the results of other studies (cf., for example, Heilmann and Löffelholz, 1998). Thus one study (Büchel and Frick, 2000), which explored the question whether foreign migrants are an economic burden to the native-born population, showed that in terms of income redistribution via the tax and benefits systems, foreign migrants are net payers to the social security system, whereas German migrants are net recipients. In terms of redistribution by the state, foreign migrants can thus be described as losers in the current system of income distribution.

Findings of the Poverty Report by the Non-Denominational German Welfare Association (Paritätischer Wohlfahrtsverband) and the German Trade Union Federation (DGB)

With the publication of the second joint Poverty Report by the German Trade Union Federation (DGB), the Non-Denominational German Welfare Association (Paritätischer Wohlfahrtsverband) and the Hans Böckler Foundation in autumn 2000 (cf. Hanesch, Krause, Bäcker, Maschke and Otto, 2000), findings were presented on migrants which go beyond the results presented in the Federal Government's Report. Based on the German Socio-Economic Panel (SOEP),[5] an analysis of the socio-economic position of various migrant groups was undertaken. In order to ensure that the major differences in legal status and access to earned and social income were taken into account, and to reveal the differences among migrants as a group, six foreign and two German migrant groups were defined, based on their divergent legal status and economic positions. The first groups were migrants from a) Turkey, b) the former Yugoslavia, c) the countries of origin (Spain, Italy and Greece), d) second- and third-generation migrants, e) asylum seekers and refugees, and f) others. The second groups consisted of a) resettlers from the former GDR, and b) ethnic German migrants from the former Soviet Union and Eastern Europe (Spätaussiedler). The West German population was defined as a control group, as almost 97 per cent of all foreign migrants in Germany live in West Germany (on the income position of foreign migrants in East Germany, cf. Mehrländer, Ascheberg and Ueltzhöffer, 1996). No statements could be made about foreign migrants with no legal residence status or refugees living in emergency accommodation and collective housing, as the SOEP only surveys persons living in registered households. This is regrettable, as these two groups face particularly high risks of poverty since they have little or no access to the legal labour market and state benefits. Unfortunately, the SOEP does not record the different types of legal status held by migrants. Nationality is only useful to a limited extent in attributing legal status to specific migrant groups. Thus Italian, Spanish and Greek migrants, as citizens of the European Union, hold an EC residence permit. The migrants included in the 'Asylum Seekers and Refugees' group hold a residence title for exceptional purposes (Aufenthaltsbefugnis), or have been granted a temporary suspension of deportation (Duldung) or permission to stay (Aufenthaltsgestattung). Most Turkish migrants should have special status in accordance with Association Council Decision No 2/76 and Decision No 1/80, although in practice, the failure to implement these Decisions adequately has resulted in many of them holding a residence permit (Aufenthaltserlaubnis) or a right of residence (Aufenthaltsberechtigung) as well, as the Central Register for Foreigners shows. No statements can be made about the legal status of the other foreign migrant groups listed.

In the following three sub-sections, the findings of this Poverty Report on trends in average household income, poverty rates, low-income rates and income dynamics over time will be presented.

Average household income As is already apparent from the findings of the Government Report, substantial differences exist between the income position of migrants and non-migrants. The income positions of individual migrant groups also vary widely. However, these differences are not immediately apparent from studies of average disposable monthly household income (Table 12.1). The income differences between migrants and non-migrants, and the heterogeneity among migrant groups themselves, only become apparent if not only the number and amount of earned incomes, the amount of capital income, and income from private and public transfers flowing into the individual household, but also the size and composition of the household are considered. Only the first factors count in calculating average household income, whereas net equivalent income (i.e. disposable household income divided on a needs-weighted per capita basis) also takes account of the factors defining household needs.

As shown in Table 12.1, net equivalent income among foreign migrants averaged DM 1,587 in 1998, compared with DM 2,074 for German migrants and DM 2,174 for non-migrants. Asylum seekers and refugees had the lowest incomes. (although these figures are based on a small number of samples), followed by Turkish migrants and second- and third-generation migrants.

Table 12.1   Poverty and low-income rates and income distribution among foreign and German migrants

			Foreign migrants in West Germany						Germany migrants in West Germany			
	Non-migrants[1]	Turkish migrants	Migrants from the former Yugoslavia	Italian, Spanish and Greek migrants	2nd/3rd generations	Asylum seekers/ refugees	Other foreign migrants	Total: foreign migrants	GDR resettlers to 1990	Ethnic German migrants	Total: German migrants	West German population
Average disposal monthly household income (in DM)												
1985	2,990	2,665	2,552	2,764	2,715		3,131	2,750		2,575	2,575	2,968
1991	3,683	3,581	3,499	3,473	3,645		4,142	3,655		3,327	3,327	3,674
1997	4,366	4,154	3,965	3,709	4,011	2,563	4,438	3,992	4,555	4,040	4,138	4,306
1998	4,353	4,370	3,895	4,173	3,715	2,839	4,890	4,111	4,143	4,354	4,315	4,321
Average disposal monthly equivalent income (in DM)												
1985	1,358	927	1,144	1,134	1,043		1,399	1,093		1,187	1,187	1,337
1991	1,788	1,198	1,426	1,379	1,381		1,922	1,414		1,604	1,604	1,748
1997	2,183	1,291	1,564	1,562	1,561	(993)	1,931	1,539	2,079	1,622	1,709	2,076
1998	2,174	1,285	1,632	1,794	1,553	(1,015)	2,088	1,587	1,906	1,596	1,654	2,074
Poverty and low-income rates												
1985 50% <	10.5	30.0	21.5	18.3	18.4	(-)	(-)	20.9		(-)	(-)	11.2
1991 75% <	34.4	70.3	49.9	52.4	51.7	(36.1)	(-)	55.0		39.1	39.1	35.9
1991 50% <	7.9	23.6	7.5	14.1	19.2	(-)	(-)	16.2		(-)	(-)	8.8
1997 75% <	32.9	67.5	51.9	54.1	52.0	(22.2)	(-)	52.4		38.7	38.7	34.9
1997 50% <	6.1	27.4	18.5	18.8	25.8	(57.2)	(-)	23.7	(-)	23.6	20.0	9.1
1998 75% <	30.2	80.9	54.5	63.2	59.9	92.4	42.6	62.9	33.8	58.5	53.8	35.6
1998 50% <	8.0	27.9	(12.5)	(9.6)	22.5	(-)	(-)	20.4	(-)	17.0	14.1	9.9
75% <	29.2	83.0	51.8	54.5	65.2	(96.1)	37.8	63.8	(30.6)	54.9	50.4	34.6
Income distribution in 1998 with reference to average disposal equivalent income												
< 50 %	8.0	27.9	12.5	9.6	22.5	(-)	(-)	20.4	(-)	17.0	14.1	9.9
51 - 75 %	21.2	55.1	39.3	44.9	42.7	(-)	30.9	43.4	(28.9)	37.9	36.3	24.7
76 - 100 %	28.3	12.5	31.5	20.5	17.1	(-)	(-)	17.2	(39.3)	32.1	33.4	27.2
101 - 150 %	28.4	(-)	15.3	19.3	12.8	(-)	36.7	15.0	(26.0)	10.4	13.3	26.0
151 - 200 %	9.6	(-)	(-)	(-)	(-)	(-)	(-)	(1.9)	(-)	(-)	(-)	8.1
>201 %	4.5	(-)	(-)	(-)	(-)	(-)	(-)	2.1	(-)	(-)	(-)	4.1

Source: SOEP 1998. Figures in brackets indicate that the sample contained between 30 and 50 persons. Samples with fewer than 30 persons are indicated by (-). We are most grateful to Jan Goebel at the German Institute for Economic Research for his assistance with the production of the tables.

Ethnic German immigrants (*Spätaussiedler*) also had an income which barely exceeded those of the above-named groups. These differences between average disposal household income and average disposal equivalent income result from the fact that migrant households have a larger number of persons living in the household, a younger age structure and therefore more children and young people compared with the average population in Germany.

Income poverty, low income and income distribution   As with the average household incomes, the poverty and low-income rates varied very widely among the various migrant groups. For the purposes of the study, the threshold value for income poverty was set at 50 per cent and for low income at 75 per cent of the average net equivalent income (arithmetical mean and old OECD scale). The lower average net equivalent incomes in Table 12.1 suggest that income poverty and 'precarious affluence' (i.e. on the brink of poverty) are widespread among German and foreign migrants. This supposition is borne out by the far higher rates of poverty and low income among migrants. In 1998, the poverty rate among foreign migrants overall exceeded 20 per cent, while the low-income rate stood at 63.8 per cent. Asylum seekers and refugees had the worst income position., although data for this group are only available from the mid-1990s. More than 90 per cent of this group survived on low incomes during the years under review, and it is assumed that well over half this group lives in income poverty. It must also be borne in mind that the SOEP data overestimate the socio-economic status of asylum seekers and refugees. Turkish migrants also face very high risks of poverty. Of more than 2 million persons with Turkish nationality living in West Germany in 1998, more than one-quarter (27.9 per cent) lived in income poverty and more than four-fifths (83.0 per cent) survived on low incomes. Second- and third-generation migrants have only a slightly reduced risk of poverty, and their poverty rates have actually increased since the early 1990s. More than 20 per cent of these young migrants lived in income poverty in 1998, while almost two-thirds survived on low incomes. Less than one-fifth of these persons had an income higher than the West German average.

By contrast, migrants from the former Yugoslavia and from Italy, Spain and Greece have relatively low poverty and low-income rates. The poverty rate among migrants from the former Yugoslavia fell to 7.5 per cent in 1991, but then rose again, while the low-income rate remained more or less stable at around 50 per cent. From 1997 to 1998, the poverty rate fell once more, standing at 12.5 per cent in 1998. Only one-sixth of migrants from the former Yugoslavia were able to achieve an above-average income. Among Italian, Spanish and Greek migrants, there was a similar decrease in the poverty rate from 1997 to 1998, which, with 9.6 per cent, was close to the overall West German rate in 1998. Nonetheless, more than half the Italian, Spanish and Greek migrants survived on low incomes and just one-quarter had an income higher than the West German average.

Overall, the poverty and low-income rates for German migrants as a whole were more favourable than for foreign migrants. However, even ethnic German migrants ((Spät-)Aussiedler) also had far higher rates in all the years under review than the average population. In 1998, 17 per cent of ethnic German migrants lived in income poverty, almost 55 per cent survived on low incomes, and only 13 per cent had an income above the average West German equivalent income. The only group of migrants with a more favourable low-income rate than the overall West German population is the group of GDR resettlers who entered West Germany before June 1990. Only around 30 per cent of them were living on low incomes in 1998.

Compared with the West German population, the group-specific income distribution among migrants is also far less favourable. With the exception of the 'other migrants', migrants rarely feature, if at all, in the upper income brackets. Whereas 38.2 per cent of the West German population had an above-average income position, the equivalent figure for foreign migrants was just 19 per cent. Among asylum seekers and refugees, just 4 per cent were able to achieve an income position which exceeded 75 per cent of the average. No one in this group exceeded the average income.

Among German migrants, the GDR resettlers have a comparatively favourable income position. Although no one of them achieved a very high income position (above 200 per cent), more than 30 per cent of them attained an equivalent income above the West German average. Of the ethnic German migrants ((Spät-) Aussiedler), on the other hand, only 13.1 per cent achieved an income position which exceeded the average disposal equivalent income.

Alongside legal status, which crucially determines access to the labour market, to education and to public transfers for some groups of migrants, the reasons for the income distribution profile lie in the composition of migrant groups. Therefore in order to gain further insights into group-specific income positions, a differentiation was carried out based on socio-demographic and socio-economic criteria. Although it is beyond the scope of this article to discuss the findings in detail, suffice it to say that – as observed for the population as a whole – persons in larger households and in households with children, persons with poorer qualifications, and persons who are not gainfully employed, as well as the unemployed and persons in low-status jobs live comparatively frequently in poverty or precarious affluence. Compared with the West German population as a whole, however, there is a far higher incidence of these unfavourable poverty-related factors among both foreign and German migrants, thus contributing to the above-average incidence of poverty among these groups.

Dynamics and mobility of poverty among migrants   The objective severity of income poverty for the individual, and how it is experienced subjectively by the person affected, depend to a crucial extent on the duration of income poverty. For this reason, as a first approach to recording the dynamics over time, Table 12.2 shows the number of years during which specific groups of migrants lived under the poverty line during the 1991-1997 period. Only those persons for whom valid income data were available for all years were taken into account.

Whereas more than four-fifths of 'non-migrants' never lived below the income poverty line during the period under review, the equivalent figure for migrants – with the exception of the ethnic German migrants ((Spät-)Aussiedler) and 'other foreign migrants' – was far lower. During the period under review, more than 60 per cent of all Turkish migrants lived in poverty for at least one year. Although this was generally no more than a short-term loss of income in 27 per cent of cases, a good one-third spent three or more years during this seven-year period in income poverty. Among the second and third generations, too, almost half the persons spent at least one year, and more than one-quarter of all persons in this group spent three or more years, in poverty. Both the Turkish migrants and the second and third generations, who lived for at least one year in income poverty, spent an average of 3.3 years in poverty during the period under review. Among migrants from Italy, Spain and Greece, the frequency of poverty was rather lower. Nonetheless, more than 40 per cent of them spent at least one year, and almost 20 per cent of them three or more years, in poverty. Of the group of migrants from the former Yugoslavia, around one-third found themselves in positions of income poverty over the short term (1–2 years) and less than 5 per cent over the long term. This surprisingly favourable finding compared with the high poverty rates since the mid 1990s can be explained by the fact that only the part of this group which is established in Germany was studied.

Table 12.2   Periods of poverty among foreign migrants during the years 1991-1997

| | 'Non-migrants' | Foreign migrants in West Germany | | | | West German population |
		Turkish migrants	Migrants from the former Yugoslavia	Italian, Spanish and Greek migrants	2nd / 3rd generations	
Never	81.6	39.2	62.6	58.6	53.1	79.0
1 – 2 times	11.9	27.0	32.9	22.6	20.3	13.1
3 – 4 times	3.8	15.6	(-)	(11.5)	12.8	4.4
5 or more	2.8	18.2	(-)	(7.4)	13.8	3.5
Ø Number of years in poverty	2.5	3.3	1.8	2.7	3.3	2.6

Source: SOEP 1998. Figures in brackets indicate that the sample contained between 30 and 50 persons. Samples with fewer than 30 persons are indicated by (-). Monthly income at the time of the survey was used as an estimated value for the whole year.

Overall, it can be noted that compared with the total West German population, the group of foreign migrants not only featured to a greater extent in the low income brackets in both years, but there was also far less mobility between the two years. Although, as other studies show, the risk of income poverty and/or welfare recipiency decreases with increasing duration of stay due to greater integration into the labour market (Büchel, Frick and Voges, 1997), given the higher number of years spent in poverty on average and lower income mobility, a high level of entrenched income poverty among migrants can be observed.

Summary and socio-political perspective

Germany is an immigration country which, for 30 years, failed to establish the legal basis for long-term immigration of foreign migrants. A migration policy which denied the existence of immigration, which introduced very restrictive rules governing the legal status of migrants, which regulated access to the labour market in line with the principle of 'prohibition with the reservation of permission' (Verbot mit Erlaubnisvorbehalt) and tightened up access to welfare benefits while restricting integration measures to German migrants greatly impeded the economic and social integration of foreign migrants. A key element of this policy was, and remains, the residence titles granted to foreign migrants and the associated restrictions on access to the labour market and welfare benefits. How far do these restrictions go? This is apparent from the 'Asylum Compromise' adopted in 1993, which reduced benefits for asylum seekers and refugees to well below the level of welfare which is recognized as the poverty line.. Over the last 30 years, the concentration of foreign migrants in lower income brackets has become entrenched – a situation which conflicts sharply with the concepts underlying an immigration society. This is borne out by the above-average rates of unemployment and welfare dependency among foreign migrants and by the far higher income poverty rates among some migrant groups. This unfavourable economic position is clearly manifested by foreign migrants' poor income dynamics and low level of mobility into higher income brackets, as well as the unfavourable income position of the second and third generations of foreign migrants.

It is to the Red-Green Federal Government's credit that it has broken away from this immigration policy, which permitted migration but did not promote integration. Elements of the Federal Government's new immigration policy since 1998 include the new Nationality Act, which entered into force on 1 January 2000, the special measures on the advancement of young foreigners as part of the urgent action programme to tackle youth unemployment, the new regulations governing labour market access for asylum seekers, for foreign nationals who have been granted temporary suspension of deportation and for foreign nationals with a residence title for exceptional purposes, and the forthcoming entry into force of a new Immigration Act on 1 January 2003. More important than these individual elements, however, is the fact that during this legislative term, there has been a more positive tone in the debate about migration in the Federal Republic: for the first time, migration has been regarded and discussed as an opportunity for, not only a threat to, the Federal Republic (on this point, cf. Angenendt, 2002; Renner, 2002).

In terms of the topics covered by this article, it will be interesting to see how the new migration policy will change the legal discrimination against foreign migrants and whether improvements in migrants' socio-economic position can be expected in future. In this context, the new Nationality Act and the Immigration Act, due to enter into force in 2003, are especially significant.

Changes brought about by the new Nationality Act

The nationality laws in force until 1999 were based on the notion of '*ius sanguinis*', which meant that citizenship entitlements were dependent on German origin. As a result, foreign migrants, despite decades of habitual residence in Germany in some cases, and their children remained foreign nationals in law and their residence status was restricted. Only after a minimum of 15 years of residence were they entitled to naturalization under certain conditions (Article 85 ff. of the Aliens Act). The entry into force of the Act to Reform the Nationality Law on 1 January 2000 made naturalization easier. The two key reforms are, firstly, that in accordance with the principle of '*ius soli*', children born in Germany to foreign parents automatically acquire German nationality by birth. The prerequisite, however, is that in accordance with Article 4 of the Nationality Act, 'one parent must have been habitually resident in Germany for eight years, and must hold a right of residence, or have held an unlimited residence permit for three years.' Secondly, adult foreign nationals now have the right to become naturalized after only eight years of residence. However, according to Articles 86 and 86 of the Aliens Act, this applies only if the foreign national is committed to the tenets of the Basic Law, holds a residence permit or right of residence, and has adequate knowledge of the German language. A further requirement is that the foreign national must give up or forfeit his or her foreign nationality and be able to support him – or herself and dependent family without claiming welfare or unemployment benefit.

These relatively restrictive conditions limit the number of potential new citizens considerably, and may explain why the number of naturalizations since the introduction of the Act has been lower than expected (on the advantages and contradictions of the new Nationality Act, cf. Dornis, 2002). Although integration and naturalization are not the same thing – as the difficulties experienced by ethnic German immigrants in integrating into German society bear out – easier access to naturalization is nonetheless a crucial step towards legal, economic and social equality with 'Germans'.

Changes expected under the new Immigration Act

With the entry into force of the Amsterdam Treaty on 1 May 1999, core areas of asylum and immigration policy have become Community responsibilities, which means that the opportunities to control the influx of various migrant groups by means of a new Immigration Act are limited. The new Immigration Act therefore primarily aims to control the influx of new economic migrants. Overall, this new Act, which bears the title 'Act to Control and Restrict Immigration and to Regulate the Residence and Integration of EU Citizens and Foreigners (Immigration Act)', has less to do with immigration than with setting out comprehensive new rules in the field of legislation applicable to foreign nationals, their residence status, access to the labour market/employment, and integration (cf. Bundesministerium des Inneren, 2002). The changes of relevance in the context of this article are the reduction in the number of residence titles, the ending of the dual permit procedure for residence and work, further cuts in benefits for asylum seekers and persons obliged to leave the Federal Republic, and the right to government-funded integration courses to promote language skills and an understanding of Germany's constitutional system.

As a result of the reduction in residence titles (especially the abolition of the 'temporary suspension of deportation' category (Duldung)) and the removal of the requirement for special permission to work, access to the labour market will be greatly eased for foreign migrants who have a residence status. Decisions on residence status will be taken by the Office for Foreign Nationals (Ausländerbehörde) after internal consultation with the Employment Administration. This means that the discrimination in labour law will be abolished, although in future, the Employment Administration is likely to adopt a restrictive approach to the granting of residence titles in order to protect 'German' workers. The restrictions on access to welfare benefits will remain in force; indeed, the timescales applicable under the Act on Assistance to Asylum Claimants will be extended (for a review of the debate about the draft law, cf. Hailbronner, 2001).

Conclusion

How will these immigration policy reforms impact on the socio-economic position of migrant groups over the long term? This can only be determined in a few years' time on the basis of differentiated income analyses. However, in the interests of a modern integration concept, the quality of the changes must be measured in future by the extent to which migrants and their children are offered economic and social prospects which enable them to participate as full stakeholders, not marginalized groups, in society.

With regard to reducing legal discrimination, the following can already be stated with certainty: for the foreign migrants living in Germany who have a residence status, access to the labour market has already eased to some extent, and this process will continue with the entry into force of the new Immigration Act. As a result, the earned incomes of foreign migrants are likely to increase. The continued restrictions on claiming social transfers, especially through the Act on Assistance to Asylum Claimants, and the risks posed to residence if welfare and unemployment assistance are claimed, will probably maintain the high rates of poverty among some migrant groups, especially asylum seekers and refugees.

Beyond the abolition of legal discrimination, it will be necessary to address the discrimination suffered by migrants in terms of their life chances. This will require targeted compensatory measures. In the interests of the immigration country and the migrants themselves, the process of immigration can only be regarded as complete and successful once migrants are no longer confined to legally, economically and socially marginalized positions. The poor socio-economic status of foreign and German migrants alike must not be accepted as permanent and as a given. This would be akin to ethnicizing social problems and conflicts which, over the long term, could threaten the social and political cohesion of German society.

Notes

1   The latter group, according to Art. 116, para. 1 of the Basic Law, are German nationals or persons of German ethnic origin who were domiciled in the former Eastern territories in Central and Eastern Europe prior to May 1945 and who left these as refugees or expellees.

2   The term 'ethnic minorities', which is often used in the English language area, is inapplicable to Germany as ethnic minorities in the English-speaking countries are generally not only part of the permanent and resident population but also have citizenship of the country of residence. In the absence of a more appropriate term, this article uses the terms 'German' and 'foreign migrants'. In some parts of the text, however, the use of the word 'foreigner' (Ausländer) is unavoidable when legal or statistical contexts are being explained.

3   The higher rates of welfare recipiency among 'foreigners' cannot be attributed to greater take-up intensity. In a study undertaken on the basis of the Socio-Economic Panel (SOEP), it was shown that the lower 'grey' figure in the take-up of support for living costs (40 per cent compared with 59 per cent for the total population) was due not to the 'migrant' factor *per se*, but to the different income, household and age structure (cf. Bird, Kayser, Frick and Wagner, 1999; Riphan, 1998).

4   The Federal Ministry for Labour and Social Affairs has now commissioned its own expert report on ethnic German migrants (Spätaussiedler) (cf. Engels et al., 2000).

5   Since its first survey in 1984, the SOEP has also covered migrants and their households. In subsequent years, persons who came to the Federal Republic to join their families, or who were born to these families (second and third generations) were automatically included in the sample. Due to the influx of migrants and the resulting changes in population structure, a specific immigrant sample was added to the general survey in 1994/1995.

References

Alt, J. and Cyrus, N. (2002), 'Illegale Migration in Deutschland: Ansätze für eine menschenrechtlich orientierte Migrationspolitik!', in K.J. Bade and R. Münz (eds), *Migrationsreport 2002*, Campus, Frankfurt am Main, pp. 141-162.

Angenendt, S. (2002), 'Einwanderungspolitik und Einwanderungsgesetzgebung in Deutschland 2000-2001', in K.J. Bade and R. Münz (eds), *Migrationsreport 2002*, Campus, Frankfurt am Main, pp. 31-60.

Artelt, C., Baumert, J. and Klieme, E. et al. (2001), *PISA 2000, Zusammenfassung zentraler Befunde*, Max-Planck-Institut für Bildungsforschung, Berlin.

Beauftragte der Bundesregierung für Ausländerfragen (2000), *Bericht der Beauftragten der Bundesregierung für Ausländerfragen über die Lage der Ausländer in der Bundesrepublik Deutschland*, Bonn.

Bender, S., Rürup, B., Seifert, W. and Sesselmeier, W. (2000), 'Migration und Arbeitsmarkt', in K.J. Bade and R. Münz (eds), *Migrationsreport 2000*, Campus, Frankfurt am Main, pp. 59-84.

Bird, J.E., Kayser, H., Frick J., Wagner G. (1999), 'The immigrant welfare effect: Take up or eligibility?', *IZA – Discussion Paper* (66), Bonn.

Brand, K. (1999), *Leitfaden zum Ausländergesetz – Stand Mai 1999*, Eigenverlag der AG TuWas, Frankfurt am Main.

Büchel, F., Frick, J. and Voges, W. (1997), 'Der Sozialhilfebezug von Zuwanderern in Westdeutschland', *Kölner Zeitschrift für Soziologie und Sozialpsychologie* (2), pp. 272-290.

Büchel, F. and Frick, J. (2000), 'The Income Portfolio of Immigrants in Germany – Effects of Ethnic Origin and Assimilation. Or: Who gains from Income Re-Distribution', *IZA-Discussion-Paper* (125).

Bundesanstalt für Arbeit (2001), *Arbeitsmarkt 2000 – Amtliche Nachrichten der Bundesanstalt für Arbeit*, Nürnberg.

Bundesanstalt für Arbeit (2002), *Arbeitsmarkt 2001 – Amtliche Nachrichten der Bundesanstalt für Arbeit*, Nürnberg.

Bundesministerium des Inneren (2002), *Entwurf des Zuwanderungsgesetzes*, Berlin (download under www.bmi.bund.de).

Bundesarbeitsgemeinschaft der Freien Wohlfahrtspflege e.V. (1998), *Stellungnahme zum Entwurf eines Zweiten Gesetzes zur Änderung des Asylbewerberleistungsgesetzes*, Bonn.

Bundesministerium für Arbeit und Sozialordnung (1998), *Übersicht über das Sozialrecht*, Bonn.

Bundesministerium für Arbeit und Sozialordnung (2001a), *Lebenslagen in Deutschland. Bericht, Der erste Armuts- und Reichtumsbericht der Bundesregierung*, Bonn.

Bundesministerium für Arbeit und Sozialordnung (2001b), *Lebenslagen in Deutschland. Daten und Fakten, Materialband zum ersten Armuts- und Reichtumsbericht der Bundesregierung*, Bonn.

DIW (1999a), 'Integration junger Ausländer in das Bildungssystem verläuft langsamer', *DIW Wochenbericht* (22/99), pp. 408-418.

DIW (1999b), 'Schul- und Berufsabschlüsse von Ausländern: Nur langsame Annäherung an die Abschlüsse von Deutschen', *DIW Wochenbericht* (26/99), pp. 483-490.

Dornis, C. (2002), 'Zwei Jahre nach der Reform des Staatsangehörigkeitsrechts – Bilanz und Ausblick', in K. J. Bade and R. Münz (eds), *Migrationsreport 2002*, Campus, Frankfurt am Main, pp. 163-178.

Engels, D., Sellin, C., Hägele, H. and Machalkowski, G. (2000), *Aussiedlerinnen und Aussiedler in der Sozialhilfe, Studie im Auftrag des Bundesministeriums für Arbeit und Sozialordnung*, Köln.

European Network Against Racism (2001), *Für eine wahre Unionsbürgerschaft*, Brüssel, (download under http://www.enar-eu.org/de/publication/citizenshipD.pdf.)

Eurostat (2002a), *Eurostat Jahrbuch 2002*, Luxemburg.

Eurostat (2002b), 'Wanderung lässt EU-Bevölkerung weiter wachsen', *Statistik kurz gefasst* (7), Thema 3, Eurostat.

Frick, J. and Wagner, G. (1996), 'Zur sozio-ökonomischen Lage von Zuwanderern in West-Deutschland', *DIW-Diskussionspapier* (140).

Hailbronner, K. (2001), 'Reform des Zuwanderungsrechts. Konsens und Dissens in der Ausländerpolitik', *Aus Politik und Zeitgeschichte* (43), pp. 7-19.

Hanesch, W., Krause, P., Bäcker, G., Maschke, M. and Otto, B. (2000), *Armut und Ungleichheit in Deutschland – Der neue Armutsbericht des DGB und des Paritätischen Wohlfahrtsverbandes*, Rowohlt Verlag, Reinbek bei Hamburg.

Hanesch, W. (2001), Der Armuts- und Reichtumsbericht der Bundesregierung: Armut und Migration, *Archiv für Wissenschaft und Praxis der Sozialen Arbeit* (4).

Heilmann, U. and Löffelholz, H.D. von (1998), 'Ökonomische und fiskalische Implikationen der Zuwanderung nach Deutschland', *RWI-Papiere* (52).

Heinhold, H. (2000), *Recht für Flüchtlinge – Ein Leitfaden durch das Asyl- und Ausländerrecht für die Praxis*, Loeper, Frankfurt.

Lederer, H.W. (1997), *Migration und Integration in Zahlen*, CD-Rom Ausgabe, Bonn.

Mehrländer, U., Ascheberg, C. and Ueltzhöffer, J. (1996), *Situation der ausländischen Arbeitnehmer und ihrer Familienangehörigen in der Bundesrepublik Deutschland*, Berlin/Bonn/Mannheim.

Münz, R., Seifert, W. and Ulrich, R. (1999), *Zuwanderung nach Deutschland – Strukturen, Wirkungen Perspektiven*, Campus, Frankfurt.

Rat der Europäischen Union (2002), *Gemeinsamer Bericht über die soziale Eingliederung - Teil 1: Die Europäische Union*, Brüssel.

Renner, G. (2002), 'Aktuelle und ungelöste Probleme des Asyl- und Flüchtlingsrechts', in K.J. Bade and R. Münz (eds), *Migrationsreport 2002*, Campus, Frankfurt am Main, pp. 179-206.

Riphan, R.T. (1998), 'Immigrant participation in the German welfare program', *Finanzarchiv* 55, pp. 163-185.

Schulz, E. (1999), 'Zuwanderung, temporäre Arbeitsmigranten und Ausländerbeschäftigung in Deutschland', *DIW-Vierteljahresheft zur Wirtschaftsforschung* (3), pp. 386-423.

Seewald, H. (1999), 'Ergebnisse der Sozialhilfe- und Asylbewerberleistungsstatistik 1997', in *Wirtschaft und Statistik* (2), pp. 96-110.

Seifert W. (1994), 'Am Rande der Gesellschaft? Zur Entwicklung von Haushaltseinkommen und Armut unter Ausländern', in *Informationsdienst zur Ausländerarbeit* (3/4), pp. 16-23.

Seifert W. (1996), 'Einwanderungsland Deutschland – alte und neue Migrantengruppen zwischen Exklusion und Inklusion', in W. Zapf and R. Habich, (eds), *Wohlfahrtsentwicklung im vereinten Deutschland*, Berlin, pp. 141-160.

Statistisches Bundesamt (2001), *Pressemitteilung vom 21.08.2001 zur Hilfe zum Lebensunterhalt*, Wiesbaden.

Stubig, H.J. (1998), 'Zur Situation von älteren Ausländern in der Sozialhilfe', *Sozialer Fortschritt* (8), pp. 210-214.

Unabhängige Kommission 'Zuwanderung' (2001), *Zuwanderung gestalten – Integration fördern*, Bericht der unabhängigen Kommission 'Zuwanderung', Zusammenfassung, Berlin.

Zimmermann, K.F. (1999), 'Aussiedler seit 1989 – Bilanz und Perspektiven', *IZA-Discussion Paper* (50), Bonn.

Chapter 13

Social protection and activation for the unemployed

Claudia Weinkopf

Introduction

Activation for the unemployed (also known as 'workfare' or 'workfirst' in English-speaking countries) has become increasingly important in recent years, both in Germany and in numerous other European countries. The aim of activation is, for example, to facilitate a return to employment as quickly as possible, to avoid long term unemployment, to reduce the high costs associated with unemployment benefits, but also to maintain or restore the employability of those affected by unemployment. There are a number of different approaches and strategies regarding activation for the unemployed; primarily these focus either on material pressures and constraints (i.e., low levels of social security, or only a short duration of unemployment benefit payments), or on effective advice and support for the unemployed. These issues are also discussed, with a slightly different emphasis, under the theme of 'Support and Demand' (Fördern und Fordern). This means that those who claim social security benefits should provide an appropriate service in return – for example, by actively looking for work, or performing work outside of the employment system that is societally beneficial. Questions regarding mobility and 'reasonableness' are an important aspect in this context, exploring, for example, issues such as whether any employment is fundamentally 'reasonable'; how low achievable income can realistically be; how far a new work place can be from one's residence; and whether the demands required by a reasonable position can be lower than an individual's existing qualifications?

In Germany, such issues have been discussed for several years and, more recently, with growing intensity. In this vein, for example, reforms on employment promotion, which came into force in early 2002 (through the 'Job-AQTIV' law), placed the activation for the unemployed at its core. Furthermore, in the spring/summer 2002, discussions were intense within the so-called Hartz Commission, a body established by the German government in response to the discovery of inaccuracies and mistakes made by the employment service in the registration of work placements, and also to provide proposals for 'modern labour market services'. The federal government has already stated that the Hartz Commission's proposals are to be implemented immediately following a successful election outcome. And, finally, questions regarding the activation for the unemployed have for some time played a central role in the debate as to whether expanding low-wage employment should be a central starting point to reduce unemployment in Germany and expand employment in the services sector – and, if so, how these should be flanked. Target groups for such measures are usually individuals with few formal qualifications, individuals in long term unemployment, and social assistance recipients. In this context, a number of model projects and programmes to test in-work benefit and wage subsidy measures in the low-income sector are also being supported.

In this paper, the fundamentally existing starting points and strategies that play a role in the context of activation for the unemployed will be analyzed in a more differentiated fashion. The initial focus will be on the design of social security for the unemployed in Germany compared to the systems in other countries, as well as on the kinds of existing regulations concerning the take-up of work and the imposition of ineligibility periods for the receipt of unemployment benefits. This will be followed by an illustration of the experience to date regarding the granting of financial incentives for the take-up of work, especially in the low-wage area. Using the experience gained so far from model projects testing financial incentives (so-called combination wages) for workers to take up low-paid employment, we will show that the effects that can be achieved using such approaches should not be overestimated, particularly since the intended target groups are evidently being reached only partially. Experience to date shows that the supply of jobs is limited in this area and that filling such positions is made more difficult, not least by supposedly lack of incentives for the unemployed to work. In addition, the approaches currently applied in Germany to intensify individual advice and guidance for the unemployed (profiling and integration agreements) are outlined. In the conclusion, consideration is given to the fact that all the activation strategies discussed must be embedded into a comprehensive labour market and employment strategy, especially since such strategies face limitations during times of high unemployment. Moreover, there are certain arguments to support the fact that comprehensive activation should keep an eye on the target of increasing employment rates. In an international comparison, for example, Germany has a lower-than-average female employment rate. A change of situation, however, requires different instruments from those that play a role in the context of activation for the unemployed.

Activation

What fundamental possibilities are there to activate the unemployed? From my point of view, discussion centres around four – partly overlapping – approaches:

- the reduction of the amount and/or duration of unemployment benefits, which is closely related to the social security of the unemployed;
- the imposition of sanctions (e.g., by imposing ineligibility periods in the event that reasonable work is refused);
- the creation of financial incentives for the take-up of work;
- an intensification of individual support.

These approaches will now be discussed in greater detail in relation to current practices and debates in Germany.

Social security during unemployment

In current political discussions, the high amount of unemployment benefit paid in Germany is often cited as a reason for the country's high unemployment. It is argued that the incentives provided for the take-up of low-paid employment in particular are too low, since the achievable net income either does not or only insufficiently exceed the previously received unemployment benefits.

If one considers the relative level of unemployment benefits in Germany, note must be taken that these benefits stand at 60 per cent or 67 per cent (for individuals with children) of previous net income, and that unemployment relief stands at 53 per cent or 57 per cent (for those with children), and that these amounts are not subject to tax. Following OECD calculations from 1996, Germany comes nowhere near the top of the list in an international comparison, but, instead, somewhere in the middle – especially where financial provision for the short-term unemployed is concerned.[1] The appropriate wage replacement rates, for example in Denmark and the Netherlands, are, in part, substantially higher (see Figure 13.1).[2]

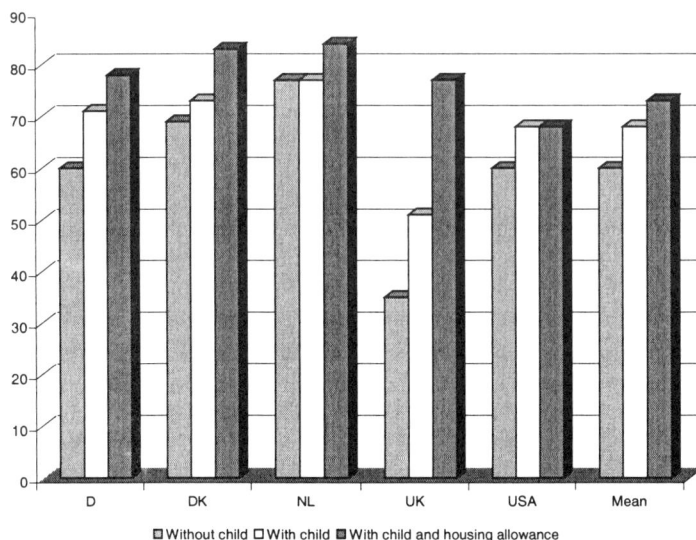

□ Without child □ With child ■ With child and housing allowance

Figure 13.1   Wage replacement rates for the short-term unemployed (1994)

Source: OECD, 1996.

Only the wage replacement rate for long term unemployment is comparatively high in Germany – both for persons with no children as also in the comparison of claims of long term unemployed persons with children, including housing benefits. But again, in the case of the latter, the level of wage replacement is higher in the Netherlands, Denmark, and even the United Kingdom than in Germany (see Figure 13.2).

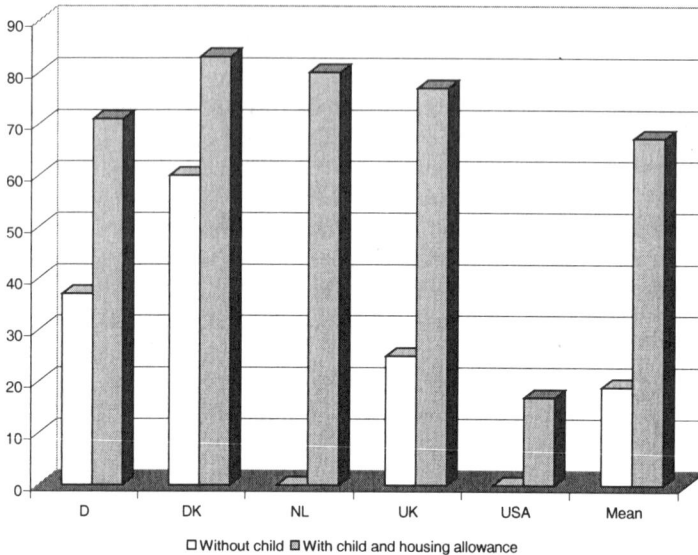

□ Without child ▣ With child and housing allowance

Figure 13.2   Wage replacement rate for the long term unemployed (60 months)

Source: OECD, 1996.

A particularly German feature is that unemployment relief is also related to the previous income from employment and amounts can therefore differ. Unemployment relief depends on previous length of employment as well as on age, and is granted after six months and for up to 32 months of the period of unemployment instead of the (higher) unemployment benefit. At the same time, however, this claim is linked to individual 'need', meaning that in couples households, for example, the income of the employed partner is taken into account, which means that claims are sometimes not granted at all. Therefore the rate provided represents an average value.

The share of those receiving of unemployment benefits provides some indication as to how restrictive the claim conditions are for granting wage replacement, although this can be influenced by the required duration of previous employment, regulations on need and, possibly, by a time restriction imposed on the claims. In Germany, this share stood at 74 per cent for the period 1995-98, according to Eichhorst, Profit and Thode (2001, p. 207), and was thus substantially lower than in Sweden (88 per cent), but also substantially higher than in France (46 per cent) and the Netherlands (48 per cent). In contrast, Germany's position regarding the share of unemployment benefits among the long term unemployed stands at 71 per cent, which is somewhere in the middle range. Significantly higher shares are found in Sweden (89 per cent), Denmark (80 per cent) and the United Kingdom (75 per cent) (Eichhorst, Profit and Thode, 2001, p. 207).

A further social security net for Germany's unemployed is the social assistance provided by the country's local authorities, or communes. In this case, the unemployed can, in the case of need, claim a socio-cultural minimum amount, as long as there are no, or only insufficient, claims for unemployment benefits. In addition, the communes offer social assistance recipients their own activation programmes, through the 'Support Into Work' (Hilfe zur Arbeit) scheme. With the growing number of unemployed social assistance recipients, the activation policy in the social assistance context has gained increasing significance in Germany.

In conclusion, it should be noted that social security for the unemployed in Germany is by no means higher than average in an international comparison. In fact, in many aspects, Germany can be found in the middle range. Nevertheless, there are calls for a reduction of the level of the wage replacement rates, and/or for a limit on the duration of unemployment relief, so that the incentives to encourage the take-up of lower-paid work can be increased. Otherwise, the argument continues, there would be the danger, especially among those unemployed who have previously worked in commercial sectors for above-average remuneration, that to accept work in lower-paid services areas would not be viable.

The Hartz Commission, too, had initially proposed cuts in the wage replacement rates as well as a time limit of unemployment relief, but, in the face of pressure from the unions, has dropped this idea. Instead, the concept presented in August 2002 includes stricter rulings on the reasonableness of work and greater flexibility, as well as a more consistent enactment of ineligibility periods, which are discussed below.

Reasonable work and ineligibility periods

The importance of the level of social protection during unemployment, in terms of the willingness of the unemployed to take up work, is by no means uncontroversial. In this context, concrete regulations regarding availability for the labour market and their practical implementation are also important. Thus, for example, Denmark and the Netherlands, which both have comparatively high wage replacement rates during unemployment, have relatively strict rules on reasonableness and other mechanisms for the consistent implementation of the 'Support and Demand' (Fördern und Fordern) principle.

Germany used to be considered a country with formally generally generous rules on the reasonableness of work. In recent years, however, these have been noticeably sharpened – most recently as part of the labour market policy reforms embodied in the Job-AQTIV law of early 2002. At the same time, statistics from the German Labour Office show that the number of imposed ineligibility periods in Germany continues to be fairly low and that by far the largest number of ineligibility periods is found in the case of employment terminated by the employer (cessation of work). By contrast, the number of ineligibility periods imposed in

1999 on the grounds of rejecting work stood at only 71,284, despite an increase over the previous year (Table 13.1). In contrast, both in terms of the overall numbers of unemployed, on average, 4.1 million in 1999, as well as the 3.739 million job placements processed by the Federal Labour Office, the total share of all ineligibility periods therefore stands at approximately 2 per cent.

Table 13.1   Ineligibility periods in Germany by reason, 1998/1999

	Termination of Employment		Rejecting employment		Expiration of entitlement to benefit	
	1998	**1999**	**1998**	**1999**	**1998**	**1999**
West Germany	203,044	209,087	47,935	56,496	8,700	11,864
East Germany	54,709	56,678	11,856	14,788	1,999	2,832
Total	257,753	265,765	59,791	71,284	10,699	14,696

Source: Bundesanstalt für Arbeit, 2000.

In an international comparison, ineligibility periods are rarely imposed in Germany. This occurs more frequently in, for example, the United States and in Switzerland (Eichhorst, Profit and Thode, 2001, p. 212). However, this could partly also be due to the fact that, at the time of this comparison, which relates to the period 1997/98, companies' demand for employees was substantially higher in these countries. A greater supply of vacancies implies tendentially greater opportunities to review the availability of those in unemployment.

On the whole, many countries apply ineligibility periods with restraint (Martin, 2000), possibly also due to potentially long-winded legal disputes. Additionally, actual implementation is influenced by the sanctions available. Against this backdrop, the Hartz Commission (2002) proposals for Germany envisage staggered future sanctions.

Fundamentally, a further element to be considered is that company vacancies can be applied only to a limited extent to review the willingness of the unemployed to work: If the employment services want to prove that they are indeed competent service providers in terms of personnel placement, they must be primarily concerned with finding suitable individuals rather than people about whose willingness and ability to work there is already some doubt. Otherwise, company assessments of the employment offices' placement services will be low, and they might in future decide not to supply details about vacancies to them. To prevent this from occurring, the employment placement services must ensure to undertake 'tailored placements'.

This problem can be avoided if opportunities to participate in labour market policy measures to monitor the availability of the unemployed are applied, which is being practiced in Germany both by the employment offices and by the local authorities with regard to their social assistance beneficiaries. The experience of the local authorities was that opportunities extended to social assistance recipients to undertake charitable or even regular work, were turned down by a number of those concerned and could also mean that these do not raise further claims.

An interesting illustration of how this might work in practice is the way in which the city of Cologne deals with young people who have neither a job nor a training place. Since mid-1999, unemployment benefits are granted to the under-25s only if they cannot accept employment or training on the grounds of ill health or similar reasons. Everyone else will only obtain social assistance benefits if they perform a corresponding service in return. Every young person in search of help is immediately offered a job, work experience, or training – i.e., already on the first day of the advice and guidance (Schwendy and Genz, 1999). This is underpinned by the consideration that allowing young people to become 'accustomed to' the receipt of unemployment benefits without providing a service in return should be avoided as much as possible. At the same time it must be noted, however, that such a strategy necessarily presupposes that there are also appropriate work opportunities. Against this background, such a strategy can tendentially only be implemented for a limited number of people, and it is important to monitor closely what happens to those who refuse help: Turning to crime or black-market work cannot be fundamentally excluded.

Recently, there have been some suggestions, for example those developed by the Munich-based ifo Institute, that propose to make adequate unemployment benefits for all social assistance recipients generally dependent on their acceptance of either low-paid employment in the private sector or work organized by the local authorities (Sinn et al., 2002).[3] It is questionable, however, whether the inherent effort and the costs required can be borne by the local authorities. A further question is how the repeatedly lamented competitive distortions already evident in a significantly lower level of publicly organized employment can be avoided with a view to small local enterprizes (Volkert, 2002).

To conclude, it must be noted sanctions for those unemployed who show a lacking willingness to work could be implemented with greater consistency. In this context, the Hartz Commission has proposed, among other things, to increase the demands on regional mobility, especially for younger single unemployed people, to make it easier to fill vacancies in regions with lower unemployment levels. Implementing sanctions is also to be facilitated so that, instead of the currently more or less standard 12-week ineligibility period, they will be staggered over a period of time.

Combination wage model projects

A further possibility to encourage the willingness to work among the unemployed and those receiving social assistance is the offer of financial incentives. Below, results to date and experience gained from such programmes and projects (in the current discussion often referred to as 'combination wages') are explained.

Over the past several years, many proposals and concepts have been developed in Germany to expand low-wage employment in order to also expand the employment opportunities especially of those with few formal qualifications and other groups with low earning potential (e.g., the long term unemployed, social assistance recipients). While some of these ideas focus on supporting companies (e.g., by subsidizing the employers' social insurance contributions), other proposals have at their core an increase in the achievable net income by granting income allowances for those in employment. Yet other proposals contain a combination of allowances both to employers and employees. After a series of calculations and simulations (Bender et al., 1999; Bender and Rudolph, 1999; Buslei and Steiner, 1999; Wagner et al., 1999) showed that the costs of across-the-board and unlimited subsidies for low-income jobs were very high while the achievable employment effect was very low, a number of model projects, limited both geographically and in terms of time, have been implemented, which are concerned exclusively with supporting new employment. The underlying idea was to test how far it would be possible to create new employment in this way.

The idea of in-work benefit to employees is being tested within the framework of the Mainz model (initially operating in selected employment office areas in Rhineland-Palatinate and Brandenburg; since March 2002, it has been operational throughout Germany). Projects on 'Einstiegsgeld' (in-work benefit) are also being carried out in Baden-Wuerttemberg,[4] in projects in Cologne and the Rhein-Sieg authority,[5] as well as in North-Rhine Westphalia's Duisburg employment office (PLUSLohn) (see Table 13.2).[6]

Table 13.2   Model projects and programmes to test income allowances

Federal State	Concept	Target group	Type of support	Duration of Support
Baden-Wuerttemberg	Einstiegsgeld (in-work benefit)	Long term unemployed, social security recipients	A share of the wages is not counted against social assistance claim	12 months
Germany-wide (since March 2002)	Mainz model	Low earners	In-work benefit	36 months
City of Cologne	Para.18, BSHG	Social assistance recipients	In-work benefit	12 months
Employment Office Duisburg	PLUSLohn	Unemployed with low benefit entitlements	In-work benefit	12 months

Source: Author's own compilation.

In all of the mentioned projects and programmes, figures on the support provided to date are on the low side and, in some cases, far lower than the originally forecast quantitative targets. This is true especially for the support based on the Mainz model, under which about 1,000 job placements had been supported in the original regions by the end of February 2002. Since employment had been terminated again in 400 cases, the number of support cases to date stood at approximately 600. Likewise, implementation at the federal level has been relatively slow since March

2002. The projects of Baden-Wuerttemberg's and North-Rhine Westphalia's social services offices have also not been able to achieve high case numbers: On average, approximately between 50 and 60 persons were supported through such projects in these local authorities up to the end of 2001.

The number of beneficiaries in the PLUSLohn project in Duisburg is noticeably higher: Between September 1998 and March 2000, 501 persons were placed into jobs (of whom 194 people received no support). Of these, 68.5 per cent were placed in temporary employment agencies (cf. Arbeitsamt Duisburg, 2001). In many cases, however, the reintegration was not sustained, as two-thirds of the placed individuals became unemployed again within the first six months. This is probably linked to the fact that the employment conditions in temporary employment agencies are generally somewhat unstable.

According to the experience to date, the hitherto low take-up of in-work benefits can be explained by several different reasons:

- Companies have not illustrated in practice the frequently argued theory of large numbers of unfilled vacancies in the low-wage area. In none of the model projects and programmes have the implementing institutions (primarily employment and social service offices, in some cases also other organizations) been informed of vacancies on a large scale.
- Where existing openings in the low-wage area could not be filled, this was, according to the experience recorded, either not at all or only in small part due to a lacking willingness to work on the part of individuals, in whose employment companies would have been interested. Rather, applicants often did not meet the employers' demands, or their work take-up failed for other reasons – such as, for example, the incompatibility of work and family life, lacking childcare facilities, or mobility problems (e.g., no access to a car, poor or non-existent public transport).
- In some cases, in-work benefit was also not utilized because the companies prefer to take advantage of wage subsidies for those hired from the target groups. To use these in tandem with granting in-work benefit to employees is not possible or permitted only in exceptional circumstances (Cologne project).

Whether and to what extent the projects have succeeded in motivating individuals to take up employment, which they would not have done without the additional allowance, and to fill vacancies that would otherwise have remained open, cannot at this stage be answered satisfactorily. If those concerned were previously long term unemployed or in receipt of social assistance (as in the case of 'Einstiegsgeld', or in-work benefit, and in the Cologne example), an additional incentive to work could be more readily assumed in these cases than in programmes with less tightly defined target groups. The latter is true especially for the Mainz model support, whose target group is defined exclusively by the level of domestic income following work take-up.

Another important question is also the extent to which those often primarily targeted to participate in such projects (i.e., those with few formal qualifications and the long term unemployed) actually benefit from this support. Initial evaluations of employment structures in the projects illustrate that this depends quite substantially on the way in which the preconditions for support are organized. Without limiting support to such groups, the proportion of long term unemployed has so far evidently been much lower: While, for example, in the Cologne model, over 70 per cent of the supported persons had previously been long term unemployed, this applies to only about one-fifth of the supported employees in the Mainz model. Smaller discrepancies can be discerned in the proportion of those with few formal qualifications (Table 13.3).

Table 13.3   Employment structure in the model projects and programmes

Model Project/Programme	Proportion of Women	Proportion of previously long term unemployed	Proportion of those with few formal qualifications
Einstiegsgeld (in-work benefit)	77 %	*	Almost 50 %
Mainz Model[7]	64.5 %	12.9 %	56.5 %
City of Cologne	42 of 81	Roughly 70 %	Almost 60 %
PLUSLohn, Duisburg	Small	*	*

*   *No data available*

Source: Author's own compilation, based on Dann et al., 2002; Hollederer et al., 2002; Czommer and Weinkopf, 2002; Arbeitsamt Duisburg, 2002.

Based on the experience to date, support for women in these projects is above average: In the Mainz model, the proportion of women constitutes 64.5 per cent, while in the case of the Einstiegsgeld (in-work benefit) project in Baden-Württemberg, it is as high as 77 per cent, which, in both cases, corresponds to the high proportion of part-time employment. In contrast, the gender proportion is virtually equally balanced in the case of the Cologne project (42 women and 39 men). In the PLUSLohn project in Duisburg, on the other hand, men are in the clear majority, which could be due to the fact that more than two-thirds of those placed worked in temporary employment, which organize operations primarily in the manufacturing sector.

A large proportion of women can be regarded as being both positive (in the sense of additional opportunities) and negative (in the sense that this could entrench, if not strengthen, the already inferior pay opportunities for women in the labour market). The latter could especially be true if, in the course of subsidizing low-pay jobs, wages in the lower income segment were lowered significantly – one aspect of the ifo proposal (Sinn et al., 2002). More positive is the encouragement of part-time work and the greater support for women with children, as demonstrated, for example, in the Mainz model, which, evidently, is especially beneficial for single mothers. Similar comments can be made about Einstiegsgeld (in-work benefit). In this context, however, it is worth asking whether similar, or even better, results could have been achieved if the funding had been used to improve childcare facilities.

Some of the model projects and programmes, implicitly or explicitly contain a preference for part-time work, in which limits to support are not related to a specific hourly rate, but to the highest achievable monthly household income. Against this background, it is not surprising that, for example in the Mainz model, the support for part-time work constitutes two-thirds of the project. In the case of the Einstiegsgeld (in-work benefit) in Baden-Württemberg, support for part-time work stood as ahigh as 79 per cent (of which 44 per cent is subject to social insurance contributions, and 35 per cent falls below the mandatory social insurance contribution level (geringfügige Beschäftigung) (Dann et al., 2002, p. 79).

For the most part, those employed within the combination-wage model projects primarily work in service-sector activities – although covering a wide range of areas. Key areas are trade, gastronomy, and cleaning services, which, given the wage structures in these areas, is hardly surprising. In the case of PlusLohn in Duisburg, most of those are placed in temporary work agencies.[8]

The issue concerning the behaviour of employees once their in-work benefit expires is still a very open question. At best, the cessation of in-work benefit can be compensated by a corresponding increase in wages (or, in the case of part-time employment, by an increase in the number of hours worked) in the company.[9]

Overall, it must be noted that, based on the experience so far with combination wages, the take-up of work of persons from certain groups can be supported, but it is still unclear how great the deadweight losses are. In addition, to date the scales achieved have been rather limited. Moreover, these instruments tend to reach those unemployed persons who are fairly close to the labour market. Individuals who have been unemployed for a very long time or who have limitations due to health, addiction or personality problems, as well as older people or those with factors that hinder their placement into work, remain tendentially excluded (Kirchmann, Spermann and Volkert, 2000, p. 18), as they are generally not directly employable without prior support of complementary measures. Among Germany's long term unemployed, however, the number of such individuals is particularly pronounced.

Individual support: Profiling and development plans

A further approach in the activation for the unemployed is the intensive advice and guidance provided for unemployed people. The aim of this strategy is to identify, on the one hand, the individual abilities and potential and, on the other, the problems preventing the take-up of employment, and to develop an individual re-integration strategy based on this information. The early recognition of problems in the sense of 'profiling' (Eberts and O'Leary, 1997) and the establishment of individual development and support programmes have already been successfully tested in Germany, for example in a number of local settings in recent years. Now the Job-AQTIV law, implemented early this year, explicitly stipulates that employment services should apply these instruments to all unemployed jobseekers.

However, until now the employment offices have had neither the time nor the capacity to put this ambitious legal requirement into practice – and not only due to the 'placement scandal', which led to the establishment of the Hartz Commission. For within the framework of profiling, considerable personnel capacity is required not only to analyse, for all unemployed persons, all the factors, circumstances or deficits restricting the possibility of immediate re-integration into the workplace, but also to subsequently set up individual development plans setting out the agreed steps necessary on the road to re-integration into the labour market. Until now, however, a large part of Germany's employment services personnel did not deal with the immediate work placement and advisory work, but rather with the determination of output evaluation and grants and a number of other activities. Against this background, additional placement personnel has already been hired by the employment offices since the early part of 2002, and the most recent Hartz Commission (2002) proposals envisage further detailed restructuring in favour of placement personnel within the employment services.

The increased involvement of third parties (e.g. training institutions, private placement agencies, etc.) already envisaged in the Job-AQTIV law is to contribute to expanding the capacity for employee placement and advice for the unemployed. Nevertheless, this will require a certain start-up period, and cannot be effectively implemented immediately. Without appropriate personnel resources, there is the danger, however, that the ambitious aim – to carry out profiling for all unemployed people and to conclude individual re-integration agreements – will become discredited. To prevent this from happening, other countries have concentrated their profiling activities on certain groups of individuals, such as, for example, under-25-year-olds, and then gradually extended this to other groups. This could also be a feasible approach for Germany.

Individually tailored advice and support can be most easily offered and carried out without complicated agreement procedures if the responsibility remains with one central authority. Until now, in Germany, different institutions have been responsible for those receiving unemployment benefits and for social assistance recipients able to work. According to the vision of the Hartz Commission (2002), this will in future be changed by means of across-the-board 'Job Centres', which will, along the lines of already existing similar institutions, be responsible for both groups and work closely with a number of official bodies at the local levels.

Conclusions

We have shown that a number of different approaches for activating the unemployed are already being applied in Germany, but that, in certain areas, there is still a deficit in implementing them. This concerns, for example, the more consistent application of sanctions in the case of a lacking willingness to take up reasonable employment, the practical implementation of the undoubtedly ambitious provisions in the Job-AQTIV law on profiling and establishment of development plans, as well as the ideas developed by the Hartz Commission (2002) that are now to be put into action.

Regarding the level of social security for the unemployed in Germany, there must be a careful balance, in our view, as to whether this should indeed be a central approach for activation. Experience collected in other countries shows that successful activation for the unemployed is also possible with a high level of wage replacement, if other possibilities for activation are consistently applied and implemented. One must also take into consideration that social security cannot only be discussed under incentive aspects, but that it simultaneously has an important socio-political function to prevent or limit poverty in a given society (cf. also the contribution by Hanesch in this volume).

Activation for the unemployed alone cannot, however, solve all of Germany's current labour market problems. For a policy of activation makes more sense the greater the number of vacancies that need to be filled. In a global labour market deficit an activating labour market policy also requires, as will be shown below, complementing opportunities to qualify and employ the unemployed so that it does not run dry. On the other hand, it would not be enough to merely discuss activation for the unemployed. For, compared to other countries, Germany also has activation deficits with regard to the employment ratio of women. In order to increase this, the instruments discussed so far are only of limited value. Rather, fundamental changes of the basic conditions, both in terms of tax and social security laws, as well as in the area of childcare, would be valuable.

Towards a broad set of measures...

Both the very heterogeneous structure of unemployment, as well as current experience gained from the current combination-wage model projects, argue quite clearly that there are no simple patent recipes for unemployment reduction, or rather, for opening up new employment opportunities in Germany. Further, it seems short-sighted to put Germany's high unemployment primarily down to incentive problems in labour availability. Measured against the employment wishes of the population there is, rather, a deficit in employment opportunities, which cannot be remedied by labour market policy instruments alone.

Labour market policy can primarily contribute to filling vacancies more quickly and to qualitatively reduce the discrepancy between demand and supply on the labour market. This requires not only measures for the activation for the unemployed, but, increasingly, also educational efforts at all levels. This is borne out by Germany's poor results in the PISA study, as well as by the incessant complaints in some economic sectors concerning the lack of suitably qualified employees.

In a labour market such as Germany's, which continues to be influenced to a large degree by specialized vocational structures, vocational training qualifications continue to be highly important. Indeed, even supposedly 'simple' service sector activities, which figure so highly in the context of the combination-wage debate, by no means make low demands on an employee's subject knowledge and social competence (for further details: Weinkopf, 2002a). Against this backdrop, it would, in our view, be extremely problematic to reduce activities aimed at qualifying the unemployed (as well as the employed) in favour of combination wages or other subsidies of low-wage jobs, as has, on occasion, been demanded.

Especially among younger unemployed, there are many arguments in favour of stronger investment in their professional qualifications, if deficits are visible. Since the majority usually enjoy a comparatively good school education (Reinberg and Walwei, 2000), it should be possible to attract them with the appropriate opportunities. Flexible and modular possibilities to gain a qualification, including a high degree of practical orientation, would seem appropriate to significantly raise the willingness to train on both sides and the ability of the vocational training market to absorb these individuals. Also, young people who find learning more challenging can be reached with appropriately tailored measures, as illustrated both by the experience of the federal government's young persons' immediate assistance programme (Jugendsoforthilfeprogramm), and by corresponding programmes put in place in a number of the federal states. Subsidized employment should be the exception rather than the rule for younger poorly qualified people, since this sends out the wrong kinds of long term signals and runs counter to the economic dynamism (Reinberg and Walwei, 2000, p. 23).

Despite their formal qualifications, older unemployed people often have particular difficulties in finding a new job, because companies in Germany have a long way to go to embrace the 'culture of work in old age'. If, among the younger and middle-aged age groups, greater emphasis were placed on promoting initial and further training, the supply pressure on the presumably continuously shrinking number of simple jobs would be reduced, which would thereby improve the employment opportunities of older people with low qualifications. Moreover, incentives still in place to exclude older employees need to be dismantled, and basic conditions and strategies need to be developed or formulated to emphasize better utilization of the know-how of older employees.

In this context, different variables of combination wages can be very suitable, but they should be limited to specific target groups and for certain periods of time. For the foreseeable future, within the scope of an activating labour market policy, it will not be possible to forego the publicly supported employment measures, which has been demanded from a number of sides, since the re-integration ratio following job creation and structural adjustment measures are comparatively low. Although the integration of the unemployed into employment must, without doubt, be the central goal of labour market policy, it nevertheless also needs support measures for those who cannot directly be integrated into the current labour market situation – in part also to maintain or increase their employability. Publicly supported employment is the only measure in which the decision on who is employed is not subject merely to business calculations and decision criteria. Rather, the employment offices have the opportunity to directly target unemployed people with specific placement barriers, who, in the framework of company hiring practices – even with the granting of integration allowances – often have no chance at all.

Measures outside of companies are also still needed to monitor the willingness to work of those unemployed about whom there are doubts, since relying on company vacancies – as explained above – contains considerable risks in this respect. Such measures should, however, be both directed at specific groups and also be limited in terms of duration. They should also primarily focus on those who, because of their age and/or their low educational and/or vocational qualifications, really do not have other opportunities. They must even be embedded into comprehensive approaches to maintain or recreate the employability of the unemployed.

...that also focus on the employment rate of women

In an international comparison, Germany not only has an above-average unemployment rate, but also a rather low employment rate, which, in addition to comparatively low proportion of older employees, primarily has to do with the below-average female employment rate. International comparisons also show that countries successful in terms of employment do not necessarily demonstrate a consistently stronger wage spread (contrary to frequent claims) but stand out by the fact that domestic and person-related services are organized to a much higher degree as public or business services (Bosch and Wagner, 2002).

Traditionally, such services have been – and still are – performed without pay in Germany, especially by women outside of the employment market. This is closely linked to the female employment rate in two respects. On the one hand, the need for external support in households and the family increases with the number of working women. On the other hand, these activities are areas in which women traditionally constitute a high proportion of employees. If employment opportunities were to be widened in this area, women would benefit to an above-average extent, which, in turn, would affect the increase of the female employment rate.

For the sustained promotion of female employment in Germany, the tax and social insurance conditions, which are still closely oriented along the family and partnership model of the 'single-earner family', would have to be modified. This affects in particular:

- married couples' tax allowances;
- free co-insurance of the non-employed partner in the mandatory care and health insurance;
- comprehensive provision for dependents in pension insurance;
- the comparatively high income level, below which marginal part-time work is not liable for the regular social insurance contributions (for more detail, cf. Bittner et al., 1998; Dingeldey, 1999).

Many other countries have withdrawn such regulations in recent years through reforms, or have introduced new ones favouring egalitarian familial employment patterns (cf. Dingeldey, 1999, pp. 121), such as, for example, individual taxation for married couples instead of a joint tax assessment.[10] Corresponding reform proposals have been repeatedly blocked in Germany in recent years, and not even the current Hartz Commission proposals (2002) take up this need for reform. Instead, an increase of the income limit for marginal part-time jobs of 500 euros has been planned in the area of domestic services.

On the other hand, in Germany (and in particular West Germany) there is considerable need to catch up with regard to the demand for childcare places and all-day school education:

- There are places in public childcare establishments for only 6 per cent of all children under the age of three. In Belgium, Denmark, Finland, France, and Sweden, the level of provision is much higher, standing at between 21 per cent and 48 per cent.
- For three- to six-year-olds, the provision in Germany, at 91 per cent, is much better; however, it must be noted that nursery opening hours are often very short and – if at all – can only be combined with short part-time work.
- The supply of childcare places for school children continues to be extremely low in Germany. Especially France (30 per cent) and Sweden (64 per cent) have a much higher level of provision in this regard. In addition to care provision for school children, the organization and scope of school teaching plays a central role. While in Germany all-day schools are an exception rather than the rule, this is completely different in other European countries. The average number of school teaching hours in Belgium, France, the United Kingdom, Italy, Luxembourg, the Netherlands and Portugal is significantly higher than in Germany (Thenner, 2000).

The childcare infrastructure undoubtedly is of central importance for the opportunities to expand female employment, which the European Commission also reiterates continually:

'Family circumstances are without doubt one of the main determinants of the overall lower employment rates for women than for men.(...) Without better childcare and a greater sharing of family responsibilities it will be impossible to close the gender gap.' (European Commission, 1998, pp. 14)[11]

A considerable expansion of all-day schools, as has been promised by all the main political parties in the last German elections, would be only a first, but nevertheless a very important step towards facilitating the compatibility of work life and family. Further measures in the area of childcare should follow; here not only a quantitative increase but also the creation of flexible and qualitatively high-level childcare is vital. Dependable care for a few hours in the morning is in no way sufficient to meet the increasing demands for flexibility made on all employees in virtually all economic sectors. Without the increased utilization of the potential of women in the labour market, the activation strategy in Germany would stop at the halfway point.

Notes

1	For the organization of social security in EU member states, MISSOC, 2001 (http://europa.eu.int/comm/employment_social/missoc2001/index_en.htm)		provides more current information. The OECD calculations used in this text are slightly older, since they are able to provide a comparison with the United States.

2   Since the OECD does not publish its concrete mode of calculation, main attention should focus on the relations rather than on the absolute level of the respectively calculated wage replacement rates.

3   The core of the proposal asks how the incentives for the take-up of low-paid jobs can be substantially increased. This is to be realized by means of massive reductions of claims for social assistance for those able to work. Those who do not find work in companies should receive only the current level of unemployment benefit, if a work organized by the local authority is taken up. Tax credits based on the American EITC are to be introduced as a complement.

4   Similar projects are also being conducted in Hesse and in Bremen. Since case numbers have until now been very low and there are no additional data on, for example, employee structures, we focus here on Baden-Wuerttemberg's experience to date.

5   Due to the low number of case numbers in the Rhein-Sieg authority, we are not focusing on this project any further. For further details, cf. Czommer and Weinkopf, 2002.

6   For details on the respective support regulations cf. Kaltenborn, 2001; Weinkopf, 2002a/b.

7   All data on the Mainz model refer to the situation in late February 2002 in the originally supported regions. Following the Germany-wide expansion of the project, the proportion of women, part-time employees, and previously long term unemployed people has risen, while the share of those with few formal qualifications (i.e., without completed vocational training) has fallen to almost 39 per cent (figures as of end of August 2002).

8   The promotion of temporary employment by means of combination wages does not seem unproblematic, since only very few companies in this area are bound by wage agreements and wages are about 40 per cent lower than the national average, according to existing information. Moreover, four-fifths of temporary work placements in Germany continue to be concentrated in industrial activities. Against this background, the promotion of jobs in temporary employment agencies work is only partially suitable to help achieve the target of expanding service sector employment in Germany.

9   In the case of in-work benefit (Einstiegsgeld) in Baden-Wuerttemberg, in the spring of 2001, two-thirds of the 71 people continued to rely on social assistance following the cessation of support, but also, with few exceptions, continued to be employed (Dann et al., 2001, pp. 71).

10 The corresponding tax law reforms in other countries occurred in two waves: In the early 1970s, there was a (far-reaching) individualization in Austria (1971), Sweden (1971), and Denmark (1970); they were followed, in the 1980s, by the Netherlands (1984) and the United Kingdom (1989), as well as Spain (1989) and Belgium (1989), which introduced partial individualization. Cf. Dingeldey, 2000, p. 25.

11 A survey of 213 female single-parent recipients of social assistance, asked for the reasons why they are not currently working, found that, in 62 per cent of all cases, inflexible or lacking childcare was a determining factor (cf. Dann, Kirchmann and Spermann, 2002, p. 173). Also Engelbrecht/Jungkunst (2001, p. 3) underline the central position of childcare in the improvement of employment opportunities for single mothers.

References

Arbeitsamt Duisburg (2001), *PLUSLohn*, Duisburg.

Bender, S., Kaltenborn, B., Rudolph, H. and Walwei, U. (1999), 'Förderung eines Niedriglohnsektors. Die Diagnose stimmt, die Therapie noch nicht', *IAB-Werkstattbericht* (6), 14. Juni 1999, Nürnberg.

Bender, S. and Rudolph, H. (1999), 'Kosten eines gestaffelten Zuschusses zu den Sozialversicherungsbeiträgen. Simulation des Zuschussbedarfs auf der Basis des Jahreszeitraummaterials der Beschäftigtenstatistik von 1997', *IAB-Werkstattbericht* (8), 11. Juni 1999, Nürnberg.

Bittner, S., Dingeldey I., Strauf, S. and Weinkopf, C. (1998), 'Für eine Reform der geringfügigen Beschäftigung', *Projektbericht des Instituts Arbeit und Technik 1998-02*, Gelsenkirchen.

Bosch, G. and Wagner, A. (2002), 'Nachhaltige Dienstleistungspolitik', in G. Bosch, P. Hennicke, J. Hilbert, K. Kristof and G. Scherhorn (eds), *Die Zukunft von Dienstleistungen. Ihre Auswirkung auf Arbeit, Umwelt und Lebensqualität*, Campus, Frankfurt am Main/New York, pp. 482-512.

Bundesanstalt für Arbeit (2000), *Geschäftsbericht 1999*, Nürnberg.

Buslei, H. and Steiner, V. (1999), 'Beschäftigungseffekte von Lohnsubventionen im Niedriglohnbereich', *Schriftenreihe des ZEW* 42, Baden-Baden.

Czommer, L. and Weinkopf, C. (2002), 'Modellprojekte zur Erprobung des § 18 Absatz 5 BSHG in Nordrhein-Westfalen', in S. Dann, A. Kirchmann, A. Spermann and J. Volkert (eds), *Kombi-Einkommen – Ein Weg aus der Sozialhilfe?*, Nomos, Baden-Baden, pp. 87-105.

Dann, S., Kirchmann, A., Spermann, A. and Volkert, J. (2002), 'Das Einstiegsgeld – eine zielgruppenorientierte negative Einkommensteuer: Konzeption, Umsetzung und eine erste Zwischenbilanz nach 15 Monaten in Baden-Württemberg', in S. Dann, A. Kirchmann, A. Spermann and J. Volkert (eds), *Kombi-Einkommen – Ein Weg aus der Sozialhilfe?*, Nomos, Baden-Baden, pp. 67-86.

Dingeldey, I. (1999), 'Begünstigungen und Belastungen familialer Erwerbs- und Arbeitszeitmuster in Steuer- und Sozialversicherungssystemen. Ein Vergleich zehn europäischer Länder', *Graue Reihe des Instituts Arbeit und Technik* 4. Gelsenkirchen.

Dingeldey, I. (2000), 'Einkommensteuersysteme und familiale Erwerbsmuster im europäischen Vergleich', in I. Dingeldey (ed.), *Erwerbstätigkeit und Familie in Steuer- und Sozialversicherungssystemen. Begünstigungen und Belastungen verschiedener familialer Erwerbsmuster im Ländervergleich*, Leske & Budrich, Opladen, pp. 11-47.

Eberts, R.W. and O'Leary, C.J. (1997), 'Früherkennung (Profiling) von Langzeitarbeitslosen und ihre Überweisung in Arbeitsmarktmaßnahmen: Erfahrungen und Lehren aus mehreren Ländern', *inforMISEP* (60), pp. 34-43.

Eichhorst, W., Profit, S. and Thode, E. (2001), *Benchmarking Deutschland: Arbeitsmarkt und Beschäftigung*, Bericht der Arbeitsgruppe Benchmarking und der Bertelsmann-Stiftung, Berlin/Heidelberg/New York.

Engelbrech, G. and Jungkunst, M. (2001), 'Arbeitsmarktanalyse: Alleinerziehende Frauen haben besondere Beschäftigungsprobleme', *IAB-Kurzbericht* (2), 16. Februar 2001, Nürnberg.

European Commission (1998), *Employment Rates Report 1998. Employment Performance in The Member States*, Brussels.

Hartz-Kommission (2002), *Moderne Dienstleistungen am Arbeitsmarkt, Vorschläge der Kommission zum Abbau der Arbeitslosigkeit und zur Umstrukturierung der Bundesanstalt für Arbeit*, 16 August 2002, no location.

Hollederer, A., Kaltenborn, B., Rudolph, H., Vanselow, A., Weinkopf, C. and Wiedemann, E. (2002), *Vom arbeitsmarktpolitischen Sonderprogramm CAST zur bundesweiten Erprobung des Mainzer Modells*, Forschungsverbund 'Evaluierung CAST', 2. Zwischenbericht, Bonn (forthcoming).

Kaltenborn, B. (2001), 'Kombilöhne in Deutschland – eine systematische Übersicht'. *IAB-Werkstattbericht* (14), Nürnberg.

Kirchmann, A., Spermann, A. and Volkert, J. (2000), 'Modellversuch „Einstiegsgeld in Baden-Württemberg". Grundkonzeption, Varianten, erste Beobachtungen', *IAW-Mitteilungen* (2), pp. 15-22.

Martin, P.J. (2000), 'What Works Among Active Labour Market Policies: Evidence from OECD Countries' Experiences', *OECD Economic Studies* 30, Paris.

OECD (1996), *Employment Outlook*, Paris.

OECD (1997), *Employment Outlook*, Paris.

Reinberg, A. and Walwei, U. (2000), 'Qualifizierungspotenziale von "Nicht-formal-Qualifizierten"', *IAB-Werkstattbericht* (10), Nürnberg.

Schwendy, A. and Genz, H. (1999), 'Arbeitsamt und Sozialamt als Partner. Erfahrungen des Kölner Sozialamtes mit einem "Bündnis für Beschäftigung"', in Stadt Köln (ed.), *Zukunft der Sozialhilfe. Gemeinsam für junge Arbeitslose*, Köln, pp. 18-28.

Sinn, H.-W., Holzner, C., Meister, W., Ochel, W. and Werding, M. (2002), 'Aktivierende Sozialhilfe. Ein Weg zu mehr Beschäftigung und Wachstum', *IFO-Schnelldienst* (9), München.

Thenner, M. (2000), 'Familienpolitik als Politik zur Vereinbarkeit von Familie und Beruf – Geldwerte Leistungen, zeitwerte Anrechte, familienunterstützende Infrastruktur und ihre Auswirkungen auf das Familienverhalten', in I. Dingeldey (ed.), *Erwerbstätigkeit und Familie in Steuer- und Sozialversicherungssystemen. Begünstigungen und Belastungen verschiedener familialer Erwerbsmuster im Ländervergleich*, Leske & Budrich, Opladen, pp. 95-129.

Volkert, J. (2002), 'Lohnabstandsgebot, Verpflichtung zur Arbeit und Sozialhilfefallen', in S. Dann, A. Kirchmann, A. Spermann and J. Volkert (eds), *Kombi-Einkommen – Ein Weg aus der Sozialhilfe?*, Nomos, Baden-Baden, pp. 11-32.

Wagner, G., Schupp, J., Zwiener, R. and Scholz, J. (1999), 'Zuschüsse zu den Sozialversicherungsbeiträgen im Niedriglohnbereich: Wenig zielgerichtet und teuer', *DIW-Wochenbericht* (27), pp. 499-509.

Weinkopf, C. (2002a), *Förderung der Beschäftigung von gering Qualifizierten: Kombilöhne als Dreh- und Angelpunkt?*, Friedrich-Ebert-Stiftung, Gesprächskreis Arbeit und Soziales, Bonn.

Weinkopf, C. (2002b), 'Subventionierte Niedriglohnjobs – (k)ein Königsweg zu mehr Beschäftigung', in G. Bosch, P. Hennicke, J. Hilbert, K. Kriftof and G. Scherhorn (eds), *Die Zukunft von Dienstleistungen. Ihre Auswirkung auf Arbeit, Umwelt und Lebensqualität*, Campus, Frankfurt am Main/New York, pp. 305-327.

Chapter 14

Activation in the Western Europe of the 1990s: Did it make a difference?

Bjørn Hvinden

Introduction

A basic idea behind activation is that it is better that people work than only live on public cash transfers. Public authorities should therefore do what they can to enable and encourage the individual to take part in gainful employment. This includes ensuring that the working of the social protection system, for instance through weakly co-ordinated provisions or a relative generosity of benefits, does not make it more difficult than necessary to achieve this objective. Different practical implications may be drawn from this general idea. More or less emphasis may be given to the goals of providing people at the margins of the labour market with better opportunities through the acquisition of new qualifications, skills and self-confidence. Similarly, more or less efforts may be addressed to tightening the cash benefit system for people out of work. The latter option may be perceived either as an alternative or a complement to providing people with new opportunities (Hvinden et al., 2001; Van Berkel and Møller, 2002).

From the late 1980s activation became – together with pension reform – one of the new key issues of reform in social protection in Western European welfare states (Clasen, 2001). In the recent policy discourse great expectations have been directed towards activation. It has not only been seen as a means of ameliorating the consequences of high and prolonged unemployment but also as an instrument to diminish economic hardship and marginalization and promote broader participation in employment more generally. In the early 1990s the Organization for Economic Co-operation and Development (OECD) launched a far-ranging review of member states' labour market situation. On the basis of this the organization formulated an ambitious reform programme for member states' policy; the OECD Jobs Strategy. One of the recommendations was to strengthen active labour market policies and reinforce their effectiveness (OECD, 1995, p. 15), based on the following rationale: 'Helping the unemployed to become competitive in the labour market is preferable to providing them only with income support' (ibid, p. 27). The OECD has later undertaken detailed reviews of the extent to which member states have reformed their policies (OECD, 1998, 1999a). Within the European Union the emerging Employment Strategy has taken up the same ideas, for instance as expressed in the agreements reached at European Council meetings in Essen 1994 and Luxembourg 1997. In the Presidency conclusions from the Luxembourg meeting a separate paragraph had the heading 'Transition from passive measures to active measures'. Here it was said that each member state would endeavour to increase significantly the number of persons benefiting from training and other active measures to improve their employability (Presidency conclusions, 1997, pp. 53-54). The Employment Strategy was later followed up through successive EU guidelines for national employment plans 1998-2002 (e.g. European Commission, 1997, 1998a, 1998b, 1999). Among other things this meant that the EU Commission and other member states were to monitor and assess the extent to which individual member states have moved towards activation.

In this article I will discuss three more specific issues:

1. First, what meanings have the term 'activation' been associated with? I will argue that we find a variety of meanings that may be interrelated but not completely overlapping.
2. Second, is it possible to demonstrate that Western European welfare states moved towards activation to any substantial degree in the course of the 1990s? I will maintain that the answer will depend on which of the meanings of 'activation' we take as our frame of reference.
3. Third, what evidence do we have about the impact of activation policies on the labour market performance of the countries in question? My conclusion is that there is some evidence for a positive relationship between strengthening of activation and improved labour market performance although the correlation is not very strong. A crucial question is what this correlation means.

Some meanings of activation

The users of the term 'activation' have not always been clear about exactly what kind of aims and reforms they have in mind. Often the user have relied on intuitive denotations and the generally more positive connotations of the word 'active' compared to 'passive'. The following is an attempt to make the differences in the underlying meanings more explicit.

*   To increase the proportion of economically active people: Generally speaking, the term may be used to refer to policy efforts to increase the proportion of people of working age who are 'economically active', that is, engaged in gainful employment. More specifically, one tends to be concerned with the proportion of people of working age who are in receipt of some sort of public income maintenance support, and usually people who have been in this situation for a prolonged period of time; e.g. as long-term unemployed or on long-term sickness leave. It may include both people who have been employed previously and those who have never been in regular work. In both categories we find unpaid family carers, usually women, who look after children or elderly or disabled family members.[1] Originally activation tended to be concentrated on the 'mainstream' unemployed, often male breadwinners who

were temporary out of work and claiming unemployment benefit. More recently activation has been widened out to other groups with a more marginal labour market position. Thus the target group now includes social assistance claimants (Lødemel and Trickey, 2001; Johansson, 2001; Hvinden et al., 2001; Heikkilä and Keskitalo, 2001; Hanesch, 2001; Saraceno, 2002), lone parents (Millar and Rowlingson, 2001) and people with disabilities (Van Oorschot and Hvinden, 2001; OECD, forthcoming).

- To increase the volume of activating policy measures: At a practical level governments may follow up their understanding of activation by offering a broad range of specific measures and targeted services meant to improve people's opportunities and prospects in the labour market. These may vary from short-term courses in active job-search to more elaborate forms of counselling, guidance, advice and coaching, testing of aptitudes, abilities and skills, referral to vocational training and education courses, subsidies to temporary or permanent jobs and other forms of job creation, help to move to other areas with more jobs, providing people with better clothes before job interviews, etc. If a higher proportion of people out of work participate in such specific measures the overall policy effort can be said to have become more 'active'. But it should be noted that the general aims of increasing labour market participation and/or diminishing economic inactivity may be pursued by other means as well; for instance through macro economic policies to increase demand, regional policies to support local business development, structural policies to stimulate technical innovation and organizational modernization, or care policies to provide more and affordable kindergartens and secure the availability of services for elderly and disabled people. Thus we may distinguish between 'activation policies' about specific activating measures in a more narrow sense and 'employment policies' about efforts to promote gainful employment and economic activity more generally (e.g. Walwei and Werner, 2001). 'Active labour market policies' (ALMP) fall somewhere between activation and employment policies. As originally set up in Sweden and other countries ALMP were an integrated part of attempts to facilitate and speed up structural change in the labour market. By means of guidance, job brokerage, job subsidization, training and retraining and financial support to move to localities where business was expanding, ALMP were meant to stimulate both labour demand and supply, and improve the match between them (Janoski, 1994; Lindqvist and Marklund, 1995; Wilensky, 1992, 2002).

- To prevent negative effects of passivity among people out of work): Sometimes policy-makers emphasize the ambition to prevent the assumed harming effects of being unemployed for prolonged periods. The experience of economic passivity is believed to be associated with social passivity more generally, diminishing the person's self-confidence and leading to feelings of insufficiency, insecurity and depression. The social distance to working life is supposed to be increasing, and as a consequence it may become more difficult for the person to return to employment when the demand eventually will increase again, creating a risk for permanent economic and social exclusion. Participation in activating measures, even if they are fairly short-term and not involving substantial learning contents should from this perspective have the potential of diminishing this risk.

- To increase the relative spending on active forms of social protection: The term 'activation' may also be adopted to characterize changes of the overall social protection system. In this context those parts of the protection system that mainly provide income maintenance for people outside gainful employment are referred to as 'passive benefits', regardless of what level of unpaid activity and participation the recipients are involved in. By contrast, 'active benefits' are construed as those parts of the social protection system that aim to make people less dependent on income maintenance support in the future. These parts could include transfer payments providing income cash benefits for people participating in vocational training, education and rehabilitation, and/or covering course fees, transport, technical equipment and other expenses related the operation of the services or measures in question (e.g. OECD, 1994). If one manages to increase the proportion of total expenditure on social protection that goes to active benefits this may be regarded as an 'activation' of the social protection system. Obviously activation in this sense may be achieved either through an increase in absolute terms in the spending on active benefits or through a decrease in absolute terms in the spending on passive benefits. In other words, an increase in relative spending on active benefits will be more remarkable if the total costs of the social protection system remain stable or become smaller, than if total costs increase at the same time.

- To give a stronger emphasis on activity requirements in income maintenance schemes: 'Activation' may also be understood as introducing a stronger element of conditionality in the granting of income maintenance benefits (e.g. Clasen et al., 2001; Hvinden et al., 2001). This involves demanding that claimants should fulfil certain activity requirements as condition for being awarded a benefit or in order to continue to receive this benefit. For instance, it has for a long time been common to require that people claiming unemployment benefit should be able to demonstrate that they are 'actively seeking work'. Similarly, people claiming incapacity benefits should be able to document that they are going through appropriate medical treatment or rehabilitation. Such requirements may be reinforced or existing requirements enforced more vigorously, for instance by demanding that people in receipt of benefits should accept to take part in the vocational training or rehabilitation courses they offered by social security or employment services, with the threat that their benefit will be reduced or stopped if they refuse. A special case of activity requirements is when claimants of means-tested social assistance are imposed the duty to carry out special work tasks in return for the financial support. The term 'workfare' should be reserved for the latter kind of activation but some authors prefer to include a broader range of activity requirements under this term (e.g. Pierson, 1994, p. 116; Geldof, 1999, p. 15; Trickey and Lødemel, 2001).

- To give stronger financial incentives to seek or remain in paid work: There has recently been a widespread concern for the assumed disincentive effects of relatively generous income maintenance benefits (e.g. OECD, 1998a; Bosco and Chassard, 1999). By disincentive effects are for instance meant situations where a person obtains the same or even a higher level of net income out of work (through the combined effect of benefits schemes and tax rules) compared with what he or she is able to achieve through paid work, or at least, where the difference between the two is fairly small. It assumed that likely consequences of this situation are that unemployed person will be less active in looking for a new job and that persons who have had their work capacity reduced (temporarily or permanently) will be less motivated to continue to work and/or go through vocational rehabilitation in order to return to work. On the basis of this form of reasoning the financial incentives to work can be improved through reducing the net replacement rate of cash benefits (the degree to which net income out of work corresponds to income in work), by reducing the duration of the period in which the benefits are payable, and/or by tightening the eligibility criteria for benefits. In order words, a way of 'activating' income maintenance schemes and their beneficiaries might simply be to undertake these and related forms of cuts.

As indicated by this short and simplified presentation the boundaries between the different meanings of activation are not very sharp and clear (Drøpping et al., 1999; Gilbert and Van Voorhis, 2001). Neither are the meanings always mutually exclusive; it is possible to combine several of them in various ways. Thus governments may adopt policies inspired by more than one of the meanings outlined here. Arguably the different meanings refer to elements that may complement each other or even serve as preconditions for each other.

At the same time one may ask whether there is any systematic or characteristic pattern in the relative weight that governments give to the various elements. For instance, governments may put the main emphasis on increasing the volume of active measures and providing people with new qualifications and better opportunities and prospects in the labour market. Alternatively, governments may put greater weight on reducing overall costs and improve work incentives by undertaking cuts in benefit schemes and/or reinforcing conditionalities. Generally speaking, one would expect welfare states with an established tradition for ALMP to favour the first option more strongly than countries with a tradition for less expansive or interventionist policies. On the other hand, financial constraints may be seen as forcing governments to limit their ambitions regarding the volume of specific active measures, as this – at least in the short-term – will increase public expenditure. Under strong budget restrictions the second option is likely to be perceived as the more attractive. Finally, it could also be that some countries will actually break with past policies, traditions or path-dependencies, adopting an innovative overall design of their policies in this area. This could also involve new and unexpected ways of combining the elements of activation we have indicated above.

A shift towards 'activation' in Western European countries?

We will examine to what extent a number of Western European countries have become more 'active' or at least experienced changes in line with one or several of the meanings of 'activation' outlined above. Here – as is often the case in cross-national research – we are constrained by the quality, completeness and comparability of existing macro-data, especially as these have been collected and presented by the OECD and the EU. One may of course raise doubt about the extent to which these data are really standardized and comparable and therefore refrain from using them. Our position, however, is more pragmatic. We will make use of the OECD and EU data as these are best available for the time being and see what overall picture we obtain by combining and analyzing them.

Table 14.1   Levels of overall labour market participation and gender gaps in labour market participation in twelve countries of Western Europe – 1990 and 2000

Country	(A) Overall rates of labour market participation (15-64 years)			(B) Gender gaps in the rate of labour market participation (15-64 years)		
	1990	**2000**	*Change 1990-2000*	**1990**	**2000**	*Change 1990-2000*
Denmark	82.5	80.0	*-2.5*	9.4	8.3	*-1.1*
Finland	76.6	74.3	*-2.3*	6.1	4.5	*-1.6*
Norway	77.1	80.7	*3.6*	12.7	8.3	*-4.4*
Sweden	84.6	78.9	*-5.7*	4.2	2.3	*-1.9*
Belgium	58.7	65.2	*6.5*	25.2	17.2	*-8.0*
France	66.0	68.0	*2.0*	17.8	12.7	*-5.1*
Germany *	69.3	72.2	*2.9*	24.5	17.9	*-6.6*
Netherlands	66.7	74.6	*7.9*	26.9	18.2	*-8.7*
Greece	59.1	63.3	*3.9*	34.2	27.4	*-6.8*
Portugal	70.9	71.1	*0.2*	23.2	15.2	*-8.0*
Spain	60.9	65.8	*4.9*	38.6	27.5	*-11.1*
UK	77.8	76.6	*-1.2*	21.0	7.7	*-13.5*

*   *1990-figures refer to the situation in the German Federal Republic before unification. The change estimates should be interpreted with caution since all countries except Finland and France had breaks in their time series affecting the homogeneity of data over time.*

Source: OECD, 2002a.

The selection of countries reviewed and compared here is also to some extent pragmatic. In principle, we are interested to achieve a complete picture as possible and would in principle like to include all EU member states plus Norway. Unfortunately up-to-date information about the volume of more specific activation measures is not available from all these countries.[2] Consequently we will focus on the twelve countries where the data – both general and specific time series – are fairly complete. We will concentrate on the changes that took place in the decade between 1990 and 2000.

Overall labour market participation: Eight of the twelve countries appeared to have a higher rate of overall labour market participation in 2000 than in 1990 (Table 14.1). The four countries experiencing a decrease in this decade, Denmark, Finland, Sweden and United Kingdom, had previously been among the countries with the highest rates of participation. The Netherlands had experienced the most notable increase in the overall rate of labour market participation. It is first of all the increased employment rate of women that has contributed to growth in overall labour market participation.

Gender equality in labour market participation: The difference in the rate of labour market participation of men and women is an important indicator of the potential for increasing the overall labour participation. The gender gap in labour market participation had become smaller in all twelve countries in 2000 compared with the situation in 1990 (Table 14.1). The changes between 1990 and 2000 tended to be most substantial in the countries with the larger gender gaps early in the period and smallest in the countries where the differences were already fairly limited. United Kingdom was to some extent an exception to this pattern since it had a medium gender gap in 1990 but the most substantial change in the following decade.

Table 14.2   Age differentials in labour market participation for men and women in twelve Western European countries – 1990 and 2000

Country	(A) Gender-specific age gaps in rate of labour market participation rate (men 25-54 years compared with men 55-64 years)			(B) Gender-specific age gaps in rate of labour market participation rate (women 25-54 years compared with women 55-64 years)		
	1990	**2000**	*Change 1990-2000*	**1990**	**2000**	*Change 1990-2000*
Denmark	25.2	26.9	*1.7*	41.9	36.1	*-5.8*
Finland	45.8	42.7	*-3.1*	45.7	39.8	*-5.9*
Norway	19.5	17.0	*-2.5*	25.3	21.9	*-3.4*
Sweden	19.2	17.9	*-1.3*	26.8	20.0	*-6.8*
Belgium	56.8	55.8	*-1.0*	50.9	57.4	*6.5*
France	49.6	52.5	*2.9*	41.8	45.3	*3.5*
Germany *	31.6	40.6	*9.0*	36.9	42.8	*5.9*
Netherlands	48.0	42.1	*-5.9*	41.8	46.5	*4.7*
Greece	34.9	36.9	*2.0*	27.2	36.2	*9.0*
Portugal	27.8	27.8	*0.0*	37.1	35.0	*-2.1*
Spain	31.8	32.6	*0.8*	27.4	40.2	*12.8*
UK	26.7	28.6	*1.9*	34.3	33.5	*-0.8*

* *1990-figures refer to the situation in the German Federal Republic before unification. The change estimates should be interpreted with caution since all countries except Finland and France have breaks in their time series affecting the homogeneity of data over time.*

Source: OECD, 2002a.

Age equality in labour market participation: A large age differential in the level of labour market participation of people of 'working age' will also indicate that there is a potential for increasing the overall labour market participation. In the case of *men*, the age gap in labour market participation decreased in five countries, Finland, Norway, Sweden, Belgium and most remarkably in the Netherlands. By contrast the age gap was considerably larger in the united Germany of 2000 than in the Federal Republic of 1990. In the case of *women*, the age gap decreased in six countries, the four Nordic countries, Portugal and the United Kingdom, between 1990 and 2000. Spain experienced a strong increase in the age gap, related to the increased labour market participation of younger women (Table 14.2).

Employment rate: The level of employment is likely to fluctuate more than the level of labour market participation but still it is significant that only half of the twelve countries had a lower rate of unemployment in 2000 than in 1990 (Table 14.3). These countries included Denmark, Norway, the Netherlands, Portugal, Spain and the United Kingdom. These same countries were together with Belgium the only ones that had diminished their rates of long-term unemployment between these two points in time (Table 14.3).

Table 14.3   The level of unemployment in twelve Western European countries – 1990 and 2000

Country	(A) Standardized rates of unemployment			(B) Estimates of the rates of long-term unemployment (12 months and more)		
	1990	**2000**	*Change 1990-2000*	**1990**	**2000**	*Change 1990-2000*
Denmark	7.2	4.4	*-2.8*	2.2	0.9	-1.3
Finland	3.2	9.7	*6.5*	0.3	2.8	2.5
Norway	5.3	3.5	*-1.8*	1.1	0.2	-0.9
Sweden	1.7	5.9	*4.2*	0.2	1.6	1.4
Belgium	6.6	6.9	*0.3*	4.5	3.9	-0.6
France	8.6	9.3	*0.7*	3.3	4.0	0.7
Germany *	4.8	7.9	*3.1*	2.2	4.1	1.9
Netherlands	5.9	2.8	*-3.1*	2.9	1.4	-1.5
Greece	7.0	11.2	*4.2*	3.5	4.6	1.1
Portugal	4.8	4.1	*-0.7*	2.2	1.8	-0.4
Spain	16.1	14.0	*-2.1*	8.7	6.7	-2.0
UK	6.9	5.3	*-1.6*	2.4	1.5	-0.9

* *1990-figures refer to the situation in German Federal Republic before unification. The estimates for the level and change of long-term unemployment should be interpreted with caution, especially as all countries France had breaks in their time series affecting the homogeneity of data over time.*

Source: OECD, 2002a, Tables A and G in Statistical Annex.

Spending on active and passive labour market measures: As mentioned above, one possible meaning of activation is the extent to which governments manage to shift the social protection system from providing income maintenance to providing active measures. The aim is to put greater emphasis on efforts to assist people in improving their degree of self-sufficiency, that is, their ability to find gainful employment and do without public financial support in the future. The OECD has sought to collect information about member states' spending on active and passive measures. In order to make this information more comparable cross-nationally the OECD presents the figures for expenditure as proportion of the gross domestic product (GDP). The idea here is that the size of the GDP determines the amount of resources a national economy has available for different purposes, and that the proportion of GDP spent on active measures is a crude expression of the priority given to activation.[3] In operational terms, 'active measures' comprise practical efforts to assist people to find or remain in paid employment and thus improve their prospects in the labour market. Such efforts range from providing possibilities for acquiring new qualifications through vocational training, guidance and information about vacancies, improving job-seeking skills, to various forms of job-creation through wage subsidies and placement in specially constructed job-openings. By contrast, 'passive measures' basically refer to cash transfers to people out of work, that is, unemployment compensation and early retirement for labour market reasons. From Table 14.4 we see that only two of the twelve countries, France and the Netherlands, appear to have achieved a substantial increase in their level of spending on active measures between 1990 and 2000. Four other countries, Denmark, Norway, Belgium and Spain, seemed to have decreased their spending on passive measures significantly in the same period.

Table 14.4   **Spending on active and passive labour market measures as proportion of the gross-domestic product (GDP) – Twelve Western European countries in 1990 and 2000**

Country	(A) Expenditure on active labour market measures as % of GDP			(B) Expenditure on passive labour market measures as % of GDP		
	1990	**2000**	*Change 1990-2000*	**1990**	**2000**	*Change 1990-2000*
Denmark	1.3	1.6	*0.3*	4.4	3.0	*-1.4*
Finland	1.0	1.0	*0.0*	1.2	2.1	*0.9*
Norway	1.0	0.8	*-0.2*	1.2	0.4	*-0.8*
Sweden	1.7	1.4	*-0.3*	0.9	1.3	*0.4*
Belgium	1.2	1.3	*0.1*	2.7	2.2	*-0.5*
France	0.8	1.3	*0.5*	1.9	1.7	*-0.2*
Germany *	1.0	1.2	*0.2*	1.1	1.9	*0.8*
Netherlands	1.0	1.6	*0.6*	2.2	2.1	*-0.1*
Greece	0.5	0.5	*0.0*	0.4	0.5	*0.1*
Portugal	0.7	0.6	*-0.1*	0.4	0.9	*0.5*
Spain	0.8	0.8	*0.0*	2.4	1.3	*-1.1*
UK	0.6	0.4	*-0.2*	1.0	0.6	*-0.4*

*　*1990-figures refer to the situation in the German Federal Republic before unification.*

Source: OECD, 1994 (Table 1.B.2); OECD, 2002b (Table H in Statistical Annex).

One may, however, raise doubts how fruitful these figures are as indicators of a turn to more activist social protection systems, if we do not take into consideration what levels of unemployment these countries experienced at the two points in time. Arguably, if two countries have the same level of spending on active efforts it is reasonable to see the country with the lowest unemployment rate as the more 'activist' of the two, *ceteris paribus*. One way to take into account that levels of unemployment were dissimilar from the start and changed differently in the countries and period under study is to standardize the expenditure figures.[4] We may calculate what the expenditure figures would have been, *hypothetically*, if all countries had an unemployment rate of ten per cent *and* spent the same amount of resources per each per cent unemployed as they did with their actual level of unemployment. We do not have strong reasons to believe that the countries would have had this level of spending if their unemployment rate had been ten per cent, as this would depend on other factors (e.g. political priorities or concerns for the deficit in government finances). Rather the point of calculating these contra-factual figures is to be able to compare the overall profile of different countries' expenditure. Moreover, the standardized figures highlight how the spending on active and passive measures has changed in the twelve countries *relative* to their levels of unemployment. The results of this standardization exercise are presented in Table 14.5.

Table 14.5   **Standardized spending on active and passive labour market measures as proportion of GDP – Twelve Western European in 1990 and 2000**

Country	(A) Standardized expenditure on active labour market measures			(B) Standardized expenditure on passive active labour market measures		
	1990	**2000**	*Change 1990-2000*	**1990**	**2000**	*Change 1990-2000*
Denmark	1.6	3.5	*1.9*	5.7	6.8	*1.1*
Finland	3.2	1.0	*-2.2*	3.6	2.2	*-1.4*
Norway	1.9	2.2	*0.3*	2.2	1.3	*-0.9*
Sweden	7.0	2.9	*-4.1*	3.7	2.8	*-0.9*
Belgium	1.8	1.9	*0.1*	4.0	3.2	*-0.8*
France	0.9	1.4	*0.5*	2.1	1.8	*-0.3*
Germany *	2.2	1.6	*-0.6*	2.3	2.4	*0.1*
Netherlands	1.7	5.5	*3.8*	3.5	7.3	*3.8*
Greece	0.8	0.4	*-0.4*	0.7	0.4	*-0.3*
Portugal	1.6	1.5	*-0.1*	0.9	2.2	*1.3*
Spain	0.5	0.6	*0.1*	1.5	1.0	*-0.5*
UK	0.8	0.7	*-0.1*	1.2	1.1	*-0.1*

*   *1990-figures refer to the situation in the German Federal Republic before unification.*

Source: OECD, 1994 (Table 1.B.2); OECD, 2002 (Tables A and G in Statistical Annex).

As a result of the standardization Denmark is added to the list of countries with a substantial increase in the spending on active measures (Table 14.5). But still most of the twelve countries had a small or no increase in the spending on active measures. Most notably both Finland and Sweden had experienced a substantial decrease in their levels of active efforts, relative to their levels of unemployment. While the employment situation had improved since the deep recession in these two countries in the early part of the decade they had not achieved to return to the level of active efforts they had in 1990. Moreover, we see that five of the twelve countries had experienced substantial decreases in the levels of spending on passive measures: Finland, Norway, Sweden, Belgium and Spain. This means that none of the three countries with a substantial increase in their active efforts had simultaneously achieved a substantial decrease in their passive spending relative to their level of unemployment. On the contrary, both Denmark and the Netherlands appeared to have had their expenditure on passive measures *increased* at the same time as their spending on active measures increased!

This outcome is paradoxical and unexpected. First of all, there had been less of a turn from 'passive' to 'active' at this level than suggested by the strong recommendations of the OECD Jobs Strategy and the EU Employment Strategy and the weight given to this kind of turn in the policy discourse in the member states. Second, there are reasons to ask whether the countries under study were more successful in undertaking cuts in their income maintenance systems than in providing new and improved opportunities for people at the margin of the labour market through participation in specific activation measures.

Cuts in income maintenance schemes: Other available information about changes undertaken in the income maintenance schemes for people out of work does indeed suggest that most of the twelve countries introduced cuts of more than one kind in the 1990s (Table 14.6). These cuts included reductions in the levels of benefits (replacement rates) and/or the maximum duration of unemployment benefit receipt, as well as stricter criteria for eligibility for benefit and/or 'work availability' or 'actively seeking work' as conditions for continued receipt of benefit. These changes are supposed to improve the financial incentives to seek or remain in paid work.

What impact did activation have on labour market performance?

In recent years a huge number of studies of the effects of activation policies and measure have been carried out. Broadly speaking these studies fall into two groups:

- Macro-economic studies of the effects on the labour market as a whole;
- Micro-economic studies of the effects on the labour market prospects and experiences of individual participants in measures.

In another paper I have reviewed the findings of a number of such studies in greater detail (Hvinden, 1999). In this context I will limit myself to the main conclusions. From these studies it seems that the impact of putting greater emphasis on active labour market measures has been uncertain and variable (see also Martin, 1998; EMCO, 2002; Walwei and Werner, 2001):

- It has so far been difficult to demonstrate beyond doubt that a shift towards active labour market measures contributes significantly to improve the efficiency of the labour market as *a whole.*
- There appears to be somewhat greater likelihood that appropriately designed active measures can improve the labour market prospects of *individuals*, even if this may take place at the expense of other job seekers who have not participated in measures. Such displacement effects may be interpreted as redistribution or sharing of the individual disadvantages and costs of unemployment. There are, however, likely to be some participants for whom the experience with the measures more has had the character of being out of the unemployment registers for some time. Some of these participants may simply find themselves temporarily 'in store', pending an up-turn in the business cycle, a restoration of their rights to cash benefits or agency acceptance of their inability to find work in the mainstream labour market.

Table 14.6   Changes in the income maintenance system for people out of work in the course of the 1990s in twelve Western European countries

Countries	*Reduced benefit levels*	*Reduced benefit duration*	*Tighter eligibility criteria*	*Tighter availability criteria*
Denmark	X	X	X	X
Finland	X		X	X
Norway		X	X	
Sweden	(x)		X	X
Belgium	X	X		X
France	(x)			X
Germany	X	X	X	X
Netherlands	X	X	X	X
Greece		X		
Portugal				
Spain	X		X	X
UK		X	X	X

Notes: Reduced benefit level: reduction in unemployment benefit levels (replacement rates) (OECD, 1999b and 1999c). Reduced benefit duration: reduction in maximum unemployment benefit duration (OECD, 1999b and 1999c). Tighter eligibility criteria: tightening of eligibility criteria for unemployment benefit (OECD, 1999b and 1999c). Tighter availability criteria: tightening of work availability criteria for continued receipt of unemployment benefit (OECD, 1999b and 1999c). X if yes, (x) if change later reversed to some extent.

Table 14.7   Composite measure (and rank) for the relative labour market performance of twelve Western European countries – 1990 and 2000

Country	1990	2000
Denmark	5.3 (4)	3.2 (3)
Finland	5.2 (3)	7.0 (7)
Norway	3.2 (2)	1.7 (1)
Sweden	1.2 (1)	3.0 (2)
Belgium	10.5 (12)	9.7 (10)
France	9.0 (10)	9.0 (9)
Germany *	5.7 (7)	8.5 (8)
Netherlands	8.5 (8)	6.7 (6)
Greece	8.7 (9)	9.7 (10)
Portugal	5.3 (4)	5.3 (5)
Spain	9.5 (11)	10.0 (12)
UK	5.5 (6)	4.0 (4)

*   *1990-figures refer to the situation in the German Federal Republic before unification.*

If we return to the twelve countries studied here, there is some evidence that a turn to more activist policies may be correlated with an improved overall labour market situation in the course of the 1990s. In order to demonstrate this we proceed in two steps.

As a first step we construct an additive index based on the ranking of the twelve countries in terms of the six aspects of labour market performance described in Tables 14.1-14.3. The country with the most desirable situation (e.g. the highest level of labour market participation) is ranked as 1, the country with the least desirable situation ranked as 12. The rank scores for each country is added together and divided by six, producing an average rank for this country. The values on this index for 1990 and 2000 are given in table 14.7. If we rank order the twelve countries according to the index we see that the relative position of Denmark, Norway, Belgium, France, the Netherlands and the United Kingdom improved between 1990 and 2000. Conversely, Finland, Sweden, Germany, Greece, Portugal and Spain obtained a lower rank in 2000 than in 1990. Most countries did not move far in the rank order though. The major exceptions were Finland that also left the top half of best performing countries in 1990s, and the Netherlands that moved into this top half.

As a second step we relate the results presented in Table 14.5 on standardized spending on active and passive measures to the changes in relative labour market performance between 1990 and 2000 (Table 14.7). The question here is whether we can detect a relationship between changes in spending profile and improved labour market performance. As can be seen from Table 14.8 a crude bi-variate analysis suggests the following:

- While all three countries with a substantially higher spending on active measures (the Netherlands, Denmark and France) improved their relative labour market performance between 1990 and 2000 this was only the case for three of the nine countries without substantial increases in active spending (Norway, Belgium and the United Kingdom). In order words, there was a positive correlation between spending substantially more on active labour market measures and improving relative labour market performance (a Pearson's correlation coefficient $r = .58$).

- Of the five countries with substantially lower spending on passive measures two improved their relative labour market performance (Norway and Belgium) while this was the case with four of the seven without substantial decrease in their passive spending (the Netherlands, Denmark, France and the United Kingdom). Thus there was a weak negative correlation between spending substantially less on passive measures and improved labour market performance ($r= -.17$).

- Finally, we can note that five of the eight countries that had achieved substantial changes in their spending profile – either through increased active expenditure or reduced passive expenditure – improved their labour market performance (the Netherlands, Denmark, France, Norway and Belgium). Only one of the four countries that had not made substantial changes in their spending profile improved its labour market performance (the United Kingdom). Thus there was as weak positive correlation between changed profile in spending on labour market measures and improved relative labour market performance ($r= .35$).

Table 14.8   Summary table: changes in spending on labour market measures and relative labour market performance in twelve Western European countries between 1990 and 2000

Profile in spending on labour market measures in 2000 compared with 1990 (relative to the level of unemployment)	Improved relative labour market performance in 2000 compared with 1990	
	No	**Yes**
Substantially higher spending on active measures		Netherlands, Denmark France
Substantially lower spending on passive measures	Finland, Sweden Spain	Norway Belgium
Neither substantially higher spending on active measures nor substantially lower spending on passive measures	Germany, Greece Portugal	UK

Given the small number of countries and the fairly short period studied here these findings should be interpreted with caution. But they do seem to suggest that a substantial increase in public spending on particular active labour measures went together with an improved overall labour market performance. On the other hand there is no evidence that to diminish spending on income maintenance for people out of work (relative to the level of unemployment) in itself contributed to overall labour market performance. Consequently the correlation between changing the profile of labour market spending (either through a substantial increase in active spending or a substantial decrease in passive spending) and improved labour market performance was fairly weak. This suggests that the way in which the profile of spending was changed has more important than achieving a change in the profile as such.

Concluding remarks

Did the twelve Western European countries studied here turn to activation in the course of the 1990s? In the beginning of this article we identified a number of different but interrelated meanings of 'activation'. The answer to the question whether the twelve countries moved in the direction of activation depends on what of these meanings we adopt or emphasize:

- In a majority of the twelve countries a larger proportion of the population of working age became economically active and in this sense 'activated'. The main factor behind this increase is the fact that more women than before became involved in gainful employment. But both the striking inter-country differences in labour market participation rates and substantial gender and age gaps in the level of participation suggests that there is substantial potential for further activation in this broad sense.
- There are also reasons to believe that the volume of activating policy measures increased in most of these twelve countries, although to different degree. If we limit ourselves to activating measures in the more specific and narrow sense (participation in vocational training, job-search courses, temporary job placements, etc.) the number of entrants into active measures (as proportion of all unemployed people) had grown most strongly in Spain, the Netherlands, Denmark and Sweden from 1990 to 2000 (OECD, 2002b, Table H).
- However, the total amount of public resources spent on activating measures in the more specific sense became substantially larger in only three of the twelve countries between 1990 and 2000, that is, in the Netherlands, Denmark and France. Activation in this sense of the term had only to a limited extent come to characterize the twelve countries. This is somewhat surprising in the light of the importance that both the OECD Job Strategy and the EU Employment Strategy and the policy discourse in member states have given to activation. One interpretation of this finding is that decision-makers in the majority of the countries have seen a more ambitious growth in activating measures as representing an undesirable increase of total social protection costs in a short-term perspective and an investment where the possible return was uncertain and/or not likely to appear until much later.
- From the same more immediate perspective governments have probably seen it as more attractive to concentrate on efforts to tighten the income maintenance system: Five of the twelve countries experienced substantial

decreases in their spending on cash benefits for people out of work, when we take into account the rates of unemployment in these countries: Finland, Norway, Sweden, Belgium and Spain. Here it is a paradox that both the Netherlands and Denmark turned out to have had a growth in this type of spending when we take into account how their levels of unemployment diminished between 1990 and 2000. One may ask whether the levels of spending on active and passive measures in these two countries will prove sustainable over time.

- It has been reported that all the twelve countries except Portugal introduced some sort of cuts in their income maintenance schemes for people out of work in the 1990s. This indicates that efforts to improve financial incentives to seek and remain in paid employment played some role in most of the twelve countries, but again, probably to different extent, given that only five countries experienced substantial decreases in the spending on passive measures, relative to their level of unemployment. We found no indication that a substantial decrease in the level of passive spending in itself improved overall labour market performance.

In the introduction we also raised the question to what extent where are any indications that the adoption of activation policies made a difference in terms for labour market performance. We found a positive correlation between spending substantially more on active labour market measures and improved labour market performance – as these factors have been measured here. Even if we take into account the few number of countries examined and the crudeness of the analysis this correlation will be encouraging by those who believe in activation policies. At the same time it is tempting to ask whether this is partly a spurious relationship. Perhaps it is not the increased active spending as such that is important but what this indicates about the governments' scope for accomplishing policy change more generally? First, this scope may be related to financial and budgetary constraints; for instance whether governments are in a position to afford to increase public spending on active measures and other provisions believed to improve employment prospects. Second, the scope for change may also be created by political factors; governments' numerical strength as well as the practical possibilities for forging alliances and striking deals with other parties and stakeholders. These factors will determine governments' ability to overcome resistance against unpopular reforms, such as making participation in active measures an obligation for people of working age who are claiming cash benefits. Finally, governments may also be faced with structural and administrative factors that facilitate or impede change. To the extent that control over relevant policy instruments are located to the same level of governance and relatively few agencies, it will be easier to initiate co-ordinated efforts to stimulate employment and activating measures, than if this authority is dispersed between different levels of governance and a greater number of agencies. In future comparative and cross-national research on activation more attention should be given to welfare states' capacity for change, restructuring and adjustment, and the factors that influence this capacity. More knowledge is also needed concerning how activation – in the various meanings outlined in this article – affects the welfare and relative autonomy of the target population of such reforms.

Notes

1 Occasionally the term activation is made to encompass efforts to encourage people to increase their participation in other forms of activity outside the home. These activities are deemed to be socially valuable or beneficial, e.g. voluntary, neighbourhood, self-help or unpaid organizational work. Participation in these activities may be seen as a good thing in itself, to be preferred to social isolation and passivity. Yet, recently the official discourse has primarily emphasized these activities as means and stepping-stones on the way into or back to gainful employment, especially for people who are at a great distance from the mainstream or ordinary labour market.

2 These countries include Austria, Ireland, Italy and Luxembourg.

3 Some authors have expressed reservations against using proportion of GDP to study changes or trends, as the GDP is likely to increase or decrease over time (e.g. Clayton and Pontussen, 2000, p. 326). But even so the GDP can be interpreted as a crude indicator of the total resources available in a country in any year. Among the countries studied here only Finland and Sweden experienced a reduction in real GDP for than one year in the 1990-97 period (OECD, 1999d, annex Table 1).

4 The European Commission has undertaken a similar standardization in recent documents, cf. EC, 1998c, p. 110 and EC, 1999c, pp. 21-23.

References

Bosco, A. and Chassard, Y. (1999), 'Shift in the paradigm: surveying the European Union discourse on welfare and work', in M. Heikkilä (ed.), *Linking welfare and work*, Luxembourg: Office for official publications of the European Communities, Luxembourg, pp. 43-58.

Clasen, J. (2001), 'Social security in the new millennium', in J. Clasen (ed), *What future for social security?*, Kluwer Law International, The Hague, pp. 1-11.

Clasen, J., Kvist, J. and Van Oorschot, W. (2001), 'On condition of work: increasing work requirements in unemployment compensation schemes, in Kautto, M., J. Fritzell, B. Hvinden, J. Kvist and H. Uusitalo (eds), *Nordic welfare states in the European context*, Routledge, London, pp. 198-224.

Clayton, R. and Pontussen, J. (2000), 'Welfare state retrenchment revisited', in C. Pierson and F.G. Castles (eds), *The welfare state reader*, Polity Press, Oxford, pp. 320-334.

Drøpping, J.A., Hvinden, B. and Vik, K. (1999), 'Activation policies in the Nordic countries', in M. Kautto, M. Heikkilä, B. Hvinden, S. Marklund, and N. Ploug (eds), *Nordic social policy: changing welfare states*, Routledge, London, pp. 133-158.

European Commission (1997), *1998 guidelines for member states employment policies*, The European Commission, Brussels.

European Commission (1998a), *1999 employment guidelines*, The European Commission, Brussels.

European Commission (1998b), *From guidelines to action: The 1998 national action plans for employment: overall assessment*, The European Commission, Brussels.

European Commission (1999), *2000 employment guidelines*, The European Commission, Brussels.

EMCO (2002), *Prevention and activation policies for the unemployed, background paper, Impact evaluation of the ESS* (European Employment Strategy), (http://europa. eu.int/comm/employment_social/news/2002/may/acti_prev_en.pdf).

Employment Observatory (1997), 'Activation of labour market policy in the European Union – comparative summary', *SYSDEM Trends* (28), pp. 4-10.

Geldof, D. (1999), 'New activation policies: promises and risks', in M. Heikkilä (ed.), *Linking welfare and work*, Office for official publications of the European Communities, Luxembourg, pp. 13-26.

Gilbert, N. and Van Voorhis, R.A. (2001), 'Introduction', in N. Gilbert and R.A. Van Voorhis (eds), *Activating the unemployed. A comparative appraisal of work-oriented policies*, Transaction Publishers, New Brunswick, pp. vii-xiii.

Hanesch, W. (1999), 'The debate on reforms of social assistance in Western Europe', in M. Heikkilä (ed.), *Linking welfare and work*, Office for official publications of the European Communities, Luxembourg, pp. 71-85.

Heikkilä, M. and Keskitalo, E. (eds) (2001), *Social assistance in Europe*, Stakes, Helsinki.

Hvinden, B. (1999), 'Activation: a Nordic perspective', in M. Heikkilä (ed.), *Linking welfare and work*, Office for official publications of the European Communities, Luxembourg, pp. 27-42.

Hvinden, B., Heikkilä, M. and Kankare, I. (2001), 'Towards activation? The changing relationship between social protection and employment in Western Europe', in M. Kautto, J. Fritzell, B. Hvinden, J. Kvist and H. Uusitalo (eds), *Nordic welfare states in the European context*, Routledge, London, pp. 168-197.

Janoski, T, (1994), 'Direct state intervention in the labor market: the explanation of active labor market policy from 1950 to 1988 in social democratic, conservative, and liberal regimes', in T. Janoski and A.M. Hicks (eds) *The comparative political economy of the welfare state*, pp. 54-92.

Johansson, H. (2001), 'Activation policies in the Nordic countries: social democratic universalism under pressure', *Journal of European Area Studies* 9(1), pp. 63-77.

Lindqvist, R. and Marklund, S. (1995), 'Forced to work and liberated from work. Historical perspective on work and welfare in Sweden', *Scandinavian Journal of Social Welfare* 4, pp. 224-37.

Lødemel, I. and Trickey, H. (eds) (2001), *'An offer you can't refuse': Workfare in international perspective*, Policy Press, Bristol.

Martin, J.P. (1998) 'What works among active labour market policies: evidence from OECD countries experiences', *OECD Labour market and social policy – occasional papers* (35), Oct. 1998, Organization for Economic Co-ordination and Development (OECD), Paris,

Millar, J. and Rowlingson, K. (eds) (2001), *Lone parents, employment and social policy*, The Policy Press, Bristol.

OECD (1994), *OECD employment outlook*, OECD, Paris.

OECD (1995) *The OECD jobs study: implementing the strategy*, OECD, Paris.

OECD (1998a), *Benefit systems and work incentives*, OECD, Paris.

OECD (1998d), *The OECD jobs strategy: progress report on implementation of country-specific recommendations*, Economics department working papers 196, OECD, Paris.

OECD (1999b), *Implementing the OECD jobs strategy: assessing performance and policy*, OECD, Paris.

OECD (1999c), *A caring world. The new social policy agenda*, OECD, Paris.

OECD (2002a), *Labour force statistics 1981-2001*, OECD, Paris.

OECD (2002b), *OECD employment outlook*, OECD, Paris.

OECD (forthcoming), *Transforming disability into ability*, OECD, Paris.

Pierson, P. (1994), *Dismantling the welfare state?*, Cambridge University Press, Cambridge.

Presidency conclusions (1997), *Conclusions of the Presidency*, the Extraordinary European Council Meeting, Luxembourg, November 20-21, 1997.

Saraceno, C. (ed.) (2002), *Social assistance dynamics in Europe*, The Policy Press, Bristol.

Van Berkel, R. and Møller, I.H. (2002), 'The concept of activation', in R. Van Berkel and I.H. Møller (eds), *Active social policies in the EU. Inclusion through participation?* The Policy Press, Bristol, pp. 45-72.

Van Oorschot, W. and Hvinden, B. (2001), 'Introduction: towards convergence? Disability policies in Europe', in W. Van Oorschot and B. Hvinden (eds) *Disability policies in Europe*, Kluwer Law International, The Hague, pp. 3-12.

Walwei, U. and Werner, H. (2001), 'Employment problems and active labor market policies in industrialized countries', in D.D. Hoskins, D. Dobbernack, and C. Kuptsch, (eds), *Social security at the dawn of the 21st century*, New Brunswick: Transaction Publishers, New Brunswick, pp. 133-170.

Wilensky, H.L. (1992), 'Active labour market policy: its contents, effectiveness, and odd relationship to evaluation research', in C. Crouch, and A. Heath, (eds), *Social research and social reform*, Clarendon Press, Oxford, pp. 315-350.

Wilensky, H.L. (2002), *Rich democracies. Political economy, public policy, and performance*, University of California Press, Berkeley.

PART IV

FAMILIES AND CHILDREN IN POVERTY AND CONCEPTS OF FAMILY POLICY

Chapter 15

Child and family poverty in Germany

Gerhard Bäcker

Background

The increasingly lively academic and political debate in Germany in the mid-1990s about the issue of 'poverty in prosperity' is characterized by the particular prevalence of poverty in households with children, found in all empirical studies. The situation is no longer dominated by poverty in old age; rather, poverty rates are higher the younger the people are. There is talk of an 'infantilization of poverty' (Hauser, 1997, p. 40). At the same time, when you look at the type of household, the risk of having to live on a low income is higher for families with several children, and especially for single-parent families.

There are many reasons for the high level of public interest in the subject of child poverty. One of the main reasons is that, because of their physical constitution and needs, children are particularly dependent on adequate and beneficial living conditions. Poverty in the early years jeopardizes the whole of one's later development. An adequate income is certainly one of the main prerequisites – although not the only one – for good development prospects and socialization conditions for children. Since in developed market economies access to almost all areas of life depends on having money – beginning with the home and the living environment, taking in food, the purchase of consumer durables and consumer goods, and ending with holidays and recreational activities – an inadequate income below the minimum subsistence level can lead to substantial restrictions in all aspects of your life. Children who grow up in poverty for a brief or long period also have no opportunity to improve their income or to provide more for themselves through their own efforts. They are dependent on their parents' income position and the strategies their parents adopt to cope with living in and escaping from poverty.

Living with children – additional outgoings and an income that does not keep up

At the centre of the data on income poverty in Germany referred to here is the income situation of people who live in households with young children. Therefore the parents as well as the children themselves are included, through the total income of the household. Where the income situation of these households can be regarded as particularly jeopardized by the people in these family households, this reflects the fact that children do not generally have an income of their own but have to be supported by their parents. From the point of view of the parents or the family group, children increase the income requirements without any assurance that the income coming in will rise to match. Indeed, the opposite is more likely to be the case. In a market economy, children and the resulting financial needs of the family have no bearing on individual remuneration, as this is based on market and performance criteria and not on needs. Moreover, the whole organization of the world of work is based implicitly on the assumption that the input of human labour must be driven by operational efficiency and working time structures. In order to succeed in work a person must be highly mobile, flexible with their time and not burdened by family responsibilities.

The birth of a first or additional child is always linked with a twofold income problem. First, costs are incurred for the appropriate maintenance of the children. The expenditure varies according to the ages of the children and may last for more than two decades; for the longer their education lasts, the higher and more protracted will be the expenditure. Second, household income does not keep up with rising needs. It will even fall if one partner, usually the woman, takes a break from work or reduces the amount of time that she works (part-time work). This loss of income, which in economic terms can be seen as an opportunity cost, has such a large impact on the living conditions of families because changes in social structures mean that the benchmark for household income and living standards is no longer the single earned income of the man, but the income of two fully employed childless partners.

The combination of increasing needs and stagnating or declining financial resources means that, as the size of a household increases, the family's needs-weighted income per head falls. From the point of view of poverty research, the crucial question is whether this decline goes all the way to the poverty and low-income threshold. A distinction must be made here between households whose income was already at or below the poverty threshold before the birth of the children (where the situation deteriorates even further) and households whose income situation deteriorates *as a result of* having children (Wingen, 1998, pp. 206). The risk of falling below the poverty threshold depends on several factors, outlined below.

The financial burden of the household increases with the *number* and *age* of the children. On the other hand, as the children grow older they become more independent, so the amount of childcare they need falls and the corresponding costs disappear (kindergarten fees, the cost of child minders etc.). Young people in job training receive trainee allowances, which add to the household income.

The capacity and willingness of mothers not to take a long-term break in their employment and to work at least part-time after giving birth is also determined by the *number* and *age* of the children. In general, continuous employment or a return to employment is easier the fewer children there are to provide for, and the older and more independent the children are. Of equal importance for the possibility of combining employment and family are the quantity and quality of opportunities for external childcare, the division of work in the home between the parents and the strength of support from social networks (help in looking after the children from grandparents, neighbours, friends etc.). At the same time, the mother's work situation depends on her academic and professional qualifications, her employment and income opportunities and the general conditions in the labour market, particularly the availability of suitable part-time jobs. From a financial point of view, the net proceeds from the additional earned income must be balanced against possible additional expenses as a result of external childcare (child minders, nannies, kindergarten fees). For someone with few qualifications or a low income (because of low hourly rates and/or short hours/part-time work), a situation may arise in which it hardly 'pays' (if at all) to take a job, and there are also advantages to doing work around the home to consider (Andreß, 1999, p. 56). Finally, the continuing differences in the employment rates of women and mothers in the western and eastern parts of Germany indicate that in the case of young children the employment of the mother is largely dependent on cultural norms and social attitudes. While for most women in West Germany motherhood and continuous (full-time) employment are mutually exclusive, the employment of both parents was and still is the social norm in East Germany.

Single-parent families face particular income risks. This family type, which is becoming increasingly common in Germany (in 1998 some 13.7 per cent of all minors lived with their single mother and 2.4 per cent with their single father (Bäcker et al., 2000, pp. 161), is characterized by the fact that *one* person, usually the mother, is largely responsible for the care and upbringing of the child or children and at the same time for providing for the family through work. Unlike married couples, single parents and their children cannot rely on a continuous share of their partner's income and the resulting benefit entitlements. Even if they manage to pull off the balancing act between bringing up children and employment, single parents are still faced with the problem that low earnings (as a result of doing less work and/or low hourly rates) or gaps in earnings through unemployment have a direct impact on household income. Although it is true that single parents can claim maintenance for the support of their children and sometimes for themselves, the problem with maintenance payments is that many fathers pay little or no maintenance for their children or spouse, or fall behind with payments. On the one hand, fathers often lack the ability to pay, and, on the other hand, many of them try to evade their payment obligations or to hide their real income. Only around a third of children receive the sum owed to them by the absent parent in accordance with the law and court judgements (see Schewe, 1996).

This general introduction to the problem should not, however, be misunderstood to mean that single-parent families in Germany are a homogenous group and run a general risk of ending up in income poverty. The living and income conditions of single parents and their children vary depending on the reasons for single parenthood, the ages of the children, individual strategies for coping, reorientation and decisions made together over time, the availability of maintenance payments or of social security benefits in lieu of maintenance, and the possibility of supporting themselves through employment.

Child poverty: some problems of methodology

In this presentation of the key findings on family poverty on the basis of the SOEP analysis (Hanesch et al., 2000), we have based the data on the methodological foundation already outlined. When looking at family and child poverty in particular, it must be borne in mind that the results are largely determined by the assumptions underlying the definition and measurement of poverty. We would therefore draw attention to certain points.

1. The concept of relative income poverty is based on the availability of resources, and takes into consideration only the income inflow. Conversely, the conditions and burdens faced in obtaining the income, the asset situation and the way the income is used are not taken into consideration. However, in assessing family income in particular it is not unimportant whether the income is obtained through the well-paid employment of the husband alone or whether, in order to achieve the same income position, the wife and even any children in vocational training have to contribute. With the asset situation it should be borne in mind that not only financial and property assets but also consumer assets are divided unequally according to age. Young families in particular have a low level of assets, which in turn means that a large proportion of their earned income has to be used for the purchase of essential furniture and equipment or other consumer durables.

2. From other studies we know that parents and their children are often supported by grandparents (see Kohli et al., 1999). It is doubtful whether these private transfers in the form of regular or irregular gifts of money or things are sufficiently taken into account in the income inflow (see Joos, 2000). On the other hand, there is every indication that parental income is not only burdened by the maintenance of children still living in the same household, but that older children frequently still need to be supported financially when they have left the household, for example to study away from home. It remains an open question whether these transfers are sufficiently taken into account empirically as a reduction in the disposable income of the parental household.

3. When calculating equivalent net income, distribution is assumed to be uniform. This means that all members of the household have the same level of prosperity. Whether or not this assumption of proportional resource allocation holds true in reality is the subject of heated debate (see inter alia Joos and Wolfgang, 1998, pp. 19; Andreß, 1999, p. 85). It could be assumed that children receive less than 'their' share because their position of power in the family is weak. On the other hand, there are various indications that parents make sacrifices in favour of their children so that their children are not affected by the financial difficulties (see Bundesministerium für Familie, Senioren, Frauen und Jugend, 1998, p. 87).

4. Finally, a major factor for the extent of child poverty is the equivalence scale shown below. Depending on the need weightings attributed to children and other members of the household, different poverty rates are obtained. A high need weighting for children leads to an increase in the incidence of poverty

among children and among households with many children. Low need weightings have the opposite effect (see inter alia Bächer, 2002, pp. 296; Kaiser, 1997; Andreß, 1999, p. 86; Weick, 1999, pp. 68).

Selected empirical findings

Average equivalent net incomes by type of household

The key question in the empirical analysis of income conditions is what income risks are faced by *members* of households in which minors live. The yardstick is the household income allocated to the members of the household according to their need weighting. First, the average equivalent net income of family households is compared with the average equivalent net incomes of all households and of non-family households.

Table 15.1   Average equivalent net income by type of household in 1998 in DM and as per cent of overall average

	West Germany		East Germany		All Germany	
	in DM	In %*	in DM	in %*	in DM	in %*
All households	2,337	100	1,708	100	2,006	100
Single < 45 years	2,489	106.5	1,935	113.3	2,405	119.8
Couple < 45 years	2,662	113.9	1,934	113.2	2,543	126.8
Single 45 - 65 years	2,683	114.8	1,648	96.5	2,497	124.5
Couple 45 - 65 years	2,684	114.8	1,919	112.4	2,505	124.8
Two-parent households with children	1,721	73.6	1,535	89.9	1,685	84.0
- Two-parent households 1 child	2,376	101.6	1,612	94.4	1,862	92.8
- Two-parent households 2 children	1,662	71.1	1,559	91.3	1,641	81.8
- Two-parent households 3 or more children	1,447	61.9	1,103	64.6	1,402	69.9
Single-parent households	1,442	61.7	1,353	79.2	1,419	70.7
- divorced/separated	1,397	59.8	1,413	82.7	1,401	69.8
- unmarried	1,258	53.8	1,313	76.9	1,284	64.0
- widowed	1,875	80.2	1,096	64.2	1,711	85.3
Two-parent households with grown-up children	1,966	84.1	1,754	102.7	1,933	96.4
Couple > 65 years	2,073	88.7	1,866	109.3	2,029	101.1
Single > 65 years	2,240	95.8	1,997	116.9	2,196	109.5

*   *Relative to the equivalent net income of all households.*

Source: GSOEP.

The object is to differentiate between the wealth positions of people in various types of household and family. If the average equivalent net income of *all* households is set at 100, the deviations displayed in Table 15.1 are obtained.

Table 15.2   **Poverty and low-income rates of all households and family households in 1998 in per cent**

	Poverty threshold 50%			Low-income threshold 75%		
	All households	Two-parent households with children	Single-parent households	All households	Two-parent households with children	Single-parent households
West Germany						
1985	11.2	14.5	35.6	35.9	46.7	67.2
1988	10.1	13.7	29.9	33.9	46.6	65.4
1991	8.8	11.4	35.3	34.9	48.2	64.2
1994	9.4	11.6	28.2	35.1	46.5	72.8
1997	9.1	11.6	29.5	35.6	48.3	67.4
1998	9.5	13.0	30.1	32.3	47.0	69.7
East Germany						
1991	4.1	3.6	17.6	22.1	24.1	47.8
1994	7.5	9.2	26.8	25.0	32.5	57.5
1997	6.3	6.5	24.2	22.8	33.0	62.1
1998	4.6	5.6	13.4	26.9	35.0	51.1

Source: GSOEP.

Two-parent households with children under the age of 18 are a good 26 percentage points below the 100 per cent level in West Germany and around 10 percentage points below in East Germany. Conversely, all types of household without children are better off. This is true in particular for middle-aged single and two-person households, whose wealth positions are significantly above the average. With family households it is noticeable how strongly the number of children determines the position. While (in West Germany) two-parent households with one child still achieve the average equivalent net income, the income level falls to 71.1 per cent of the average with two children and to 61.9 per cent with three or more children. The income situation also proves to be unfavourable in one-parent households, which only achieve a level of 61.7 per cent. There are marked differences between the various types of one-parent household. The income situation is worst when the head of the household is a single mother, in which case the equivalent net income amounts to only 53.8 per cent (West Germany) or 76.9 per cent (East Germany) of the average. Divorced or separated parents are only a little better off with levels of 59.8 per cent (West Germany) and 82.7 per cent (East Germany). In contrast, *widowed* parents (whose children are on average older) do better with 80.2 per cent (West Germany). This puts them above the level of two-parent households.

If we compare the situation in East Germany with West Germany, it is noticeable that for two-parent households with children the deviations from the general household equivalent income are smaller than in the west. This may be due to the fact that the rate of employment of mothers in East Germany is still significantly higher than in West Germany. The position of one-parent households is also better than in the west. However, this type of family is still considerably below the average equivalent net income in East Germany.

Table 15.3   Poverty rates of family households according to different equivalence scales in per cent

	Poverty threshold 50%			
	West Germany		East Germany	
	Two-parent households with children Equivalence scale 1: 0.7: 0.5	Two-parent households with children Equivalence scale 1: 0.5: 0.3	Two-parent households with children Equivalence scale 1: 0.7: 0.5	Two-parent households with children Equivalence scale 1: 0.5: 0.3
1985	14.5	8.9	-	-
1988	13.7	9.3	-	-
1991	11.4	7.6	3.6	3.1
1994	11.6	6.5	9.2	7.1
1997	11.6	7.4	6.5	3.8
1998	13.0	8.3	5.6	3.6

Source: GSOEP.

Poverty rates according to household and family composition

What interests us above all is what proportion of each type of household falls into the income groups 'less than 50 per cent of average' (poverty) and 'less than 75 per cent of average' (low income). Table 15.2 shows that between 1985 and 1998 family households fell below both the 50 per cent poverty threshold and the 75 per cent low-income threshold far more frequently than all households. In 1998 the poverty rate (50 per cent threshold) for all households in West Germany was 9.5 per cent, compared with 13.0 per cent for two-parent families and 30.1 per cent for one-parent families. The gaps are even more pronounced for the 75 per cent low-income threshold. In 1998 the corresponding rates in West Germany were 32.3 per cent for all households, 47 per cent for two-parent families and 69.7 per cent for one-parent families. The gap of more than 30 percentage points calculated from the differences between the 50 per cent and 75 per cent thresholds, which (with fluctuations) is characteristic of the whole trend in the poverty and low-income rate since 1985, shows that a very high proportion of family households occupy the area between 51 per cent and 75 per cent of the average equivalent net income (precarious affluence). Single-parent households run an extremely high risk of falling into poverty. In 1998 almost one third of households in this group were below the 50 per cent threshold, and two thirds were below the 75 per cent threshold.

As already mentioned, the poverty rates of family households change if the equivalence scale is modified. We have calculated comparisons between the revised OECD scale with the equivalence weightings of 1.0 (head of household), 0.5 (other household member) and 0.3 (children under 15 years) and the scale we have used with need weightings of 1, 0.7 and 0.5. The results can be seen in Table 15.3. With the revised OECD scale the values throughout are 3 to 4 points lower than on the old scale.

Table 15.4 provides a more detailed sub-division of poverty and low-income rates and their development over time according to various household compositions. The household compositions are arranged according to various household and life cycle phases. All two-person households *without* children show a much lower than average incidence of poverty. For such households in West Germany the poverty rate in 1998 was between 2.6 per cent (couples between 45 and 65 years) and 5.6 per cent (couples under 45 years). Rates for single-person households were similarly below average with poverty rates between 3.9 per cent (single between 45 and 65 years) and 8.9 per cent (single under 45 years).

Table 15.4   Poverty rates by household composition – West Germany

	1985	1988	1991	1994	1997	1998
	< 50%	<50%	< 50%	< 50%	< 50%	< 50%
West Germany						
Single < 45 years	11.9	10.0	6.9	6.5	7.4	8.9
Couple < 45 years	2.7	4.2	2.6	6.0	3.7	5.6
Single 45 - 65 years	7.3	8.0	6.0	7.9	5.8	3.9
Couple 45 – 65 years	3.2	3.4	4.0	5.0	3.5	2.6
Two-parent households 1 child	8.1	7.6	9.4	8.9	7.5	7.8
Two-parent households 2 children	13.9	17.3	8.7	7.4	11.4	13.0
Two-parent households 3 or more children	32.3	21.7	20.9	25.7	21.6	24.7
Single-parent households	35.6	29.9	35.3	28.2	29.5	30.1
Two-parent households with grown-up children	8.1	5.6	5.4	10.2	10.0	8.8
Couple > 65 years	7.8	6.7	5.4	3.2	2.8	3.5
Single > 65 years	7.2	7.9	6.5	5.6	6.3	6.1

Source: GSOEP.

This compares with family households which had the following poverty rates: two-parent households with one child – 7.8 per cent; two-parent households with two children – 13 per cent; two-parent households with three or more children – 24.7 per cent. This again clearly illustrates that two-parent households with one child still have a lower incidence of poverty than the average for the population as a whole, but two-parent households with two children are slightly above average and two-parent households with three or more children are significantly above average.

Single-parent families can be broken down into various groups. A distinction can be made between separated/divorced parents, unmarried parents and widowed parents. With regard to both the poverty threshold (50 per cent) and the low-income threshold (75 per cent), single mothers and their children are the worst off.

Table 15.5   Poverty rates by household composition – East Germany

	1985	1988	1991	1994	1997	1998
	< 50%	<50%	< 50%	< 50%	< 50%	< 50%
East Germany						
Single < 45 years			9.6	9.7	5.8	10.5
Couple < 45 years			8.1	2.7	4.7	2.7
Single 45 - 65 years			1.4	5.8	20.3	6.9
Couple 45 - 65 years			2.1	1.3	1.7	3.2
Two-parent households 1 child			2.5	7.1	5.8	3.5
Two-parent households 2 children			4.0	9.3	5.0	3.6
Two-parent households 3 or more children			5.8	16.5	14.7	22.7
Single-parent households			17.6	26.8	24.2	13.4
Two-parent households with grown-up children			2.8	9.6	4.9	1.3
Couple > 65 years			1.3	1.0	1.6	1.2
Single > 65 years			2.2	3.9	2.3	0.6

Source: GSOEP.

In West Germany in 1998 this category showed a poverty rate of 38 per cent and a low-income rate of 87.7 per cent (see Table 15.5). The income situation of separated and divorced parents is also extremely difficult. For this category the rates were 29.4 per cent and 71.4 per cent. The situation is much better for widows with minors, with a poverty rate of 11.4 per cent and a low-income rate of 35.1 per cent. The higher average age of the children and the entitlement to social security benefits in lieu of maintenance (widow's and orphan's pensions) alleviates the situation.

As far as the differences between east and west with regard to poverty and low-income rates are concerned, it is possible to say that the incidence of relatively poor income situations, not only overall but also among family households, is substantially lower in East Germany (measured against the income level in East Germany) than in West Germany. It is also noticeable that in the east the incidence among two-parent households with children is slightly above the average. Admittedly, in East Germany, as in the west, a high proportion of single-parent households can expect a poor income situation, but the income risk is less marked than in the west.

Table 15.6   Poverty rates in family households – West Germany

Family composition	1985 < 50%	1988 <50%	1991 < 50%	1994 < 50%	1997 < 50%	1998 < 50%
West Germany						
Married couple with children	14.6	13.7	10.6	10.8	11.9	13.4
Unmarried couple with children	11.1	13.8	26.2	22.0	18.5	20.6
Single parent: divorced/separated	36.9	35.6	32.4	31.9	31.0	29.4
Single parent: unmarried	45.0	29.3	43.1	22.8	48.9	38.0
Single parent: widowed	26.4	22.7	21.2	3.3	6.5	11.4

Source: GSOEP.

Table 15.7   Poverty rates in family households – East Germany

Family composition	1985 < 50%	1988 <50%	1991 < 50%	1994 < 50%	1997 < 50%	1998 < 50%
East Germany						
Married couple with children			3.7	7.8	5.0	5.5
Unmarried couple with children			3.8	26.2	13.3	3.3
Single parent: divorced/separated			22.3	19.2	22.3	7.1
Single parent: unmarried			4.7	38.0	29.1	17.4
Single parent: widowed			( )	( )	( )	( )

Notes: ( ) = Sample size 0 – 30; (X) = Sample size 31-50.

Source: GSOEP.

If we look at the results over the whole period covered by the SOEP, we can see (in spite of fluctuations in individual values) a large degree of consistency in the poverty and low-income rates (Figure 15.1). *No increase* in family poverty can be seen. The following conclusions can be drawn. Couples with three or more children were able to improve their position gradually up to the beginning of the 1990s, but this began to deteriorate again after 1993. The poverty rate for two-parent households with one child runs largely parallel to the poverty rate for all households. On the other hand, the poverty rate of single-parent households fluctuates strongly, although the fluctuations remain around the 35 per cent level.

The analysis will be supplemented with findings on the impact of the number and age of the children on the incidence of poverty. The age of the children (Table 15.6), defined here as the age of the youngest child, has a noticeable impact on the poverty and low-income rates of both two-parent and single-parent households in West Germany. The lower the age of the youngest child, the higher the rates. When interpreting the results it must be borne in mind that the age of the youngest child alone does not provide adequate information about the composition of the family.

The youngest child could be the first and so far the only child in the starting phase of the family, or it could be the last sibling in a large family now consolidating its position.

As already mentioned, for family households the number of children is a very significant factor in the risk of falling below the poverty threshold in terms of disposable income. Table 15.7 confirms that families with many children are particularly threatened with poverty.

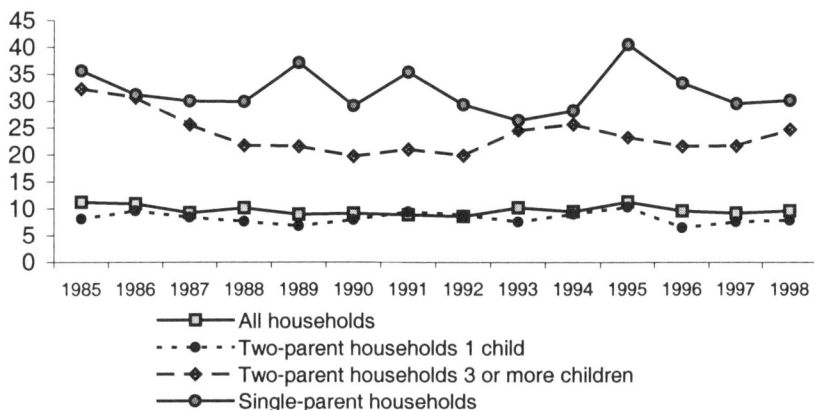

Figure 15.1   Poverty rates of family households 1985-1998, West Germany

Family households and employment

The level of employment of family members is a key factor in the level of poverty risk in family households (see Becker, 2002, pp. 126; Grabka and Kirner, 2002, pp. 527). Table 15.8 shows that in two-parent households with children the incidence of poverty is low if both partners are in employment. In 1998 the rate in West Germany was 3.7 per cent. The risk increases in leaps and bounds if one of the partners is not in employment – whether due to unemployment, a break in employment or the discontinuation of employment. Thus the need-weighted incomes of 18.8 per cent of all people living in single-income households with children are below the 50 per cent threshold. The problem is even greater if both partners are unemployed, in which case 41.8 per cent are below the poverty threshold.

Table 15.8   Poverty and low-income rates in per cent according to the age of the youngest child, 1998

Age of children	Poverty threshold Low-income threshold	Two-parent households with children		Single-parent households	
		West Germany	East Germany	West Germany	East Germany
0 – 6 years	< 50 %	15.3	7.4	30.7	(26.4)
	< 75 %	54.4	48.1	74.2	(61.1)
7 – 14 years	< 50 %	13.0	2.9	29.0	8.6
	< 75 %	45.3	29.4	64.5	54.0
15 – 18 years	< 50 %	10.7	7.7	22.4	(10.5)
	< 75 %	41.5	34.5	64.7	(36.7)

Notes: ( ) = Sample size 0 – 30; (X) = Sample size 31-50.

Source: GSOEP.

Table 15.9   Poverty rate in per cent according to the number of children, 1998

Number of children	Poverty threshold Low-income threshold	Two-parent households with children		Single-parent households	
		West Germany	East Germany	West Germany	East Germany
1 child	< 50 %	7.8	3.5	28.1	6.3
	< 75 %	34.0	25.3	66.2	38.8
2 children	< 50 %	13.0	3.6	24.8	7.7
	< 75 %	52.4	37.3	75.8	57.3
3 or more children	< 50 %	24.7	22.7	44.5	(45.6)
	< 75 %	63.9	66.6	74.4	(79.9)

Notes: ( ) = Sample size 0 – 30; (X) = Sample size 31-50.

Source: GSOEP.

It is worth noting that the poverty rate in households of employed single parents (15.1 per cent in West Germany in 1998) is lower than the poverty rate in single-income two-parent households (18.8 per cent) (Table 15.11). However, when looking at these findings it is important to remember that the employment of both partners is closely related to the *number* of children (Table 15.9). If there is only one child it is easier for the woman to work, while the additional needs are limited. With several children it is more difficult to work and generate another income, while the resulting limited income is divided among more people. These interrelated effects are an important factor in explaining the large differences in poverty rates between two-parent households with one and two incomes.

Child and family poverty in Germany and the shortfalls in family policy

The high risk of poverty for single-parent and two-parent families with large numbers of children is a poor advertisement for the German welfare state, where the protection and promotion of families and children is an important principle explicitly mentioned in the Constitution. It is clear that the social security system of the welfare state is not sufficiently capable of compensating for the income problems of families. However, the main reason for this is not that the overall financial dimensions of family policy are too small, but that the structures and principles of the benefit system in Germany produce the wrong trends. The following problems can be identified:

- Although child allowance has been substantially increased in Germany in recent years (from 2002, depending on the number of children, it amounts to €154 per month for the first, second and third children, and €179 per month from the fourth child upwards), it only partially covers the costs arising for the care and upbringing of children. The result is that households in the lower income bracket have to resort more frequently to supplementary benefit because of child costs (Table 15.10).
- As an alternative to child allowance, child-related tax concessions can be claimed. This benefits households with high incomes because the tax allowance provides more relief for them than child allowance.
- In a number of benefits German social and family policy focuses on the promotion of marriage. However, as the number of single parents increases, a growing proportion of married women remain childless and, even for married mothers, the period of child-rearing grows shorter, the logic of a purely marriage-oriented benefit is called into question. The problems of a marriage-oriented family benefit are most clearly seen in the tax law (see Kirner, Schöb and Weick, 1999). For tax purposes the married couple are not assessed separately, but jointly. This gives rise to substantial financial advantages since the tax liability of two half incomes is lower than that of one whole income of the same size. The advantages are larger the larger the difference between the incomes of the two spouses, or the higher the income of the sole-earner. It is particularly advantageous if the wife does not work at all and has no income of her own. Since this relief is linked solely to the legal status of 'marriage', it also applies if there are no children to provide for or if the children have already left home. Moreover, the advantage of income splitting is not available to single parents or any families on low incomes who pay little or no tax

and cannot therefore benefit from tax relief. However, as seen above, earned income and the need-weighted income per head are particularly low in the starting phase of a family.

Table 15.10   Child allowance 1996-2002

	Child allowance in DM/€			
	First child	Second child	Third child	Fourth child and each additional child
1996	200	200	300	350
1997	220	220	300	350
1998	220	220	300	350
1999	250	250	300	350
2000	270	270	300	350
2001	270	270	300	350
2001*	138	138	154	179
2002*	154	154	154	179

*   *In €.*

• Although the risk of poverty in families depends crucially on employment opportunities for women and mothers, the German welfare state continues to favour the non-employment of mothers and does too little to allow child-rearing and employment to be combined. A crucial precondition for the objective of allowing women to work and to remain in employment and continue their professional development even after the birth of children is the provision of adequate day-care facilities for children of all ages with opening times that match working hours. In particular, single mothers who want to have their own earned income and do not want to remain dependent on supplementary benefit for a long period are reliant on such facilities. In the provision of day-care facilities a distinction can be made between West and East Germany (see Bäcker et al. , 2000, pp. 210). In East Germany it may be said that comprehensive provision of all-day kindergartens and places in crèches and after-school centres was taken for granted in GDR days. West Germany on the other hand lags far behind. Although the full provision of kindergarten places has been largely achieved, these are mainly for mornings only. This positive development contrasts with a still inadequate provision for small children up to the age of three. An equally unsatisfactory childcare situation exists for children of school age. Schools in Germany are purely morning facilities, which see themselves as having the task of providing education but not of providing childcare.

Table 15.11 Poverty and low-income rates in family households according to employment

	Poverty rate 50%						Low-income rate 75%					
	1985	1988	1991	1994	1997	1998	1985	1988	1991	1994	1997	1998
West Germany												
Single-parent households												
In employment	21.0	17.7	18.4	7.9	16.5	15.1	51.9	52.7	54.1	61.4	55.9	53.6
not in employment	48.8	56.7	53.7	51.0	55.2	44.5	80.3	86.7	80.8	89.0	86.9	86.2
Two-parent households with children												
A: in employment	6.3	7.3	4.8	3.6	2.9	3.7	29.9	34.1	35.4	20.5	31.3	29.6
B: in employment												
A: in employment	16.7	13.3	14.6	13.7	16.6	18.8	55.0	51.6	57.6	57.6	59.5	61.3
B: not in employment												
A: not in employment	54.8	64.1	54.6	45.7	44.3	41.8	84.0	93.0	99.6	89.0	96.6	85.1
B: not in employment												
East Germany												
Single-parent households												
in employment			8.9	10.8	13.8	3.9			36.3	33.4	46.6	31.3
not in employment			46.8	49.6	42.9	26.0			85.7	90.7	87.6	84.1
Two-parent households with children												
A: in employment			2.7	4.1	1.5	1.6			17.1	15.1	14.8	14.5
B: in employment												
A: in employment			4.1	10.6	9.5	7.3			38.1	51.3	52.0	57.4
B: not in employment												
A: not in employment			26.5	59.6	34.1	18.2			55.1	98.6	92.8	85.1
B: not in employment												

Notes: ( ) = Sample size 0 – 30; (X) = Sample size 31-50.
Source: GSOEP.

All-day schools or schools with afternoon care are still rare and are totally non-existent among primary schools. The provision of places in after-school centres in West Germany is also very low with a supply ratio of 3.5 per cent. Overall, the childcare situation in West Germany is very deficient and thus represents a considerable impediment to combining employment and family in an acceptable way.

References

Andreß (1999), *Leben in Armut – Analyse der Verhaltsweisen armer Haushalt mit Umfragedaten*, Westdeutscher Verlag, Opladen, Wiesbaden.

Bäcker, G. (2002), 'Armut trotz Sozialhilfe? Zum Verhältnis von Einkommensarmut und Hilfe zum Lebensunterhalt', in S. Sell (ed.), *Armut als Herausforderung – Bestandaufnahmen und Perspektiven der Armutsforschung und Armutsberichterstattung*, Duncker & Humblot, Berlin, pp. 287-308.

Bäcker G., Bispinck, R., Hofemann, K. and Naegele, G. (2000), *Sozialpolitik und soziale Lage in Deutschland*, Vol. II, Westdeutscher Verlag, Wiesbaden.

Becker, I. (2002), 'Frauenerwerbstätigkeit hält Einkommensarmut von Familien in Grenzen', in *Vierteljahreshefte zur Wirtschaftsforschung* 71, No.1, pp. 126-146.

Bundesministerium für Familie, Senioren, Frauen und Jugend (1998), *Zehnter Kinder- und Jugendbericht, Bericht über die Lebenssituation von Kindern und die Leistungen der Kinderhilfen in Deutschland*, Bonn.

Grabka, M. and Kirner, E. (2002), 'Einkommen von Haushalten mit Kindern: Finanzielle Förderung auf erste Lebensjahre konzentrieren', in *DIW-Wochenbericht* (32), pp. 527-536.

Hanesch, W., Krause, P., Bäcker, G., Maschke, M. and Otto, B. (2000), *Armut und Ungleichheit in Deutschland*, Der neue Armutsbericht der Hans-Böckler-Stiftung, des DGB und des Paritätischen Wohlfahrtsverbands, Rowohlt Verlag, Reinbek bei Hamburg.

Hauser, R. (1999), *Ziele und Möglichkeiten einer sozialen Grundsicherung*, Nomos-Verlag, Baden-Baden.

Joos, M. (2000), 'Wohlfahrtsentwicklung von Kindern in den neuen und alten Bundesländern', in Ch. Butterwegge (ed.), *Kinderarmut in Deutschland – Ursachen, Erscheinungsformen und Gegenmaßnahmen*, Campus, Frankfurt am Main, pp. 89-108.

Joos, M. and Meyer, W. (1998), 'Die Entwicklung der relativen Einkommensarmut von Kindern in Deutschland 1990 bis 1995', in J. Mansel and G. Neubauer (eds), *Armut und soziale Ungleichheit bei Kindern*, Leske & Budrich, Opladen, pp. 19-33.

Kaiser, J. (1997), 'Wirtschaftliche und soziale Lage von Niedrigeinkommensbeziehern', in *Wirtschaft und Statistik* (9), pp. 325-343.

Kirner, E., Schöb, A. and Weick, S. (1999), 'Zur Einkommenssituation von Hanshalten mit Kindern. Entscheidung des Bundesverfassungsgerichtes erfordert Reform der staatlichen Förderung von Ehe und Familie', in *DIW-Wochenbericht* (8), pp.67-87.

Kohli, M., Künemund, H., Motel, A. and Szydlik, M., 'Familiale Generationenbeziehungen im Wohlfahrtsstaat. Die Bedeutung privater intergenerationaler Hilfeleistungen und Transfers', in *WSI-Mitteilungen* (1).

Schewe, C. (1996), 'Zur Zahlungsmoral von unterhaltspflichtigen Elternteilen', in *Sozialer Fortschritt* (9), pp. 325-330.

Wingen, M. (1998), *Familienpolitik*, UTB-Verlag, Stuttgart.

Chapter 16

Why are day care vouchers an effective and efficient instrument to combat child poverty in Germany?

C. Katharina Spiess and Gert G. Wagner

Child poverty – a special problem for poverty research

There is a broad consensus today that child poverty is highly unacceptable to society. This is partly because, as a rule, children have no active influence over the onset of poverty, and cannot do anything to help overcome it.[1] Moreover, the developmental deficiencies of children that may be linked to poverty can be only partly compensated for, and have a number of long-term effects.[2] Children who live in poverty for an extended period are particularly disadvantaged and as the duration of poverty increases, the compensation options (e.g. the availability of financial resources to fall back on) decrease (see Piachaud, 1992, p. 81 or OECD, 2001). Case studies for Germany, such as the ones from Hock et al. (2000) show that strategies for overcoming poverty among adult members of the household do not necessarily enhance the well-being of the child.

Now that there is more empirical evidence, from the Poverty Report (Armutsbericht) published by the Hans Böckler Foundation (see Hanesch et al., 2000) and the Federal Government's Poverty and Wealth Report (Armuts- und Reichtumsbericht) (BMA, 2001), that child poverty is a growing problem in Germany, the question of how family poverty can be combated has come to the fore in political discussions. The increasing poverty trend is especially evident in the growing proportion of single parents drawing social assistance: in 1975, just 17 per cent of all West German households on social assistance were single parents, while the figure for 1998 had risen to around 26 per cent (see BMA, 2001, annex: Table II.14).[3]

Instruments for combating child poverty

Against this empirical background of high poverty rates among family households in Germany, various models for combating child poverty have been publicly debated in Germany, and also discussed to some extent in academic circles. Most of the strategies are linked to an increase in child allowance (Kindergeld). In the political sphere, The Green Party have developed a specific proposal to increase child allowance for low-income family households. The Greens' proposal for a 'basic income for children' (Grüne Kindergrundsicherung) involves a means-tested child allowance supplement – which will not, however, reduce eligibility for social assistance – of up to 102 euros per child per month (see for example, Otto et al., 2001 and Otto and Spiess, 2002).[4] This 'basic income for children' should be guaranteed, independent of employment status.

In contrast to this, other programmes, such as the 'Mainz Model' (Mainzer Modell) introduced all over Germany from March 2002, do link a child allowance supplement to employment. Under this plan, a supplement is paid to 'low earning families' and single parents, provided that they move from unemployed to employed status. This supplement amounts to 25, 50 or 75 euros per child up to 18 years old, depending on income.

What these proposals have in common is that they represent monetary transfers that are intended to effect a direct improvement in the income position of family households. These transfers are not 'earmarked', which means that – in the words of economic theory – the 'economic actors' can use this transfer according to their own preferences. Beside monetary transfers like this, child poverty can also be decreased or prevented through in-kind transfers (cf., for example, OECD, 2001)[5]. However, this kind of transfers are given a far lower priority in the German debate on child poverty.[6]

In-kind transfers are generally purpose-specific transfers; from an economic point of view, they can lead to inefficiencies, in that they undermine 'consumer sovereignty' by stipulating how recipients must use the transfer (see also Besharov and Samari, 2000, pp. 213). However, with purpose-specific transfers it is possible to ensure that the public resources used to fund them are actually utilized for their intended purpose. In the context of combating child poverty, purpose-specific respectively 'earmarked' transfers could include food stamps, housing benefits, free school lunches, health insurance cover further training options for the parents or day care vouchers (see also section 5).

Causes of child poverty

In Germany, political discussion about appropriate instruments for combating child poverty often ignores the causes of families' poor income position, even though the causes of child poverty have long been known to poverty researchers.[7] The Federal Government's Poverty and Wealth Report, for example, identifies unemployment and low income as particular factors behind child poverty. Other problems come from inefficient behaviour in acquiring goods and services; separation and divorce, and the birth of another child (BMA, 2001, XXIV).

In this chapter, we argue that the choice of appropriate instruments for combating child poverty must also tackle these root causes of child poverty. Divorce and fertility levels are much less susceptible to political influence than individual employment. Incentives can be created, and the relevant conditions put in place, to encourage employment; in other words, causes like 'low income' and 'unemployment' can be tackled politically. However, these factors themselves are due to a variety of factors, arising – as is well-known – on the demand side of the labour market as well as the supply side.

Given that children of single parents are especially impacted by poverty (see also e.g. Jenkins et al., 2002a, 2002b), the search for the causes of unemployment must focus especially – but not exclusively – on this group. If we do so we see that apart from a lack of suitable demand in the labour market, it is often impossible for single parents to take up employment because of a lack of childcare facilities. This finding applies particularly to West Germany, where the provision of places at day care centres lags far behind the East German states and neighbouring European countries like France and Denmark (see e.g. Büchel and Spiess, 2002, and Beckmann and Engelbrech, 2002). Various empirical surveys show that the reason many mothers are not employed can be found in this low level of childcare provision. In 2001, for example, 89 per cent of mothers of pre-school children in Germany cited insufficient child-care facilities as the reason for being not employed. For mothers with pre-school children, the corresponding figure was 75 per cent (see Team Perspektive Deutschland, 2002).[8]

Further criteria for the selection of efficient and effective instruments

However, in choosing adequate instruments for combating child poverty (and here adequate must mean both efficient and effective)[9] we must include not only the causes of child poverty but also two further criteria.

First, instruments for combating child poverty must ensure that they actually benefit the children. Discussion on combating family poverty often looks only at the family as a whole, which income analyzes in particular interpret as a perfectly homogeneous unit of consumption, without explicitly going down to the level of the children. This phenomenon can also be observed in other countries:

> '...most research on welfare programs, [...], has focused on the way that parents respond to incentives created by welfare, rather than on its effects on children' (see Currie, 1998, p. 177).

But consideration of the effects on children is especially important in that any effective political measure must ensure that it enhances the well-being of the specific target group, otherwise it cannot be described as effective.[10]

Second, instruments for combating child poverty must have a lasting effect; in other words they must not only work in the short term but also in the medium and long term. This means that instruments for combating child poverty should ideally be preventive, in the sense of inhibiting poverty in the medium to long term.

In light of these three criteria for selecting instruments for combating child poverty, we argue that 'earmarked' transfers to support the attendance of day care centres are a practical instrument.[11] This is an efficient and effective instrument as the public support of good day care promotes both employment and income (addressing acute poverty) and the education of the children themselves (addressing chronic poverty). This does not mean that monetary transfers per se are the wrong way to combat child poverty, but in the German context in particular, where child allowance is high by European standards (see European Commission, 2002),[12] we must ask what additional instruments which are efficient and effective for combating child poverty could be considered.

Even transfers earmarked for a specific purpose must be deployed in the most efficient and effective way possible. We show below that these should be issued to those in need in the form of day care vouchers.

Day care vouchers as an instrument for combating child poverty

Day care vouchers as an instrument for combating child poverty address one of the most significant causes of child poverty. They are intended to enable single parents especially, but also couples where a single parental income is insufficient, to take up employment. In contrast to monetary transfers which may even cause parents to reduce the amount of paid work they do,[13] day care vouchers facilitate employment – starting with the search for a suitable job.

Second, compared to not 'earmarked' transfers like increased child allowance, day care vouchers ensure that public funds genuinely benefit the transfer's target group, namely the children themselves. This benefit comes in the form of good education if the day care centres provide good quality. Vouchers guarantee that parents cannot put the money towards other consumer ends. This is highly relevant, for – as noted above – empirical studies have demonstrated that the strategies adopted by adult members of the household to overcome poverty do not necessarily give the highest priority to the children's well-being (see Hock et al., 2000). Also, studies in the USA show that in-kind transfers do more to enhance children's well-being than monetary transfers (see Currie, 1998).[14]

Apart from this 'effectiveness' argument there are 'efficiency' arguments in favour of vouchers. Compared to other ways of promoting attendance at day care centres by subsidizing the supply side – i.e. care providers – this form of support ensures that it addresses the demand side, thus the actual target group for the transfer.

Thirdly, attendance at a good quality day care centre, made possible by the voucher, is linked not only to a number of short-term effects, but also medium- and long-term benefits. For the children,[15] a good standard of education in a day care centre can lead to a better long-term outcome, particularly for children from socio-economically disadvantaged families. In the medium term, this is reflected, for example, in greater success at school, and over the long term, in reduced welfare dependency and higher incomes.[16] Empirical evidence for this can be found especially in various US studies (see Spiess, 1998 and OECD, 2001, pp. 35). In Germany, the results of the most recent PISA study have shown (see Baumert, 2001) how important it is for children from socio-economically disadvantaged families in particular to experience good education even at pre-school age. However, it should be noted that the positive effects of attendance in day care centres only occur where the care provided is of high educational quality (see for example the overview of various studies on this topic in ECCE, 1999).

Crucial elements of day care vouchers

How should a system of childcare vouchers be set up, and what would be the consequences of introducing them in Germany?

Until now, attendance in day care centres in Germany has been subsidized through the granting of support to non-profit institutions such as the churches, or else the state itself has provided day care centres for children. In 1998, 45 per cent of day care centres were municipality-run facilities and 55 per cent were run by the non-profit providers, usually the majority of funding from the municipality and some funding from the State (Bundesland) (see for example, Kreyenfeld et al., 2001). The planning, which determines how many centres and places in centres are required is the responsibility of the municipality. Youth services departments (Jugendämter) are usually responsible for the allocation of places.

As we mentioned above we propose that this system of promoting the supplier should be replaced by support for the demand side in the form of specifically targeted 'subject transfers', namely day vouchers, and that the public funds provided for day care should be increased (see Kreyenfeld et al., 2001 and Spiess 2002a, 2002b).[17]

Day care vouchers should be given to parents with children of nursery, pre-school and school age. The value of the voucher should be based on the income of the parents. Higher-value vouchers should be given to parents on low incomes than to family households on higher incomes. Thus the transfer to low income families should be higher than to high income families.[18] This aspect is particularly important in terms of combating poverty.[19]

As a voucher system has other objectives beside combating child poverty – such as generally improving the work-life balance of parents or ensuring equality of opportunity for children (see also Kreyenfeld et al., 2001), it should not only go to families on low incomes. This would also reduce the risk of stigmatizing families on low incomes if they were the only group receiving the vouchers.

For the vouchers to meet the criterion of sustainability, it is essential that they should only be redeemable against childcare in licensed day care centres. These licensed or accredited facilities must be able to demonstrate a high quality of education. This could be regulated via minimum quality standards laid down for the whole country, which all facilities must meet. Vouchers are not viable without sound quality checking of day care providers.[20]

Day care vouchers could be combined with quality assurance instruments, aimed primarily at implementing consistent and nationwide quality standards, and giving parents a means of judging the quality of a day care centre better than they can in the existing system.[21] This could be achieved by a 'quality seal' scheme, as suggested by Spiess and Tietze (2002).

Parents could get the vouchers from the youth services departments and choose, from among the licensed facilities, the day care centre that best meets their needs. This aspect of matching supply to demand[22] also plays a key role in preventing and reducing child poverty: The demands of a paid job are greater than the current legal entitlement to a day care place in Germany allows for (see Article 24a, Child and Youth Welfare Act (Kinder- und Jugendhilfegesetz)). This legal entitlement generally guarantees only four hours' care per day, whereas even for part-time work (if taking account of the journey to and from work), more extensive care provision is needed, which would also allow for more flexible working hours of the centres (on this point, see also Kreyenfeld et al., 2001).

Day care providers could redeem the vouchers at the youth services departments run by all municipalities in Germany, and obtain reimbursement. Day care vouchers should not be transferable, in order to avoid a 'black market' in vouchers.

The vouchers should cover all of the costs (both operational and investment costs) of a day care place. As the costs of a day care place vary depending on age, the value of the voucher should be based on the age of the child.

In practice, the price of a day care place is determined to a substantial extent by quality. Setting the value of the voucher must therefore be done in tandem with setting quality standards. Moreover, the value must be specified in terms of the amount of time for which care is required This assumes, firstly, that the quality and quantity of care to be provided have been defined at policy level, and secondly, that the relationship between the cost and the quality of institutional care is known.

One of the options within the voucher system is to decide whether the voucher should be defined in terms of the price or the time period of care. If the voucher is defined in terms of price, this ensures only that the voucher has a specified value; whether parents use it for 10, 20 or 40 hours of day care per week is their own decision. However, parents have differing childcare needs; parents who work part-time need only around 20 to 30 hours per week of child-care outside the home, whereas parents who work full-time need up to 50 hours. If price-based vouchers were to be issued, the obvious assumption is that parents in part-time jobs would spend the whole value of the voucher for only 20 hours care, while mothers in full-time work would have to use the voucher for 50 hours' worth of child-care A difference in the educational quality of the care given to children of full-time and part-time working mothers could then result. For this reason, it is preferable to issue vouchers based not on price but on the amount of time in care.

In principle, vouchers could be financed either from taxes or by 'parafiscal' mean's of a special social security system responsible for any kind of family respectively child support. However, if financing were through taxes, the Federal Government should also be involved, to guarantee permanency of funding.[23] In 2002, for the first time in the German history of child and youth welfare, the Government announced just such a federal investment programme. For a period of four years from 2003 on, 4 billion euros are to be made available for full-day day care.[24]

However, experience from other countries supports the view that social security systems, i.e. insurance-type contribution payments, guarantee more consistent a high level of service than systems financed from taxes. In periods when public funds are tight, experience shows that tax-funded services are more likely to be cut (see, for example, Atkinson, 1988) than contributions to a particular social security system, such as a pension or health care insurance system are to be diverted. If we follow this line of argument, then the funding of day care should be part of the financing of all child-related services provided by the state, and managed through a social security system particular for families. It is essential that this such a system should be organized like the existing pension and health care insurance systems in Germany and financed through contributions. Thus, we could imagine a child insurance scheme with contributions for the adult population of Germany.[25]

Concluding remarks

To summarize: We believe day care vouchers are an effective and efficient instrument for combating child poverty – based on theoretical and empirical considerations. They address a significant cause of child poverty, they ensure that the public funds made available actually benefit the children, and they are effective not only on a short-term but also on a medium and long-term basis, because they are linked to the provision of high-quality education, which must be regulated by the state.

To what extent this strategy might also prove to be an effective anti-poverty instrument has not yet been evaluated systematically.[26] In Germany, the City of Hamburg will be the first federal state to introduce day care vouchers from 2003 (see Arlt, 2001). In any case it is necessary to carry out an independent and systematic evaluation of this first attempt of implementation.

Notes

1   See e.g. OECD (2001)
2   For U.S. studies, see e.g.. Duncan and Brooks-Gunn (1997), or Gregg et al. (1999); for German works, see e.g. Schönig (2000), and Hock and Holz (2000).
3   For a detailed description of income poverty in family households in Germany, see e.g. Hanesch et al. (2001), BMA (2001), Becker (2002), Otto and Spiess (2002), and Jenkins et al. (2000a, 2000b).
4   For a similar proposal to the Greens' 'basic income for children' from the academic sphere, see Hauser and Becker (2001). Hauser and Becker suggest a means-tested supplementary child allowance, which would make up the difference, for the bottom income class, between the existing child allowance and the overall benefit needs of the child, and would reduce gradually with increasing income. These authors also recommend an additional means-tested supplementary parental leave benefit. An increase in the parental leave benefit for the first years of the child's life is also suggested by Grabka and Kirner (2002).
5   On the effect of in-kind transfers in combating income poverty, see also e.g. Smeeding (1977).
6   The debate in other countries differs here; for example, OECD discussions on child poverty treat monetary transfers and in-kind transfers – as equally valuable instruments in combating child poverty (see OECD, 2001, pp. 36).
7   However, there are few empirically based analyzes of the consequences, and particularly of the instruments for reducing child poverty in Germany. A good international example of this type of analysis is e.g. Duncan and Brooks-Gunn (1997).

8   For earlier studies giving evidence of this, see e.g. evaluations based on the German Welfare Survey for the years 1994 and 1998 (Statistisches Bundesamt, 2000).

9   Effective means the economical achievement of goals.

10 A side effect of this arrangement of earmarked transfers direct to target groups is also that it is easier to evaluate this measure, as it is possible to measure directly whether the desired objective has been reached. Non-earmarked, monetary transfers do not allow this comparatively simple evaluation (see Currie, 1998, p. 185).

11 Hence our suggestion to follow the Anglo-American tradition, where many programmes for promoting childcare in daycare centres are linked to the goal of reducing income poverty in families (for an overview of the situation in the U.S.A., see e.g. Spiess, 1998).

12 In 1999, Germany had the highest level of child allowance in the EU, after Luxembourg.

13 Rønsen (2001) has shown that in Norway for example, monetary transfers to parents have led to mothers reducing their hours of work.

14 For a discussion on childcare vouchers versus monetary transfers, see also Beshariv and Samari (2001, pp. 197).

15 On the parents' side it should be noted that continuous employment leads to opportunities to earn a higher income in the long term (see e.g. Beblo and Wolf, 2002).

16 For other 'outcome measures', see among many others e.g. Currie (1998).

17 For a detailed discussion of the advantages of supporting the demand side over the supply side, see Kreyenfeld et al. (2001).

18 An analysis of distributional effects of day care subsidies in the current public system does show that this is not the case at present although most German states do have income dependent day care fees (see Spiess et al., 2002a).

19 Parker (1989) points out for example: A voucher system aimed at preventing a situation where lower income households do not have the same access to daycare centres, must favour the bottom income groups. Empirical examples also show that social segregation in day care centres where attendance is funded via a voucher is not so pronounced as in the cases of subsidizing supplies (centres) (see Besharov and Samari, 2000).

20 See also Parker (1989) and Besharov and Samari (2000).

21 Perhaps the existing German 'quality definition and checking system' could be retained. Certainly, quality assurance and control should be performed by an independent body. In the current German system, municipalities and states, in their pivotal role in funding daycare centres for children, have per se no pronounced interest in high standards of quality, as these are generally associated with higher costs. This gives rise to the danger that they may not carry out adequate quality assurance (for more detail, see Spiess and Tietze, 2002).

22 This aspect is a decisive advantage of supporting the 'economic actor' over the 'object'; see Kreyenfeld et al. (2001) and Spiess (2002a, 2002b).

23 In the existing system of financing, there is no assurance of lasting and permanent funding, because of large fluctuations in municipalities' budgets (for this aspect, see also Kreyenfeld et al., 2001).

24 See official statement on family policy by Gerhard Schröder to the German parliament, 18th April 2002. In autumn 2002 it is anticipated that these funds will be made available to develop all-day schools (see e.g. Bulmahn, 2002). At this point we do not intend to discuss further whether the right priorities have been set, in the light of the deficiencies at the pre-school stage recently suggested by PISA; but see Spiess et al. (2002b).

25 For a similar suggestion from the 1960s, see Schreiber (1964). In its most recent report, the academic advisory board to the Federal Ministry for Family Affairs, Senior Citizens,

Women and Youth proposes setting up a family fund (Wissenschaftlicher Beirat beim Bundesministerium für Familie, Senioren, Frauen und Jugend, 2001). Day care vouchers could also be paid for out of such a fund.

26 In the USA and Canada for example, vouchers are issued in various states/provinces (see Steuerle et al., 2000, Appendix 17A Survey of Voucher Use). One of the few evaluations we know of relating to a day care voucher system in an American state does not however address poverty policy issues directly (see Parker, 1989).

References

Arlt, S. (2002), 'Das Hamburger "Kita-Gutschein-System"', in Bundesvereinigung Evangelischer Tageseinrichtungen für Kinder (eds), *Neue Ansätze zur Finanzierung von Kindertageseinrichtungen – von der Objekt- zur Subjektfinanzierung*, Stuttgart, pp. 54-64.

Atkinson, A. (1988), 'Sozialversicherung und Einkommenssicherung', in G. Rolf, P. Bernd Spahn and G. Wagner (eds), *Sozialvertrag und Sicherung*, Frankfurt and New York, pp. 221-240.

Baumert, J. et al. (eds) (2001), *PISA 2000: Basiskompetenzen von Schülerinnen und Schülern im internationalen Vergleich*, Opladen.

Beblo, M. and Wolf E. (2002), 'Die Folgekosten von Erwerbsunterbrechungen', in *Vierteljahreshefte zur Wirtschaftsforschung* (1), pp. 83-94.

Becker, I. (2002), 'Frauenerwerbstätigkeit hält Einkommensarmut von Familien in Grenzen', *Vierteljahreshefte zur Wirtschaftsforschung* (forthcoming) 71(1), pp. 126-146.

Beckmann, P. and Engelbrech, G. (2002), 'Vereinbarkeit von Familie und Beruf: Kinderbetreuung und Beschäftigungsmöglichkeiten von Frauen mit Kindern', in G. Engelbrech (ed.) *Arbeitsmarktchancen von Frauen*, Nürnberg, pp. 263-281.

Besharov, D.J. and Samari, N. (2000), Child-Care Vouchers and Cash Payments, in C. Steuerle, E. Van Doorn Ooms, G. Peterson, R. D. Reischauer (eds) *Vouchers and the Provision of Public Services*, Washington D.C., pp. 195-223.

Büchel, F. and Spiess, C.K. (2002), 'Form der Kinderbetreuung und Arbeitsmarktverhalten von Müttern in West- und Ostdeutschland', *Schriftenreihe des Bundesministeriums für Familie, Senioren, Frauen und Jugend* 220, Kohlhammer, Stuttgart.

Büchel, F. and Spiess, C.K. (2002), 'Müttererwerbstätigkeit und Kindertageseinrichtungen - neue Ergebnisse zu einem bekannten Zusammenhang', in *Vierteljahreshefte zur Wirtschaftsforschung* (1), pp. 96-114.

BMA (Bundesministerium für Arbeit und Sozialordnung) (2001), *Der erste Armuts- und Reichtumsbericht der Bundesregierung: Lebenslagen in Deutschland*, Bonn.

Currie, J. (1998), 'The Effect of Welfare on Child Outcome', in R. A. Moffitt (ed.) *Welfare, the Familiy, and reproductive behavior*, Washington, D.C., pp. 177-204.

Duncan, G.J. and Brooks-Gunn, J. (eds) (1997), *Consequences of Growing Up Poor*, Russel Sage Foundation, New York.

Europäische Kommission (2002), MISSOC, *Gegenseitiges Informationssystem zur Sozialen Sicherheit in den Mitgliedstaaten der Europäischen Union. Situation am 1. Januar 1999 und Entwicklung*, Europäische Kommission Generaldirektion Beschäftigung, Arbeitsbeziehungen und soziale Angelegenheiten (Referat V/E/2), http://europa.eu.int/comm/employment_social/soc-prot/missoc99/ (as at: August 2002).

European Child Care and Education (ECCE) – Study Group (1999), *European Child Care and Education Study. School-age Assessment of Child Development: Long-term impact of Pre-school Experiences on School Success, and Family-School Relationships, Final Report for Work Package # 2*, Submitted to European Union DG XII. Science, Research and Development RTD Action: Targeted Socio-Economic Research, Berlin.

Grabka, M. and Kirner, E. (2002), 'Einkommen von Haushalten mit Kindern: Finanzielle Förderung auf erste Lebensjahre konzentrieren', in *DIW-Wochenbericht* (32), pp. 527-536.

Gregg, P., Harkness, S. and Machin, S. (1999), 'Child Development and Family Income', *York Publishing Services for the Joseph Rowntree Foundation*, York.

Joos, M. and Wolfgang, M. (1998), 'Die Entwicklung der relativen Einkommensarmut von Kindern in Deutschland 1990 bis 1995', in J. Mansel and G. Neubauer (eds), *Armut und soziale Ungleichheit bei Kindern*, Leske & Budrich, Opladen, pp. 19-33.

Habisch, A. (2000), 'Gesellschafts-Ordnungspolitik – Gestaltung institutioneller Arrangements für die Bürgergesellschaft des 21. Jahrhunderts', in J. Bernhard, A. Habisch and E. Stutzer (eds). *Familienwissenschaftliche und familienpolitische Signale*, Max Wingen zum 70. Geburtstag, Vektor Verlag, Grafschaft, pp. 89-98.

Hanesch, W., Krause, P., Bäcker, G., Maschke, M. and Otto, B. (2000), *Armut und Ungleichheit in Deutschland. Der neue Armutsbericht der Hans-Böckler-Stiftung, des DGB und des Paritätischen Wohlfahrtsverbands*, Rowohlt Verlag, Reinbek bei Hamburg.

Hauser, R. and Becker, I. (2001), *Lohnsubventionen und verbesserter Familienlastenausgleich als Instrumente zur Verringerung von Sozialhilfeabhängigkeit*, Sonderdruck aus Private Versicherung und Soziale Sicherung. Festschrift zum 60. Geburtstag von Roland Eisen, Metropolis Verlag, Marburg.

Hock, B., Holz, G. and Wüstendörfer, W. (2000), *Folgen familiärer Armut im frühen Kindesalter – Eine Annäherung anhand von Fallbeispielen*, Dritter Zwischenbericht zu einer Studie im Auftrag des Bundesverbandes der Arbeiterwohlfahrt, ISS-Eigenverlag, Frankfurt am Main.

Hock, B. and Holz, G. (2000), *Erfolg oder Scheitern? Arme und benachteiligte Jugendliche auf dem Weg ins Berufleben*, Fünfter Zwischenbericht zu einer Studie im Auftrag des Bundesverbandes der Arbeiterwohlfahrt, ISS-Eigenverlag, Frankfurt am Main.

Jenkins, S. P., Schluter, C. and Wagner, G. (2002a), 'Child poverty in Britain and Germany', *Report Series, Anglo-German Foundation*, London.

Jenkins, S. P., Schluter, C. and Wagner, G. (2002b), 'Children in Poverty – A British-German Comparison for the 1990s', in *Economic Bulletin* 39(3), pp. 95-98.

Kreyenfeld, M., Spiess, C.K. and Wagner, G. (2001), *Finanzierungs- und Organisationsmodelle institutioneller Kinderbetreuung*, Luchterhand, Neuwied Berlin.

Kreyenfeld, M., Spiess, C.K. and Wagner, G. (2002), 'Kinderbetreuungspolitik in Deutschland: Möglichkeiten nachfrageorientierter Steuerungs- und Finanzierungsinstrumente', in *Zeitschrift für Erziehungswissenschaften* (2), pp. 201-221.

Lauterbach, W. and Lange, A. (1998), 'Aufwachsen in materieller Armut und sorgenbelastetem Familienklima', in J. Mansel and G. Neubauer (eds) *Armut und soziale Ungleichheit bei Kindern*, Leske & Budrich, Opladen, pp. 106-128.

Leibfried, S., Leisering, L. et al. (1995), *Zeit der Armut. Lebensläufe im Sozialstaat.* Suhrkamp, Frankfurt am Main.

Mansel, J. and Neubauer, G. (1998), 'Kinderarmut – Armutsrisiko Kinder', in J. Mansel and G. Neubauer (eds) *Armut und soziale Ungleichheit bei Kindern*, Leske & Budrich, Opladen, pp. 7-18.

OECD (2001), *Starting Strong. Early Childhood Education and Care*, Paris.

Otto, B., Spiess, C.K. and Teichmann, D. (2001), *Berechnung des Grünen Kindergrund-sicherungsmodells und einer Gegenfinanzierung durch ein Ehegattenrealsplitting*, Kurzgutachten für die Bundestagsfraktion von Bündnis90/ Die Grünen. DIW-*Gutachten*.

Otto, B. and Spiess, C.K. (2002), 'Die Grüne Kindergrundsicherung. Welche Familien würden davon profitieren und in welchem Maße?', in *Sozialer Fortschritt* 51(5), pp. 11-118.

Parker, M.D. (1989), 'Vouchers for Day Care of Children: Evaluating a Model Program', in *Child Welfare*, LXVIII 6, pp. 633-642.

Piachaud, D. (1992), 'Wie mißt man Armut?', in S. Leibfried and W. Voges (eds) Armut im modernen Wohlfahrtsstaat, *Sonderheft der Kölner Zeitschrift für Soziologie und Sozialpsychologie*, Westdeutscher Verlag GmbH, Opladen, pp. 63-87.

Rønsen, M. (2001), 'Market Work, Child Care and the Division of Household Labour', *Statistics Norway Report* 2001/3.

Schönig, W. (2000), 'Langzeitarbeitslosigkeit und Kinderarmut', in C. Butterwegge (eds) *Kinderarmut in Deutschland*, Campus Verlag, Frankfurt am Main, pp. 197-219.

Schreiber, W. (1964), *Kindergeld im sozio-ökonomischen Prozeß. Familienlastenausgleich als Prozeß zeitlicher Kaufkraft-Umschichtung im Individual-Bereich*, Kohlhammer, Köln.

Smeeding, T. (1977), 'The Antipoverty Effectivness of In-Kind-Transfers', in *Journal of Human Resources*, XII 3 pp.361-378.

Spiess, C.K. (1998), 'Staatliche Eingriffe in Märkte für Kinderbetreuung. Analysen im deutsch-amerikanischen Vergleich', Campus Verlag, *Reihe Wirtschaftswissenschaften*, Frankfurt am Main/New York.

Spiess, C.K., Kreyenfeld, M. and Wagner, G. (2002a), 'A Forgotten Issue: Distributional Effects of Day Care Subsidies in Germany', forthcoming in *European Early Childhood Education Research Journal*.

Spiess, C.K., Büchel, F. and Frick, J.R. (2002b), 'Kinderbetreuung in West- und Ost-deutschland: Sozioökonomischer Hintergrund entscheidend', in *DIW-Wochenbericht* (31), pp. 518-524.

Spiess, C.K. (2002a), 'Bedarfsorientierung von Kindertageseinrichtungen – was heißt das und wie erreichen wir sie?', in *Zukunft Familie* (2), Forum Familie der SPD (ed.), own publisher, Berlin, pp. 45-60.

Spiess, C.K. (2002b), 'Gutscheine – ein Ansatz zur Finanzierung und Steuerung im Kinder-tagesstättenbereich', in D. Dohmen and B.A. Cleuvers (eds) *Nachfrageorientierte Bildungsfinanzierung – Neue Trends für Kindertagesstätte, Schule und Hochschule*, Bertelsmann Verlag Bielefeld (Schriftenreihe zur Bildungs- und Sozialökonomie 1), pp. 33-50.

Spiess, C.K. and Tietze, W. (2002), 'Qualitätssicherung in Kindertageseinrichtungen – Gründe, Anforderungen und Umsetzungsüberlegungen für ein Gütesiegel', in *Zeitschrift für Erziehungswissenschaften* (1), pp. 139-162 .

Statistisches Bundesamt (2000), *Datenreport 1999*, Bonn.

Steuerle, C.E., Van Doorn, O., Peterson, G. and Reischauer, R.D. (2000), (eds) *Vouchers and the Provision of Public Services*, Washington D.C.

Team Perspektive Deutschland (2002), Projektbericht zur größten Online-Umfrage Deutschlands, Eine Initiative von McKinsey, stern.de und T-Online, http://www.perspektive-deutschland.de/ergebnisse/index.shtml (as at: 18. Juli 2002).

Wissenschaftlicher Beirat beim Bundesministerium für Familie, Senioren, Frauen und Jugend (2001), 'Gerechtigkeit für Familien. Zur Begründung und Weiterentwicklung des Familienlasten- und Familienleistungsausgleichs', *Schriftenreihe des Bundesministeriums für Familie, Senioren, Frauen und Jugend* 202, Stuttgart.

Chapter 17

Social policy strategies to combat income poverty of children and families in Europe

Bea Cantillon and Karel Van den Bosch

Introduction

In the EU there is growing concern about poverty among children, and among families with children. In most OECD countries, income poverty among children now exceeds that among the elderly, who traditionally were the demographic group most at risk of poverty (Jäntti and Danziger, 2000). However, the policy response of most industrialized countries in the past decades towards poverty among the elderly – extending coverage and levels of pension benefits – is less obvious as a policy option as regards poverty among families with children. There are two basic reasons for this. First of all, there is a consensus that increases in social spending are to be avoided, in view of the expected upward pressure on government budgets resulting from the ageing of the population in the coming decades. Secondly, in contrast to the elderly, families with children are supposed to be 'self-reliant', i.e. to be able – in normal circumstances – to earn sufficient income through their own efforts to escape poverty. Benefit dependency is seen as economically inefficient, as socially and morally degrading, and also as ultimately an ineffective route to escape poverty.

Given this starting point, this paper tries to reach some general policy recommendations for combating income poverty among children and families. It is organized as follows. In the next section, I identify which families with children are most at risk of poverty. Single parents obviously belong to this category, but – what is less well known – so do families with three or more children. In the third section, I discuss some of the new social risks leading to child poverty, which are related to low skills and to the current impossibility of many parents to combine care for children and paid work. In the fourth and final section, I suggest some possible policy responses which would support families in meeting the direct and indirect costs of children.

Incidence of poverty across family types

It is now generally well known that one-parent families (virtually synonymous with lone-mother families) tend to face a much high risk of poverty than two-parent families in almost all OECD countries (e.g. Bradbury and Jäntti, 2001a). Figure 17.1 confirms this once again. It also shows, however, that in several European countries, the poverty rate among large families with three or more children is equally high as that among single-parent families. This is the case in Belgium, Spain, Finland (though at a comparatively low level), Italy, and the UK. The poverty risk of large families generally exceeds that of childless non-aged families, except in the Nordic Countries and The Netherlands. By contrast, couples with only 1 or 2 children are less at risk of poverty compared to the average childless household, except in Italy and the UK.

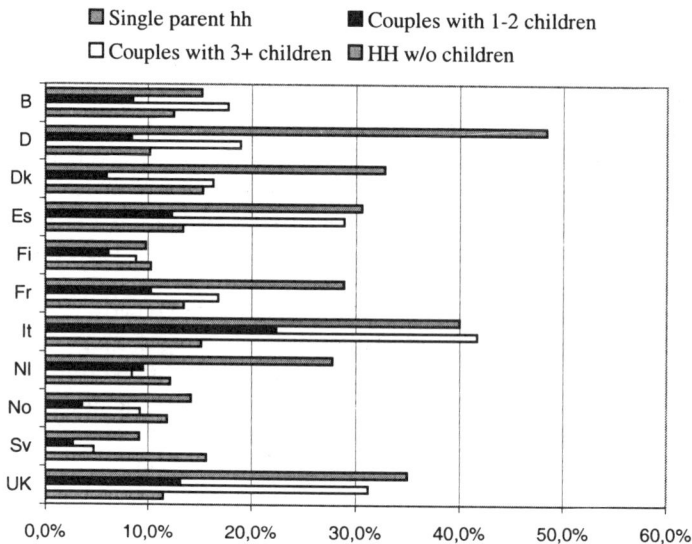

Figure 17.1   Poverty rates (headcount) among the non-aged in several European countries in de mid-nineties, by family type

Note: See Appendix for details on method. B=Belgium, D=Germany, Dk=Denmark, Es=Spain, Fi=Finland, Fr=France, It=Italy, Nl=The Netherlands, No=Norway, Sv=Sweden, UK=United Kingdom.

Source: Own calculations from the Luxembourg Income Study.

The significance of this finding is emphasized by the fact that in many European countries, large families are (still) more numerous than one-parent families, and in addition contain more children per family.

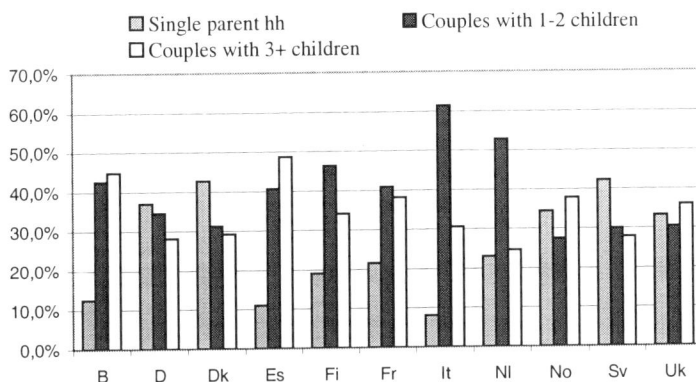

Figure 17.2 legend: Single parent hh; Couples with 1-2 children; Couples with 3+ children

Figure 17.2 Distribution of children in poverty across family types in several European countries in the mid-1990s

Note:　See Figure 17.1 and Appendix for methods and definitions.
Source:　Own calculations from the Luxembourg Income Study.

The implications of this are revealed in Figure 17.2, which shows the percentage distribution of poor children across family types. In several countries (Belgium, France, Spain, Italy), the proportion of poor children who live in two-parent families with 3 or more children is much larger than the proportion living in lone-parent families. The contribution of one-parent families exceeds that of large families only in the low-poverty countries Denmark and Sweden, and in Germany, where one-parent families are at a very elevated risk of poverty, both compared to other countries, and compared to other German families.

Of course, an important, if not the main proximate cause of poverty among families with children is no, or inadequate involvement in the labour market. However, as Figure 17.3 shows, the labour market situation of poor families with children varies drastically by family type. (Figure 17.3 excludes Finland, Norway and Sweden, where child poverty rates are very low.) Most of the poor single parents are not in work (with the exception of Germany), and therefore, in many countries getting them into a job may be generally an effective way to get them out of poverty. On the other hand, in most countries the majority of large families in poverty have at least one worker (Belgium, The Netherlands and the UK are exceptions). Poverty among large families without any worker is extremely high, but such households are relatively few in number. Most of the couples in poverty with many children are single-worker families – and this is incidentally true for all couples with children in poverty.

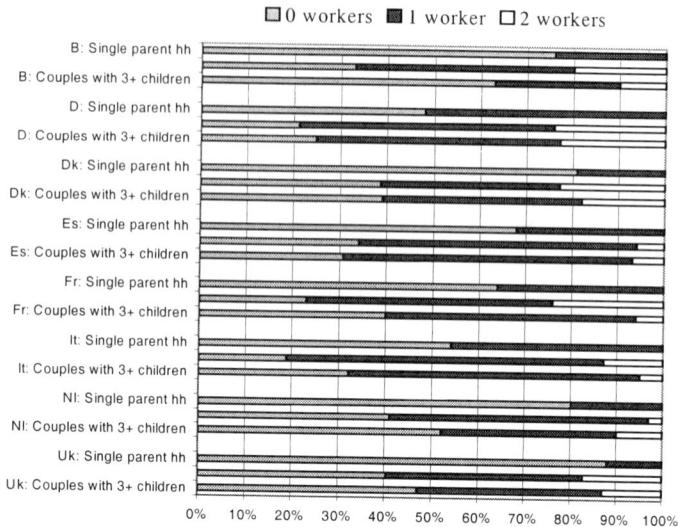

☐ 0 workers ■ 1 worker ☐ 2 workers

Figure 17.3 **Distribution of poor families with children across number of workers, by family type, in several European countries in the mid-1990s**

Note: See Figure 17.1 and Appendix for methods and definitions. Only workers among the head and spouse or cohabitor are counted.

Source: Own calculations from the Luxembourg Income Study.

New social risks and the causes of poverty among families with children

In many European countries, the male breadwinner model used to be the norm, where the father went into the labour market and earned a wage which was deemed to be sufficient to support his family and cover the monetary costs of children. In this model, the mother stayed home to take care of the children. The time costs of children were therefore internalized in the household and socially 'invisible'. Poverty resulted if there were many children to feed, or if the wage-earner fell ill, became unemployed, or was otherwise incapable of working. The traditional social insurance welfare state was designed to cover these risks, through family benefits, and sickness, invalidity and unemployment social insurance schemes. Although reality nowhere and never totally conformed to the male breadwinner model, the traditional social insurance welfare state worked reasonably well in the years of nearly full employment (for men), and limited labour market participation of married women, during the sixties and seventies. Yet, benefits, especially unemployment benefits were often too low to escape poverty.

Today, these causes of poverty are still important. But they are being overshadowed by new social risks, resulting from long-term social and economic changes. The key terms here are individualization, technological development and globalization. Without entering into the difficult debate on the nature and relative importance of these phenomena, we can still identify three observable developments, which lead to new social risks for families with children.

1. In virtually all European countries, as a result of their improved education and of the women's emancipation movement, married women and mothers are increasingly performing paid work outside the home. This implies that children are no longer self-evidently taken care of by the mother at all times during the day and during the working week. In contemporary welfare states 'care work' has become socially visible, and has a *price-tag*: care that was previously provided naturally and without remuneration by female homemakers has increasingly been commodified on the private and public service market. Conversely, a choice to take care of children within the family has now an important opportunity cost, viz. the loss of the mothers' wages. As one-earnership is (at least partly for many persons) a choice, it cannot be insured following the traditional social insurance methods.

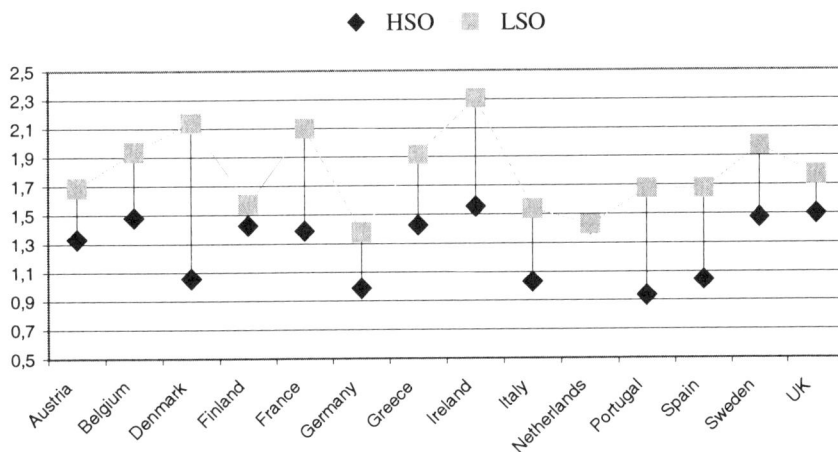

Figure 17.4   Average number of children of women aged 26-45 by educational level, in a number of European countries

Note: HSO: Higher Secondary Education; LSO: Lower Secondary Education, or less. All women aged 26-45 are included, irrespective of marital status, position in the household and whether they have children or not. Children are persons living in the same household as the woman, and are related to the woman as child, step-child or foster child (irrespective of age).

Source: European Community Household Panel, wave 1997.

2. Persons with relatively low education have an increasingly difficult time on the labour market. As the number of traditional well-paying jobs for low-skilled men in manufacturing has steadily declined, such persons are increasingly found in the service sector, where wages are lower, and job security is limited. Moreover, low skilled men tend to marry low skilled women (educational homogamy). Therefore, the action taken by many couples in response to changing economic circumstances – increased labour market participation by the wife – is less open and less effective for these persons.

These developments create a category in society, which is at very high risk of poverty in all countries. These are mothers with low education (Cantillon et al., 2001). Whereas highly educated mothers are generally in paid work, even in the most traditional European societies such as Spain and Italy, this is much less true for low-skilled mothers. The employment gap between well educated women and their less well educated sisters is conspicuously wide in the Continental and Southern European countries, although it is significant even in the social-democratic welfare states of Scandinavia. For women with few marketable skills, the opportunity costs of the care of children often exceed the relatively small wages they can command in the market. The comparison of paid work outside the home versus care work inside the home becomes even more skewed if the low-skilled mother is entitled to a social benefit, even if it is only a small one. These tendencies are reinforced by the fact that in most European countries, women with low education have on average more children to care for than women who are highly educated (Figure 17.4).

3. While lone parenthood is perhaps not more common now then in earlier decades, the proximate causes of becoming a single mother have changed. Widowhood has become less important, and divorce (and intentional lone motherhood) have become more common, implying that there are more lone parents with young children. The major cause of poverty and chronic welfare dependency among lone mothers with modest earnings-capacities is their inability to combine full-time work and childcare. Moreover, the technique of social insurance is not well-suited to protect against the risk of divorce and one-earner ship (in contrast to the risk of widowhood).

Policy recommendations

Designing a policy package to combat income poverty among children and families is not an easy matter. Policies must respond to both the old and the new social risks leading to poverty. Also, their cost must remain within reasonable budgetary limits, and measures taken should encourage, rather than discourage working.

This said, one of the most clear conclusions coming out of cross-country comparative research into poverty and welfare states is that low poverty requires high social spending (Bradbury and Jäntti, 2001b; Cantillon et al., 2002). There are some obvious, but also some less obvious reasons for this.

One of the more obvious reasons is that a generous child benefit system must be part of any anti-child poverty policy package. Child benefits should cover the direct costs of children, and should preferably depend on the number and age of children, but preferably not on the parents' income. Figure 17.5 shows that family allowances have an important poverty reducing effect in many countries (the main exceptions are Italy and Spain, who at the time the data were collected had no child allowances that were not means tested, and Sweden, where poverty before family allowances is very low to begin with.) Figure 17.5 also reveals that the poverty reducing effect is particularly pronounced for the most vulnerable categories, viz. single parent households, and families with many children. Belgium and France manage to bring back rather high pre-family allowance poverty rates for large families to levels that are near those of families with one or two children.

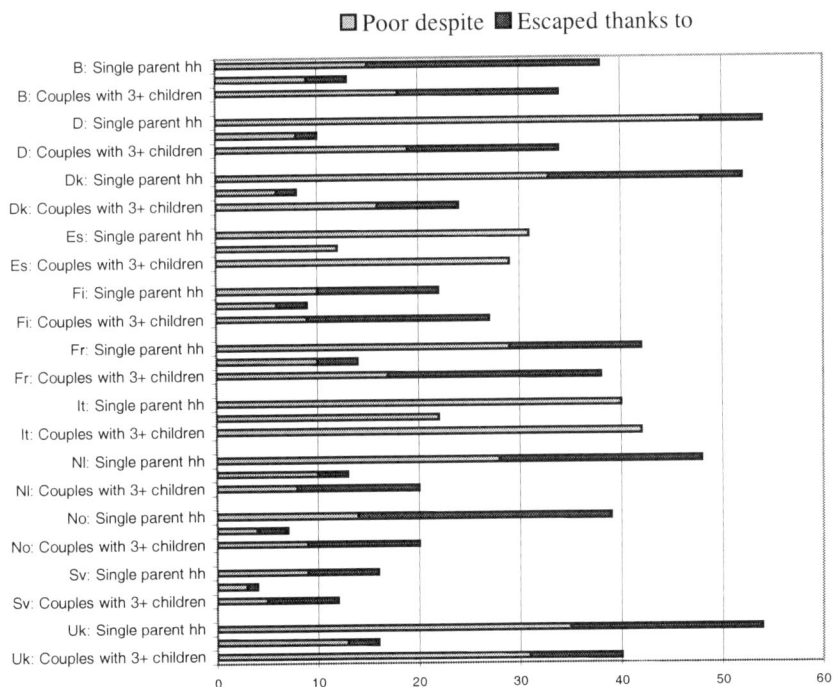

Figure 17.5 **Poverty reducing effect of family allowances: proportion of households who have escaped poverty thanks to family allowances**

Note: Family and child allowances include any family or child related allowances, as long as they are not means tested. See Figure 17.1 and Appendix for methods and definitions.

Source: Own calculations from the Luxembourg Income Study.

However, introducing or raising family benefits is not the only strategy needed to combat poverty among children. This is illustrated in Figure 17.6, where the introduction of a universal basic child benefit is simulated. The benefit is set at such a level, that the total cost is a given percentage of aggregate income of the non-aged (the latter is shown on the horizontal axis of Figure 17.6). One can see that the introduction of such a benefit would substantially reduce poverty rates among children in all countries where it does not exist now (or where such benefits are small), and that, conversely, the elimination or reduction of such a benefit would significantly increase poverty rates in other European welfare states. The effect is particularly pronounced for the UK, suggesting that in that country many households with children are living near the poverty line.

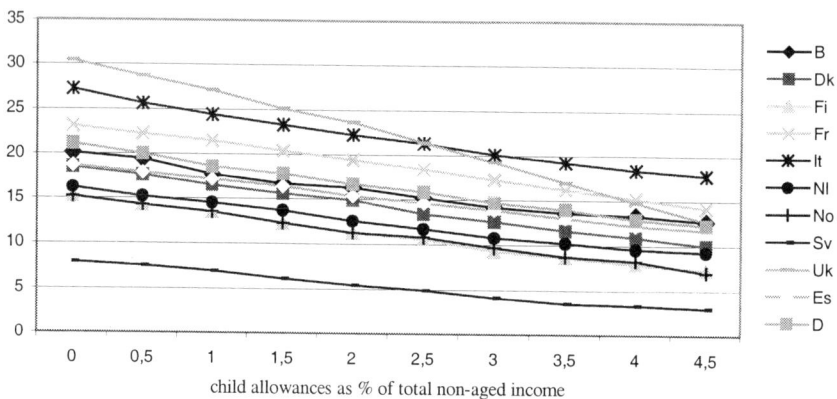

Figure 17.6   Simulated poverty rates of children at a range of levels of a basic child benefit, in a number of European countries

Note: Family allowances were calculated as a fixed amount per child, such that the total equals the indicated proportion of total income of the non-aged. Other income was adjusted, such that aggregate income remained constant. See Figure 17.1 and Appendix for methods and definitions. See also Van den Bosch (2002) for more details on the simulation method.

Source: Own calculations from the Luxembourg Income Study.

Figure 17.6 also shows that even if all countries would increase their spending on family allowances to relatively high levels, important differences in child poverty rates between countries would remain, with Italy and the UK still having a large proportion of poor children. Partly, this reflects the inadequacy of other social transfers in a number of countries, which are either too low, or have a too limited coverage. Modern welfare states should not forget to protect their citizens against the old social risks, such as sickness and invalidity, and in particular unemployment, through adequate replacement incomes.

However, for reasons indicated above, poverty among children cannot be eliminated by social transfers alone. Most families with children should be able to earn the largest part of their income through their own efforts. For economic as well as social reasons, the male breadwinner model is no longer tenable. This implies that policies should be designed to enable all women, including those with limited skills, to combine paid work and care, and to enter the labour market and earn a decent wage (Solera, 2001). Such a strategy would contain a number of elements.

A central element in this strategy would be the provision of child care at prices that every parent can afford. In many countries, there is a very limited supply of formal child care for pre-school children, or it is offered at market prices, which only women with high earnings potential are able and willing to pay. Many mothers rely on social networks (family, neighbors) to take of their young children while they are working, but for those who are not so fortunate, the unavailability of childcare often keeps them at home. Expanding the supply of affordable childcare should therefore be a priority.

At the same time, it is probably wise to recognize that not every mother (or father) will want to work full-time and during all the years her or his children are growing up. It is therefore essential that employment policies

'should aim at gearing working conditions to family circumstances as well as at a better distribution of work over individuals' active life span, while taking due account of the possibilities and needs of each family phase.' (Cantillon et al., 2001, p. 463)

This may be realized through the expansion of part time work, flexible working hours (on the mothers' terms, not only on the employers terms), and facilities to take days off work for taking care of sick children.

Another important element in such a policy package would be a system for parental leave, which would enable mothers (and fathers) to stay home for a number of months or years in order to look after their children, while keeping a formal link to their former job. At present, many mothers leave the labour market after their second or third child, never to return again. Parental leave systems should be designed such that parents have the right to come back to a specific job, so that they can regenerate their human capital.

Of course, those women, especially low-skilled women, who enter the labour market, should find jobs waiting for them. The private and public services sector offers the greatest opportunities for expanding the number of jobs. There is a latent market in care for the elderly, in domestic help, etc., which could be made manifest through selective policies to reduce the cost of labour (job subsidies, reductions in taxes and social contributions). Also, in order to reconcile the needs for a decent wage with the limited market earnings potential of some mothers and fathers, refundable tax credits for families with low wages should be provided.

The need for such policies as outlined above is often recognized. What is less often recognized is that it is equally important to contain tendencies towards greater wage inequality, and a worsening position of low wage earners. As Figure 17.7, perhaps surprisingly shows, there is a clear positive relationship between low-pay incidence and child poverty: the fewer persons are paid low wages, the fewer children are in poverty.

The reasons for this relationship are at this moment not entirely clear. The seemingly obvious explanation, that if many breadwinners receive low wages, their children are living in poverty, holds only very partially. Certainly in European countries, most low wage earners not the sole breadwinner in their family, but secondary earners such as married women and older children. Another possible explanation is that extensive welfare states, which reduce child poverty, also compress the wage distribution: high taxes discourage high-wage earners from putting in many additional hours, while high benefits discourage those with low potential wages to enter the labour market at all (Alvarez, 2001). A third possible explanation is that both a high level of social expenditure and a compressed wage distribution emanate from widely shared value systems emphasizing solidarity and equality. Such values might at once support pay norms and collective agreements (Atkinson, 1999, p. 68), as well as universal and generous benefits. Exploring this relationship is an important task for future research.

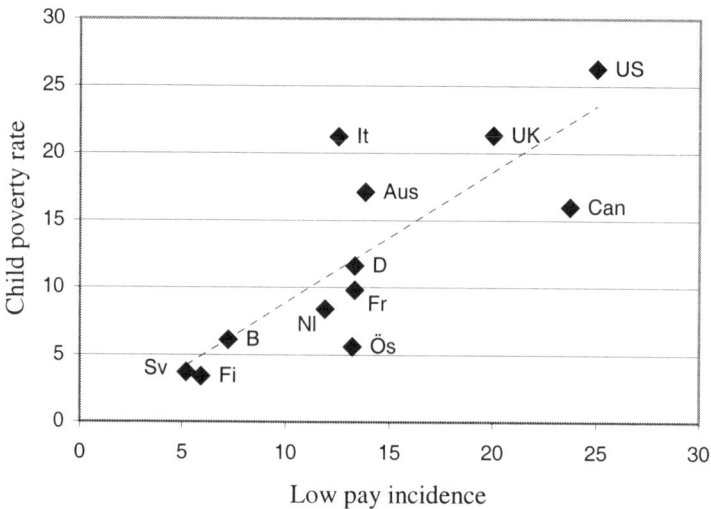

Figure 17.7   The cross-country relationship between the incidence of low pay, and the extent of child poverty

Source: Low pay: OECD (1998) Employment Outlook; poverty: Bradbury and Jäntti, (2001a).

What the cross-country comparisons certainly show is that extensive welfare states with adequate benefits and services, which are a precondition for combating child poverty, cannot co-exist with large wage inequalities. Therefore, governments concerned with poverty among children and families should not let market inequalities increase unchecked, expecting welfare state arrangements to 'mop up' any problems that the market creates or leaves unsolved. Reducing market inequalities should go hand in hand with improving social services and benefits.

Conclusion

This paper tries to present some general policy recommendations for combating income poverty among children and families. It starts by noting that in most European countries single parents and families with three or more children are the family types most at risk of poverty. Many of these poor families with children lack any worker, but a large proportion of poor children live in single-worker families. I discuss some of the old and new risks which lead to income poverty for families with children. The central point here is the current impossibility for many parents to combine care for children and paid work, at a time when dual earnership is become the social and economic norm. Many lone parents, but also many low-skilled married women are unable to earn a decent wage, either because jobs offering such wages are unavailable, or because they cannot reconcile a job with their caring responsibilities.

An adequate social policy package to combat poverty among families with children, would include first of all adequate child benefits and social insurance replacement incomes. Secondly, such a package should enable all women, including those with limited skills, to combine paid work and care, and to earn a decent wage. This requires affordable child care, in-work arrangements for parents, and parental leave systems to allow parents to come back to a job, after a period of staying home to look after their children. Finally, it is suggested that governments concerned with child poverty should not only develop welfare state arrangements, but also limit market inequalities.

Annex: Data, methods and definitions

Most original results in this contribution are based on the Luxembourg Income Study. The datasets used are:

Country	Year	Dataset Identification
Belgium (B)	1997	BE97
Germany (D)	1994	GE94
Denmark (Dk)	1997	DK97
Spain (Es)	1990	SP90
Finland (Fi)	1995	FI95
France (Fr)	1994	FR94
Italy (It)	1995	IT95
The Netherlands (Nl)	1994	NL94
Norway (No)	1995	Nw95
Sweden (Sv)	1995	SW95
United Kingdom (UK)	1994	UK94

See the LIS website (www.lisproject.org) for information about these datasets. LIS data for the EU countries Ireland, Austria and Luxembourg were not used. The latest Irish data are from 1987, the Austrian data appeared to lack crucial information on some income components, and Luxembourg was regarded as being too small.

Poverty is defined as equivalent disposable household income below the poverty line. The equivalence scale used is the modified OECD one, with weights of 1 for the first adult, 0.5 for other adults, and 0.3 for children. The poverty line is set at 60 percent of median equivalent disposable household income, calculated across all individuals, in each country. Households with zero or negative incomes were excluded from all analyses, as variation in the prevalence of these incomes across country is likely to reflect differences in income data collection and imputation methods, rather than in the real economic situations of households.

Children are all persons under age 18, but excluding heads and spouses. Single-parent families are defined as households where the head is without a spouse or cohabitor and there are also children present; other persons may also live in such a household. Couples with three or more children are households where the head has a spouse or is cohabiting, and there are at least three persons under age 18. Couples with one or two children are all other families with children. Non-aged are all persons below age 65. The precise definition of a worker differs from country to country. I have tried to include everyone who is working in self-employment, or has a contract as an employee, including those that are temporary not working, (e.g., due to short-term illness).

References

Alvarez, P. (2001), 'The politics of income inequality in the OECD: The role of second order effects', *Luxembourg Income Study Working Paper* (284), Syracuse University, Syracuse.

Atkinson, A. (1999), 'The distribution of income in the UK and OECD countries in the twentieth century', *Oxford Review of Economic Policy* 15(4), pp. 56-75.

Bradbury, B. and Jäntti, M. (2001a), 'Child poverty across the industrialized world: evidence from the Luxembourg Income Study', in K. Vleminckx and T. Smeeding (eds), *Child well-being, child poverty and child policy in modern nations: What do we know?*, Policy Press, Bristol, pp. 11-32.

Bradbury, B. and Jäntti, M. (2001b), 'Child poverty across twenty-five countries', in B. Bradbury, S. Jenkins and J. Micklewright (eds), *The dynamics of child poverty in industrialized countries*, University Press, Cambridge, pp. 62-91.

Bradshaw, J., Ditch, J., Holmes, H. and Whiteford, P. (1993), *Support for children. A comparison of arrangements in fifteen countries*, UK Department of Social Security, Research Report 21, London.

Cantillon, B., Ghysels, J., Mussche, N. and Van Dam, R. (2001), 'Female employment differences, poverty and care provisions', *European Societies* 3(4), pp. 447-469.

Cantillon, B., Marx, I. and Van den Bosch, K. (2002), *Welfare state protection, labour markets and poverty: lessons from cross-country comparisons*, Paper presented at the 9th BIEN International Congres, Geneva, 12-14 September 2002.

Esping-Andersen, G. (1990), *The Three Worlds of Welfare Capitalism*, Polity Press, Cambridge.

Iversen, T. and Wren, A. (1998), 'Equality, Employment and Budgetary Restraint. The Trilemma of the Service Economy', *World Politics* 50, pp. 507-546.

Jäntti, M. and Danziger, S. (2000), 'Income Poverty in Advanced Countries', in A. Atkinson, and F. Bourguignon (eds), *Handbook of income distribution*, Elsevier. (Handbooks in economics; 16), Amsterdam.

Korpi, W. and Palme, J. (1998), 'The Paradox of Redistribution and Strategies of Equality: Welfare State Institutions, Inequality, and Poverty in the Western Countries', *American Sociological Review*, pp. 661-687.

Marx, I. and Verbist, G. (1998), 'Low-paid work and poverty: a cross-country perspective', in S. Bazen, M. Gregory and W. Salverda (eds), *Low-wage employment in Europe*, Elgar, Cheltenham.

OECD (1998), *Employment Outlook*, OECD, Paris.

Oxley, H., Dang, Th.-Th., Förster, M.F. and Pellizari, M. (2001), 'Income inequalities and poverty among children and households with children in selected OECD countries', in K. Vleminckx and T. Smeeding (eds), *Child well-being, Child poverty and child policy in modern nations: What do we know?*, Policy Press, Bristol, pp. 371-405.

Solera, C. (2001), 'Income transfers and support for mothers' employment: the link to poverty risks', in K. Vleminckx and T. Smeeding (eds), *Child well-being, child poverty and child policy in modern nations: What do we know?*, Policy Press, Bristol, pp. 459-484.

Van den Bosch, K. (2002), *Convergence in poverty outcomes and social income transfers in member states of the EU*, Paper for the XV World Congress of Sociology in Brisbane, July 2002.

Vleminckx, K. and Smeeding, T. (eds) (2001), *Child well-being, child poverty and child policy in modern nations: What do we know?*, Policy Press, Bristol.

Index